CLARENDON LAW SERIES

INTRODUCTION TO COMPANY LAW

SECOND EDITION

PAUL DAVIES

Allen & Overy Professor of Corporate Law
University of Oxford

OXFORD
UNIVERSITY PRESS

OXFORD

UNIVERSITY PRESS

Great Clarendon Street, Oxford OX2 6DP

Oxford University Press is a department of the University of Oxford.
It furthers the University's objective of excellence in research, scholarship,
and education by publishing worldwide in

Oxford New York

Auckland Cape Town Dar es Salaam Hong Kong Karachi
Kuala Lumpur Madrid Melbourne Mexico City Nairobi
New Delhi Shanghai Taipei Toronto

With offices in

Argentina Austria Brazil Chile Czech Republic France Greece
Guatemala Hungary Italy Japan Poland Portugal Singapore
South Korea Switzerland Thailand Turkey Ukraine Vietnam

Oxford is a registered trade mark of Oxford University Press
in the UK and in certain other countries

Published in the United States
by Oxford University Press Inc., New York

First published 2002
Second edition published 2010

British Library Cataloguing in Publication Data

Data available

Library of Congress Cataloging-in-Publication Data

Davies, P. L. (Paul Lyndon)
    Introduction to company law / Paul Davies.—2nd ed
    p.cm
    Includes bibliographical references and index.
    ISBN 978-0-19-960132-5 (hardback: alk. paper)—
    ISBN 978-0-19-920776-3 (pbk.: alk. paper)
    1. Corporation law-Great Britain. I. Title.
    KD2057.D38 2010
    346.41′066—dc22   2010031491

Typeset by Newgen Imaging Systems (P) Ltd., Chennai, India
Printed in Great Britain
on acid-free paper by
Clays Ltd., St Ives plc

ISBN 978-0-19-960132-5 (Hbk.)
ISBN 978-0-19-920776-3 (Pbk.)

Preface to the Second Edition

The first edition of this book appeared in 2002. A lot of company law activity has occurred in the intervening eight years, most obviously the blockbuster Companies Act 2006. For a book whose objective remains the same as in 2002—to provide an overall structure for thinking about company law for people coming to the subject for the first time—the 2006 Act is much less significant than it would be for, say, a practitioners' text. However, if I ever thought that a second edition would simply be a matter of changing the section numbers in the first edition, I was quickly disabused. A number of reasons for the non-cosmetic changes can be identified.

The most obvious change is that Chapter 10 now deals with a different subject matter: international company law rather than small companies. My estimation is that the former topic, which includes the important question of the appropriate role for the European Community in the company law area, is now of more importance to students of company law than the latter. Ideally, I would have added a chapter on international company law and retained the small companies chapter, but I did not want to make the second edition longer than the first. In any event, many of the crucial issues relating to small companies, such as the unfair prejudice remedy, are already covered in other chapters.

Chapter 8, dealing with majority and minority shareholders, still has the same subject matter but is structured rather differently, because my views on the matter have changed over the intervening period. The same is true, on a lesser scale, at various points in many of the chapters, especially those dealing with the centralized management. In other cases, I simply thought that I now had developed better ways of explaining the same views as I have always held.

However, overall the structure of the second edition is very similar to that of the first. My computer tells me, for what it's worth, that the book's overall length is 2 per cent less than that of the first edition.

My debts to colleagues working in the field are many and various, especially to my co-authors of the second edition of the *Anatomy of Corporate Law* (2009). I tried to acknowledge my other intellectual debts in the Preface to the first edition, but it was impossible to do so in any reasonable compass, and I will not undertake the task again. However, I should like to express my thanks to colleagues at both LSE (where I worked until recently) and at Oxford (where I now work) for providing a stimulating intellectual environment and, in the case of Oxford, for making re-entry so easy.

PLD
Jesus College, Oxford
St Philip and St James' Day, 2010

Contents

Table of Cases

Tables of Legislation

UK Secondary Legislation

Non-statutory

European Treaties and Legislation

Directives

List of Abbreviations

AGM	annual general meeting
AIM	Alternative Investment Market
AktG	Aktiengesetz
ASB	Accounting Standards Board
BERR	UK Department for Business, Enterprise, and Regulatory Reform
BIS	UK Department for Business, Innovation, and Skills
BOFIs	banks and other financial institutions
CDDA	Company Directors Disqualification Act
CEO	chief executive officer
CIC	Community Interest Company
CJEC	Court of Justice of the European Community
CLR	Company Law Review
DGCL	Delaware General Corporation Law
DRR	Directors' Remuneration Report
DTR	Disclosure and Transparency Rules
EEA	European Economic Area
EGM	extraordinary general meeting
ESV	enlightened shareholder value
FRC	Financial Reporting Council
FSA	Financial Services Authority
FSHC	firm-specific human capital
IA	Insolvency Act
IAS	International Accounting Standard
IASB	International Accounting Standards Board
ISC	Institutional Shareholders' Committee
JV	joint venture
LLP	limited liability partnership
LP	limited partnership
LR	Listing Rules
LSE	London Stock Exchange
ltip	long-term incentive plan
NED	non-executive director
SE	Societas Europaea
SPE	European Private Company
SSRN	Social Science Research Network
TFEU	Treaty on the Functioning of the European Union

I

The Core Features of Company Law

WHAT IS COMPANY LAW ABOUT?

Those coming to the study of company law for the first time are often put off by the bulk and range of legal materials which appear to be relevant. The main source of statutory material, the Companies Act 2006, contains over 1,300 sections and 16 Schedules. This is the latest in a line of Acts which can be traced back to the emergence of modern company law in the middle of the nineteenth century. The first modern Act was the Joint Stock Companies Act 1844, introduced by one of the great statesmen of the nineteenth century, William Gladstone, when he was President of the Board of Trade. This Act ushered in the crucial principle that citizens should be empowered to form companies by going through a relatively simple bureaucratic procedure, presided over by a state official, the Registrar of Companies. Previously, incorporation had been available securely only by following the cumbersome routes of obtaining a private Act of Parliament or a Royal Charter.[1]

However, not all of company law is in the 2006 statute. Some parts of it, though less than before the 2006 Act, are still in the common law, and judicial interpretation is crucial in some areas which are in the statute. So, there is a significant body of case-law to be mastered as well. Even some of the statutory rules relevant to the company's operations are not to be found in the Companies Act at all but in the Insolvency Act 1986. Many problems, which lie undiscovered or can be ignored whilst the company is a going concern, become the focus of detailed analysis once the company is no longer able to pay its way. In consequence, some central issues of company law tend to be seen through the lens of insolvency law, as we shall see in subsequent chapters. Of increasing importance, as well, are the Financial Services and Markets Act 2000 and rules made under it

---

[1] These two routes to incorporation still exist but are rarely used, at least by trading companies, but examples of companies incorporated in this way can still be found.

by the Financial Services Authority.[2] These regulate companies which have raised finance from the public to further their activities and whose securities are traded on a public market, such as the Main Market of the London Stock Exchange or its Alternative Investment Market (AIM) for less seasoned companies or on the increasing number of competitor markets. Finally, in some areas, such as that just mentioned of publicly traded companies, European Community law now takes a lead role, so that the interaction between Community and domestic law needs to be understood.

The main purpose of this book is to argue that, despite appearances, company law is not a vast catalogue of unrelated and tedious rules, but rather that it can be seen to be organized around the solution of a relatively small number of fundamental problems. This gives rise to the core features of company law, which are identified in this chapter. Later chapters will analyse how the core features have been implemented in the main parts of British company law and how that law seeks to solve any consequential problems. The aim of the book as a whole is to equip the student with a set of intellectual tools which can be brought to bear on, and to analyse, any part of the subject. One significant advantage of this approach is that, on an initial pass, much of the detail of the law can be ignored. Once the underlying structure of the law has been laid bare the student of the subject can return to particular areas and bury him- or herself in the details of a particular topic to the extent that inclination or need dictate.

But first of all, what is a company? For the lawyer, it is an organizational form, provided by the law, through which the suppliers of the various inputs necessary to achieve a certain objective can come together and coordinate their activities. Those activities are usually of a business nature and designed to earn profits. It will be assumed in this book, unless otherwise stated, that this is the case, though in fact the British company can be, and is, used for some non-business or non-profit-making activities as well. In other words, those who form a company do not have to commit themselves as to the sort of activity they intend to carry on through it.[3]

The company is the most successful organizational form made available by the law for business activities, and one of the aims of this book

---

[2] At the time of writing the institutional future of the FSA is uncertain. Under government plans announced in June 2010 it seems likely that the functions of the FSA which we consider in this book will be transferred to a new Consumer Protection and Markets Authority.

[3] s 7(2) of the Companies Act 2006 simply states that 'a company may not be formed for an unlawful purpose'. Companies formed to promote charitable objectives are by no means uncommon. All references hereafter, unless otherwise stated, are to the 2006 Act.

is to explain why this should be. However, it is not the only form. Partnerships of various types—ordinary, limited, and limited liability— are alternative choices, at least for small businesses.[4] Moreover, there are organizational forms for particular types of activity, such as building societies, cooperative societies, and community benefit societies.[5] Even the trust can be deployed for commercial ends. The company is, thus, not without competitors, but at least since the end of the nineteenth century it has been the most popular choice of legal form for businesses of some size and for many small businesses as well. As of the end of March 2009 there were nearly 2.7 million companies on the British registers of companies maintained by Companies House.[6] Of these some 2 million had an issued share capital of £100 or less (which can be taken as a proxy for being a small business), whilst there were only 16,500 limited partnerships and 38,500 limited liability partnerships on the register.[7] These figures do not tell us anything about the numbers of ordinary partnerships, which are not required to be registered. There are many of these—recent figures put the number at 462,000—but ordinary partners do not have limited liability.[8] Thus, the figures suggest the dominance of the corporate form amongst those who engage in business with one or more other persons.

The British company also faces competition from organizational forms made available by EU law, though neither of the forms currently available has proved popular in the UK.[9] More significant is competition from companies formed in other jurisdictions but operating in the UK, of which

[4] However, the partnership form is available only to those carrying on a business with a view to making a profit. The difference between a limited partnership (LP) and a limited liability partnership (LLP) is that in the former the liability of only some of the partners is limited. There must be at least one 'general partner' without limited liability—though that general partner may be a limited liability entity! The LP is the vehicle of choice for private equity and hedge fund investment funds and the LLP for professional services firms, for example, law firms. On limited liability see below in this chapter.

[5] The last two organizational forms were known as industrial and provident and friendly societies until renamed by the Cooperative and Community Benefit Societies and Credit Unions Act 2010.

[6] BERR, *Statistical Tables on Companies Registration Activities 2008–2009*, Table A1. Companies must register in England and Wales, Scotland, or Northern Ireland. There is no such thing, technically, as a 'British' or 'UK' company, even if the Companies Act 2006 now applies across all three jurisdictions.   [7] Ibid, Tables E2 and E4.

[8] BIS, Statistical Press Release (URN 09/02), 2009, Figure 2 provides the figure for partnerships. It also shows that there were 3 million sole traders, suggesting that most sole traders do not seek to make use of a legal vehicle to separate their business from their personal assets or to obtain limited liability.

[9] As of 2009 there were 205 European Economic Interest Groups and 14 European Public Limited Companies registered at Companies House: BERR n 6 above, Table E3.

nearly 9,000 had an established place of business in the UK in 2009.[10] We will discuss these forms of competition further in Chapter 10.

Thus, the company has proved a very successful legal form for carrying on business. But, whose activities does it help to coordinate? British company law focuses on the coordination of three groups of people: shareholders,[11] directors (and to some extent senior managers who are not directors), and creditors. The law seeks to regulate both the relations between these three groups (for example, shareholders as against directors or creditors as against shareholders) and within these groups (for example, majority as against minority shareholders or secured as against unsecured creditors). It also seeks to regulate, to some extent, the mechanisms by which people join or leave one of these groups as well as their rights and duties once they have joined a group. Thus, the law is interested in the processes by which investors come to be shareholders or creditors of a company as well as their legal status once they have acquired shares or lent money to the company.

However, it is clear that a successful business needs to coordinate the activities of a wider range of people: employees, suppliers, and customers, at the very least. So, let us look first at those whose inputs company law does concern itself with and then try to explain those inputs which are not coordinated by company law.

Shareholders invest in companies in exchange for shares. What rights are attached to the shares depends principally, not on the law, but on the contract entered into by the investors with the company: the basic principle here is freedom of contract. One has to look at the terms of issue of the shares to see what rights the shareholder obtains. Companies may issue more than one 'class' of shares, with different rights being attached to the different classes. However, the core shareholder, the 'ordinary' shareholder, generally receives little in the way of financial entitlements in exchange for the investment. The ordinary shareholder may have expectations of dividends and capital gains arising out of an increase in the market price of the share but no legal entitlement to them. What the ordinary shareholder does normally receive is the right to vote, ie potentially they control the company. However, it is perfectly lawful for a company to issue non-voting ordinary shares (but at the risk that it will not be able to sell them at a good price). Further, it may issue shares, often called

---

[10] Ibid, Table E1.

[11] More accurately its 'members', since a company need not have shareholders, but must have members. However, in line with our concentration on business corporations, we will normally proceed on the basis that the members are shareholders.

'preference' shares, which do carry a fixed legal entitlement to a dividend (and perhaps other rights), but for this reason preference shareholders are often not granted voting rights.

Shareholders may acquire their shares from the company, ie the company 'issues' or 'allots' the shares to the investor in exchange for a consideration provided to the company by the investor. In the case of a publicly traded company that investment will normally be in the form of cash, but the consideration could be in kind, eg the provision of assets which the company needs for its business. Or the shares may be acquired from an existing shareholder, with the consideration moving from the selling investor to the acquiring one. In the case of publicly traded companies the existence of trading in the shares on a public market (stock exchange) makes this second form of entry into and exit from the company very easy. In other cases, selling the shares may be more problematic in practice. What the shareholder can rarely do is insist the company buy the shares back; even if the company wishes to buy the shares back it may face constraints on so doing, designed to protect creditors.[12] Thus, one may say that, once the investment is made, it is 'locked into' the company, in the sense that it cannot be unilaterally withdrawn from the company by the investor. Of course, this provides a form of stability for the company on the financing side of its activities.

The directors typically manage, or arrange for the management of, the company, constituting themselves into a 'board' of directors for that purpose. This is a pretty uncontroversial statement, but one cannot find it in the Companies Act 2006. As we shall see in Chapter 5, British company law leaves it up to the shareholders to decide on the division of business functions between themselves and the board. However, in large companies there are powerful, indeed irresistible, pressures toward extensive delegation of powers of management to the board. In such companies the board may further delegate important functions to senior, but non-board, managers. There may, or may not be, much overlap between the directors and the shareholders. Where there is a large shareholder body, there will be little overlap, one of the purposes of the board being to move business decision-making into the hands of a small group of people. Where there is a small shareholding body, there may be considerable overlap: indeed in such cases, all the shareholders may be directors of the company. Then, the division between shareholders and the board looks rather artificial.

---

[12] See below Ch 4.

A person who wishes to invest in a company may prefer not to do so by becoming a shareholder in it but by lending money to it. In this case too the relationship between company and lender is primarily contractual, but the loan contract typically gives the lender very different rights from those of a shareholder. Although lenders' rights can be structured as variously as shareholders' rights, the lender will typically be entitled to the return of the amount lent at a fixed date (the 'maturity' date) in the future, so that the loan is locked in only for a period and not indefinitely, as with an investment by way of a share issue. Consequently, the need to refinance loans which are coming to maturity can constitute a major problem for companies' chief financial officers, especially if the credit market has moved adversely to the company since the loan was taken out. Substitution of shareholder-provided finance may be the only solution in very tight credit markets. Equally, the lender will normally have an entitlement (and not just an expectation) of a periodic return, through an interest payment of a fixed amount.

Moreover, these claims of the lenders will rank ahead of any claims which shareholders have against the company. For this reason and because of their lack of financial entitlements as against the company, ordinary shareholders are often referred to as supplying 'risk' or 'equity' capital to the company. By contrast, the lender will only very unusually have voting rights in the company or be considered a member of it. The point is of theoretical, even ideological, significance, because the train of thought which makes the shareholders the members of the company leads naturally to making the shareholders' interests predominant within company law. To the Victorian drafters of the companies legislation it was as natural to vest ultimate control of the company in the shareholders (members), at least as the default rule,[13] as it is still to us to think that the members of a cricket club or a students' union should be the ultimate repository of authority in those organizations.

Loans may be made either by a bank (or a group of banks acting together in a 'syndicated' loan) or be raised on the capital markets from multiple investors. In the latter case, the lender will usually have one thing in common with the shareholder. This is the easy transferability of the lender's rights. The company will raise the amount it needs by issuing what are usually termed 'bonds' (or 'notes' or even 'paper' in the case of shorter-term

---

[13] A default rule is one which is applied by the law in a particular situation unless the parties involved agree upon a different rule. The law may make it easy or difficult for the parties to agree upon something different. Because of the dominance of ideas of freedom of contract in company law, default rules are one of its characteristic features.

loans), which can be traded on a public market in the same way as shares. The choice between bank loans and bonds is essentially a commercial one, but a significant boost was given to the bond markets when the 'credit crunch' beginning in late 2007 caused bank lending to dry up or, at least, to be very much reduced. Of course, only large companies have access to the bond markets, so that small and medium-sized companies could not use this way around the problem.

The category of creditors is, of course, very much larger than that of long-term creditors. Employees will be creditors in respect of their unpaid wages, as are unpaid suppliers and customers who have paid for goods or services in advance. But why should company law deal with creditor/ company relations? In the case of the shareholder relationship, the answer is clear. The shareholder is, in essence, a creation of company law and so it is appropriate that company law should regulate shareholder/company relations. But debtor/creditor relations exist in all sorts of contexts where neither party is a company. The answer is provided by the company law doctrine of limited liability (discussed below) which gives the rationale for, but also determines the scope of, company law's interest in company/ creditor relations. As we shall see, limited liability permits the company to act opportunistically towards its creditors in ways which are not open to those without limited liability. Company law necessarily responds to this issue, as we see in Chapters 3 and 4. However, insofar as aspects of the company/creditor relation are not unique to company debtors, the general law can be left to deal with the issue.[14]

The reasons given for the partial interest of company law in creditor/ company relations can be used to explain its non-interest in the relationship between other groups and the company. Relations between the company and its suppliers and customers can be left to general commercial and consumer law. Whatever the rights and obligations of suppliers and consumers, they should not turn on whether the other contracting party is a company or some other form of trading entity. There is no reason, it can be argued, why a consumer should have greater (or lesser) rights of redress against a corporate supplier than one that is a partnership. If this were the case, the law would distort the choice of legal forms for business.

---

[14] There are two exceptions to this statement, both relating to security interests. First, there is a special registration system of charges created by companies (see Part 25 of the Act) and, second, companies can create a form of security interest, the 'floating charge', not available to non-corporate borrowers. However, it is far from clear that these rules should apply uniquely to companies. See Law Commission, *Registration of Security Interests: Company Charges and Property other than Land*, Consultation Paper 164 (2002) and *Company Security Interests: A Consultative Report*, CP 176 (2004).

This argument is pretty widely accepted. However, it is controversial when it is applied to employees. Should company law ignore the company/ employee relationship? British company law pretty well does, ie the rules of employment and labour law apply irrespective of the legal form of the employing enterprise. German law takes a different view, applying special rules so as to require the representation of employees on the boards of large companies. The overall impact of the British approach is to give employees less influence in relation to the setting of corporate strategy than does German law. The argument that the matter should be left to employment law applying to all legal entities does not quite work in this area. First, if the issue is conceived to be one of employee influence in large businesses, the dominance of the corporate form for large businesses means that the distinction between rules applying to all legal forms and those applying only to companies comes close to being meaningless.[15] Second, and more important, it is possible that rules making the board strongly accountable to the shareholders will have an adverse impact on the ability of the management to generate long-term, flexible relationships with the employees. If this is true, then even if there is no issue of employee representation at board level, it might still be important to adjust director/shareholder relations because of their spill-over effect in the employment sphere. We look at these issues in Chapter 9. In the meantime we can note that the level of responsiveness of company law to company/employee relations constitutes one of the great dividing lines among the company laws of modern economies.

THE CORE CHARACTERISTICS OF COMPANY LAW

It is suggested that there are five core characteristics around which it is possible to organize an introductory analysis of company law. The New Zealand Law Commission has identified four of them in the following terms.[16]

- Recognition of the company as an entity distinct from all its shareholders.

- Limited liability for shareholders.

- Specialized management, separate from the shareholders.

- Ease of transfer of the shareholder interest.

---

[15]   It is true that there are some large limited liability partnerships, but LLPs are in general subject to rules derived from corporate (not partnership) law.

[16]   Law Commission, *Company Law Reform and Restatement*, Report No 9 (Wellington, New Zealand, 1989), para 22.

In addition, it is suggested that there is a fifth characteristic, which the Commission perhaps omitted because it thought it too obvious, but which is in fact the most controversial feature of modern company law, at least in terms of the wider public debate. This is:

• Allocation of rights of control over the company to the members of the company.[17]

Let us say a little about each of these now. They will be fully examined in the later chapters of this book.

SEPARATE LEGAL PERSONALITY

The notion that the company is a legal person separate from its shareholders, directors, creditors, employees, indeed from anyone else involved in it, is fundamental to the conceptual structure of company law. Functionally, it is also important because it facilitates, even if it does not require, the provision by company law of other core features such as limited liability and transferable shares. The Act provides that, upon registration of the company, the subscribers to the memorandum of association, which is the formal registration document stating that its signatories wish to form a company,[18] are transformed from a collection of individuals into 'a body corporate' by the name stated in the certificate of incorporation, whose first members the incorporators are.[19] It thus follows that separate legal personality is an inevitable consequence of the incorporation of a company.

However, the separate legal personality of the company complicates some areas of legal reasoning, because an additional legal person has to be fitted into the analysis of legal relations between and among shareholders, directors, and creditors. In other words, company law does not typically establish legal relations directly between or within these groups, but instead mediates them through the company. Thus, normally directors will owe duties to the company rather than to the shareholders; shareholders may have rights against the company rather than against the directors. There are good functional reasons for proceeding in this way, for the company acts as a sort of 'central counterparty' for all these relationships, rather than, for example, shareholders having to contract directly with each other or with each director—and to re-contract whenever there is a change of shareholder or director. Nevertheless, conferring legal personality on the company sometimes leads people to treat the company as

---

[17] Even in Germany the shareholders are not excluded from control of companies where board level representation of employees is mandated, but they are required to share it.
[18] s 8. This is pretty much all the memorandum does now state. Before the 2006 reforms, it had a much larger mandatory content.   [19] s 16(2).

if it were a natural legal person rather than the artificial one that it is, and to attribute to it 'interests' which it cannot possibly have.[20] So, whilst it is almost impossible to avoid talking at some point about 'the interests of the company', one needs to remember that this is really a shorthand for one or more of the groups of natural persons who have legal relations with the company and who certainly can have interests. In the UK the 'company' typically means its members/shareholders.

LIMITED LIABILITY

Limited liability means that the rights of the company's creditors are confined to the assets of the company and cannot be asserted against the personal assets of the company's members (shareholders). Hence the common expression 'limited liability companies'. However, this is really a misnomer. The liability of the company is not limited at all. Creditors' rights can be asserted to the full against the company's assets. It is the liability of the members which is limited.

Separate legal personality facilitates limited liability in that it makes it easier to distinguish business assets (owned by the company) from personal assets (owned by the members), though it is not impossible to find effective ways of drawing this line in bodies which do not have separate legal personality. While the company is a going concern, separate legal personality can be said to guarantee limited liability. If a third party has a contract and the counter-party to the contract is a company as a separate legal person, English common law draws the consequence that liability on the contract is confined to the company and its assets and will not extend to the members of the company and their assets.[21] In English law, the real bite of the limited liability doctrine is revealed not in the context of a possible direct legal relationship between the creditor and the shareholders on the transaction giving rise to the debt or liability, because such a relationship is not recognized. Rather, the importance of limited liability shows itself in the legal relationship between the company and its members if

---

[20] If the company is really a legal person separate from any of the groups of natural persons who are involved in its business, can one even say that it is contrary to the interests of the company that it should be wound up (ie dissolved)?

[21] See *Maclaine Watson & Co Ltd v Department of Trade and Industry* [1988] BCLC 404, 456–7, CA. At common law there is thus a clear dichotomy: either a body is incorporated and it is liable to third parties and its members are not; or it is an unincorporated association with no legal personality and its members are liable. Some civil law systems, including in this context the Scottish law of partnership, recognize 'mixed' bodies, where the body is incorporated and liable but the members are nevertheless also (secondarily) liable (see Partnership Act 1890, s 4(2)).

the company becomes insolvent because it has insufficient assets to meet the overall claims of its creditors. In insolvent liquidation the question arises whether the liquidator, who now runs the company in place of the directors, can claim a contribution to the company's inadequate assets from its members. However, since an unpaid creditor has the power to put the company into compulsory liquidation[22] and since the liquidator owes his or her primary duties to the company's creditors, in fact the creditors will normally be the parties in interest if the liquidator is able to bring such contribution claims against the members.

Perhaps surprisingly, one cannot find the answer to the question of whether the members have limited liability in this further and crucial sense (ie as against the liquidator) in the Companies Act. It is necessary instead to turn to the provisions of the Insolvency Act 1986. Section 74 begins with the proposition that in a winding up the members are indeed liable to make such contribution as is needed to cover the company's debts and liabilities. Fortunately for the shareholders, however, the section goes on to provide that, in the case of a company which has issued shares, no further contribution is required from the shareholders beyond the amount, if any, which is still owing to the company for the shares.

Thus, by a combination of separate legal personality (whilst the company is a going concern) and the provisions of the Insolvency Act (if it becomes insolvent), limited liability is effectively guaranteed to the members of companies. However, it is not obligatory to have limited liability. The Companies Act permits the incorporators to choose an 'unlimited company'.[23] In such a company the shareholders have the protection of the doctrine of separate legal personality, but the contribution principle of s 74 of the Insolvency Act applies to them in full force. Thus, so long as the company is solvent, the shareholders of an unlimited company need have no dealings with its creditors, but if the company goes into insolvent liquidation they should expect the liquidator soon to appear on the scene, seeking contribution to the company's assets. For this reason, perhaps, very few unlimited companies have been formed, even though unlimited companies are more lightly regulated than limited companies: of the companies on the register in 2009 fewer than 5,000 were unlimited companies.[24]

---

[22] Insolvency Act 1986, ss 122–4.

[23] s 4—provided it is formed as a private company.

[24] Above n 6, Table A2. In particular, unlimited companies do not have to file accounts, ie make them publicly available (s 448) and they are free to reduce their share capital without following any prescribed statutory procedure (s 617—prohibition on alteration of share capital applies only to limited companies).

In the previous paragraphs we have concentrated on the protection afforded to shareholders by the doctrine of limited liability. However, if the principle is that the creditors' claims are normally to be confined to the assets of the company, one might conclude that the assets of the directors (and indeed of employees and other groups) should be protected from the creditors' claims as well. As we shall see in Chapter 2, the legal techniques by which the protection of limited liability is extended to directors are entirely different from those by which it is extended to shareholders, and the protection of directors is conceptually less securely based than it is in relation to shareholders.

CENTRALIZED MANAGEMENT

In companies of any size it is hardly surprising that the management of the company is not left with the shareholders but is entrusted to a small group of managers. Partly, this is a question of speed and cost. A large shareholding body can be convened fairly only after reasonable notice (say two weeks at a minimum) and at some expense. Partly, it is a question of expertise. Shareholders in large companies, even if they are professional fund managers, may be experts at taking investment decisions but are not necessarily skilled at managing companies. Individual investors may not be highly skilled at either, since their main occupation in life may be something entirely different. Partly, it is a question of motivation. A shareholder who knows he or she will be one of a body of, say, 1,000 shareholders taking a particular decision may be tempted not to invest much time in working out the correct answer to the question, but rather to free-ride on the efforts of the others—but all the shareholders will be subject to the same incentive to shirk and so none may prepare properly. The dynamics of small group decision-making, which will govern decisions of the managers, are entirely different.

However, the arguments in the previous paragraph do not constitute a convincing case that company law should require a centralized management structure. One might say that, if these arguments are forceful, companies will develop their own structures, provided only they are given the legal freedom to do so. Such contractual structures could be customized to the needs of particular companies and, indeed, some companies, for example small ones, might decide that they did not need a centralized management structure at all: the shareholders might be a small enough group for them to constitute also the managers. As we shall see in Chapter 5, British law does indeed give the shareholders considerable freedom as to how they organize the internal governance structure of the company and how they divide powers up between the shareholders and the board. In this respect it is more flexible than many other systems.

However, on one point British company law is prescriptive. Section 154 of the Companies Act requires public companies to have at least two directors and private companies to have one.[25] The Company Law Review floated the idea that British company law should follow the example of many US states and permit small companies to dispense with the separate board of directors,[26] but on consultation the idea did not prove attractive.

There is no doubt that the statutory requirement for a board of directors has some advantages. In particular, when it is desired to regulate the top management of companies, whether by common law or statute, the board provides a focus for the attachment of the relevant rules. As we shall see, there is a very substantial corpus of statutory and common rules applying to directors, the analysis of which traditionally constitutes a major part of company law courses. This explains why managers as such play a relatively small role in company law, no matter how large they may loom in the business schools. At centre stage, as far as the law is concerned, are the directors, either individually or collectively as a board of directors, though some of the directors will normally also be full-time managers of the company (usually termed 'executive' directors).

Apart from requiring directors, the law says very little about who the directors should or should not be. No qualifications are required for acting as the director of a company,[27] though directors can now subsequently be disqualified from so acting on various grounds.[28] The Act used to have a mandatory maximum age for directors, but this has now gone to be replaced by a mandatory minimum age—16.[29] Further, whilst a company may be a director of another company, a company must have at least one director who is a natural person.[30] Both rules have enforcement rationales: under-age directors may be able to escape liability—either in law or in practice—whilst certain sanctions cannot be applied to corporate directors.

However, in relation to companies traded on public markets, as we shall see in Chapter 7, the traditional abstention of the law from regulation of

---

[25] The distinction between public and private companies is explained below at p 15.

[26] See eg Delaware General Corporation Law §351.

[27] Except the negative one of not being an undischarged bankrupt: Company Directors Disqualification Act 1986, s 11.

[28] So everyone is entitled to at least one bite of the cherry of being a company director. See below Ch 4 at p 90.

[29] s 157. s 185 of the Companies Act 1948 set a retirement age of 70 for directors of public companies. [30] s 155.

who directors are and what they do is coming under some strain. The notion that, at least in listed companies, management is too important a matter to be left entirely to the directors and shareholders is beginning to gain ground, but so far it has expressed itself in the Corporate Governance Code rather than in the Companies Act.

SHAREHOLDER CONTROL

We have already noted that the Victorian draftsman regarded the shareholders, as members, as the ultimate repository of authority in the company. What concretely does this mean in terms of control rights for the shareholders? There are three principal areas of shareholder control: control over the company's constitution; control over the company's management; and control over the company's economic surplus. Let us say a little about each of these.

Control over the company's constitution

The central component of the company's constitution[31] is its 'articles of association'. The articles freely regulate all those matters which are not subject to rules laid down in legislation or common law and also determine the applicable rule where the statutory or common law rule is a default rule.[32] Since the tradition of British company law has been either to regulate only a few matters relating to the internal organization of the company through mandatory rules and to regulate others via default rules, the articles are a crucial source of rules for the company. Although low down in the hierarchy of sources of rules applicable to the company, the articles will in many cases provide, even today, the rule which is relevant for the governance of the company. An important example of the role of the articles, as we shall see in Chapter 5, is to determine the division of powers between the shareholders and the board.

The importance of the articles is demonstrated by their treatment in the Act. First, all companies are required to have articles of association,[33] presumably on the basis that a company's internal governance arrangements will be incomplete without them. Second, although the company is free to have what articles it wishes, since modern company law first emerged the legislature has provided 'model' articles which companies are free to adopt, in whole or in part, rather than develop customized

---

[31] The term also includes certain resolutions of the company, notably special resolutions: s 17.   [32] See n 13 as to the meaning of a default rule.
[33] s 18(1).

articles.[34] This reduces transaction costs on formation, though, as we shall see in Chapter 8, it also creates the risk that the articles will not accurately reflect the governance assumptions upon which the company was in fact established. However, the Act puts some force behind the model by making it a default rule that the model articles apply unless the company chooses, wholly or in part, to have something different.[35] Third, the articles are a public document, since they must be delivered to the Registrar of Companies on formation of the company.[36]

However, the crucial point for present purposes is that the shareholders have control of the articles. Clearly those who form the company (the incorporators) and become its first members choose the initial articles of association. However, subsequent amendments of the articles are also under the control of the shareholders. Not only must the directors secure the approval of the shareholders for any amendment of the articles, so that the shareholders have a veto over amendments to the constitution, but it is open to the shareholders to initiate changes to the articles, even if the directors are opposed to the change.[37] Amendments require a special resolution, ie a three-quarters majority of those voting. Given the significance of the articles in determining the governance arrangements of British companies, shareholder control over the articles is by the same token a significant feature of the law.

This is the appropriate point to note an important choice which the incorporators must make on formation and which will determine the model articles applicable to their company. This is the choice between forming a 'public' and a 'private' company.[38] The public/private distinction is regarded as being so important that it is reflected in the suffix which most companies are required to have as part of their name. A public company must carry the words 'public limited company' or 'plc' after its name and a private company the word 'limited' or 'ltd' (or their Welsh equivalents). The formal distinction between the two types is that a private company commits a criminal offence if it offers its shares (or other securities) to the public, whereas a public company is free to do so, provided it complies with the (now extensive) rules on public offerings of

[34] The current models are set out in the Companies (Model Articles) Regulations 2008/3229. There are different models for different types of company. A, long overdue, innovation was the introduction in 2008 of separate models for public and private companies limited by shares. The model articles can be traced back to 1856.   [35] s 20.

[36] s 9(5)(b). As must subsequent amendments: s 26.

[37] s 21. See Ch 5 at p 114 for further discussion of the distinction between initiation rights and veto rights. In Delaware, by contrast, changes to the company's 'charter' can be initiated only by the board: DGCL §242(b).   [38] s 9(2)(d) and see n 34 above.

securities.[39] However, although a public company may offer its shares to the public, it does not follow from the status of being public under the Act that it has done so. On the contrary, more public companies have not made such offerings than have.[40] The Companies Act definition of being public can thus give rise to confusion, because in common parlance (and among securities lawyers) a 'public' company refers to the narrower category of companies whose securities are traded on a public market (such as a stock exchange). In this case, not only has there been a public offering of shares but those shares have been introduced to trading on a public market. In order to try to avoid this confusion, this book will reserve the term 'public company' for companies that are public in terms of the Act's definition and use the phrase 'publicly traded companies' to refer to those which are public in the securities lawyer's use of the term.

However, the distinction under the Act between 'public' and 'private' companies is more fundamental than it seems at first sight. The Act regulates the former more closely, not only in relation to the transaction of issuing shares to the public (if such has occurred), but also more generally, as we shall see throughout this book. Choosing to be a public company is thus taken as a proxy for being a company whose affairs need to be somewhat more closely regulated by the Act, whether or not there has in fact been a public offering of shares. Yet, the legislature never moved beyond drawing the public/private distinction within a single Companies Act to developing separate legislative frameworks for the two types of company, as is common in continental European countries, where there are separate Acts for public and private companies.

Overwhelmingly, companies are private: only 0.4 per cent of companies on the effective register in 2008 (fewer than 10,000) were public companies (though they included the economically most important companies).[41] It is thus within the private category that the widest range of sizes can be found. A small number of private companies are very big economically. However, the majority of private companies have turnovers which are small. The Company Law Review found that 65 per cent of companies which were actively carrying on business had an annual turnover of less than £250,000, which is a very small amount.[42] Most of

---

[39] s 755.

[40] Figures suggest only about one-quarter of British public companies have their securities traded on public markets.

[41] Above n 6, Table A2. The 'effective' register subtracts from the total number of registered companies those in the course of removal.

[42] Company Law Review, *Developing the Framework*, Consultation Document 5 (London: Department of Trade and Industry, 2000), para 6.8. Turnover is a measure of the value of the

these will have been owner-managed companies.[43] A pattern of a small number of (economically) large companies and a larger number of (economically) smaller companies is to be expected. If large companies are the result of the search for economies of scale or scope, then there are necessarily going to be rather few such companies in existence at any one time. On the other hand, if the entrepreneurial spirit is vigorous, one would expect a constant supply of new companies seeking to exploit fresh opportunities which the more leaden-footed large companies cannot quickly seize.

Control over management

Control of the company's constitution and control of its management are separate but linked issues. Thus, the company law of a country might prescribe minutely the division of functions between shareholders and the board and the decision-making procedures within companies (so that shareholder control over the constitution was of little importance) but might nevertheless give the shareholders the power to appoint and dismiss the directors (so that it would be appropriate to say that they had control over the management). Or, contrariwise, it might leave the division of powers to be determined by the shareholders, but make it difficult for shareholders to remove directors from office. British law confers both types of control on the shareholders. Control over the articles gives the shareholders control over the division of power between them and the directors and the statute provides that the shareholders may at any time and for any reason by ordinary majority remove any or all of the directors from office.[44]

Entitlement to the surplus

The third element of control which we identified was control over the distribution of the surplus made by the company. The shareholders' entitlement to the surplus earned by the company results from the combined operation of two features of company law. The first is the principle that the directors have no authority—and possibly the company has no capacity—to distribute the company's assets to anyone other than the members of the company except in discharge of legal claim upon the

---

business done by a company during a period; it is not a measure of the company's profit which would have been much less, perhaps even non-existent. The payments were voluntary in the sense that the employees had neither a statutory nor a contractual entitlement to them.

[43] 70 per cent of companies have only one or two shareholders: ibid para 6.9.

[44] s 168.

company or in order to further the company's business.[45] This principle is strikingly displayed by the need to make special statutory provision permitting a company which is ceasing to trade to pay voluntary severance payments to its employees. Since the payments are not in satisfaction of any legal claim on the company and a company which is ceasing to trade has no need to generate goodwill amongst its workforce, such payments were held to be unlawful at common law.[46] However, even the modern statutory provisions permitting such payments require shareholder approval for them, thus underlining the point that surplus is for the shareholders to dispose of.[47]

If payment of surplus to non-members is difficult, except with shareholder consent, the answer to the second question of whether the members have an entitlement to the surplus when the company is a going concern[48] depends mainly upon the rights a particular class of shareholders has against the company. In fact, companies tend to be extremely cautious in granting legally enforceable entitlements to dividends to ordinary shareholders, as we have seen above.[49] Thus, the board usually has an extensive legal discretion whether it pays out a dividend or invests the surplus in new projects. Broadly, the same is true of other mechanisms whereby a company might return surplus to the shareholders, for example, by way of share buy-backs.[50]

Thus, it may be too strong a thing to say that the shareholders have a 'right' to the corporate surplus, but one can say that the law contains a structure which will encourage the surplus to flow in the shareholders' direction, unless the board is, unusually, dependent upon neither the shareholders' votes nor their willingness to subscribe for new share issues in the future. The above argument may seem implausible in the light of the recent, though now less frequently mentioned, emphasis on 'shareholder value'. The answer is that the law supports shareholder value (insofar as it does) through the mechanisms which make the board responsive to the interests of the shareholders (discussed later in the book) rather than through creating legal entitlements to the surplus.

---

[45] Of course, the company's business might consist in part of giving money away, for example, in the case of a charitable company making grants to support certain activities. Here the problem dissolves, precisely because the company's authorized activities include giving money to non-members.   [46] *Parke v Daily News* [1962] Ch 927.

[47] s 247; IA 1986, s 187.

[48] The same principle applies on a winding up. Any surplus available after the creditors have been paid is to be distributed among the members 'according to their rights and interests' which will be defined in the company's constitution or the terms of the share issue: IA 1986 s 107.   [49] At p 4.

[50] See below Ch 4 at p 80.

Although the principle of shareholder control is well established in British law, nevertheless it is controversial, at least in some quarters and especially where that control is immediate or exclusive. There are arguments for loosening management accountability in the direction of the shareholders in order to permit management to be freer to take into account non-shareholder interests or in favour of requiring shareholders to share accountability with other groups, most obviously employees. We shall attempt to face head on the questions raised by this clash of values in Chapter 9. Modern theories of 'stakeholding' in companies pose a powerful challenge to the shareholder monopoly of managerial control.

TRANSFERABILITY OF SHARES

The ability of the shareholder to transfer her shares to another investor is crucial for investment strategy, since the 'liquidity' thus created enables the investor to adjust her investment portfolio to meet changing market conditions, for example by moving into the shares of a company operating in a different sector of the economy or out of shares altogether and into another investment class. It is also valuable for governance purposes: the company may function more smoothly if a dissatisfied investor (or one who simply needs cash) is able to leave the company rather than remain as a carping minority. However, transferability of shares to another investor also carries the implication that, as is indeed the case, repurchase of the shares by the company is not normally the way in which liquidity is provided. In other words, once an investor has made a purchase of shares, she is 'locked into' the company in the sense that the investment cannot be withdrawn on the simple initiative of the shareholder, as it can be, at least as the default rule, in a partnership.

Lock-in of investment

Suppose an investor buys shares from a company when that company makes a public offering of its shares. At that point money will move from the investor to the company and the investor will become a shareholder in the company. Later the shareholder may wish to sell her shares. It is rare for such a sale to be effected by way of a repurchase of the shares by the company. Indeed, until relatively recently the law prohibited a company from purchasing its own shares. Now, repurchases are permitted, provided the company follows the prescribed procedure, designed mainly to protect the interests of creditors,[51] but it is not normally obligatory for the company

---

[51] See Ch 4 at p 80.

to repurchase a shareholder's shares when the latter requests it. It is the board which decides (though possibly under shareholder pressure) to put in place a buy-back programme, and so the shareholder cannot count on one being available at the particular time she wishes to divest her shares. Given the flexibility of British company law, it is no surprise to learn that shareholders can contract for the right to sell their shares back to the company (thus giving rise to so-called 'redeemable' shares), but redeemable shares are also based on company consent (albeit given ex ante rather than ex post) and are in any case rather rare in the form in which they give the shareholder a put option against the company.[52]

Thus, the law strongly steers the shareholder who seeks liquidity to rely on the market to find a substitute investor rather than to expect the company to buy back the share. This approach, of course, promotes stability in the resources available to the company. If the company had to provide liquidity for its investors, its own assets would need to have a higher level of liquidity than under the current rules and could not be invested so easily in long-term projects. One can thus see why it is in the interests of a company which has made a public offering of its shares to secure that its shares are admitted to trading on a public market. This will enormously increase the efficiency of the process whereby shareholders in the company may dispose of their holdings to other investors, if they wish to do so. By extension, the availability of a market in the shares will also increase the willingness of investors to buy the shares in the initial offering by the company.

The lock-in of the shareholder's investment in the company and the provision of liquidity through the market for shares are also facilitated by the concept of separate legal personality. Since the assets employed in the business are owned by the company and not by the shareholders, even collectively, a disposal of the investor's interest in the company, measured by the share, does not involve any transfer of those underlying business assets.

Transferability in the market

Given the importance of transfers in the market as the primary method for providing liquidity to investors, it is perhaps surprising that company law does rather little to guarantee ease of transfer of the share from the shareholders' point of view. It could hardly give the shareholder a general right to transfer the shares, in the sense of imposing upon someone else the duty

[52] It is possible instead or in addition to contract for the share to be compulsorily redeemable by the company as against the shareholder.

to buy them at a fair price.[53] However, potential investors who are in a particularly strong bargaining position may be able to secure such a provision in the company's constitution or in a separate contract with the company or the other shareholders when making their investment—at least in the case of private companies. Nor does the law guarantee to the shareholder the existence of a market upon which the shares can be traded, though, as we have just seen, it may be in the interest of companies which raise funds from the public to ensure that a market is available. In fact, for many private companies, there probably is no market, or no adequate market, for the company's shares. In such a case, the shareholder may find herself in an unfortunate position, unable to exit the company or able to do so only at an unrealistically low price. In such a case, not only is the investment locked in, but so is the investor.

However, company law does not even guarantee that, if a buyer can be found, the shareholder may transfer the shares without the consent of others involved in the business. There is certainly a presumption that shares are issued by a company on the basis that they are freely transferable, but that presumption may be rebutted by express provisions in the company's constitution or the terms of issue of the shares.[54] In fact, in small companies, which are in effect incorporated partnerships, restrictions on the free transferability of shares are common, as the drafters of the company's constitution try to recreate in the company context the rule which normally obtains in a partnership, namely, that the admission of a new partner requires the consent of the existing partners.[55] In fact, until 1980, to qualify as a private company the Act required that restrictions be placed by the company on the free transferability of its shares, though that is no longer the case. Any guarantee of transferability without consent is to be found, not in company law, but in the rules governing the operation of securities markets. The law requires that access to at least the top tier of public markets should be available only to classes of security which are freely transferable.[56]

THE CORE FEATURES AND COMPANY SIZE

We have now identified five core, structural features of company law. They are: separate corporate personality; limited liability; centralized management under a board structure; shareholder control; and free

---

[53] Though this is a remedy heavily used in unfair prejudice cases: see below Ch 8.
[54] s 544. [55] *Re Smith & Fawcett Ltd* [1942] Ch 304.
[56] FSA, Listing Rule 2.2.4(1).

transferability of shares. The attentive reader will have noticed, however, a curious attribute of these core features: it is possible to establish a company which fails to display all but one of the core features. That feature is separate corporate personality, which flows ineluctably from the fact that, upon registration, the statute incorporates the company. The statute itself provides the option to form unlimited liability companies and in any event limited liability and the other three features can in fact be avoided by appropriate provisions in the company's constitution or contracts with the company or its shareholders.

The attentive reader will also have observed that the companies most likely not to display the four optional core features are the smallest ones. Take Smith & Jones (Decorators) Ltd, incorporated by Ms Smith and Mr Jones, who were and remain its only shareholders, to run a small decorating business. The money to fund the business they have probably borrowed from the local bank, which has required Smith and Jones to give personal guarantees of its repayment. So, at least in relation to this major commitment, they do not have the benefit of limited liability. Smith and Jones, as the company's only shareholders, have appointed themselves its only directors and probably are not much aware, when they take decisions, whether they are doing so as shareholders or as directors. As shareholder/ directors they do all the managing this small company requires, so that there are no senior managers who are not directors. In fact, there is unity of shareholding, board membership, and management in this company, rather than centralized management separate from the shareholders. The articles provide that the consent of all the existing shareholders is needed for the admission of a new member and that, if an existing shareholder wishes to sell his or her shares, they must first be offered to the other existing shareholders; and, of course, the shares in the company are not traded on a public market. So there is no free transferability of shares.

It might be thought, however, that this is clearly a company where shareholder control applies. Smith and Jones have all the shares, clearly control the board since they are the board, and no doubt take for themselves by way of dividend or directors' remuneration as much of the company's economic surplus as they think is prudent in the light of its needs for working capital or capital for expansion. At a deeper level, however, one may doubt this is an example of *shareholder* control. Let us suppose, as would be common, that upon registration Smith and Jones agreed to subscribe each for one £1 share in the company, and they have not subsequently increased their holdings. So, Smith and Jones have acquired these control rights for the payment of a mere £2—or, rather, the obligation to pay £2, for the shares have probably been issued as not paid up.[57] Why should the bank be prepared to finance a company where the controllers have contributed apparently so little? The answer probably is because Smith & Jones' business plan reveals that they are going to be the people who get and do the work which the company is set up to carry on. In effect, they have been given control rights, not because they have made a major equity investment in the company (they clearly have not), but because they have promised to work for it. This small company displays a form of workers' control or, if you prefer, the shares have been allocated to them, not in exchange for capital contributions, but in exchange for an implicit promise to devote their full energies to developing the business. Smith and Jones are not shareholder-capitalists but shareholder-workers or shareholder-entrepreneurs.

Of course, it is equally easy to identify companies which display all five of the core features in a straightforward way. Such companies tend to be at the other end of the size spectrum from Smith & Jones (Decorators) Ltd. Companies, such as BP, whose shares are traded on public markets will fall within this category. They are likely to have hundreds, perhaps thousands or even tens of thousands, of shareholders, none of whom has given any personal guarantee of the company's debts or liabilities; the board is clearly distinct from both the shareholders and the senior management of the company; and the shares are freely transferable from both the shareholders' and the company's point of view. As far as the law is concerned, the shareholders also control the company in the ways defined above. However, by way of contrast with Smith & Jones Ltd, the sheer number of the shareholders raises a serious question whether the difficulties the shareholders will face in coordinating their actions mean that in fact they are incapable of exercising the control the law confers upon them. We shall examine this question in Chapter 5.

In addition to companies whose shares are traded on public markets, it is likely that nearly all public companies display the five core features, although the absence of a public market may make it more difficult for a shareholder to find a purchaser for her shares. Finally, a substantial number of private companies will also display the five core features. A good example might be a company, originally built up by an entrepreneur, who has now died, and the shares are held by various members of later generations of the founder's family. They may still have a keen financial and emotional

---

[57] Only public companies are required to take payment for the shares at the time of allotment, to the extent of one-quarter of the nominal value of the share and the whole of any premium: s 586.

interest in the fortunes of that company but may have decided not to run it themselves but rather to hire professional managers to do so, the senior of which managers they will have placed on the board. In such a case one can identify centralized management distinct from the shareholders but, in contrast to the publicly traded company, the problems of shareholder coordination are much easier to deal with and the accountability of the board to the shareholders will be real. Indeed, the shareholders may place one or more of the family members on the board in a non-executive capacity in order to improve the flow of information from the management to the shareholders. Where this has happened, the shareholders, directors, and managers will be distinct, but overlapping, groups. However, in the absence of a public market, free transfer of shares may again be a difficulty. Moreover, the family may be committed to keeping control of the company in their hands, even if some non-family members have been admitted as shareholders, and may have included provisions in the company's constitution or may have entered into a shareholders' agreement which formally restrict the transferability of the shares.

The above are only examples (or models) of types of company. In practice a bewildering variety of configurations can be found. However, both in this chapter and later in the book, it is worth keeping these simplified models in mind when testing the impact of particular legal rules. Proceeding up the size hierarchy, we have identified: the owner-managed company; the large private company; the public company whose shares, however, are not publicly traded; and the public company whose shares are traded on a public market and whose activities are thus regulated in addition by the rules of that market.

As far as the core features are concerned, there is a clear correlation between the size of the company and the likelihood of its displaying all five core features. It is suggested that this is not a random fact. As companies become larger, their needs for capital to carry on their business are likely also to increase, to the point where the public may be invited to provide risk capital to the company, either directly or via intermediaries such as pension funds or insurance companies. Public shareholders are unlikely to want or be able to manage the company, so centralized management emerges, and they are likely to be significantly more willing to invest in the company if they can subsequently dispose of their shares on a market and if they benefit from limited liability. Finally, having provided investment with no legal guarantee of a return, they are likely to want the power to remove the management if it proves unsuccessful.

The point about the core features of company law is not that they are mandatory for companies but that they are made available to all companies.

The core features facilitate the growth of businesses within the corporate form for, as the business expands, the core features can be taken up and applied, without the particular business having to change its legal form. This is perhaps the strongest argument for allowing very small businesses to have access to the corporate form, even though it is far from clear that they really need the core features. Indeed, in the early days of modern company law, such access was frowned upon. The policy of the mid-Victorian companies legislation was that small businesses should adopt the partnership form and only medium-sized and large businesses the company form. Thus, an upper limit of twenty was placed on the number of people who could form a partnership; beyond that they had to form a company.[58] By contrast, incorporation with limited liability was restricted to associations of at least twenty-five and later at least seven members.[59] Thus, below seven members the partnership form was obligatory; between seven and twenty either could be chosen; above twenty only the corporate form was available.

The story of the subversion of this legislative policy of using the number of members as a proxy for the size of a business and of excluding small businesses from the corporate form is one of the best known in the history of British company law. From the beginning company practitioners set about undermining this policy, by the use of nominee shareholders,[60] mainly in order to give small businesses the advantages of limited liability. The House of Lords set its seal of approval on this development in one of its most famous decisions in our field, *Salomon v A Salomon & Co Ltd*[61] and the legislature decided to accept the defeat and did not seek to reverse *Salomon*. From that time onwards even the smallest one-person business has had access to the corporate form.[62]

Despite the wide availability of the corporate form to businesses of different sizes, it is clear that the corporate form comes into its own in the case of large businesses—large as a matter of the scale of their economic

---

[58] Companies Act 1856, s 4. The rule was abolished in 2001.

[59] Seven was the number chosen in the 1856 Act, the Limited Liability Act 1855 having originally stipulated the higher number.

[60] A nominee shareholder is one who holds the shares on behalf of another, often as a bare trustee. So, the seven-member requirement could be subverted in practice by having one beneficial holder and six other shareholders who held their shares, usually only one share each, on behalf of the beneficial holder.   [61] [1897] AC 22.

[62] The minimum number of members had gradually been whittled away to two when in 1989 Council Directive 89/667/EEC required the UK formally to introduce one-member private companies. However, because of the previous possibility of using nominee shareholders, this was a change of form, not substance. The 2006 Act now allows single-member public companies: s 7(1).

activities or large in terms of the number of investors (or both). In such cases the company is likely to be structured so that all its core features are displayed. Herein lies the comparative advantage of the company over other forms of business organization. For small businesses the company may face competition from the partnership in its various forms, but at the other end of the spectrum it reigns supreme.

NOT–FOR–PROFIT COMPANIES

Although this book is primarily about companies formed for the purpose of carrying on business for a profit, the flexibility of the corporate vehicle is such that it can be used for carrying on not-for-profit activities. One form of the company is specifically adapted for this purpose. This is the company 'limited by guarantee'.[63] Such a company has members but they are not shareholders, because a guarantee company issues no shares. Instead, its members must agree to contribute an amount (usually minimal) to its assets if the company is wound up as insolvent. The company limited by guarantee is, however, able to display the core features identified above, notably that of limited liability, except that there is less likely to be an economic surplus to distribute or, even if there is, its distribution to the members may be prohibited by the company's constitution.[64] Because of the existence of this form of the company (with members who are not shareholders) the generic term used in the Act to refer to those who are associated in the company is 'member', not 'shareholder', even though in most companies the members are shareholders.

It may be wondered why so many 'not-for-profit' companies choose to incorporate as companies limited by guarantee rather than as share companies. After all, shares can be issued with a nominal value as low as 1p, and it is difficult to think that the obligation to pay a few pence on joining (as opposed to undertaking the obligation to pay a few pence on winding up if the company is insolvent) would alter many people's decision whether or not to join the company. In some cases, regulation is the answer. Thus, if a charity wishes to incorporate as a company, it is normally easier to do so as a guarantee company. Even where there is no

---

[63] s 3. It will be a private company if incorporated today.

[64] The phrase 'not for profit', which is not a term of art in British law, is used to refer both to the companies which do not aim to make a profit and to those which do so aim but which prohibit its distribution to the members.

regulatory pressure to use the guarantee form, it seems that ceasing to be a member is a much easier process to handle in a guarantee company where there is no share to be dealt with, which must either be repurchased by the company (which, as we saw above, is a process highly regulated by the Act) or transferred to a new member, which is a cumbersome process in private companies. Instead, the admission and departure of members of a guarantee company can be governed solely by the company's own rules.

In addition, the Act permits companies limited by guarantee (but not companies limited by shares), which are charities or which pursue certain defined public-interest objectives and whose constitutions prohibit the distribution of economic surplus to the members, to dispense with the obligation, which would otherwise apply to them, to include the word 'ltd' at the end of their name.[65] However, guarantee companies are not obliged to pursue not-for-profit objectives and, conversely, companies which have issued shares may also be used in the not-for-profit sector. Thus, the tenants of a block of flats may incorporate a company limited by shares in order to see to the upkeep of the common parts. That is clearly not a charitable or even a public interest objective. Equally, however, such a company may not be seeking to make a profit. Its aim may simply be to balance over time the receipts from the tenant-members by way of maintenance charges and expenditures on cleaning, decorating, and repairs.

The role of the company in the not-for-profit area is an increasingly important one. With the growing reliance by government on non-governmental organizations for the delivery of some kinds of social services previously provided directly by the state, charities, and other bodies, such as housing associations, find themselves entering into contractual commitments of an increasing size. They thus have an incentive to incorporate in order to gain in particular the benefits of limited liability. These pressures have led to the development in recent years of legal vehicles more specifically adapted to not-for-profit ends than the company limited by guarantee. Thus, in the case of charities a specialized form of corporate body (the Charitable Incorporated Organization) is to be made available to this end.[66] In 2004 the legislature created the Community Interest Company (CIC) which is a specialized form of the limited company for the pursuit of non-charitable but community

---

[65] s 60 and the Company and Business Names (Miscellaneous Provisions) Regulations 2009/1085, reg 3.

[66] The basic framework is in the Charities Act 2006, but needs implementing regulations.

objectives, which does allow some limited distribution of the economic surplus.[67]

THE STRUCTURE OF THE BOOK

Having identified the core features of company law and the range of uses to which the company vehicle can be put, it might be thought that the rest of this book should consist simply of analysing the way in which the core features are implemented in company law, noting as one goes along the types of company which do not make use of a particular core feature and seeking to explain why this should be. Indeed, discharging these tasks will constitute a substantial part of the rest of this book. However, the task is somewhat more complex than the above description might suggest, for the following two reasons.

First, the values which underlie the core features cannot be presented as overriding policy objectives which must defeat in all circumstances countervailing values. Take, for example, the doctrine of limited liability, ie the rule that creditors' claims are limited to the company's assets. As we shall see in a later chapter, one powerful argument in favour of limited liability is that it encourages the purchase of shares by people who do not want to be involved in the management of the company. However, it is also a doctrine which may permit, or even encourage, opportunistic behaviour on the part of the controllers of the company as against its creditors, for example, by spiriting out of the company assets which the company was represented as owning when the credit was advanced to the company. It is not in the interest of shareholders in general for limited liability to be used in this way, because such behaviour may make it more expensive for companies to raise credit. For example, if abuse of the doctrine of limited liability were rife, banks lending to companies might be prepared to do so only at higher interest rates than they would obtain if the shareholders' liability were not limited. So, the task for company law is not simply to implement limited liability. The task is not even necessarily to balance the interests of investors and creditors, though it may come to that if no better strategy can be identified. The most challenging task is to design a set of rules which achieves the desired benefits of limited liability (encouraging shareholder investment) whilst reducing or even eliminating the occasions for opportunistic behaviour as against creditors which those rules might otherwise generate. The task is a demanding one, both in

---

[67] Companies (Audit, Investigation and Community Enterprise) Act 2004, Part 2 (still in force). There were some 3,500 CICs in existence in early 2010.

relation to limited liability and the equivalent issues arising under the other core features.

Second, the five core features do not inhabit separate universes. On the contrary, they interact with one another, so that the ideal solution for the implementation of one feature may score very poorly when considered from the standpoint of its promotion of another feature. We have already noted that shareholder control over management may be maximized by placing a wide range of decisions in the hands of the general meeting, but that such a rule would at the same time substantially deprive the company of the benefits of centralized management. For small companies, where centralized management is not a desideratum, this solution may be feasible. In large companies, on the other hand, general shareholder decision-making would be a disaster, and in such companies the law must try to devise techniques which provide the benefits of shareholder control without at the same time imposing greater costs by way of loss of the benefits of centralized management.

As we proceed through the book and consider the five core features (separate legal personality, limited liability, centralized management, shareholder control, and free transferability of shares), we will become aware that *three* relationships recur in our analyses. These three relationships are:

- the relationship between the shareholders as a whole and the board of directors;
- the relationship between majority and minority shareholders; and
- the relationship between the controllers of the company (whether directors or shareholders) and those other groups whose contribution is potentially vital to the success of the company, such as investors, lenders, employees, suppliers and customers.

The relationships which are the focus of attention vary according to the core feature and type of company we are concerned with. Thus, in a publicly traded company centralized management raises issues mainly concerned with the first relationship (how can the directors be made accountable to the shareholders?) but the solution to that problem may affect relationships in the third category (too close an accountability to the shareholders may discourage, for example, employees or suppliers from making appropriate investments in their relationship with the company). In a large private company accountability to the shareholders will be easier to provide because the shareholdings are likely to be more concentrated, but with concentrated shareholdings there is a greater risk that some of the shareholders will obtain control and run the company without regard to the interests of the non-controlling shareholders, thus raising issues under the second relationship.

In short, the task of most of the remaining chapters is to analyse the way in which the law seeks to provide the benefits, and avoid the costs, of the core features of company law by focusing, across the range of companies, on the relationships among the corporate actors upon which the weight of the law's policy falls.

2

Corporate Personality

In the first chapter we saw that the idea of the company as a separate legal person facilitates two core features of company law.[1] These are the limited liability of the shareholders and the transferability of a shareholder's interest in the company to another person. Separate legal personality makes it easier to distinguish business assets from personal assets, a distinction upon which limited liability depends. It also permits shares, which belong to the members, to be transferred from one person to another, whilst the property and contractual rights and obligations of the company, ie its business assets and liabilities, remain unaffected. With hard work and ingenuity, limited liability and the transfer of interests can be (and have been)[2] achieved without separate legal personality, but only at a much higher cost of transacting, and so separate legal personality is the efficient rule. There is often debate within legal systems about the range of legal vehicles which should be treated as having separate legal personality, and legal systems differ somewhat on this point among themselves,[3] but it is notable that no modern legal system fails to make readily available to businesses formed for commercial purposes a legal vehicle which has separate legal personality.

For this reason, contemporary debate in company law focuses on the problems generated by the acceptance of separate legal personality for the company, rather than upon the question of whether it should, in principle, be made available. In this chapter we shall examine two such issues. The

---

[1] Above p 9.

[2] Thus, before the legislature created a simple form of incorporation by registration in the middle of the nineteenth century, business people aimed to achieve these features by means of the 'deed of settlement company', a form of partnership in which the assets of the business were held by trustees. See *Gower's Principles of Modern Company Law* (6th edn, London: Sweet & Maxwell, 1997), 28–32.

[3] A matter on which different stances have been taken by legal systems is whether the partnership should have separate legal personality, an issue upon which, even within Great Britain, different views are taken in England and Wales (no separate legal personality) and Scotland (legal personality). See Law Commission and Scottish Law Commission, *Partnership Law: A Joint Consultation Paper* (2000), 6–9 and Part IV.

first, which we shall analyse only briefly at this stage, is what exceptions, if any, should be made to the rule of separate legal personality. The second, which will occupy the bulk of the chapter, is how a company, which is an artificial person, can be said to act or to know anything.

THE EXCEPTIONS TO SEPARATE LEGAL PERSONALITY

Given the functions within company law of separate legal personality, it is obviously a matter of great interest to company lawyers if the legislature or the courts ignore the doctrine of separate legal personality, with the consequence that shareholders are made liable for the company's debts or the free transfer of shares is impeded. However, we intend to deal with this aspect of separate legal personality primarily in those chapters where we discuss limited liability and the transferability of shares. Especially in relation to limited liability,[4] we shall see that there is a narrow set of situations where, for good reason, the corporate veil is pierced (as the hackneyed phrase has it) and shareholders are held responsible for the company's debts or other liabilities. The reason for postponing discussion is that these examples of piercing the corporate veil can be analysed sensibly only within an overall understanding of the role of limited liability.

This leaves the more general issue of disregarding the separate legal personality of the company without any impact on the liability of the shareholders or the free transferability of shares. When in *Salomon v A Salomon & Co Ltd*[5] the House of Lords emphasized the importance of the separate legal personality of companies, it did so, not only for the purposes of limited liability, but for all legal purposes. However, although this is the starting point for analysis, the courts have held that in some situations the separate legal personality of the company should be ignored. In fact, the list of such instances is now impressively long.[6] For example, it was held in one case that, for the purposes of compensation under compulsory purchase legislation, a parent company was entitled to compensation for disturbance to its business arising from the compulsory purchase of premises, even though the premises belonged to a subsidiary company.[7] In this case there was no question of the shareholder (the parent) being liable for the debts of the company (the subsidiary); rather, the parent benefited from the lifting of the veil. Much effort has been expended by company

---

[4] See Ch 4 below.   [5] [1897] AC 22.
[6] See eg *Palmer's Company Law* 2.1519–20, giving a dozen categories of case where this happens.   [7] *DHN Food Distributors Ltd v Tower Hamlets LBC* [1976] 1 WLR 852.

lawyers in trying to explain these instances. It is suggested that no single explanation for these cases will be found and that in any event company lawyers are not well equipped to provide the explanation or explanations.

I make this apparently radical suggestion on the basis that it is possible to decide whether to ignore the separate legal personality of the company in this class of case only on the basis of an understanding of the purpose of the rule which is alleged to require this step to be taken. This is true whether the rule in question is statutory, common law, or contained in a contract. Is the rule, whatever its origin, inconsistent with the recognition of the company's separate personality? Often a company lawyer will not have much to offer to the debate.

An example, from labour law, may help to make the point clear. One function of employment law is to help redress the balance of power between the employer and the dependent or subordinated worker by imposing mandatory standards below which the parties to the employment contract cannot agree to go. Suppose, however, the employer is a small company of which the worker, party to the employment contract with the company, is also the only shareholder and only director. Should the mandatory rules of labour law apply to such a contract? Is the worker here subordinated or, if one ignores the separate personality of the company, 'really' his or her own boss? The point is not always as easy to resolve as this way of putting it might suggest,[8] but my argument is that resolution of the problems is a matter for employment lawyers and the vital interests of company law are not implicated, whichever way the decision turns out. The principal issue at stake in these cases is the scope of the protection to be afforded to the worker as against the employing company. However that question is answered, the shareholders of the employing company will not be made responsible for the company's obligations.

Thus, the upshot is that the limited liability aspects of piercing the corporate veil will be discussed in later chapters and the non-company law aspects will not be further discussed.

HOW DOES A COMPANY ACT AND KNOW?

Although the company is a separate legal person, because it is an artificial person it is capable of acting and knowing only if the acts or knowledge of human beings are attributed to it. Thus, one needs to know whose actions or knowledge and in which situations shall be treated as the company's.

---

[8] For the latest in a long line of recent cases on the matter see *Secretary of State for Business, Enterprise and Regulatory Reform v Neufeld* [2009] BCC 687, CA.

This question arises in two principal situations. The first is where the question to be answered is whether a company has entered into a transaction, typically a contract. The second is where the question to be answered is whether the company has committed a wrong, either civil or criminal. The answers are crucial for those involved with companies, whether internally or externally. Shareholders and managers need to know who can bind the company legally as to its future conduct or involve the company in legal responsibility for actions (in the sense that the company's assets are placed at risk for the satisfaction of the claims of third parties). Conversely, those seeking to deal with companies or affected by the actions of those operating within the corporate organization need to know whether their transaction with the company is secure and whether they can hold the company liable for wrongs done to them.

An important further issue also arises. Those within and without the company need to know whether that corporate liability, if it arises, exists as well as or in place of liability on the person connected with the company. As we shall see, the law takes a radically different view on this issue in the case of contracts (generally only corporate liability), torts (generally both personal and corporate liability), and crime (where the regime depends on the seriousness of the crime).

There is a broad spectrum of possible approaches to the issue of attribution, ranging from treating the acts done or liabilities incurred by all the agents and employees of the company as those of the company to confining the company's responsibility to the actions of its constitutional organs, ie the board or the shareholders' meeting. As we shall see, British company law makes full use, in different contexts, of the range of possible answers.

A related issue is to determine how, precisely, the process of attribution works. There are two broad approaches. One is to establish that an individual has incurred a liability and then to attribute that *liability* to the company because of the relationship which exists between the company and the individual and because there is a sufficiently close connection between that relationship and the circumstances in which the liability was incurred. The best-known example is the rule of vicarious liability. For example, an employee commits a tort in the course of his employment or agency and the employing company is held liable to the victim, not because it has committed the tort but because it is the employer of the tortfeasor.[9]

---

[9] This is the current orthodoxy as to how vicarious liability works, but see R Stevens, Note, (2007) 113 LQR 31, arguing that vicarious liability also operates by attributing acts, not liability, to the principal.

The alternative is to treat the *acts or knowledge* of individuals as acts or knowledge of the company, on the basis of which the liability of the company is assessed. Here the company is the primary bearer of the liability; establishing whether the individuals have incurred the liability is not a necessary step in establishing the company's liability (though the individuals may well be liable). For example, a statute may impose a duty only on employers. To decide whether an employing company has broken that duty it will be necessary to decide whose acts or knowledge (from among the individuals operating within the organization) should be attributed to the company, but those individuals will not themselves be in breach of duty because they are not employers.[10]

This second technique of attribution has a broader impact if it is combined with that of 'aggregation'. Here, the acts or knowledge of a number of individuals within the organization are attributed to the company, so as to make the company liable, even though no single individual possesses the combination of acts and knowledge which serve to make the company liable. By this technique, the company is put under legal pressure to have effective systems in place not only to monitor potential wrongdoing by its agents or employees, but also to distribute the knowledge of any one employee to all those within the organization for whom it may be relevant, so that they may avoid illegality. However, in some cases aggregation defeats the purpose of the rule, which may be aimed at confining, not distributing, information within organizations. Here, companies need to be provided with a defence against aggregation. An example from the area of financial services is the oddly named 'Chinese wall'. If a conglomerate financial services company has effective barriers in place to prevent 'inside information' moving from one part of the company to another, its liability for insider dealing will be assessed on the basis of the compartmentalization produced by the barriers.[11]

It will be clear that, under the traditional analysis of vicarious liability, the persons whose actions brought about the change in the company's legal position will themselves be liable. Under the approach of attributing acts to the company, however, the matter is left open and could be decided either way without affecting the company's liability.

---

[10] Even in this example the individuals might incur various forms of secondary liability, such as aiding and abetting the company.

[11] Insider trading is trading in securities on the basis of price-sensitive information which is not publicly known. However, if an investment bank has effective barriers in place to prevent such information moving from, say, its corporate finance department to its dealing department, the liability of the dealers will be assessed on the basis of what is done and known in the dealing department alone. See FSA, *Code of Market Conduct*, para 1.3.5.

CONTRACTING

PRIMARY RULES OF ATTRIBUTION

As far as contracting is concerned, the law displays two outstanding features. The first is that it allows a wide range of persons to commit the company to contracts, whilst giving the company control over the choice of the persons to whom this power is given. The second is that it treats the resulting rights and duties as existing, normally, only between the third party and the company, and not also or instead between the third party and the person acting on behalf of the company.

The most obvious answer to the question of who can commit the company to contracts is that the company's constitutional decision-making bodies can do so. Lord Hoffmann has referred to rules imposing liability upon a company in this way as the 'primary rules of attribution'.[12] On this view, the actions of the board of directors or of the shareholders (normally acting by resolution) will be treated as actions of the company. If the board approves a contract between a third party and the company, there is not usually any doubt that the company is bound by the contract.

Even on this limited approach to attribution, however, the matter is not entirely free from difficulties. Take a person contracting with the board over a matter which the company's articles say is one reserved for decision by the shareholders.[13] Is the company bound by the agreement? The modern tendency, as we shall see further below, is to treat the company's articles as an essentially internal document and to relieve the third party of the need to concern itself with its provisions. Thus, section 40 permits a good faith third party to treat the board's power to bind the company as unlimited by the articles and makes bad faith so difficult to prove that very few third parties will fail to benefit from this provision. In consequence, third parties dealing with the board normally do not need to concern themselves with such restrictions on the board's powers.

However, no similar protection exists for those contracting with the company through the shareholders (where the constitution gives contracting power to the board). This is perhaps to be explained on the grounds

---

[12] *Meridian Global Funds Management Asia Ltd v Securities Commission* [1995] 3 All ER 918, 923, PC.

[13] Another risk for third parties is that the apparent directors have not been properly appointed under the procedure laid down in the company's articles. s 161 confers validity on directors' actions even if this is so (and in certain other cases), but the section protects a narrower range of third parties than does s 40 because it does not apply to those put on notice of the defect: *Morris v Kanssen* [1944] Ch 346, CA and [1946] AC 459, HL.

that, in all but the smallest companies, the advantages of centralized management[14] mean that the company's constitution routinely allocates contracting powers exclusively to the board, so that third parties should have a very different set of expectations about the contracting powers of the board, on the one hand, and the shareholders, on the other.[15] In very small companies a concerned third party can probably protect itself by obtaining the unanimous consent of all the shareholders.

However, even with these problems solved, the primary rules of attribution are not enough. Any large company will find the primary rules of attribution inadequate, for their implication is that only contracts approved by the board will bind the company. That may suit a small company, but the board of any large company is likely to find its efficiency heavily diluted if it has to spend its time approving all the company's contracts, no matter how trivial, rather than getting on with its main activity of setting and monitoring the company's business strategy. An efficient legal system must provide a mechanism whereby those lower down the company's hierarchy can bind the company contractually. Thus, further (secondary) rules of attribution are needed. Here, however, company law has not developed its own comprehensive set of rules. Instead, it relies on the general rules of agency to define the legal position of both the company and those who act on its behalf. However, these rules apply to companies with certain special twists. The following briefly analyses the application of agency law to companies, with emphasis on the special twists.

SECONDARY RULES OF ATTRIBUTION: AGENCY AND AUTHORITY

The rules of agency permit, but do not require, the company to disperse contract-making powers throughout the organization. Typically, in all but the smallest companies the company's articles will empower the board to, and the board will, delegate contract approval powers to senior managers, who are not directors, and they may be empowered to make a sub-delegation to more junior levels.[16] Only the good sense of the board and the senior management constrains the choice of those whom they authorize to contract on behalf of the company and determines the limits placed on their authority to contract.

---

[14] See above Ch 1 at p 12.
[15] In some cases the board's decision on a contract may need shareholder approval (see Ch 5 below), but even in such a case the third party will be dealing with the board.
[16] See eg art 5 of the Model Articles for public companies.

Where a duly authorized agent of the company contracts on its behalf, the result is a contract between the third party and the company (the principal); the agent is normally not a party to the contract. This coincides with the expectations of those who work for companies, whether as directors or managers, and, it is suggested, of those who deal with companies. Both groups would be surprised if contracts made by managers in the course of their duties and on behalf of the company were to render the managers personally liable or entitled on the contracts, unless, of course, they and the third party chose to make the manager a party. Within company law the only significant exception to this position concerns contracts made on behalf of companies not formed at the time of the contract, typically a contract made with a third party by persons who are in the process of forming a company. In such a case section 51 treats the contract as one made with the persons purporting to act for the company, unless it is agreed that the agents shall not be liable.[17] In short, in this narrow situation the default rule that the agent is not party to the contract is reversed.

Agency is thus a highly flexible and efficient instrument for the allocation of contracting powers within the company. The main problems in agency law arise when the agent is not actually authorized by the principal to act on its behalf, but is believed by the third party to be so. This may arise because the so-called agent is not authorized to act at all on the principal's behalf or because, although authorized, the agent's authority was restricted in some way and the agent exceeded that authority. The starting point must be that the company (as any other principal) is not bound in such a situation. Otherwise, the company would not be able to control the allocation of contacting power within its organization. Neither the third party's mistaken, even if honest, belief about the agent's authority nor the agent's mistaken, even if honest, belief about the scope of his authority should by themselves be sufficient to impose on the company a contract to which it did not consent. However, it may be that the company has in some way misled the third party into thinking that the agent was authorized to act on behalf of the company. In such a case, the law protects the legitimate expectations of the third party by holding the company to a contract which it did not, in fact, authorize.

---

[17] This is better than the common law result which was that, in many cases, there was no contract at all: not with the company, because it did not exist, and not with the agents because they did not purport to contract personally. Thus, the third party's expectations were entirely defeated. Even so, it would be an improvement to make it possible for the company, once formed, to ratify the contract and relieve the agent of responsibility.

The typical way in which a company misleads a third party as to an agent's authority is by appointing the agent to a position, of which it can be said that persons in that position normally have a certain authority, but the particular company has restricted the particular agent's power in some unusual way. In fact, as Lord Diplock pointed out some years ago, the doctrine of usual authority is even more important than this description might imply. Even where it is highly likely that the agent has actually been authorized to enter into the contract in question, the third party will probably not enquire whether this is so, but, in order to reduce transactions costs, will instead rely on the appearance of things.[18] The scope of the doctrine of usual authority thus defines the boundaries of efficient contracting with the company.

The principle of usual authority is easy enough to state at a general level, though there may be factual arguments in particular cases as to what is the usual authority of a person holding a particular type of position.[19] For company lawyers it is important to note that the courts have been reluctant to accept that a single director has an extensive usual authority to contract on behalf of the company.[20] Directors are expected to discharge their duties at board meetings, ie collectively, and so although the board as a whole may have very wide management powers, third parties are not entitled to read across these powers to individual directors. This increasingly anachronistic doctrine, however, may be less important than it seems, because it seems to focus on non-executive directors. If the director holds in addition an executive position in the company, for example as managing director, the usual authority of that executive (which is likely to be broad) is what counts, not that of the associated directorship.

Another common way in which the company[21] may hold out a person as having authority to contract is by representation to the third party,

---

[18] *Freeman & Lockyer v Buckhurst Park Properties (Mangal) Ltd* [1964] 2 QB 480, CA. The whole judgment is worth reading.

[19] A particularly thorny issue is whether an agent who does not have usual authority to contract can nevertheless bind the company on the grounds he had usual authority to convey to the third party the decision of the person within the company who does have authority to contract: see *First Energy (UK) Ltd v Hungarian International Bank* [1993] BCLC 1409, CA; *ING Re (UK) Ltd v R&V Versicherung AG* [2007] 1 BCLC 108.

[20] *Houghton & Co v Nothard, Lowe & Wills* [1927] 1 KB 246, CA. By contrast, the usual authority of the company secretary has been expanded: *Panorama Developments Ltd v Fidelis Furnishing Fabrics Ltd* [1971] 2 QB 711, CA.

[21] But who is the company? Certainly someone with actual authority to make the representation, but there seems no reason why it should not be someone with ostensible authority to make the representation, provided the representor's ostensible authority can be properly founded. In theory, this could give rise to an infinite regression, but it is unlikely that more than two or three layers of authority would emerge in practical situations.

by words or conduct, that the agent does have authority (even though, as between the company and the agent, no such authority has been conferred). This is in fact simply a more generalized version of the principle of usual authority, where the holding out arises from the appointment of the agent to a particular position. It is common to use the term 'ostensible' authority to refer to both the particular and the general ways in which a holding out may be founded.

RESTRICTIONS IN THE COMPANY'S ARTICLES

The above is general agency law. However, we need to come back to the specific company law question of the impact of restrictions, contained in the articles of association, on the general agency rules. These restrictions may be of two kinds. First, the articles may purport to confine the company's capacity to engage in business to certain defined areas—though this is less common today than it was. Although a third party's contractual rights are no longer at risk from this purported restriction on the company's capacity,[22] the restriction on corporate capacity can be seen as also limiting the agent's authority. This is on the basis that an agent of the company cannot have actual authority to do that which the company does not have capacity to do.

Second, the articles of association may place restrictions on an agent's authority to act on behalf of the company, even in areas where the company is free to act. Thus, the articles might say that no manager, without board approval, may enter into a contract on behalf of the company if the liability under it exceeds £50,000.

Company law has always shown some scepticism towards arguments that the company can protect itself through provisions in its constitution against claims from good faith third parties purporting to contract with it. Early on, it developed the 'indoor management rule'[23] to give some protection to third parties in such situations. However, that rule did not really do the job, in large part because it did not protect those who actually knew of the limitation in the constitution or knew enough facts to be put on enquiry as to whether there was a relevant limitation in the constitution. The risk that a court might, ex post, treat a third party as having known enough to have been put on enquiry meant that, for many third parties, the only safe course was to conduct, ex ante, that enquiry into the company's constitutional arrangements, thus providing certainty at the expense of higher transaction costs. This weakness was exacerbated by the doctrine

---

[22] s 39.
[23] Associated with the case of *Royal British Bank v Turquand* (1856) 6 El & Bl 327, HL.

of constructive notice, which treated the third party as knowing what was in the articles (because the articles are a public document) even if in fact the third party was ignorant of them.

However, the trend in the current law and in reform proposals is to turn the company's constitution into an entirely internal document which has no impact upon the question of whether the third party may enforce its transaction with the company. In other words, articles are no longer seen as an appropriate way of conveying information about agents' authority to third parties contracting with the company. This is the exact opposite to the principle which underlays the idea of constructive notice arising from public filing. The company may still limit the authority of its agents as it wishes, provided it brings those limitations to the attention of third parties, but it cannot use the constitution to achieve the necessary notification.

However, this policy is only partially implemented in the current law. Section 40 provides that 'in favour of a person dealing with the company in good faith, the power of the directors to bind the company and to authorize others to do so, is deemed to be free of any limitation under the company's constitution'. As we have already noted, the section also adopts a narrow view of what constitutes 'bad faith'. However, this section protects unambiguously only those third parties who contract with the company via the board, ie those who rely on the primary rules of attribution, or with sub-board agents who stay within the authority which has been conferred upon them by the board, even if the board conferred that authority in breach of the articles. It is not clear that it helps third parties contracting with agents who go outside the authority conferred upon them, directly or indirectly, by the board. If the section does operate so narrowly, the third party may have to rely on the common law 'indoor management' rule in many cases. As we have seen above, this is far too narrow a basis for the implementation of a policy of third party protection, especially in the light of the doctrine of constructive notice. The 'indoor management' rule does indeed give third parties some protection against the impact of constructive notice, but only, it seems, if their constructive (or actual) knowledge of the articles leads them to suppose that the agent might have had authority to act. It provides no protection where the actual or constructive knowledge clearly indicates that the agent did not have authority.[24]

---

[24] In other words, where the agent has ostensible authority, the third party can assume that it survives contrary provisions in the articles, unless those provisions inevitably destroy the appearance of authority. In *Turquand* (above n 22), where the articles provided that the board had authority to borrow only such sums as had been authorized by the shareholders, the third party dealing with the directors was entitled to assume that such authority had been given

The CLR had proposed a more radical reform so that the statute would straightforwardly provide that 'in determining any question whether a person has ostensible authority to exercise any of a company's powers in a given case, no reference may be made to the company's constitution'.[25] Thus, in relation to the secondary as well as the primary rules of attribution for contracting authority, the relevant rules would operate untrammelled by the provisions of the company's articles, and the policy of promoting security of transactions for third parties would be pressed home. It is perhaps a pity that this approach was not adopted.

TORTIOUS LIABILITY

VICARIOUS LIABILITY AND TORT

At their core, contracts are voluntary legal instruments. It is consistent with this view that companies should be free to specify which persons shall be empowered to act as their agents for contracting purposes, that companies should be able effectively to limit the authority of those agents (provided the limitations are conveyed to third parties by an appropriate means), and that the resulting contractual rights and duties should exist only between company and third party. As we have seen, agency rules largely achieve this result in relation to the company's contracting powers. However, these are not necessarily an appropriate set of rules for the attribution of liability where the act done by the person is wrongful, either civilly (normally because it is a tort) or criminally. Here, one might expect the person who acts normally to be liable (even if the company is also liable) and for the rules which determine whether the company is also liable to attach less importance to the company's freedom to arrange its affairs so as to avoid liability. As we shall see, this is the pattern one finds in relation to tort liability as a result of the application of the doctrine of vicarious liability, whereas in relation to criminal liability, where the doctrine of vicarious liability is controversial, the proper state of the law is a matter of controversy.

The secondary rules of attribution in relation to the tortious liability of the company again rely on general legal doctrines—this time vicarious liability rather than agency rules. However, as with agency vicarious liability needs to be examined in the particular context of company law in

---

by the shareholders (though in fact it had not). If the articles had said the directors had no borrowing powers, the common law would not have helped the third party.

[25] CLR, *Final Report* (July 2001), Vol 2, ch 16, draft clause 16(7).

order to establish whether it helps or hinders the implementation of the core features of our subject. The doctrine of vicarious liability operates widely so as to make the company liable in tort. It applies to torts committed by both agents and employees.[26] It makes the employer or principal (for our purposes, the company) liable to the victim for the tortfeasor's conduct. The employee or agent is the tortfeasor (and thus is liable to the victim of the tort) but, because of the relationship existing between the agent or employee and the company, the company is also liable. In fact, company and individual are joint tortfeasors.[27] The nature of the doctrine of vicarious liability is such that it is not necessary to prove that 'the company' has committed a tort. What has to be shown is that the agent or employee committed the tort; the company then has liability for the tort attributed to it by the doctrine of vicarious liability provided the requisite relationship existed between the company and the tortfeasor.

Much of the case-law on vicarious liability turns on the definition of that appropriate relationship. The traditional formulation was the employer (company) would be liable if the employee or agent had committed the tort 'in the course of their employment', but not otherwise. More recent case-law has expanded the concept so that the company is now liable if there is a 'sufficiently close connection' between the employee's or agent's conduct and the company's business. The effect has been to open up corporate liability for acts which were clearly not authorized by the company and were not for its benefit.[28] By the same token, the ability of the company to limit its tortious liability has been restricted. If employees or agents are not given certain functions at all, the scope of the company's vicarious liability can be limited. However, if there is a business case for the company to engage in certain activities, it is difficult for the company to do so without accepting the associated risk of vicarious liability, even for unauthorized and, from the company's point of view, counter-productive acts. The company must instead monitor closely the acts of the employees and agents it assigns to those tasks.

---

[26] That the vicarious liability of principals for the acts of agents is as wide as that of employers for employees was asserted by the House of Lords in *Heatons Transport (St Helens) Ltd v TGWU* [1972] 3 All ER 101, 109. In the company context, the matter is less important than it might be, because nearly all those with authority to contract on behalf of the company will also be its employees.

[27] *New Zealand Guardian Trust Co Ltd v Brooks* [1995] 1 WLR 96, PC.

[28] *Lister v Hesley Hall Ltd* [2002] 1 A C 215, HL (sexual abuse of children in a care home by the staff employed to look after them); *Dubai Aluminium Company Ltd v Salaam* [2003] 2 AC 366, HL (partners vicariously liable for knowing assistance, given by one of their number, in breach of trust). See S Deakin 'Enterprise Risk: The Juridical Nature of the Firm Revisited' (2003) 32 *Industrial Law Journal* 97.

Indeed, one rationale for this wider vicarious liability is that the company, as with any employer, is in the best position to monitor the activities of agents and employees and the potential tortious liability gives the company a strong incentive to engage in monitoring.[29] An employer, for example, may refrain from hiring incompetent workers or agents, put in place proper training programmes, design working practices which reduce the chances of wrongdoing, and discipline workers who do not conform to those practices. If none of these is possible in a particular case, then vicarious liability helps to ensure that the costs of engaging in a particular business are internalized within the business and then passed on to the consumers of the company's output through its pricing policy. In short, the company does not enjoy the same freedom to fine-tune its vicarious liability in tort as it has in relation to the power of its agents to bind it contractually. In particular, an instruction given to an agent or employee not to engage in certain actions, even if that restriction is well publicized, will not necessarily operate to restrict the company's vicarious liability in tort.

PRIMARY RULES OF ATTRIBUTION

Given the width of vicarious liability in the law of tort, the primary rules of attribution for tort liability have received less attention from claimants and the courts, as indeed have secondary rules of attribution based on any theory other than vicarious liability. Corporate tort victims normally do not need to look beyond vicarious liability. However, in some, atypical, cases vicarious liability is not enough to determine the particular legal question arising between the litigants. It is clear that there are situations in which the acts of an individual are attributed to the company so as to make the company directly liable (the individual possibly being also liable). Tort law itself has developed the somewhat imprecise doctrine of the 'non-delegable duty' which operates in this way in respect of 'independent contractors' who are neither employees nor agents of the employer.

Within company law, the primary rules of attribution may produce a similar result. Thus, if the board of directors authorizes the commission of a tort on the company's behalf, the company will be treated as having committed that tort, as will the directors who authorized it.[30] Precisely

---

[29] See R Kraakman, 'Third-Party Liability', in P Newman (ed), *The New Palgrave Dictionary of Economics and the Law* (London: Macmillan, 1998), Vol 3 at p 583. This justification also probably explains why vicarious liability is less readily imposed outside the employer/employee or principal/agent relationship, because in relation to other groups the monitoring argument works less well.

[30] Those who authorize the commission of a tort are liable as secondary parties. But, short of authorization, a director is not liable for a tort committed by another director, agent, or employee of the company: *C Evans & Sons Ltd v Spritebrand Ltd* [1985] 1 WLR 317, CA.

when the acts of the board or the shareholders will be 'identified' with the company so as to make the company liable directly is a matter of some debate and has been discussed more fully in relation to criminal liability (see below). It has been said that the company is directly liable where the 'directing mind and will of the company' has authorized or committed a tort.[31] This is not a very helpful phrase, except that it does indicate that direct liability arises in a much narrower set of circumstances than vicarious liability. It seems that the company should be liable for torts authorized by the shareholders in a general meeting, as well as by the board, and it has been held that the doctrine applies to acts of a managing director or a sole beneficial shareholder in the conduct of the company's business, which were not endorsed at a meeting.[32]

TORTIOUS LIABILITY OF INDIVIDUAL ACTORS

Where the company's liability is based on vicarious liability, it is clear that the individual is liable as well. Indeed, on the conventional view, without individual liability there will be nothing for which the company can be liable vicariously. However, one can ask whether it would be better to follow the agency pattern and treat the acts of the individual as the acts of the company alone, so that individual liability would not arise. Not surprisingly, the issue has emerged in recent years in that part of our law where the division between contract and tort is contestable. Where the rules of tort and contract overlap, it is not surprising that a major issue has arisen in respect of company agents as to whether the governing principle should be the contract/agency one of no personal liability or the opposite tort notion.

Take the area of negligent misstatements. If a director in pre-contractual negotiations makes a negligently false statement and that statement becomes (only) an implied term in the subsequent contract between the third party and the company, the company will be liable on the promise that the statement is true and the director, not being a party to the contract, will not. If, on the other hand, the negligent misstatement is regarded as a tort, the director will be liable as tortfeasor and the company will be vicariously liable for the director's tort. Indeed, the point applies more generally to the negligent provision of services under a contract with a company: if the action is brought in contract, the company will be the only available defendant; if in tort, the individual who has negligently provided the services on behalf of the company may be liable as well. This

---

[31] *Lennard's Carrying Co Ltd v Asiatic Petroleum Co Ltd* [1915] AC 705, HL.

[32] *H L Bolton (Engineering) Ltd v T J Graham & Sons Ltd* [1957] 1 QB 159, CA (a landlord and tenant, not a tort, case); *Stone & Rolls Ltd v Moore Stephens* [2009] 2 BCLC 563, HL.

distinction matters little if the third party sues the company (which is liable on either analysis) but it does matter if the third party sues the director, as the third party may well wish to do, for example, if the company is insolvent. Thus, we need to see how the courts have handled the issue of the personal liability in this context.

The House of Lords held in *Williams v Natural Life Health Foods Ltd*[33] that the correct approach to the issue of the liability of corporate agents in tort is to rely on the general requirements of the law of tort relating to negligent misstatements and the negligent supply of services. In particular, it is a central ingredient for liability in these torts that a defendant must have assumed personal responsibility for the statement or services before liability in tort will be imposed. In the case of those acting on behalf of companies, such personal responsibility will not be taken to have been assumed unless the individual can be said to have conveyed to the third party, by words or conduct, that she was assuming personal responsibility. Merely to be the director or employee of a company is insufficient to lead to a finding of assumption of personal responsibility, even if that individual's expertise is the crucial resource available to the company for the effective delivery of the promised services.[34] The default rule is that the individual is assuming responsibility only on behalf of the company, so that the company can be sued as a primary tortfeasor because the individual's acts are attributed to it, but the individual cannot, because an essential ingredient for liability in these torts is missing.

Thus, in the case of torts arising out of the negotiation or performance of contracts on behalf of companies, the decision in *Williams v Natural Life Health Foods* amounts to saying that the appropriate distinction is not that between liability in tort and liability in contract. Rather, the better distinction is between relationships voluntarily entered into by third parties with the company and obligations toward the whole world imposed by law upon everyone, including those acting on behalf of companies. In the former case, where the third party contracts with the company, the default rule should be that the person acting on behalf of the company is not liable, whether the cause of action is framed in contract or in tort. That

---

[33] [1998] 1 WLR 830, HL. The case concerned negligent advice given by the director of a franchising company about the likely success of a proposed franchised health food shop. This general issue emerged in recent years first in the New Zealand courts. For an excellent analysis of these New Zealand decisions see D Goddard, 'Corporate Personality: Limited Recourse and its Limits', in R Grantham and C Rickett (eds), *Corporate Personality in the 20th Century* (Oxford: Hart Publishing, 1998), at 44–55.

[34] However, the test is an objective, not a subjective, one and so is open to the influence of the courts' policy perceptions.

default rule may be altered (where the company's agent accepts either contractual or tortious responsibility) but, unless the agent agrees to the contrary, the legal liabilities are those of the company alone. In the case of imposed obligations, say where the individual steals the third party's goods, the individual will be liable in tort, whether he is acting on behalf of a company or not.

Thus, in the *Williams* case, the House of Lords dealt with a company law problem without creating a specific company law rule but rather by relying on the general rules of tort law about assumption of responsibility.[35] Such an approach has one clear advantage. It enables all those acting on behalf of the company, whether directors or employees, to benefit from the protection of the rule.[36] A situation where there is one rule for directors and officers and another for employees is thus avoided. As with agency law, the same rules apply across the company's hierarchy of workers. On the other hand, the court's reasoning makes it clear that the conclusion in favour of the individual does depend upon the existence of another person (the company) which can be said to have assumed responsibility for the services and upon which the third party can be said to have relied. If there is no other legal entity, as in the case of a partner in an ordinary partnership (at least in England and Wales), the individual who has provided the services negligently will be treated as assuming responsibility for them (if anyone has done so). Thus, the *Williams* decision does constitute a consequence of, or at least build on, the doctrine of the separate legal personality of the company.

The *Williams* decision may also be seen as effectuating another company law doctrine, that of limited liability, at least if one takes the broader view of limited liability discussed in Chapter 1.[37] On this broader view, limited liability means that the person dealing with the company is confined to the company's assets for the satisfaction of his or her claims. On this view of limited liability, the doctrine should protect the assets of those acting for companies as much as it protects shareholders' assets. From

---

[35] For this reason, a director (or other individual) can be liable for fraudulent statements made on behalf of the company without assumption of responsibility, for that is not a requirement for the tort of deceit. See *Standard Chartered Bank v Pakistan National Shipping Corp (No 2)* [2003] 1 AC 959, HL. This seems right: corporate personality should not be a shield for fraud.

[36] However, the courts have been reluctant to give immunity in negligence to professionally qualified employees working in organizations. See *Phelps v Hillingdon BC* [2001] 2 AC 619, HL (educational psychologist employed by LEA); cf *Edgeworth Construction Ltd v M D Lea & Associates Ltd* [1993] 3 SCR 206 (Supreme Court of Canada)—individual engineers of an engineering company held not liable. In other words, in such cases the courts have found an assumption of responsibility. [37] Above p 12.

this perspective, to allow parties to contracts with the company to enforce their claims against the personal assets of agents or employees of the company is to permit them to escape from the terms of their bargain, just as much as in the case of enforcement against the personal assets of the shareholders. Clearly, the decision in *Williams* is a crucial element in the rules whereby British law provides this protection beyond shareholders. In particular, the *Williams* decision has provided comfort to those conducting business through small companies who may be, not only the company's dominant shareholder and director, but also its principal employee. To protect the personal assets of such people from contractual claims but not from tortious claims arising out of the same voluntary transactions with the company would be to deprive them substantially of the benefits of operating through a company with limited liability. However, the comfort so provided does depend upon the view the courts take of the role of assumption of responsibility in the general law of tort relating to negligent statements or the negligent provision of services. It is always possible that general tort law will be pushed in a direction unfavourable to directors of companies without the impact of such a development on the doctrine of limited liability being uppermost in the judge's minds.

A somewhat similar issue (of individual tortious liability linked to corporate contracts) arose in *Said v Butt*,[38] involving in this case contractual performance rather than formation. Suppose the board decides not to honour a contract the company has entered into. The company will be liable for breach of contract, but the directors will not (because they are not parties to it). However, can the directors be sued in tort by the other party to the contract for inducing breach by the company of its contract? This first instance judgment of some antiquity suggests not. The court in effect made an exception to the scope of the tort of inducing breach of contract, perhaps not just for companies but in all cases where an agent acts on behalf of a principal in a way which puts the principal in breach of contract. This seems correct and in line with the reasoning in *Williams*: the contracting party should be confined to the company's assets for the satisfaction of its claims.

CRIMINAL LIABILITY

Legal systems differ in their approaches to the principles which determine the criminal liability of companies. Some (such as Germany) historically have treated guilt as something which can be attributed only to

---

[38] [1920] 3 KB 497.

human beings, so that companies escaped criminal liability. At the other end of the spectrum, some (such as federal law in the United States) apply the doctrine of vicarious liability to crimes in much the same way as they have applied it to torts. Modern British law has no conceptual difficulty with the principle of corporate criminal liability, but, on the other hand, it has been unwilling to accept broad secondary rules of attribution in the criminal sphere. Vicarious liability, as we have seen, is a form of strict liability as far as the company is concerned. The common law, which has traditionally insisted upon a guilty mind as an essential element of crimes, has therefore been reluctant to find companies guilty, whether on the basis of vicarious liability or the attribution of mental states of individuals to the company.

However, criminal law in the UK is not just common law. Parliament has created many crimes, some based upon strict liability, and, where the statute has imposed strict liability, the courts have been willing to treat acts of employees and agents as acts of the company for the purposes of criminal liability. Crucially, this approach has extended to those crimes which impose strict liability but subject to a 'reasonably practicable' defence. This development is important, practically as well as theoretically, because one of the main sources of such 'hybrid' duties is the Health and Safety at Work Act 1974, which imposes duties upon employers not to conduct their undertakings in such a way as to expose employees or members of the public to risks to their health and safety. If a corporate employer, though its employees or agents, conducts its business in such a way as to create such a risk, then, subject to the reasonable practicality defence, it will be guilty of an offence, irrespective of whether any of its individual employees are guilty. To hold otherwise, Steyn LJ thought, would be to allow corporate employers to escape liability where individual employers or partnerships would be liable.[39]

None of this provides any guidance for crimes requiring a particular mental state. However, some sixty years ago the British courts applied the doctrine of 'identification' (discussed above) to crimes of this type: where a person or persons who constitute the 'directing mind and will' of the company have committed a crime, the company will be treated as liable as well because such people 'are' the company.[40] It has remained rather unclear who can constitute the directing mind and will. Lord Diplock

---

[39] *R v British Steel plc* [1995] 1 WLR 1356, CA: company guilty through the negligence (though probably not criminal negligence) of its employee.

[40] *R v ICR Haulage Ltd* [1944] KB 551, CCA. This was the application to the criminal law of the idea first developed in *Lennard's Carrying Co Ltd v Asiatic Petroleum Co Ltd* (above n 30).

thought it was only those authorized by the articles to exercise the company's powers, ie that the doctrine provided only a set of primary rules of attribution for crimes involving a guilty mind.[41] This may still be the test for common law crimes, but it is now clear that in the case of statutory offences requiring a guilty mind the question to be asked is who, for the purposes of the statute, is to be treated as the directing mind and will of the company.[42]

Despite these developments, the company is likely to escape criminal liability for serious common law crimes, unless the board or the shareholders have authorized the criminal conduct in question. This was widely regarded as unsatisfactory in relation to serious accidents caused by failures by company managements to put in place and enforce proper supervisory systems. Under the identification doctrine, only if someone at a very senior level in the company could be shown to have committed the criminal offence would the company be liable as well. In particular, the limited scope of the doctrine of identification made prosecutions of companies for involuntary manslaughter by gross negligence[43] difficult to conduct, even though it is a common charge against individual defendants.[44]

There were two possible ways forward from this unsatisfactory state of the law. One was to re-examine the arguments in favour of a general rule of vicarious liability for criminal offences. The deterrence and internalization of costs arguments, which we noted above in relation to vicarious liability in tort,[45] apply in principle to criminal liability as well. Indeed, if, as seems likely, the enforcement agencies of the state find it more difficult to detect and prove criminal wrongdoing within large organizations than do private claimants alleging tortious conduct, the argument in favour of vicarious liability is stronger in relation to crimes than torts. It is likely that the large company, through its internal disciplinary and monitoring techniques, is in a better position to deter criminal behaviour on the part of its employees than are the organs of the state, which may find it difficult to penetrate large organizations. Vicarious criminal liability could

---

[41] *Tesco Supermarkets Ltd v Nattrass* [1972] AC 153, HL.

[42] *Meridian Global Funds Management Asia Ltd v Securities Commission* [1995] 3 All ER 918, PC. In that case the acts of a senior investment manager, who was not a director, were attributed to the company. In *Re Supply of Ready Mixed Concrete (No 2)* [1995] 1 AC 456, HL, it was the acts of local managers, acting in defiance of express orders from senior management, whose actions were attributed to the company.

[43] *Attorney-General's Reference (No 2 of 1999)* [2000] QB 796, CA.

[44] See Home Office, *Reforming the Law on Involuntary Manslaughter: The Government's Proposals* (May 2000), para 3.1.6: only three successful prosecutions and all of small companies, where it is more likely that the person responsible at the operational level also holds a 'directing mind and will' position within the company.   [45] Above p 44.

provide a powerful incentive to companies to make compliance with the criminal law a central goal of the company's overall strategy (a 'culture of compliance').

However, there is a risk that vicarious criminal liability, just like vicarious tortious liability, could create perverse incentives. Under vicarious criminal liability the company, on the one hand, has an incentive to detect criminal conduct, so that it can control it; on the other, detection of crimes increases the risk that liability will be imposed on the company. One way of counteracting these perverse incentives is for the courts to grant to those companies which do introduce effective compliance systems substantial discounts on the normal fine if, as will inevitably happen under even the best control systems, an employee does commit a criminal offence in the course of her duties, provided the company cooperates with the investigations by the public authorities. This is in essence the approach of the federal criminal law in the United States.[46]

An alternative approach, however, was advocated by the English Law Commission.[47] This built on the technique used in the Health and Safety at Work Act to create criminal duties which apply to companies and whose breach by the company can be demonstrated by attributing acts and omissions of relevant officers and employees to the company, whether or not those individuals are held to have committed a crime. Responding in particular to the difficulty of convicting a company of involuntary manslaughter, the Commission proposed the creation of a new offence of 'corporate killing'. These proposals eventually reached the statute book in the shape of the Corporate Manslaughter and Corporate Homicide Act 2007.

This Act creates a criminal offence where a company causes a person's death as a result of the way its activities are organized or managed where that organizational or management failure amounts to a gross breach of a duty owed by the company to the deceased. The crucial point is that no individual has to be picked out whose acts constitute the offence of manslaughter and who fits the criteria for identification with the company, as under the common law approach. The company can be convicted on its organizational failings alone, provided those failings can be identified as the responsibility of its senior management. Thus, organizational, rather than individual, failure becomes a basis for criminal liability, provided

---

[46] J C Coffee, 'Corporate Criminal Responsibility: An Introduction and Comparative Survey', in A Eser, G Heine, and B Huber (eds), *Criminal Responsibility of Legal and Collective Entities* (Freiburg: Jus Crim, 1999).

[47] The Law Commission, *Legislating the Criminal Code: Involuntary Manslaughter*, Law Com No 237 (1996).

Corporate Personality

that failure occurred at a senior level in the company. The sanction is an unlimited fine on the company (ie the shareholders) plus a power for the court to order that the company publicize its conviction (and so a reputational sanction) and an order that the company remedy the managerial failings revealed in the case. However, as recommended by the Law Commission, no additional criminal rules are created for directors and senior managers: the Act concerns itself only with the criminal liability of the company.

CONCLUSION

It is clear that the attribution rules for companies are complex, mainly because of the range of situations with which it is necessary to deal. However, they are fundamental. Whenever a statement is made about a company 'doing x' or 'deciding y', it is probable that there is an implicit reference to one or more of the rules of attribution. They form the bedrock of company law, even if their structure is still not fully defined. With hindsight, it can be seen that giving the company separate legal personality was the bold and imaginative but technically easy conceptual step. Giving that person the means of thought and action has proved a legally much more complex undertaking.

3

Limited Liability and Channelling Creditors' Claims

CONCEPTIONS OF LIMITED LIABILITY

We saw in Chapter 1 that the company's separate legal personality facilitates the task of identifying and separating the assets and liabilities which are properly attributable to the business carried on by the company and those which are properly attributable to the individuals who have invested in the company (shareholders) or who manage it (directors and others). The company owns the former; the shareholder or director the latter. The corporate set-up is in marked contrast with the position of a sole trader, where there is no difference in point of ownership between the business and personal assets and liabilities of the trader (even if he must make an internal administrative effort to keep them separate for tax and perhaps other purposes). The ordinary partnership is a hybrid situation: the assets and liabilities of the business run by the partnership are held by the partners jointly; the non-partnership assets and liabilities by the individual partners.

Having made this distinction between corporate and non-corporate assets, the law is in a position to proceed to the next step, which is the provision of limited liability (though one can have separate legal personality without limited liability, as in the unlimited liability company[1]). Although 'limited liability' is a well-known phrase, at least three (not necessarily mutually exclusive) meanings can be attached to it. At its narrowest, limited liability means that that claims of the company's business creditors cannot be asserted against the assets of the shareholders. As we also saw in Chapter 1,[2] the doctrine of separate legal personality secures this result so long as the company is a going concern. In the case of insolvency, which is where the matter is at its most pressing, protection of the shareholders is

---

[1] Above Ch 1 at p 22.   [2] At p 10.

effected by limiting the claims the liquidator can make against the share-holders for a contribution to the company's assets—in fact, the Insolvency Act ensures that no further contribution is required if the shares are fully paid up.[3] Thus, an investor in shares secures through limited liability a cap on his downside liability if the company's business proves unsuccessful. The investor may lose the whole of his investment—but no more than that. By contrast, the ordinary shareholder's exposure to the upside of the investment is normally unlimited: there is no cap on the returns if the business is outstandingly successful (though the shareholder normally has no entitlement to have the economic surplus distributed to him at any particular time).

A somewhat broader version of the first proposition states that the claims of the business creditors can be asserted only against the assets of the company. Putting the proposition this way makes it clear that the assets of not only the shareholders but also of others connected with the company, notably its managers and other agents, are to be shielded from the claims of creditors. This is in fact very largely the position in British law, though that result is achieved through very different legal mechanisms from those which protect the shareholders. As we saw in the previous chapter, in the case of voluntary transactions which the company enters into with third parties, the director or other agent normally escapes liability on the contract because the law of agency produces contractual relations only between the company as principal and the third party. Thus, agency law, coupled with the separate legal personality of the company, protects directors and other agents from personal liability on corporate contracts. As to insolvency, since they are not members, at least in their capacity as director or agent, the liquidator has no claim at all against them for a contribution to the assets of the insolvent company (unless they have engaged in fraudulent or wrongful trading, which we discuss in the next chapter).

It might be thought that the (extensive) liability of agents in tort cuts against this view of directors and managers being shielded from creditors' claims. It was suggested in the previous chapter that the exposure to tort claims was justifiable because tort liability is liability for wrong-doing. It would be odd if the individual escaped liability for wrongful conduct because that conduct occurred in the course of a company's business rather than outside it, especially given the ease with which companies can be incorporated. In consequence, the second proposition

---

[3] IA s 74(2)(d).

should be understood as referring to directors' and agents' protection against the claims of creditors arising out of contractual relations with the company.[4]

The third aspect of limited liability we need to examine is the corollary of the first. Just as the company's creditors cannot assert their claims against the assets of the shareholders, so the creditors of the shareholders cannot assert their claims against the assets of the company. This again flows from the separate legal personality of the company. The shareholder may pledge his shares to secure a personal loan and the lender may seize those shares if the loan is not repaid, but this gives the creditor no claim against the assets of the company, which are not owned by the shareholder.[5] Thus, when the majority shareholder in the travel firm, Thomas Cook plc, filed for bankruptcy in 2009, the shares held by this large shareholder, which had been pledged to the shareholder's creditors, were seized by the latter and later sold in the market to a variety of new investors. All this occurred without the assets of Thomas Cook or its ability to trade being impaired.[6]

Limited liability is often regarded as a surprising doctrine, almost a departure from the normal order of things, insofar as it confers protection on shareholders.[7] Certainly, there is an apparently strong contrast between the position of the small entrepreneur who carries on business as a sole trader or through a traditional partnership, who does not have the benefit of limited liability, and one who uses the company vehicle to conduct the business. The privileged position of the user of the corporate form might thus be thought to need justification. Why should the user of the corporate form be able to shelter personal assets in a way the sole trader or partner may not? One might answer this point by saying that the law makes limited liability available to anyone who wants it, through the 'one-person' company (recognized in practice for more than 100 years)[8] or through the newly introduced Limited Liability Partnership. Nevertheless, since limited liability throws risks onto creditors which they otherwise would

---

[4] As we saw at pp 45–48 there is some difficulty in drawing the line between voluntary transactions (where agents should not be liable personally) and wrongdoing (where they should).

[5] In the case of a partnership, which does not have separate legal personality, an express statutory provision is needed to produce a similar result: Partnership Act 1890, s 31.

[6] *Sunday Times*, 6 September 2009 (available on <http://business.timesonline.co.uk/tol/business/industry_sectors/leisure/article6823311.ece>).

[7] Protection of directors and agents against creditors is much less controversial, perhaps because it is not a protection confined to the agents of companies. The third aspect of limited liability, as a corollary of the first, stands or falls with it.   [8] See above p 25.

not have to carry, the question remains why the principle is so widespread and whether it ought to be so.

THE RATIONALES FOR LIMITED LIABILITY

ENCOURAGEMENT OF PUBLIC INVESTMENT

Historically, the argument for limited liability which had the strongest impact upon the Victorian legislature was that, without it, companies would not be able to raise from the public the large amounts of capital needed for major projects, of which the paradigm example at that time was the construction and operation of a new railway line.[9] Unlimited liability throws upon investors in companies' shares the risk of the loss of the whole of their personal wealth if the company becomes insolvent. Potential investors might respond to that extra cost of investment in one of three ways, all of which, it was reasonable to think, would reduce the pool of risk capital available to companies. First, they might simply seek other forms of investment, say company bonds,[10] rather than their shares. As bondholders, the investors would merely be creditors of the company, rather than members of it. As creditors, they would not be liable for the company's debts; on the contrary, as creditors they might be in a position to apply the principle of unlimited liability against the company's shareholders for the satisfaction of their own claims. However, loans are a less flexible form of financing than share capital,[11] and so the effect of unlimited liability would be to decrease the amount of risk capital available to companies, even if the total amount of finance were not reduced.

Second, unlimited liability would increase the costs to investors of port-folio diversification. Every investment in an additional company would increase the insolvency risk to the investor's wealth. Unlimited liability for shareholders would thus create an incentive for shareholders to con-centrate, rather than diversify, their shareholdings, but such concentra-tion would itself make it more difficult for investors to protect themselves against other sorts of risk. Risks that a particular company might turn out

---

[9] Limited liability was made available in the Limited Liability Act 1855, some eleven years after the first modern companies Act, the Joint Stock Companies Act 1844. Thus, for eleven years there was a general system of incorporation by registration but without limited liability. This shows that the Parliament of the time was well aware that limited liability was not a neces-sary feature of incorporation.　　　[10] On the meaning of 'bonds' see above p 6.

[11] Mainly because the interest on loans is normally payable periodically, no matter how badly the company is doing, whereas ordinary shareholders are entitled only to such dividends as the directors declare. See Ch 1 above at p 6.

to have bad management or that some sectors of the economy might do better than others, for example, can best be met by sensible diversification of the investor's shareholdings across a number of companies. However, under unlimited liability the additional costs of diversification would reduce the incentives for risk-averse investors to buy shares.

Third, unlimited liability creates a powerful incentive for shareholders to monitor closely the actions of the management of the company. If the whole of one's personal wealth is potentially at risk from the actions of the board, a review of the performance of the company at the annual general meeting of shareholders may seem inadequate. However, close monitoring of the board is both costly for individual shareholders (who may have other and more pressing calls on their time) and for the shareholders collectively, as it is likely to deprive the company of the benefits of centralized management. Those not in a position to engage in close monitoring would thus be less willing to buy shares and those who could do so would be willing to pay less for the company's shares because they would know that a monitoring obligation was in effect attached to them.

It could be argued that this emphasis on the raising of capital from 'the public' is today misplaced, since the role of the individual shareholder has declined. It is true that the percentage of the ordinary shares of companies listed on the London Stock Exchange which were held by individuals fell from 54 per cent in 1963 to 10 per cent in 2008, whilst that held by pension funds, insurance companies, unit trusts, investment trusts, and other financial institutions (the 'institutional investors') rose substantially,[12] and so it could be said that an increasing proportion of individual investment is channelled to the market via collective intermediaries. However, it is not clear how far this undercuts the arguments for limited liability, ie whether indirect investment would protect individual investors against the costs of unlimited liability. First, individual direct investment is still important and encouraged by governments (consider privatization issues) and is also important outside the large listed companies (consider investment by wealthy individuals in medium-sized private companies). Second, unlimited liability for the institutions would reduce the returns to investment via intermediaries and thus provide an incentive for direct investment, which, in the case of small investors, makes portfolio diversification more difficult. In any event, in the worst case unlimited liability might still reach through the institution to the personal assets of the investor, say where the

---

[12] See below Ch 5, Table 1.

investor is a member of the institution, as in an investment trust,[13] unless limited liability were reinstated at this point.

FACILITATION OF PUBLIC MARKETS IN SHARES

We have already noted the important role which public share markets play in enabling companies to raise capital. Such a market provides liquidity for the investor, whilst preserving the company's assets intact. Providing liquidity to the investor means providing a market on which at any time he can readily and cheaply sell his shares at a price (or within a narrow range of prices) which is publicly known. Under a regime of unlimited liability, however, the value of the shares would depend, not only on information about the company's performance available to the market, but also on the relative wealth of the shareholders. For example, if the shares over time traded into the hands of poor shareholders, the value of the shares to a wealthy shareholder would go down, because of the greater risk to his assets.[14] So, establishing the price of the shares would require the analysis of a whole new range of information and, in addition, that price would vary according to the shareholder's personal wealth. This would be likely to reduce the liquidity of the market, especially as reliable information about the wealth of fellow shareholders might be difficult to obtain.[15]

It is clear that neither of the above arguments provides strong grounds for applying the limited liability doctrine to the whole range of companies. If a company does not have its shares listed on a public market, the second argument falls away. The first argument has a rather broader impact. It could be said to facilitate investment not only in companies which offer their shares to the public, but, by extension, in all companies which wish to have equity investors who are not closely involved in the management of the business. This would include many large private companies as well as public companies. Even so, the argument is inapplicable to an owner-managed company, where close involvement in the management of the

---

[13] An investment 'trust', despite its name, is a company whose shares are traded on the market and whose assets are invested in the securities of other companies (and possibly other categories of investment asset).

[14] This assumes that the shareholders are jointly and severally liable to the creditors, so that the creditor could sue the wealthiest shareholders for the total liability and the latter would then seek to recover a contribution from the poor shareholders, which might or might not prove feasible. The result would be different under a regime of proportionate liability in which the shareholder was liable only for that proportion of the creditor's loss which his shareholding bore to the total equity capital.

[15] P Halpern, M Trebilcock, and T Turnbull, 'An Economic Analysis of Limited Liability in Corporate Law' (1980) 30 *University of Toronto Law Journal* 117 seem to have been the first fully to articulate this particular argument.

company is not seen by the shareholder as a burden but as an entitlement, and which may not raise significant amounts of risk capital in any event.

Nor do the arguments developed above have much application within corporate groups, unless they are very loosely structured. The arguments may support limited liability for the parent company's shareholders but not *within* the group, ie as between one group company and another of which it is a shareholder. However, are there other arguments in favour of limited liability which might have a broader impact?

PARTITIONING OF ASSETS

Given the limited scope of the above two rationales for limited liability, it is not surprising that recent theoretical efforts have focused on trying to identify a broader rationale for limited liability. Important work by Professors Hansmann and Kraakman has led to the proposition that the third version of limited liability identified above provides the most general benefit from and justification for limited liability.[16] As we noted at the beginning of this chapter the idea of a partitioning of assets starts from the insight that corporate personality and limited liability do not function only so as to shelter the personal assets of the shareholders from the creditors of the company. They also function so as to shelter the assets of the company from the creditors of the shareholder ('entity shielding'). Thus, if a shareholder becomes insolvent, the personal creditors may seek to assert their claims against the insolvent person's shares but not against the assets of the company which issued the shares. In this way separate legal personality and limited liability permit a partitioning of a person's business assets (which become the assets of the company) and a person's non-business assets (which remain his own). These two classes of asset (held by separate legal persons) may then be used as security to raise finance from separate groups of creditors, the company's assets to raise finance for the business and the personal assets finance for the shareholders' other activities. The business creditors will face no competition from the personal creditors in relation to the company's assets; and the personal creditors will equally face no competition from the business creditors in relation to the non-business assets.[17] This result can be defended from an efficiency perspective. The business creditors need monitor only what the company

---

[16] H Hansmann and R Kraakman, 'The Essential Role of Organizational Law' (2000) 110 *Yale Law Journal* 387 and eid. and R Squire, 'Law and the Rise of the Firm' (2006) 119 *Harvard Law Review* 1333.

[17] This assumes that the company controllers cannot easily intermingle their business and personal assets by freely moving assets into or out of the company. Legal strategies to prevent such behaviour are analysed in Chapter 4.

does with its assets and the personal creditors need monitor only what the shareholders do with their personal assets. Thus, the monitoring costs of the creditors are reduced.[18]

Equally, within the corporate group, limited liability permits the allocation of assets to legally separate companies and the pledging of those assets in support of particular business ventures to appropriately skilled creditors. Although creditors of a subsidiary might seem better off if they could claim on the assets of any of the companies in the group, they do in fact obtain a benefit from maintaining the separate legal personalities of the companies. Excluding creditors of other group companies from claims on the assets of the subsidiary relieves creditors of that subsidiary of the need to monitor the activities of the group as a whole, and thus reduces monitoring costs.

It is to be noted that the above arguments assume that monitoring of corporate management is an activity engaged in by creditors and not only by shareholders. The creditors' monitoring role in companies is less widely recognized by company lawyers than the shareholders' role, because company law has designed institutional mechanisms which express the shareholders' monitoring function (annual reports by directors to shareholders; shareholders' meeting; duties owed by the board of directors), whereas the creditors' monitoring role is largely, if not wholly, expressed in the provisions of private contracts. Nevertheless, it should not surprise us that creditors who have advanced large amounts to companies wish to be informed about and, in some degree, to control what the management of those companies does with the resources advanced and that they wish to put themselves in a position to take appropriate action if a substantial risk emerges that the loan may not be repaid.[19] In fact, in companies with dispersed shareholding bodies the creditors may be more effective monitors of management than the shareholders, and shareholders may then to some degree free-ride on the efforts of large creditors.[20] We discuss creditor monitoring further below.

---

[18] It is sometimes said that limited liability cheapens enforcement in a second way, namely, it means that the company's creditors do not have to face the prospect of obtaining enforcement against a large body of shareholders whose personal circumstances will vary. This seems a weak argument. Unlimited liability would not *require* the company's creditors to sue the shareholders, whilst the doctrine of joint and several liability (above n 14) allows the creditors, if they do sue, to pick out the wealthiest and make them liable for the whole of the debt.

[19] This will be the case even if the loan is secured on the assets of the company. It is likely to be cheaper for lenders to prevent the company from defaulting on the loan than to seek repayment after default.

[20] See eg J Drukarczyk and H Schmidt, 'Lenders as a Force in Corporate Governance: Enabling Covenants and the Impact of Bankruptcy Law', in K Hopt et al (eds), *Comparative Corporate Governance* (Oxford: Clarendon Press, 1998).

THE COSTS OF LIMITED LIABILITY

Despite the above real benefits of limited liability for shareholders, no one pretends the doctrine does not have costs. These potential costs are most evident when those who benefit from limited liability also have control of the company's management. In that situation the controllers face a strong temptation to use their control power in an opportunistic[21] fashion so as to benefit themselves as shareholders. At its simplest, they may shift assets into the company when they need to raise credit and out of the company when the time comes for repayment; but there are many other examples of opportunistic conduct. By contrast, there is little reason to be worried about a non-controlling shareholder's exemption from responsibility for the company's liabilities, at least so long as we are prepared to accept that lenders of money to the company are not responsible for the company's liabilities.[22] The modern view that shareholders do not own the company, but only their shares, makes their limited liability a less surprising doctrine for passive shareholders than it was previously thought to be.

There are two paradigm cases of the combination of control and limited liability, though they are very different from one another. One is the small company where, at its extreme, the shareholders and the directors may be the same people, so that control of the company is directly in the hands of the beneficiaries of limited liability. Almost at the other end of the spectrum is the corporate group. No large business today is carried on through a single company. Rather a string of parent, subsidiary, subsidiary, and associated companies exist behind a single name. Even a quite modest business may be carried on through one or more linked companies. However, each of these companies is a separate legal person and its shareholders (ie one or more other companies in the group) benefit in principle from limited liability as much as individual shareholders in a free-standing company do. Take a simple example of a parent company which holds all the shares of a subsidiary company. Parent and subsidiary are separate legal persons. The parent has complete control of the subsidiary: the directors of the subsidiary will be the nominees of the parent and

---

[21] This term is used to refer to self-interested behaviour which involves some element of deception, misrepresentation, or bad faith. See O Williamson, *The Economic Institutions of Capitalism* (New York: Free Press, 1986). The term is not a legal term and the law may or may not characterize a particular example of opportunistic behaviour as illegal.

[22] Doctrinally, this is because lenders to the company do not become its members. If they do intervene substantially in the affairs of the company, they might attract liabilities towards other creditors as 'shadow directors' under the doctrine of wrongful trading (below p 86), though the courts are not astute to impose such liability.

may even be the same persons as the directors of the parent company, so that the subsidiary board has no independent business discretion. Yet, the parent in principle benefits from the doctrine of limited liability as against the creditors of the subsidiary. Again the combination of limited liability and control may lead to opportunistic behaviour on the part of the parent company, for example, assigning risky activities to the subsidiary but not endowing it with adequate assets to carry those risks.

As is so often the case with company law, the task of the law is to preserve the benefits associated with limited liability whilst constraining opportunistic use of the doctrine. A number of approaches to this task are conceivable. However, there is also the initial question of whether the law needs to engage in the task of constraining opportunism at all. It could leave creditors to protect themselves, largely by contract, against the risks of opportunistic behaviour. In this strategy company law is not entirely without a role, because it could be used to place creditors in a position where they can bargain effectively with companies, for example, by requiring disclosure of relevant information. However, the greater weight of the policy for dealing with opportunism in this strategy lies with private rather than public ordering. We shall analyse creditor self-help in the rest of this chapter before turning to the legal rules which directly constrain opportunism in the next.

CREDITOR SELF-HELP

LIMITED LIABILITY AS A DEFAULT RULE

Although limited liability is now available to the smallest company,[23] it is not a mandatory rule. Those who do not like its implications may seek to contract out of or around the rule. In other words, the question is not whether limited liability is the best policy but whether limited liability coupled with freedom of contract is the best policy.

The most dramatic demonstration of the default status of the limited liability rule is freedom of parties to dispense with it entirely. The Act permits incorporators to establish companies which do not have limited liability,[24] and thus to opt out of limited liability across the board. In fact, this facility is little used. More significant in practice is opting out of the limited liability rule in particular transactions. Thus, in owner-managed companies, where the arguments for limited liability are perhaps least persuasive, limited liability in practice is often not available in respect of such

---

[23] See above Ch 1 at p 25.   [24] See above Ch 1 at p 11.

companies' major liabilities. To revert to our small company, Smith & Jones (Decorators) Ltd,[25] the loan which that company raised from the local bank in order to begin business was likely to have been available only on the terms that Ms Smith and Mr Jones gave personal guarantees of the repayment of the loan by the company, which guarantees were secured on their personal assets, notably a charge on their dwellings.[26] In this situation the bank has contracted out of limited liability: by contract, it has reinstated its right to assert its claim against the personal assets of the shareholders, should the assets of the company prove insufficient to satisfy the liability.

In fact, the choice between limited and unlimited liability is a choice between two default rules. Even if the legislature had never passed the Limited Liability Act 1855, it would have been possible for companies to contract in particular transactions on the basis that the creditor would not pursue the assets of the shareholders. So, the choice between limited and unlimited liability is a choice of starting points for private contracting. The basis of the choice should be the one which will most often suit the parties' needs *without* further substantial contracting, because in this way the costs of doing business are reduced. The standardization of modern economies on the limited liability rule suggests that the correct choice in this case is clear.

CONTRACTING AROUND THE CONSEQUENCES OF LIMITED LIABILITY

However, it would be wrong to see the role of private contracting as confined to opting out of limited liability. Contract has an equally important role in dealing with the *consequences* of transacting on the basis of limited liability. Most of these techniques are not specific to contracting with companies but rather are applicable to contracting with any counterparty whose solvency is in doubt.[27] In general, too, they are not techniques of company law but of commercial or property law, and so are excluded from most courses on company law. Nevertheless, they deserve to be

---

[25] Above p 22.

[26] Since the matrimonial home is often the most substantial personal asset an entrepreneur possesses, it is not surprising that the law reports now contain many cases dealing with the legal problems generated by entrepreneurs who have charged that home without obtaining the fully informed consent of their spouse. See eg *Royal Bank of Scotland v Etridge (No 2)* [2002] 2 AC 773, HL.

[27] One should also avoid the fallacy of thinking that, absent limited liability, the creditors' problems would evaporate. There are plenty of devices whereby natural persons entering into contracts can seek to put their assets beyond the reach of their creditors.

mentioned briefly. A lender doubtful of the borrower's ability to repay may take security over some or all of the company's assets.[28] This course of action does not expand the pool of assets which the creditor can pursue (in the way that a personal guarantee does), but it does give the security-holder priority over other creditors in the event that the company's assets prove inadequate.

Alternatively, or in addition, the lender may seek to control the actions of the corporate borrower by inserting provisions in the loan contract, requiring the lender's prior consent to certain courses of action which the lender judges might adversely affect the prospects of the loan being repaid.

> The theory is that a lender providing capital acquires an interest in the preser-vation of that capital, thereby conferring an entitlement to some voice, how-ever muted, in the management of the business in order to protect that interest. Unlike equity shares, debt does not have a right to vote for management. That 'vote' is conferred by covenants, the breach of which results in the sanction of an event of default, thereby encouraging compliance.[29]

The variety of protections for creditors which can be created in this way is large, and there is no need to explore them in detail here. Among the more common are restrictions upon the creation of security over the company's assets in favour of future creditors (the 'negative pledge' clause); restric-tions on the borrower's disposing of its assets; and requirements that the company continue to meet certain financial tests relating to its liquidity, solvency, or capital adequacy.[30]

Finally, a supplier to a doubtfully solvent customer may refuse to give credit (by requiring cash against delivery); may contract only on the basis of a higher than normal interest rate; or may seek to retain title in the goods, even after delivery, until the point at which payment is made. Restrictive action on the part of creditors is often triggered by a down-grade issued by a credit rating agency. Thus, if a major credit rating agency reduces the rating it gives to a large company's debt, that will have a major impact upon the cost to that company of raising loans; and the company's

---

[28] The floating charge, which is a technique of company law, is dealt with below at p 66.

[29] Philip R Wood, *International Loans, Bonds and Securities Regulation* (London: Sweet & Maxwell, 1995), 31. 'Covenant' in this connection means simply an obligation in the loan agree-ment other than one relating to payment and not an undertaking under seal. Note that Wood is here using 'capital' in a more general sense than it is used in the phrase 'legal capital'.

[30] See S Smith and J Warner, 'On Financial Contracting: An Analysis of Bond Covenants' (1979) 7 *Journal of Financial Economics* 117; W Bratton, 'Bond Covenants and Creditor Protection: Economics and Law, Theory and Practice, Substance and Process' (2006) 7 *European Business Organization Law Review* 39.

management can be expected to seek to maintain the confidence of rating agencies. Or the supplier may take out insurance against non-payment by the customer: the sudden reduction in the availability of such insurance had an adverse, though temporary, impact on supply chains in the recent 'credit crunch'.[31]

Thus, the scope for creditor self-help is wide. Nevertheless, three issues of principle arise. First, what can company law do to facilitate the processes of creditor self-help? Second, does creditor self-help, whilst solving some problems associated with the limited liability rule, generate any consequential problems for company law? Third, can creditor self-help deal with all the problems generated by the limited liability rule, ie can it be regarded as the sole solution? We will look in turn briefly at the first two issues in the remainder of this chapter and the third issue in the next one.

A ROLE FOR COMPANY LAW: FACILITATING CREDITOR SELF-HELP

The main contribution which company law makes to creditor self-help is in relation to disclosure of information. At a basic level, the Companies Acts have always attached great importance to the principle that companies with limited liability should signal this fact in a very public way to those who may deal with them. Except in rare cases, the Act requires limited companies to incorporate into their names the appropriate suffix ('plc' for public companies or 'ltd' for private ones or their Welsh equivalents), without which the Registrar will not incorporate the company;[32] it requires the company to give publicity to its name at all its places of business and on its correspondence;[33] and it prohibits the use of the term 'limited' by persons which are not limited liability companies.[34]

At a more fundamental level the Companies Act requires disclosure to the public of the company's annual financial statements and other reports, as discussed in Chapter 5.[35] Nevertheless, it can be argued that the information contained in the public accounts is often out of date,[36] and many large lenders no doubt require the production of more up-to-date information as part of the pre-contractual bargaining process.

---

[31] To the point where the government introduced a temporary scheme under which suppliers could purchase additional protection to that available in the public market from the state.

[32] ss 58–9. See Ch 1 above at p 1.   [33] Part 5, Ch 6.

[34] s 65 and regulations made thereunder.   [35] Below p 115.

[36] Private companies have nine months from the end of the financial year to file their accounts, public companies six months (s 442), and a public company whose securities are admitted to trading on a 'regulated' (top-tier) market four months (FSA, Disclosure and Transparency Rule 4.1.3).

THE FLOATING CHARGE

Moving beyond disclosure of information, we noted above that most of the legal techniques which creditors use to protect themselves against limited liability are not specific to company law. They are means of protection against debtors of uncertain financial status, whether that uncertainty derives from limited liability or some other source. However, there is one technique which was developed specifically in the company context. This is the floating charge.[37] This is a form of security which was developed by company practitioners in the nineteenth century and is available only to companies and, now, limited liability partnerships. It has a threefold significance. First, it permits companies to give security over classes of asset which otherwise it would be difficult to pledge; second, it enables lenders to attach a significant additional sanction to the restrictions a company may have accepted in the loan contract; third, through its enforcement mechanism it brings the charge-holder into the governance of the company.

On the first point, the difficulty with a fixed charge is that it requires lender assent to the disposal of the assets charged and thus is inappropriate for the charging of assets which are turned over in the course of a business. It is relatively easy to have a fixed charge on a factory but almost impossible to have one over the raw materials and half-finished products being worked on in that factory. A floating charge avoids these problems by not attaching to specific assets until some event occurs which causes the charge to 'crystallize'. Until that point the charge 'floats over' the assets charged and the company can deal freely with them, at least in the ordinary course of its business, as if they were unsecured. Of course, the floating charge is not as good a security from the creditor's point of view as the fixed charge, because the creditor runs the risk that the class of assets covered by the floating charge will prove to be less substantial at the point of crystallization than was expected at the point of creation. Nevertheless, it has the undoubted merit of permitting the company to charge a type of asset which would otherwise have little value as security.

Second, English law now seems to have reached the position that the creditor has a very free hand to specify the events which will cause the charge to crystallize. It seems not to be necessary that the event be one which puts the repayment of the loan or the security in jeopardy; and

---

[37] For a more detailed discussion than is possible here, especially on the distinction between fixed and floating charges, see P Davies (ed), *Gower and Davies Principles of Modern Company Law* (8th edn, London: Thomson, 2008), 1162–82 and 1196–215 (chapter by S Worthington).

the event may operate automatically so as to bring about crystallization. This puts the lender in a powerful position. It can attach the sanction of crystallization to the non-performance of any of the obligations which the loan contract lays upon the company as to the way in which it conducts its business. It is common for lenders to say that the loan becomes repayable if these restrictions are breached; it can now add the sanction of crystallization of the charge, which much increases the chances that the lender will in fact recover the money owing.[38]

Third, default has an impact, not only, via crystallization, on property rights over the company's assets, but also upon the company's governance. The existing board of directors is replaced by an administrator, in effect appointed by the charge-holder, who henceforth runs the company.[39] Consequently, once the administrator is appointed, the centralized management of the company is vested in him or her and the holder of that office becomes the focus of the rules relating to the conduct of the company's management.

CONTRACTING FOR GOVERNANCE RIGHTS

So far, we have looked at the ways in which company law facilitates creditor self-help in terms of mandatory disclosure of information and the floating charge. There is one other significant contribution by company law to creditor self-help. This is something we have remarked upon already, ie the flexibility of the company's constitution.[40] This enables the creditor to secure representation within the governance organs of the company, whether or not a floating charge has been created or there has been a default under it, if that seems to the creditor an appropriate course of action. Thus, by contract the lender may secure the right to nominate a director to the board. There is nothing in company law which requires directors to be selected by the shareholders. However, this is an area in which the law has not quite caught up with its own flexibility. Thus, the shareholders by ordinary majority can remove a director at any time,

---

[38] *Re Brightlife* [1987] Ch 200. See also *Re Permanent House (Holdings) Ltd* [1988] BCLC 563, where the 'events of default' included 'the making by the [lender] at any time hereafter of a demand upon the Company for repayment of all or any of the monies hereby secured'. Note that, of course, the word 'default' is not used here in the same sense as in the phrase 'default rule'. In 'event of default' default means a failure to meet an obligation; a 'default rule' means the rule which applies in the absence of contrary choice, but there is no implication of an obligation to make an alternative choice.

[39] In the case of floating charges attached to large-scale issues of debentures the former power to appoint a receiver still obtains. The receiver's duties run to the charge-holder alone; the administrator's to all creditors.   [40] Above Ch 1 at p 14.

whether that director was appointed by them or not,[41] and the nominator has no redress other than that which it has stipulated for in the contract (which might include, of course, the right to call for repayment of the loan and to appoint an administrator). Equally, the courts have insisted that the nominee director owes duties to the company, as any other director, rather than to the nominator. They have not even, within that formula, accepted the proposition that the nominee director should be permitted to give special consideration to the interests of the nominator.[42] One wonders whether this injunction is observed in practice; even if it is, the nominee director may provide at least a useful channel of information to the nominator about the company's activities. Alternatively, if the lender wants up-to-date information, it can stipulate for it in the loan agreement.[43]

OPPORTUNISTIC BEHAVIOUR BY
SECURED CREDITORS

Creditor self-help aims, largely by contract, to restrict the scope for opportunistic behaviour on the part of the controllers of companies which the limited liability doctrine permits. The very success of self-help, however, may generate consequential problems. First, the techniques of self-help may create scope for opportunism on the part of secured as against unsecured creditors. This was recognized by the legislature as an issue at an early stage, for the combination of the fixed and floating charge enables the secured creditor to scoop the pool of the company's assets, to the potential detriment of the unsecured creditors. Consequently, the legislature gives certain unsecured debts (mainly employees' claims to wages and contributions to occupational pension schemes) statutory priority over the floating, though not the fixed, charge.[44] The preference used to be accorded to various claims by the state, but these have been almost all removed, to the benefit of the general unsecured creditors.

However, the above preferences benefit only certain categories of unsecured creditor. A general, if limited, preference was provided in 2003: where the assets of the company are subject to a floating charge, then, except where the assets realized have a very small value, a proportion of the assets realized must be set aside for the unsecured creditors and not

---

[41] See Ch 5 below at p 124.   [42] See Ch 6 below at p 183.

[43] Cf *New Zealand Guardian Trust Co Ltd v Brooks* [1995] 1 WLR 96, PC, where the directors of the borrowing company were required by the debenture trust deed to certify every three months to the trustee for the lenders that, having made due enquiry, nothing had occurred which to their knowledge and belief adversely affected the interests of the lenders.

[44] Insolvency Act 1986 ss 40 and 386 and Sch 6.

paid to the floating charge-holder.[45] Finally, the Insolvency Act renders a floating charge invalid if it is created in the period shortly before insolvency, except to the extent that the charge-holder provides new consideration to the company. This prevents the powerful, but unsecured, creditor using the floating charge to elevate itself to the position of secured creditor when it sees that insolvency is probable, a particular risk if the creditor is closely connected with the management of the company.[46]

Second, the self-help possibilities, especially the floating charge and its associated enforcement mechanisms, have proved so effective that they can create the converse of the problem they aim to solve, namely, the potential for opportunistic conduct on the part of secured creditors as against the management of the company. This arises from the fact that the charge-holder may be able to use the contractually specified events of default to replace the existing board at a time when there is still a good chance that the company will be able to trade out of its difficulties. So far, however, the legislature has not sought to address this issue.

Thus far, we have looked at the considerable scope which creditors have for self-help and at the problems creditor self-help may cause. What we have not done is ask the question of whether self-help can sensibly be relied upon to deal with all the problems which limited liability causes for creditors. We turn to this issue in the following chapter.

---

[45] IA s 176A. The maximum deduction from the floating charge-holder's entitlement is £600,000.

[46] IA 1986, s 245. The relevant period is normally one year before the insolvency, but *two* years if the creditor is connected with the company.

4

Limited Liability
The Limits of Creditor Self-Help

THE CASE FOR MANDATORY RULES

In the previous chapter we discussed the role of self-help on the part of creditors to protect themselves against the opportunistic behaviour by controllers of companies which limited liability permits and even encourages. We saw that there was in fact considerable scope for such self-help mechanisms and that, probably, the extension of the limited liability rule to all companies, large and small, was rendered tolerable only because of the availability of self-help. However, we now need to look at creditor self-help more critically. Two questions need to be asked. Can we be confident that self-help is in fact capable of addressing all forms of opportunistic behaviour generated by limited liability, or is there a role for mandatory rules to supplement self-help? Obviously, if self-help is ineffective in relation to a particular problem, we may need to consider whether mandatory legal rules could do a better job.[1] However, even if self-help is capable of addressing a particular problem linked to limited liability, one still needs to ask whether that problem can be regulated more effectively by mandatory rules than by creditor self-help.

It is suggested that there are three arguments in favour of the law making some use of mandatory rules against opportunism arising out of limited liability. As we shall see, these rationales for mandatory rules have been accepted to some extent in British law, so that the picture of complete reliance on creditor self-help to counter opportunism is not an accurate portrayal of that system. First, some creditors are not well-placed to protect themselves. The obvious example is those who had no

---

[1] Of course, it is illogical to argue that, because creditor self-help cannot work, mandatory rules will be effective. It is possible that some costs of limited liability are unavoidable; in that case, the question is simply whether the benefits of the rule outweigh its costs.

prior relationship with the company before they became its creditors, into which category fall many victims of torts committed by companies. A pedestrian knocked down by a company's vehicle, driven negligently, will not typically have had any prior opportunities to negotiate contractual protections with the company. Some other types of creditor are perceived as not able to contract effectively with the company on a self-help basis, for example, individual employees injured by the company's negligent conduct of its business, despite apparent opportunities for ex ante bargaining. Those who are not able to make use of the self-help contractual mechanism may be referred to as 'non-adjusting' creditors.[2]

Second, and most important in practice, it may be more efficient to use mandatory legal rules or to provide a mandatory framework for bargaining between company and creditors, even if such rules and procedures could be generated by private contracting. Where the legislature is able to predict in advance which particular rule or type of machinery will be effective in dealing with a particular form of opportunistic behaviour, it will be less costly for the legislature to specify it than for each set of contracting parties to have to grope their way, perhaps imperfectly, towards that solution. Thus, if the legislature thinks that creditor protection across the board requires that a particular level of resources should be kept in the company and not distributed to shareholders by way of dividend, it may so specify, and creditors who desire a higher level of protection may bargain for it. However, it is no easy task for the legislator to predict in advance that a particular legal rule will be the best way of dealing with a particular problem. Company law is full of examples of, or proposals for, over-broad rules, with adverse side-effects, to deal with problems which can best be solved in other ways.[3]

Third, some forms of opportunism generated by limited liability may involve conduct which, whether it occurs in the company context or not, is regarded as unlawful. A good example is fraud. Of course, the normal civil and criminal rules against fraud could simply be, and often are, applied to fraud in the conduct of the affairs of a company. However, it is possible that the efficiency of the criminal and civil law relating to fraud could be increased by the development of rules applying specifically to fraud in companies. These special rules can then be tailored to the particular features of company law, for example, so as to fit in with the processes for the liquidation of companies.

---

[2] J Armour, 'Legal Capital: An Outdated Concept?' (2006) 7 *European Business Organization Law Review* 5.   [3] See the discussion of minimum capital rules below p 75.

GENERAL RULES AGAINST DEBTOR OPPORTUNISM

Thus, there may well be a case for supplementing self-help with legal protection. Whether in any particular situation that case is made out will depend upon further analysis. Before engaging in such analysis there is one further preliminary point which needs to be made. In our discussion in the previous chapter[4] we have seen that many of the self-help techniques available to creditors can be used against all unreliable debtors, whether companies or not. Since this is a book on company law, however, we did not consider such general self-help techniques in detail. Equally, mandatory rules designed to deal with debtor opportunism may be aimed at all debtors, whether companies or not; and, similarly, the detail of these rules falls outside the scope of this book. Nevertheless, these other categories of rule deserve brief mention, if only to set the context in which company law operates.

For example, we have just noted that the self-help seems of limited value in relation to involuntary creditors, typically the victims of certain types of corporate torts, and it might be thought that there is a major role for mandatory rules of company law to protect involuntary creditors. Indeed, one way of dealing with this problem would be to create a rule specific to company law. Professors Hansmann and Kraakman have proposed the abolition of limited liability and the reintroduction of personal liability for shareholders in such cases, albeit on the basis of proportionate liability.[5] In Britain, by contrast, the matter is hardly debated. This might be because tort judgments in the UK have not reached levels which threaten the viability of companies, unlike in the US, so that victims who obtain judgment generally get paid. Alternatively, it might be that the legislature has taken the view that the insolvency of tortfeasors is not just a problem of company tortfeasors but is one that applies across the board. It may be that enforcing tort judgments against companies is not significantly more uncertain than enforcing them against individuals and partnerships. Limited liability may be a problem in relation to corporate tortfeasors but there may be significant, if different, problems of enforcement against personal defendants. If this is the case, then limited liability does not constitute the whole of the problem and removing it would be only a partial solution. Some other solution should be found which applies to all tortfeasors. This is indeed what one finds when the legislature requires

---

[4] Above p 63.
[5] In the article cited above p 59 at n 16. On the difference between joint and several liability and proportionate liability see above p 58 n 14.

potential tortfeasors to take out insurance. Two examples will suffice. The Employers' Liability (Compulsory Insurance) Act 1969 requires employers, whether corporate or not, to insure against liability for bodily injury or disease sustained by employees in the course of their employment.[6] A similar scheme operates in relation to third-party liability for motor accidents, whether those responsible are companies or not.[7]

The problem of voluntary creditors who cannot bargain effectively can be dealt with in the same way. Thus, the issue of employees who have wages outstanding on the insolvency of their employer is a problem not confined to companies, and the relevant legislation, creating a fund from which unpaid employees are reimbursed, applies to all employers.[8] Nevertheless, this piece of labour law, as with the examples of compulsory insurance mentioned above, does in fact operate in the particular areas covered so as to mitigate for employees of corporate employers the incentives to opportunism which limited liability creates.

Coming closer to company law, the Insolvency Act 1986 aims to control the temptations which beset all debtors, whether corporate or otherwise, to put assets beyond the reach of their creditors in the period before insolvency supervenes. See for example the sections of that Act controlling transactions by debtors with their assets at an undervalue in the pre-insolvency period (a way of giving away assets to someone friendly to the debtor) or conferring a preference on one creditor (perhaps linked with the debtor) over the others.[9]

Our task, however, is to analyse the role of company law in providing mandatory rules to control company opportunism. Creditor protection issues can arise in many diverse contexts in company law. In this chapter we shall confine our attention to three sets of rules where creditor protection has traditionally been thought to be a primary concern of company law. The first set consists of those rules which either require a company to have a certain level of assets at its disposal before it commences business or which restrict the ability of the company, after it has commenced business, to move assets out of the corporate 'box' and into the hands of the

---

[6] Since the amount of the compulsory cover is set at £5m per occurrence, the legislature presumably viewed the problem as one linked to the size of the business rather than to its legal structure. See Employers' Liability (Compulsory Insurance) Regulations 1998/2573, reg 3.

[7] Road Traffic Act 1988, Part VI, as supplemented by the Third Parties (Rights against Insurers) Act 2010.

[8] Employment Rights Act 1996, Part XII. The coverage of the reimbursement right is rather limited, but the principle is there.

[9] On undervalue transactions and preferences see IA 1986, ss 238–41 (applying to companies) and ss 339–42 (similar provisions for individuals); common remedial provisions are in ss 423–4.

shareholders. The current rules implement these restrictions by reference to a company's 'legal capital', though other approaches are available and have been advocated for the UK, as we shall see. Since under a regime of limited liability the creditors' claims are confined to the company's assets, such rules have an intuitive plausibility about them, but we shall see on examination that they have their own costs as well.

The second set of rules are those which aim to reduce opportunism on the part of company controllers which takes the form of adding to the company's liabilities at a time when there is little hope that there will be sufficient assets in the company's coffers to meet the creditors' claims when they fall due. The risks to creditors from such behaviour are clear; what is perhaps less clear is why company controllers should engage in such behaviour.

Finally, we look at the rules governing opportunism towards creditors within corporate groups and especially the position of involuntary creditors in such situations.

LEGAL CAPITAL RULES

WHAT IS LEGAL CAPITAL?

In company law, 'capital' is used in a restricted sense which does not coincide with the broader way in which it is used in ordinary speech or even by company financiers. My dictionary defines 'capital' (in the financial sense) as 'wealth available for or capable of use in the production of further wealth'.[10] For company lawyers, however, legal capital is the value of the consideration which the shareholders have provided to the company in exchange for their shares. Thus, if the shareholders have contributed cash and other assets to the extent of £10,000 to the company in exchange for their shares, then £10,000 is the value of the company's legal capital. Of course, the company may have acquired a further £10,000 from some other source. A bank may have lent £10,000 to the company, but that money does not count as legal capital, even though it can well be said to be wealth available for the production of further wealth. Immediately after selling its shares and receiving the loan from the bank, the company may have £20,000 in its bank account, but only £10,000 counts as the company's legal capital.

The reason for restricting the definition of legal capital in this way reveals its creditor protection function. Suppose the company becomes

---

[10] *Collins English Dictionary* (1982).

insolvent. The shareholders have no claim, on a winding up, to the return of their contributions to the company until all the creditors' claims have been satisfied. This is the principle of 'shareholders last'.[11] Therefore, it can be argued that the greater the amount that the shareholders have contributed to the company in exchange for its shares, the more likely it is that the creditors will be repaid. As it is sometimes put, the shareholders' contributions constitute a 'cushion' for the creditors against the risk of default by the company. The bank, on the other hand, as a creditor, will have a claim on insolvency for the return of the £10,000 which will compete with the claims of other creditors,[12] and so its contribution should be excluded from the legal definition of capital.

There are three possible ways in which a legal system could use the concept of legal capital to protect creditors. The first is a way which would give the creditors a very high degree of protection, but at a cost to enterprise which is so great that no legal system adopts it. The second is a way which British law utilizes only grudgingly and partially, under pressure from EC law. The third has long been part of its thought patterns. The first two techniques are forms of minimum capital requirement; the third is referred to as 'capital maintenance'.

MINIMUM CAPITAL

The first protective technique for creditors would be to require companies, before commencing business, to raise a certain minimum amount of capital and to put that minimum amount on one side so that it could be made available to meet the claims of the creditors, should the company become insolvent.[13] Such a policy would genuinely turn capital into a fund for the protection of creditors. This would be all well and good if capital were an inexpensive commodity, but it is not. To require companies to raise, and pay for, but not to be able to deploy to profit-earning ends, a significant amount of capital would be to make the corporate form very unattractive for business. So, no legal system imposes this as a mandatory rule. Instead, the company is free, and expected, to deploy the consideration raised on

---

[11] IA 1986, ss 107 and 143.

[12] Indeed, as we saw above (p 68) the bank is likely to have secured its loan with a fixed and floating charge and thus repayment of its loan will be given priority over the claims of unsecured creditors. It is conceivable that the unsecured creditors would fare better in the liquidation if the company had never taken on the secured loan in the first place.

[13] An alternative device might be to require the company to take out a bond (a form of insurance) to a certain amount, so that, upon insolvency, the guarantor of the bond would pay the prescribed amount to the creditors. This device is sometimes used in construction contracts to protect the client against the insolvency of the builder during the construction process. As such, it is an example of creditor self-help.

the sale of its shares in the conduct of the company's business. Within a very short time, the £10,000 mentioned above will have been used to pay wages, rent premises, and to buy equipment and raw materials and so on. Whether at the end of its first (or any subsequent) trading period the company's net assets (assets less liabilities) are worth more or less than the value of its initial capital will depend, obviously, on how successfully the company has traded.

Nevertheless, there is a weaker form of this initial capital policy which could be implemented, and this constitutes the second policy. This would be to require a company to have received in exchange for its shares a certain minimum value (the 'minimum capital') before it commences business, but not to require this capital to be put on one side but instead to permit it to be used in the company's business. In Britain no such requirement is laid upon private companies. However, public companies, following the Second Company Law Directive,[14] must have allotted shares with a nominal value of at least £50,000, of which at least one-quarter must actually have been paid over to the company, before the company commences business.[15]

This weaker form of the policy may rescue the corporate form for business enterprise, but there are two good reasons for thinking that a minimum share capital requirement in this form does not do much to protect creditors. To start with, in economic terms the adequacy of the minimum capital figure must depend on the riskiness of the company's business, which varies from one company to another, so that in most cases a single figure will be either inappropriately high or inappropriately low. The latter gives creditors the illusion of protection; the former creates barriers to entry and thus restricts competition. The low figure stipulated by the legislature for public companies suggests that, given this choice, it will opt

---

[14] Council Directive 77/91/EEC, OJ 1977 L26/1, as amended. This Directive applies only to public companies. The minimum capital requirement for public companies also necessitated the introduction of rules for valuing non-cash consideration and prohibiting certain speculative forms of consideration: see ss 584–7 and 593–7.

[15] Part 20, Ch 2. The 'nominal' or 'par' value of the share is the value attributed to it by the company when the class of shares of which it is part is created, for example, a £1 share or a 10p share. Shares may not be issued for less than their nominal value (a practice known as 'discounting': s 580) but may be issued for more. In the latter case, the additional amount received by the company is referred to as a 'premium' and, in British law but not all other EU systems, is treated for almost all purposes as part of the company's capital. Since the nominal value need bear no relation to the consideration the company is likely to receive when it issues the shares (except that the former must be less than the latter), the whole system is rather confusing. Where the premium is treated in the same way as the nominal capital, the concept of a nominal value could with advantage be abolished. Minimum capital and capital maintenance rules can be formulated, if it is desired to have them, without reference to nominal values.

for illusion. The minimum capital idea could be taken seriously, as it is for banks and insurance companies.[16] Here capital requirements are related to risk, are updated as the company's business profile changes, and are enforced by a regulator (the Financial Services Authority). In the case of companies not posing a systemic risk to the economy, it is very doubtful whether the benefits of creating such a structure for all companies would be worth the costs.

Further, the very fact that in this weaker form of the minimum capital policy the consideration received on the issue of the shares can be used in the company's business substantially undermines the creditor-protection rationale for the requirement. If all goes well, the net value of the company's assets will exceed the value represented by the consideration received for the shares. By contrast, if all goes badly and, by definition, if insolvency supervenes, all will have gone badly, the value of the company's actual assets will fall below the value of the consideration initially received. Thus, the minimum initial capital requirement does not guarantee that the company will have any particular amount of assets available to meet the claims of its creditors at any later period and in particular upon insolvency.[17] At best it can reduce the chances of insolvency occurring, but, as noted above, the amount of the required capital is not well designed to this end because it is not risk related.

The minimum capital requirement would have a stronger bite if it were combined with a requirement that the company cease trading when its net assets value fell below the minimum capital or some proportion of that value. However, that might result in companies which were in fact viable being required to cease trading, to the detriment of their shareholders and employees, as well as possibly to some of their creditors.[18] This is because companies which are balance sheet insolvent (assets less than liabilities) may still generate enough cash to pay their debts as they fall due, so that on a cash-flow basis they are solvent and may indeed be able to trade their

---

[16] And even more seriously after the 'credit crunch' of 2007–9. See H Schooner and M Taylor, *Global Bank Regulation* (New York: Academic Press, 2010) chs 8–9.

[17] So legal capital in a company limited by shares does not perform the function of the guarantee given by the members in a company limited by guarantee. See above p 26, though even here the guarantee is usually derisory.

[18] Cf s 656, which merely requires the directors of a public company to call a shareholders' meeting if the net value of its assets falls below half the value of its issued and paid-for (not minimum) capital. The Limited Liability Act 1855 reflected a stronger policy: a company which lost three-quarters of its initially issued capital had to cease trading and be wound up (s 13). However, s 656 could perform a valuable signalling function, by indicating publicly the state of the company's balance sheet, except that the secured creditors are likely to have intervened long before s 656 is triggered.

way back to balance sheet solvency. In any event, as we shall see below in relation to wrongful trading, rules which require action to be taken if the company's balance sheet or cash-flow position reaches a certain state can exist independently of whether there is an initial minimum capital requirement in the law. The law could leave the company to raise whatever capital from shareholders it wishes, but intervene if the business plans do not work out.

CAPITAL MAINTENANCE

The third approach to the use of the concept of capital, and the one long adopted by British law, is in fact to leave companies free to raise what capital they will, both prior to commencing business and subsequently, but then to use the value of the capital in fact raised as a mechanism to regulate the freedom of the company's controllers to move assets out of the company.[19] This is the doctrine of 'capital maintenance'. Thus, unlike some US state laws, the UK does not reject legal capital as a regulatory tool entirely, as is sometimes mistakenly thought. Litigation about distributions made to shareholders in breach of the rules is not uncommon.[20] Under the 'capital maintenance' approach, the value of the capital in fact raised from shareholders is used to set a bar for the value of the assets which the company can distribute to its shareholders. This is a somewhat more plausible use of the capital concept than the minimum capital requirement, where it is used to determine whether the company can begin business. It is more plausible because an obvious piece of opportunism is for a company to raise money from creditors on the basis that the company holds assets to a certain value but later to distribute some of those assets to the shareholders, to the detriment of the creditors' chances of being repaid.

More precisely, the capital maintenance rule says that a public company cannot make a distribution of assets to its shareholders unless the value of the company's net assets (ie assets less liabilities) after the distribution has been made will exceed the value of the initial and subsequent capital contributions received from its shareholders.[21] It is not enough that, after the distribution, the company's assets should equal its liabilities (the so-called 'bare' net assets test). The assets must exceed the liabilities by the amount

---

[19] This policy is now obviously qualified by the minimum capital requirement for public companies.

[20] Whether legal capital is the best test for the legality of distributions is discussed below.

[21] s 831. Private companies are treated slightly more generously: see s 830. This permits the company to distribute the full amount of its profits even though it has suffered an as yet unrealized loss, because only realized losses are set against gains (which also must be realized to count).

of the company's legal capital (ie a 'net assets plus margin' test, the margin being provided by the amount of the legal capital). If the company cannot meet this requirement, it may make no distribution to its shareholders but the company is not prohibited simply for this reason from continuing to trade.

The capital maintenance rules thus restrict more extensively the freedom of controllers of companies to move assets out of the company and into the hands of the shareholders than would a bare net assets test. It could be argued that the capital maintenance rules replicate for the company when it is a going concern the principle which applies on an insolvency: shareholders are entitled to payments only if the creditors' claims have been met (or 'shareholders last'). As near as can be with a going concern, that result is replicated by prohibiting a distribution which would reduce the value of the company's net assets below that of the shareholders' contributions. Of course, the protection is not fully equivalent. After making a lawful distribution, the company's trading may deteriorate and it may fall into insolvency, but the prior lawful distributions cannot normally be recovered from the shareholders in that situation. The only completely 'safe' rule for the creditors is one which permits distributions to shareholders only in a winding up. However, such a rule would reduce the attractiveness of equity investment (by delaying returns to shareholders) and increase the company's cost of capital, as investors reduced the price they were willing to pay for shares. As far as I know, no modern system imposes such a rule, though, of course, the shareholders are free to adopt it in, for example, a 'one-shot', limited duration company.

Let us see how the principle, as embodied in the Companies Act, plays out in respect of some typical ways in which assets may be moved out of a company.

DIVIDENDS AND SHARE BUY-BACKS

First and obviously, the principle is applied to dividends declared by the company: their payment must not leave the company with net assets less than the value of its legal capital, at least in the case of public companies.[22] A dividend is a payment, usually in cash,[23] made by the company to its

---

[22] And companies are prohibited at common law from making gratuitous dispositions of their assets, other than by way of limited charitable and similar donations, other than in the ways permitted by the Act. See *Aveling Barford Ltd v Perion Ltd* [1989] BCLC 626.

[23] Dividends in the form of shares in the company are possible, in which case they are called 'scrip' dividends, as are dividends in the form of tangible assets, though these are known mainly in closely held companies.

shareholders, in the case of listed companies usually twice a year,[24] the amount of the dividend being expressed as a percentage of the nominal value of the shares. The maximum amount of the dividend is fixed by the directors in most companies, though the shareholders can reduce the amount proposed.[25] This makes the dividend sound like a payment of interest, but, at least for ordinary shares, the amount of the dividend is not fixed, as it would be on a loan, but is decided each year, in the light of the company's financial position, by the board, who may decide to make no distributions, and subject to the Act's capital maintenance rules.

The same principle is also applied to public companies in respect of the other main way for a company to return assets to its shareholders whilst it is a going concern, that is, by offering to buy back a proportion of its shares. Until relatively recently, it was thought to be inconsistent with the capital maintenance rules to permit a company to buy back its shares at all.[26] A shareholder who wished to liquidate her investment could do so only by finding another investor to step into her shoes. Hence the importance of the core feature of the free transferability of shares.[27] However, it has now been realized that capital maintenance does not require a complete ban on share buy-backs, which have in fact become a reasonably common way for companies to return unwanted assets to their shareholders or to implement a scheme to replace equity finance with debt finance.

The law recognizes that buy-backs can be funded in two ways which do not offend capital maintenance. First, they may be funded out of the proceeds of a fresh issue of shares, in which case the consideration received for the new shares simply replaces the repurchased shares in the company's legal capital. Here, one class of shares in effect replaces another. In practice, such buy-backs are relatively uncommon.

More radically, a company with unwanted assets may fund a buy-back, without a new share issue, out of distributable profits. Since the funds

---

[24] Usually referred to as 'interim' and 'final' dividends, respectively.

[25] Model articles for public companies, art 70(2).

[26] This general principle is still stated in s 658(1). Significantly, the section does not apply to companies with unlimited liability. It is now subject, however, to the buy-back rules discussed below. Moreover, British company law has also accepted the legality of redeemable shares. These are shares which are issued on the basis that either the company or the shareholder (or both) can require the shares to be bought back on certain terms at some date in the future. Unlike the buy-back provisions discussed below, the redemption of redeemable shares is contractually compulsory. From the creditors' point of view redeemable shares are less of a threat than repurchases of shares because it is clear from the outset that redeemable shares may not be a permanent part of the company's capital (and the terms of the redemption are required to be publicly available: s 685). They are not discussed further here because the rules on financing redemptions track those for buy-backs: see ss 687–8.   [27] Above p 19.

used for the buy-back could have been distributed to the shareholders, say by way of dividend, it might be thought that the creditors could have no objection to their use in this alternative way. However, there is a further point. Once the shares have been bought back, the value of the consideration which the company then holds in exchange for its shares will have been reduced, ie its legal capital will have been reduced. In consequence, the freedom of the company to make distributions to its shareholders in the future will be increased, because, under the dividend rules just considered, the amount of the margin which the company must hold above an exact balance of assets and liabilities will be less. This might be thought to represent a threat to the creditors' interests. However, this point can be dealt with by requiring the value of the company's legal capital to be maintained at its pre-buy-back level, so that the company's freedom to make dividend payments in the future is not increased.[28] These are precisely the rules applied by the Act to buy-backs by public companies, and the creditors' consent to such action on the part of the company is not required.[29]

The rules about maintaining the company's legal capital in a buy-back assume, as used to be required, that the shares bought back are cancelled. However, subject to certain restrictions, a company may now hold on to the shares it repurchases (put them in its 'treasury') and later resell them on the market. Treasury shares do give rise to certain regulatory concerns,[30] but these are not centrally creditor protection concerns. If the shares bought back are not cancelled, the company's capital yardstick is not reduced. If the shares are later sold by the company, at whatever price,[31] the creditors benefit because the company receives from investors assets on which the creditors, potentially, have a claim prior to that of the shareholders.

The buy-back rules are applied more leniently to private companies, because, subject to conditions, they can finance buy-backs 'out of capital'. Take a private company built up by an entrepreneur who has now reached retirement age and wishes to sell his stake in the company to finance that retirement. If, as is likely, there is no public market in the shares, the other

---

[28] Technically, this is done by requiring the company to create an undistributable reserve in its accounts. Thus, legal capital may consist of three things: the value received by a company corresponding to the nominal value of the shares; any additional consideration, which will be reflected in the share premium account (see n 15 above); and capital redemption account used to maintain the capital yardstick if shares are repurchased out of profits.

[29] ss 692 and 733.   [30] Part 18, Ch 6.

[31] Since the company is selling shares which already exist rather than issuing new shares, the rule about not issuing shares at less than their nominal or par value (above n 15) does not apply.

shareholders cannot personally afford to buy out the founder, and the company has insufficient undistributed profits to acquire the founder's stake, the only solution may be to sell control of the company to a larger, perhaps publicly traded, company or to a venture capitalist. In order to help such companies remain independent, the Act permits share repurchases out of capital. Of course, on traditional thinking such a course of action is a threat to the creditors, since the net assets of the company will be reduced below the level of the company's capital, and for the future, once the shares have been bought back and cancelled, the company's capital level will be set at a new and lower point. In order to protect creditors the Act deploys three devices.[32] (i) The directors proposing a repurchase out of capital must make a statutory declaration of solvency, stating that after due enquiry they are of the opinion that the company will be able to pay its debts as they fall due for at least a year after the repurchase. A director who signs a solvency statement without reasonable grounds for believing it to be true commits a criminal offence.[33] (ii) The directors' declaration must be approved by the company's auditors as reasonable. (iii) Any creditor may apply to the court to have the repurchase prohibited or approved subject to conditions aimed at protecting the interests of the creditors.

REDUCTION OF CAPITAL

It can be seen from the above discussion that the function of the capital maintenance rules in controlling distributions to the shareholders depends upon the amount of the company's capital being a figure which is not subject to manipulation by the company, either through its board or the general meeting. If that amount could easily be reduced by the company, its constraining impact on distributions would vanish. However, there may be good reasons in particular cases for the company to 'reduce its capital'. In considering these reasons, it is important to be clear, at the outset, what a reduction of capital involves. It does not involve, necessarily, a reduction of the assets of the company by returning them to the shareholders, though that may be involved in particular cases. What is reduced in a reduction of capital is the value attributed in the balance sheet to the consideration received by the company in exchange for its shares. It is an accounting change, not necessarily a change in the assets

---

[32] Part 18, Ch 5.
[33] s 715. This is an imprisonable offence even though the basis of liability is negligence. Civil liability, whether to the company or to creditors, is not specified in the statute, though civil liability to the company could be built on the general duties discussed below in Ch 6.

held by the company, but, because of the relevance of the balance sheet to the legality of distributions, it is an accounting change with 'real world' implications for the company's future freedom to make distributions.

The company may need to reduce this figure because it is proposing to return unwanted assets to its shareholders and does not have the necessary distributable profits to do so. On the other hand, it may have lost its assets in the course of normal trading and simply wish to bring the capital figure in its accounts into line with its actual position.[34] In this latter case, once the capital figure has been reduced, profits earned in the future, which would otherwise have had to be retained to build up the assets of the company to the level of the former capital 'cushion', are now distributable on the basis of the lower legal capital. Indeed, this may be the very reason for the reduction: a rescuer may not be willing to inject fresh equity into the company unless any profits made thereafter are immediately distributable. However, it is the reduction of the figure for share capital which is the necessary precondition to these distributions and it is on the legality of the reduction, rather than the subsequent distribution, that the law concentrates.

The Act now contains two procedures whereby the company can exceptionally reduce the amount of its capital, one (the traditional one involving confirmation of the proposal by the court) being available to all companies and the other (out of court) available only to private companies.[35] Given the risks to the creditors of a reduction of capital, both procedures are hedged about with protections for them. In the general procedure, the protection is provided mainly by the need for court approval, but, where the reduction proposal involves a return of assets to the shareholders, creditors who can show 'a real likelihood' that the reduction would result in the company being unable to discharge the claim or debt when it falls due become in effect entitled to have their debts repaid or secured as a precondition for court approval.[36] In the case of the (newly introduced) procedure for private companies, the main protection, as with a share buy-back out of capital, is the directors' solvency statement to which criminal liability for negligence is attached.[37] The aim of both sets of rules is to protect existing creditors, whilst future creditors will contract on the basis of the company's new capital position.

---

[34] These two examples are given in s 641(4)(b), but that section permits a reduction of capital 'in any way'.

[35] Part 17, Ch 10. The Second EC Company Law Directive requires creditor access to the court in the case of reduction of capital by a public company.

[36] s 646, as amended. The court can override this prima facie entitlement: s 645(3).

[37] s 643. However, auditor verification is not required.

CONCLUSION

The current capital maintenance rules have received a bad press in the UK in recent years. No one doubts that, in a system of limited liability, there needs to be some restriction on the freedom of company controllers to move assets out of the company for the benefit of the shareholders and to the detriment of the creditors. Indeed, all modern company law systems have such rules. The question is whether a distribution rule based on legal capital is the best that can be devised.

One obvious point of criticism is that the margin above net assets required for a lawful distribution is set by a historical figure, ie the amount the company happens to have raised from its shareholders in the past. It is far from obvious that this is an appropriate yardstick. The evidence from those creditors who contract for customized protections in their loan contracts is that they focus on maintaining the level of assets in the firm at the time of the loan or on the company continuing to meet in the future certain financial tests of its health (such as maintaining a certain ratio between its earnings per share and its dividend per share (for example a ratio of 3) even if the statutory tests would permit the distribution of a larger amount).[38] This evidence suggests that the linkage between creditor protection and legal capital is, whilst not fanciful, not optimum. In some cases it may be too low a protection (as in the case where a lender advances money to the company on the basis of the assets it currently holds and which reflect many years of successful trading and only modest distributions) and in other cases too high, as where the company's future cash flow is so strong that payment now which reduces the company's net assets below its legal capital is not a danger to creditors.

The implication of this line of argument is that the law should shift away from a rule fixing the distributable profit by reference to the company's legal capital and opt instead for a standard, which could be applied more flexibly to the circumstances of the case.[39] Professor Rickford has suggested a generalization of the standard which is already deployed in relation to private companies' repurchases of shares out of capital and out-of-court reductions of capital, ie the solvency certificate. Under this proposal the legal capital test for distributions would be replaced by a solvency test.[40] This approach is conceptually superior to that based on

[38] John Armour, 'Share Capital and Creditor Protection: Efficient Rules for a Modern Company Law' (2000) 63 *MLR* 355, 373–7.
[39] On the rules/standards distinction see below p 114.
[40] J Rickford (ed), 'Reforming Capital: Report of the Interdisciplinary Group on Capital Maintenance' (2004) 15 *European Business Law Review* 1, and J Rickford, 'Legal Approaches

legal capital. It has two possible defects. First, it may not appeal to directors themselves, because of the liabilities attached to negligent solvency
statements (assuming that this liability would be substantial and take
both criminal and civil forms).[41] Whatever the deficiencies of the current
system, it has the undoubted merit from the directors' point of view that a
payment which falls within what the balance sheet indicates is the permitted amount of the dividend is unlikely to be challenged successfully. The
director can rely on an accurate balance sheet, verified by the auditors,
as providing a safe haven from liability, whereas the solvency test would
require judgment from the directors, and so the liability risk would be
greater.[42]

The second risk is that the judgment of the directors, in cases where
they are effectively accountable to the shareholders, might be biased in
favour of distributions, a bias which is not present in the current bright-
line rule, derived from the accounts. In most cases, of course, companies
distribute far less to shareholders than the amount permitted by law, but
the risk of overpayment might be a real one where the company has been
trading unsuccessfully. It has been suggested that mitigation of both risks
could be achieved by building back into the solvency test a qualification
based on the accounts, ie that after the distribution, the company should
be required to satisfy the 'bare' net assets test.[43] This would not amount to
a restoration of the legal capital test, but it would restore the balance sheet
as an important element in defining the legally permitted pay-out.[44] This
might provide some comfort to both directors and creditors, by providing a firm underpinning for the directors' judgment. However, reforming the legal capital test for distributions would require revision of the

to Restricting Distributions to Shareholders: Balance Sheet Tests and Solvency Tests' (2006)
7 *European Business Organization Law Review* 135.

[41] The civil liabilities attaching to directors for wrongful payments of dividends can be
substantial. See *Bairstow v Queen's Moat Houses plc* [2001] 2 BCLC 531, CA, where the wrongdoing directors were ordered to restore to the company £78.5 million paid away in unlawful
dividends. The award was made in a counterclaim by the company in proceedings for wrongful
dismissal initiated by the claimants!

[42] In extreme cases payment of a distribution which is lawful by reference to the balance
sheet might be a breach of fiduciary duty, even under the present law, as where the company's
finances suddenly deteriorate after the end of the financial year but before the dividend is paid,
but this will be a rare situation.

[43] W Schön, 'Comment: Balance Sheet Tests or Solvency Tests—or Both?' (2006) 7 *EBOR*
181. For the definition of the 'bare' net assets test see above p 78.

[44] This step would also take account of David Kershaw's pertinent point that the accounting
standards upon which the accounts are based have a creditor protection value: 'Involuntary
Creditors and the Case for Accounting-Based Distribution Regulation' [2009] *Journal of
Business Law* 140.

Second EU Company Law Directive (at least for public companies, where the issue is most pressing) and, after an unsatisfactory investigation, the Commission set itself against any such reform.[45]

FINANCIAL ASSISTANCE

Usually linked to the concept of legal capital is the rule that a company may not give financial assistance towards the purchase of its own shares, whether before or after the purchase.[46] In fact, as currently formulated, this rule does not have any necessary connection with legal capital. A company may not give such assistance even if it does so out of distributable profits. Nor is it clear that creditor protection provides a satisfactory rationale for the rule. It catches, for example, a loan by a company to a sound investor on above-commercial terms to buy shares in the company, but fails to catch a loan to a doubtful borrower on easy terms to gamble at the local casino. In any event, the 2006 Act made it no longer applicable to private companies, including companies formerly public but which become private before providing the assistance. Complete abolition of the rule is prevented by the Second Company Law Directive.

CONTROLS ON OPPORTUNISM NOT LINKED TO LEGAL CAPITAL RULES

WRONGFUL AND FRAUDULENT TRADING

We examined above the rules which limit opportunistic behaviour on the part of companies by restricting the board's freedom to make distributions of assets to the shareholders. However, the controllers of a company may reduce the value of the company's net assets not only by shifting assets out of the corporate 'box', but also by taking on additional liabilities. Net assets equals assets less liabilities, so the net assets figure will decline if either the company's assets go down or its liabilities go up. To deal with an increase in liabilities a broader rule than one controlling distributions is needed.

There is, however, an initial puzzle here. One can see that shareholders may benefit if corporate assets are distributed to them, but how do they (or

---

[45] KPMG, *Feasibility Study on an Alternative to the Capital Maintenance Regime Established by the Second Company Law Directive* (Berlin, 2008). For a critique of the KPMG approach see K Fuchs, 'The Regulation of Companies' Capital in the European Union: What is the Current State of Affairs?' [2011] *European Business Law Review* (forthcoming).

[46] Part 18, Ch 2.

the directors) benefit from the company taking on additional liabilities, if there is no concomitant distribution? The answer to the question can be found by considering the situation of a company which is nearing insolvency. By taking on extra liabilities (obtaining goods on credit or not paying money due to the Inland Revenue or to the company's pension fund, for example) the directors may put the company in a position where it is able to continue to function for a period of time. During that period it may be possible to extricate the company from its financial difficulties so that it returns to profit, thus preserving the directors' jobs, and is able to pay dividends to its shareholders. On the other hand, if the period of continued trading does not resolve the company's difficulties and the company simply goes into insolvent liquidation, limited liability will ensure that it is the creditors rather than the shareholders who bear the downside risk of the decision to continue to trade and the agency rules discussed in Chapter 2 will similarly protect the directors. To put the matter more formally, the shareholders will be in favour of any project which has a reasonable probability of a pay-off which will take the company out of balance sheet insolvency, even if the project's expected value, given the probabilities, is less than the investment required to finance it, so that it would not normally be undertaken.

How should the law handle this situation? One rule might be to require companies whose assets are less than their liabilities to file for insolvency. However, such a rule might be both over- and under-inclusive. If there is a reasonable prospect of the company being able to trade out of its difficulties and it can currently pay its debts as they fall due, it would be to the benefit of all concerned with the company (shareholders, employees, creditors) that trading should continue.[47] By contrast, a company whose assets exceed its liabilities but is trading unsuccessfully and has no prospect of recovering should cease to trade before it dissipates any more of its assets.

An alternative approach is to try to readjust the structural bias in the trading decision. The bias arises, as noted, from the fact that the downside risk of continued trading falls entirely on the creditors, whilst the shareholders are exposed only to the upside benefits of the decision to continue to trade. The directors are likely to be systematically more in favour of continuing to trade than they would be if the shareholders were exposed to both risks and benefits of the trading decision. The same arguments

---

[47] Some jurisdictions, however, do impose this rule. See P Davies, 'Directors' Creditor-Regarding Duties in Respect of Trading Decisions Taken in the Vicinity of Insolvency' (2006) 7 *European Business Organization Law Review* 301 at 311.

apply, moreover, where the controlling directors' main interest lies not so much in the value of their shares as in the opportunities for gainful employment which the company provides for them. In both cases, limited liability permits the director/shareholders to externalize the costs of continued unsuccessful trading onto the creditors of the company, whilst permitting them to capture the benefits if the continued trading is successful.

Where the directors take on extra liabilities, knowing that the company will be unable to discharge them or are reckless in this regard, company law has long contained a rebalancing mechanism. It prohibits conducting the affairs of a company with intent to defraud creditors (or indeed for any fraudulent purpose). Any person party to such conduct, whether or not a director of the company, commits a criminal offence[48] and can be made civilly liable.[49] The civil liability bites only if the company is wound up and takes the form of permitting the liquidator to apply to the court for an order that the parties to the fraudulent conduct make a contribution to the assets of the company, for the benefit of its creditors. The remedy is thus a collective one, by the liquidator on behalf of the creditors, not one vested in individual creditors. If the party to the fraudulent conduct is a shareholder of the company, such a court order thus involves removing the protection of the limited liability rule which would otherwise be applicable.

However, fraud, because it involves dishonesty, is difficult to prove; and, even if it can be proved, covers only a small part of the opportunistic conduct against which it is arguable creditors deserve protection. Given the incentive structure outlined above, the directors are likely to convince themselves that the continued trading will be successful and the creditors will be repaid, so that the problem is one of self-deception on the part of the directors rather than fraud committed on others. After the problem was revisited by the Cork Committee[50] the legislature enacted a rule which attempts to eliminate the structural bias identified above even when fraud is not present.

The crucial conceptual shift made by section 214 of the 1986 Act, as compared to the fraudulent trading provisions, is to create the potential of civil liability[51] for directors who negligently have decided to continue to

---

[48] s 993.   [49] IA 1986, s 213.

[50] Report of the Review Committee on Insolvency Law and Practice, Cmnd 8558 (London: HMSO, 1982), ch 44.

[51] Primarily by way of a liability to contribute to the assets of the company but also, where the director is in addition a creditor of the company, by subordinating his claim as creditor to the claims of all the other creditors of the company: IA 1986, s 215.

trade. A director who ought to have realized that the company had no reasonable prospect of avoiding insolvent liquidation is liable to be ordered by the court to make a contribution to the assets of the company if the company does in fact go into insolvent liquidation, unless he 'took every step with a view to minimising the loss to the company's creditors as . . . he ought to have taken'. In short, the section imposes upon directors a duty of care, which is measured objectively and enforced by the liquidator on behalf of the creditors.

The choice by the legislature to review directors' conduct by reference to a general standard of negligence was no doubt deliberate. The legislature did not wish to lay down precisely when a company should cease trading. Sometimes continued trading will be in the best interests of the creditors; sometimes not. As Park J once said: 'Ceasing to trade and liquidating too soon can be stigmatised as the coward's way out.'[52] It is the directors' responsibility to assess whether compliance with section 214 requires cessation of trading (as it often will) or continuance in business. The purpose of section 214 is to reverse the structural bias in favour of the shareholders by internalizing the risks of loss, as well as the chances of gain, in directors' decision-making processes when their company nears insolvency.[53] Unlike some of the rules analysed in the section on capital maintenance, here the legislature is not attempting to specify the substantive outcome but to restructure the decision-making process of the directors.

Whether section 214 will succeed will depend on two main things. The first is whether liquidators can raise the funds to enforce the wrongful trading liability. Changes made in 2006 permit the liquidator to recover litigation costs as part of the liquidation expenses ahead of any payment to the holder of a floating charge, who thus is the real person at risk of the costs of the litigation, but who is protected by provisions requiring the charge-holder's consent or the consent of the court to the initiation of section 214 proceedings.[54] The second is the ability of the courts to adjust the liability standard so that it neither discourages the directors of viable companies from continuing in business nor encourages those whose business is not viable to continue. We discuss the risk of 'hindsight bias' further

---

[52] *Re Continental Assurance Co of London plc* [2001] Bankruptcy and Personal Insolvency Reports 733.

[53] In line with this, the court in *Re Produce Marketing (No 2)* [1989] BCLC 520 suggested that the maximum amount of the contribution the directors should be asked to make to the company's assets is the amount of the extra liability incurred by the company towards its creditors as compared with the position had the directors acted properly.

[54] IA 1986, s 176ZA and Insolvency Rules 4.218A–E.

when we discuss directors' general duty of care in Chapter 6, but so far the courts have not displayed a tendency towards such bias (though there has been little litigation).

There is one final feature of the wrongful trading provisions which should be noted. Although the rule addresses opportunism generated by limited liability, section 214 operates at the end of the day to make the directors personally liable, not the shareholders. However, this should not surprise us. Continuing to trade is a management decision, even if it is taken in the interests of the shareholders. Thus, the section targets directors' decisions, whilst picking up shareholders who instruct the board what to do by applying its provisions to shadow directors.[55]

Despite the innovations made by section 214 it is arguable that the section operates too late to provide complete protection for creditors' interests. The section applies only where the company has reached the position that there is no reasonable prospect that the company will avoid insolvent liquidation. It can be said that the directors may be tempted to take action which is adverse to the creditors' interests before that point is reached, for example, where it is likely that the company will become insolvent, even though it cannot be said that it has no reasonable prospect of avoiding this fate. There is in fact some authority to the effect that directors' fiduciary duties to act in the best interests of the company require them to balance the interests of shareholders and creditors at a point before the section would bite. The issue was not clarified in the 2006 Act but rather was left to development by the courts.[56]

Liability for wrongful trading and other ex post legal rules discussed below constitute a further justification for the traditional lowly place accorded by British law to minimum capital rules. Rather than insist on a doubtfully relevant legal capital rule being satisfied before the company begins trading, British law pays more attention to the ex post control of opportunistic trading decisions which may be taken subsequently, including by those whose companies were initially capitalized inadequately.

DISQUALIFICATION OF DIRECTORS

Is there a case for conferring a role in this area upon the public authorities, in order to protect the public from the activities of those who act inappropriately as directors? The law has long taken the view that certain types of financial behaviour ought to disqualify a person from being a director of a company (or otherwise involved in its management), so that undischarged

---

[55] Shadow directors are discussed below at p 148.
[56] Davies, above n 47 at pp 327–9.

bankrupts are prohibited from being directors of companies.[57] The Cork Committee[58] recommended a considerable strengthening of the disqualification provisions, whose enforcement lies in the hands of the public authorities (in the shape of the Insolvency Service). That body may make applications to court for a disqualification order or may accept a disqualification undertaking given by a director out of court. These provisions may operate so as to restructure the decision-making processes of directors, even though they generate no monetary benefit for creditors, by holding out the threat of disqualification against directors who take on risks that are unreasonable for the creditors.

The Committee concentrated in particular on the extension of the provisions for the disqualification of the directors of insolvent companies on grounds of 'unfitness'.[59] A disqualified director is prohibited from being involved in the management of companies, whether as a director or otherwise, unless the court consents, for a period of time, which in the case of unfitness disqualification is a minimum of two years and a maximum of fifteen. Infringement of the prohibition is a criminal offence, but it also renders the person personally liable for the debts of the company incurred during the period of infringement.[60] This is consistent with the notion that the disqualification order should not be a ban on engaging in business but a ban on doing so through a company and with the benefit of limited liability. Unfitness, of course, is a very general term but for present purposes it is important to note that a major category of unfitness which the courts have identified is directors' attempting to trade out of difficulties on the backs of the creditors. Thus, in a leading case the Court of Appeal affirmed that paying only those creditors who pressed for payment and taking advantage of those creditors who did not in order to provide the working capital which the company needed was a clear example of unfitness.[61]

The Insolvency Service has been reasonably active in securing disqualification orders or, increasingly, undertakings. Around 900 disqualification undertakings are notified annually to Companies House and towards 150 disqualification orders.[62]

---

[57] Company Directors Disqualification Act 1986, s 11.   [58] Above n 50, ch 45.

[59] CDDA 1986, s 6. A court which declares that a director has engaged in wrongful or fraudulent trading may also disqualify that person for up to fifteen years (s 10). No doubt, in most cases such a director could also be disqualified under s 6, but s 10 permits the court to disqualify without the intervention of the Insolvency Service. There are various other grounds for disqualification.   [60] Ibid, ss 1, 2, and 15.

[61] *Re Sevenoaks Stationers (Retail) Ltd.* [1991] Ch 164, CA.

[62] BERR, *Statistical Tables on Companies Registration Activities 2008-9*, Table D1. Getting on for 200 disqualification orders are made annually by courts on their own initiative in criminal proceedings, often involving fraud, against directors.

PHOENIX COMPANIES

In the above account we have assumed that the opportunism of the company's controllers was displayed only in relation to a single company, but there is evidence of what one might call 'serial wrongful trading'. The Cork Committee quoted evidence from a Consumer Protection Officer about persons who set up companies with vestigial capital; immediately run up debts, often by taking deposits from consumers for goods or services which are never delivered; transfer the assets of the first company at an undervalue to a second company; allow the first company to cease trading, with its creditors confined to that company's inadequate assets; and then begin the process all over again with the second (or third or fourth) company.[63] So, like the Phoenix,[64] the second company rises from the ashes of the first. The Cork Committee hoped to combat such behaviour with the introduction of directors' liability for wrongful trading and speedy disqualification of directors on grounds of unfitness, as already discussed.[65] It also proposed one further reform (now ss 216–17 of the Insolvency Act 1986) designed to deprive such people of the freedom to use the same name to carry on the business of the second company as had been used for the first. Repeating the name across the successive companies is a common part of Phoenix schemes, designed to disguise, especially from the creditors of the second company, the insolvency of the first enterprise, so that they think they are dealing with the first, and still flourishing, company. A director of an insolvent company (whether involved in a Phoenix scheme or not) is prohibited from carrying on a second business under the name used for or by the first company, unless the court consents, and such an act both constitutes a criminal offence and renders the director personally liable for the second company's debts (though the second company is not liable for the first company's debts).

The Company Law Review found that, despite these reforms, the problem of the Phoenix company persisted. The problem seemed to be mainly one of enforcement of the existing law, rather than its reform. If the assets of the first company are meagre, the liquidator does not have the resources to embark on wrongful trading litigation or even to investigate the affairs

---

[63] Above n 50 at para 1741.

[64] A legendary Arabian bird said to set fire to itself and rise anew from its ashes every 500 years. The comparison is inapt only to the extent that the average Phoenix company is likely to last 500 days rather than 500 years.

[65] And also through the introduction of regulation of the profession of 'insolvency practitioner', since the effective implementation of a transfer of assets to the new company requires the consent of the liquidator of the old one.

of the company in any depth. Without investigation by the liquidator no information is likely to emerge upon which the Insolvency Service could base disqualification proceedings.[66] It is equally difficult for the Registrar or the Insolvency Service to monitor breaches of the names provisions, if the second company is formed with a different name from that of the first but in fact trades under a similar name.[67]

CONCLUSIONS

What conclusions can be drawn from these three examples of the use of mandatory rules to control opportunistic conduct on the part of the controllers of companies, by reference to doctrines other than legal capital? First, it is suggested that they confirm the suggestion made in the previous chapter[68] that the risks of opportunistic behaviour are particularly strong when limited liability is combined with control of the company. Wrongful trading, conduct rendering directors unfit to continue in that role, and the Phoenix syndrome are predominantly problems of small companies, where the directors of the company are also those who are in a position to take the lion's part of the company's economic success (whether by way of dividends as shareholders or fees as directors or salary as employees of the company). Such company controllers have the strongest incentive to exploit whatever advantages limited liability gives them as against the creditors of the company, if the company falls into financial difficulties.

Second, the creditors likely to get hurt in the case of such small companies include those who are financially unsophisticated and incapable or unable to take advantage of the self-help remedies outlined in the previous chapter. The use of mandatory rules of company law to protect them can thus be justified under the first rationale identified at the beginning of this chapter.[69]

---

[66] Liquidators (and others dealing with insolvent companies) are obliged to report matters coming to their attention which suggest unfitness to the Service: CDDA s 7(3) and (4) (and Regulations made thereunder), but since the Service does not pay for the liquidator's services, it cannot ask him to investigate matters which it is not in the financial interests of the creditors to have investigated. In any event, in some cases of Phoenix companies it is not in any creditor's interest even to secure the appointment of a liquidator, and so all that happens is that eventually the company is struck off the register of companies by the Registrar, without any investigation of the company's affairs, because the Registrar concludes from persistent non-filing of accounts that the company is no longer carrying on business: s 1000.

[67] Company Law Review, *Completing the Framework* (November 2000), para 13.104. A company need not trade under its corporate name and there may be legitimate reasons for not doing so. s 216 in fact applies to trading as well as registered names, but it is very difficult for the public authorities to detect whether a company is using a trading name which is different from its registered name.   [68] Above p 61.

[69] Above p 70.

Third, with regard to civil liability the design of an appropriate set of rules to make the directors personally liable to the creditors collectively is relatively straightforward, as we have seen with the wrongful trading provisions. The difficulty is ensuring that such liabilities are meaningful in practice, for the liquidator has no public funds to pursue wrongful trading actions. He can use only the assets of the company which would otherwise be available for distribution to the creditors, and will naturally be reluctant to divert them towards litigation except when he can be sure that the result will be to enhance the financial position of the creditors he serves. The most promising course of action for the liquidator is often to assign the cause of action, in exchange for a share of the eventual proceeds, if any, to a specialist claims agency which can spread the risks of non-success over a portfolio of similar claims from other companies—though there are some legal uncertainties with this process.

Fourth, the difficulties of private enforcement give scope for public law controls on opportunistic behaviour. However, effective enforcement is not guaranteed simply through the involvement of the public authorities. Although the Insolvency Service is active, it is beyond its capacity to police continuously the 70 per cent of all companies which have only one or two shareholders, even if such a level of official monitoring of business activities were regarded as tolerable by society. Since the chances of detection are only moderate, it is probably right to deploy fairly substantial sanctions against those who are caught. In this way one can justify the possibility of imposing disqualification for periods of up to fifteen years[70] and the threat of custodial criminal sanctions against those who breach the disqualification orders.

Fifth and finally, discussion of the effectiveness in practice of the wrongful trading and disqualification provisions is in order because they may be regarded, functionally, as a substitute for the minimum capital rules which British law lacks, at least for private companies. Where there is no or only nominal equity financing for the company's business, its resources come in one way or another from the company's creditors, by way of bank loans, goods, and services supplied on credit, facilities taken on lease rather than outright purchase, and so on. If the business does not prosper, the creditors' interests will be threatened immediately.[71] The

---

[70] Only about 10 per cent of the disqualification orders or undertakings fall within the 'upper bracket' of disqualification for 10–15 years, but the proportion of such orders has been rising over the previous five years: Insolvency Service, *Annual Report and Accounts 2008–09*, Chart 6.

[71] In fact, a company with no legal capital probably becomes insolvent on a 'balance sheet' test (are assets more than liabilities?) the moment it begins to trade, unless it is very lucky, which is no doubt why the statutory test for compulsory winding up is the 'going concern' test,

wrongful trading and disqualification provisions may be said to make feasible in public policy terms the adoption by companies of what might be thought to be, from the creditors' perspective, risky financial structures. Those risks are moderated by the imposition of a legal duty on the directors towards the creditors and the threat of future exclusion from use of the corporate form. Ex post control is less of a drag on enterprise than minimum capital rules but ex post controls require more enforcement effort than conditions applicable to the formation of a company.[72]

GROUPS OF COMPANIES

As we saw when we explored the rationales for limited liability at the beginning of the previous chapter, those based on encouraging investment in shares or on facilitating the operation of public markets in shares do not explain why the company law permits the operation of the limited liability principle within groups rather than simply as between the group as a whole and the outside world. However, the rationale based on the partitioning of assets and creditor monitoring is applicable within groups. Thus, the main policy questions are questions such as whether the law should permit the assignment of risky activities to a particular company in a group so that the claims of the creditors are confined to the assets of that particular company (and do not extend to the assets of other companies in the group). Alternatively, should the group be permitted to allocate a particularly valuable asset to a non-trading subsidiary, thus shielding it from the creditors of the trading companies in the group? The asset-partitioning argument, and its associated incentives for creditor monitoring, would suggest that in principle such segregation of assets and liabilities should be permitted. As ever, creditors who are uncomfortable with this situation and are in a position to protect themselves by contract can negotiate guarantees from other companies in the group, in particular from the parent company.[73]

---

ie whether the company can meet its debts as they fall due: IA 1986, s 122(1)(f) and 123(1)(e). A company whose assets are less than its liabilities may nevertheless have plenty of cash with which to discharge the immediate claims on it.

[72] For an energetic argument that ex post controls cannot do the whole job and that access to the corporate form with limited liability should be made more difficult see A Hicks, *Disqualification of Directors: No Hiding Place for the Unfit?*, Association of Chartered Certified Accountants, Research Report 59 (London, 1998).

[73] Cf *Re Polly Peck International plc (in administration)* [1996] 2 All ER 433, where a Cayman Islands subsidiary company without significant assets was formed and issued bonds to the amount of 700m Swiss francs, in order to avoid the costs of listing the bonds in London, a situation which was acceptable to the purchasers of the bonds only because the parent company, then a substantial company, guaranteed the obligations of the subsidiary. But courts are not astute to treat statements by parents to creditors of subsidiaries as contractual

The essence of the idea of a group of companies is that two or more companies, although separate legal entities, are managed as a single unit, though the management arrangements are likely to vary considerably in the degree of initiative accorded to subsidiaries. The legal structure of the group, as well, may display enormous variations. In particular, the parent company may control the subsidiary on the basis of holding all the subsidiary's shares (a 'wholly owned' subsidiary) or simply a majority of them or it may even be able to control the decisions of the subsidiary without holding a majority of its shares.[74] Where the subsidiary is not wholly owned, the law needs to think about the position of the 'outside' shareholders in the subsidiary as well as the subsidiary's creditors, a matter we consider in Chapter 8. Further, parent (or 'holding') companies may spawn strings of subsidiaries, as where P has a subsidiary S1 which has its own subsidiary SS1, which thus becomes an 'indirect' subsidiary of P. If P has another direct subsidiary, S2, which also has its own subsidiary SS2, one may need to think also, for example, about the relations between S1 and S2 or between SS2 and S1 or between any of the group members. In short, group structures provide company lawyers with the most complex factual situations to analyse.

However, two things are clear about the British law relating to groups. The first is that the issue of liability within groups is not addressed specifically in the companies legislation. The second is that the courts have allowed the separate legal personality doctrine of the *Salomon* case[75] to operate within the group structure, so that in general the partitioning of assets and liabilities to particular subsidiary companies is permitted—and, indeed, frequently done. On the first point, it is sometimes suggested that the legislation has not addressed the issue specifically because British company law lacks the necessary conceptual apparatus. This is clearly not the case. Where the Act wishes to impose rules on groups of companies, it is fully able to do so. It does so in relation to group accounts and took this step many years before group accounts became mandatory under Community law—in fact, before the Community was created.[76] Again, a number of the duties imposed by statute on directors are extended to 'shadow directors', defined as 'those in accordance with whose directions or instructions the directors of a company are accustomed to act'.[77] This

---

promises: *Kleinwort Benson Ltd v Malaysia Mining Corp Bhd* [1989] 1 All ER 785, CA ('letter of comfort' treated as being a statement of present fact, not a promise about future conduct).

[74] For example, where a substantial but minority corporate shareholder has the right to appoint the majority of the subsidiary's board.   [75] Above p 25.

[76] ss 398–408. The Act contains definitions of parent and subsidiary companies and, slightly wider, parent and subsidiary undertakings (ss 1159 and 1162) but the differences need not detain us here.   [77] s 251.

definition embraces a wide range of persons who exercise control within a company without themselves being directors. Among such persons may be a parent company which instructs the directors of a subsidiary how they shall conduct the business of the subsidiary.[78] However, the Act shows some caution about imposing liabilities on shadow directors which might disrupt intra-group arrangements.[79]

Nevertheless, the shadow director example is particularly important in the context of this chapter, because among the statutory provisions extended to shadow directors are those relating to wrongful trading, discussed in the previous section.[80] Thus, section 214 may operate to impose liability upon a parent company to the creditors of the subsidiary. One can see that the Companies Act has no difficulty with the idea that, exceptionally, parent companies should be liable for the debts of their subsidiaries. What the wrongful trading provisions do not create is a routine liability of this type, flowing simply from the fact of the existence of a parent and subsidiary relationship. Something more is required, and in the case of section 214 that additional thing is the failure of the parent company to treat the management of the subsidiary as having an independent existence, plus negligent disregard by the parent of the interests of the subsidiary's creditors in the period before insolvency.

A similar conclusion flows from an analysis of the common law rules which sometimes permit the courts to ignore the separate legal personality of the subsidiary. We have already encountered the common law doctrine of 'piercing the veil'.[81] We noted that this doctrine is particularly important when it operates to remove the protection of limited liability, because one of the primary functions of separate legal personality doctrine within company law is precisely to facilitate the implementation of limited liability. As far as groups are concerned, the courts have varied somewhat over time in their willingness to pierce the veil, but the latest authority is quite restrictive. This is *Adams v Cape Industries*,[82] a particularly important case

---

[78] See *Re Hydrodan (Corby) Ltd* [1994] 2 BCLC 180, where the judge was prepared to view a company as the shadow director of an indirect subsidiary. This was on the basis that the parent could be shown in fact to give the indirect subsidiary the instructions the section requires. However, the judge was not prepared to hold that the directors of the parent became shadow directors on the basis of instructions given in the course of their functions as directors of the parent. To the same effect *Re Paycheck Services 3 Ltd* [2009] 2 BCLC 309, CA.

[79] s 251(3)—not imposing the general fiduciary duties of directors on a parent company even if it is a shadow director of its subsidiary.

[80] The provisions relating to disqualification on grounds of unfitness are also extended in this way.   [81] Above p 32.

[82] [1990] Ch 433, CA. In fact, the central company in the case (CPC) was not a subsidiary of the defendant, since its shares were held by an independent third party, though CPC was

because it involved the failure of an attempt to pierce the veil on the part of involuntary creditors of the subsidiary.

The claimants were allegedly the victims of asbestos-related diseases which had been caused by products put into circulation by the subsidiary. In a robust judgment the court was clear that the fact that a group was conducted as a single economic entity did not mean that the normal operation of the principles of separate legal personality and limited liability were to be set aside. Cape was not to be exposed to liability on the grounds that it 'ran a single integrated mining division with little regard to corporate formalities as between members of the group'. So, the parent company could make the other members in the group dance to its tune without losing the benefits of limited liability as against those companies. Moreover, a questionable motive did not deprive Cape of these benefits: it retained them even if 'the purpose of the operation was in substance that Cape would have the practical benefit of the group's asbestos trade in the United States, without the risk of tortious liability'. It was, the court thought, a legitimate use of the group structure to bring this result about.

Cape was at risk of being held liable for the actions of a subsidiary only if the group arrangements were a 'façade'. The tests to be passed for this conclusion to be reached were not explored in detail, but they seemed to involve a complete abandonment of the formalities of company law vis-à-vis the subsidiary. As we have seen, the fact that Cape controlled the business policy of a subsidiary would not turn it into a façade in the sense meant by the court. Cape would have to go well beyond that, as it had with a Liechtenstein subsidiary, which was 'no more than a corporate name', having no employees or officers of its own but using those of other group companies. Thus, at common law the requirements for piercing the veil are more demanding than those contained in the statutory definition of a shadow director. Whereas domination of the subsidiary's board is likely to satisfy the statutory definition of a shadow director, the common law seems to regard a separate if compliant board as sufficient to maintain the separate legal personality of the dominated company.[83] Of course, under the statute being a shadow director does not by itself trigger liability, only the potential for it.

---

closely associated with Cape and the discussion in the case proceeded on the basis that the rules applicable to subsidiaries proper were the relevant ones.

[83] In *Yukong Line Ltd of Korea v Rendsburg Investments Corp of Liberia* [1998] 1 WLR 294 the court seemed to accept that there could be no question of piercing the corporate veil in respect of a liability which had not yet arisen (ie where the controllers had shifted assets out of a company, in anticipation of a liability). The creditors should establish the liability, take control of the company, and cause it to sue the former directors and recipients of the assets.

However, even at common law the claimants' position may be stronger if the control exercised by the parent over the activities of the subsidiary can be argued, not to make the parent liable for the debts of the subsidiary, but to create a direct duty (in tort) owed by the parent towards the claimants. Thus, it has been argued that where a parent company prescribes the health and safety policies of its subsidiaries, it comes under a duty of care in tort towards the employees of the subsidiary and local inhabitants to take reasonable care to protect them in respect of their health and safety. In such a case the common law of tort acts in a way which is parallel to section 214, as extended by the shadow director provision.[84]

It is clear that British law is at one end of the spectrum as far as the regulation of liability within groups is concerned. Other countries, as different as Germany and New Zealand, have specifically addressed the group issue in legislation. If such legislation were to be introduced in Britain, a large number of policy choices would have to be made.[85] The legal techniques for modifying limited liability are not confined to making the parent (or other group companies) generally liable for the debts of its subsidiary. In some cases it might be more appropriate to confine the creditors' claims to the assets of the subsidiary but to make the parent liable to the subsidiary to the extent that it has caused harm to the subsidiary's financial interests or to protect the subsidiary's creditors by restricting the freedom of the parent to shift assets out of the subsidiary into the hands of the parent, say, by way of dividend.[86]

A further set of choices relates to whether the group law would be mandatory or optional. It might seem odd to make liability towards a subsidiary optional for a parent company. Why should the parent ever choose it? However, separate legal personality has some costs for the management of corporate groups, as well as for group creditors. In particular, the fact that the duties of the directors of each group company are owed in principle to that company and not to the group as a whole may restrict the flexibility of group management. Thus, there might be some scope for a 'deal' whereby the parent benefited from the removal of some or all of the legal obstacles

---

[84] See *Connelly v RTZ Corporation plc* [1998] AC 854, HL and *Lubbe v Cape plc* [2000] 1 WLR 1545, HL, which decided, however, only the question whether the claims should be heard in the English courts and not the existence or breach of the tortious duty. The second case involved the same company as in the *Adams* case, but the facts related to its South African subsidiaries.

[85] For discussion of these issues, see Corporate Governance Forum, *Corporate Group Law for Europe* (Stockholm, 2000).

[86] All these techniques can be found in the German *Konzernrecht*, introduced in 1965.

to running the group on an integrated basis in exchange for undertaking certain obligations towards the creditors of subsidiaries.[87]

Finally, there would be a choice between making the modification of limited liability a general feature of group law or something which cut in only upon the insolvency of a group company. The New Zealand legislation operates on the latter basis, giving the court a wide 'just and equitable' discretion to make a solvent group company liable for the debts of another insolvent group member or to require the liquidation of two or more group companies to be consolidated.[88]

At present such discussion is not well developed in the UK, at least at the level of policy makers. The British legislature has yet to be convinced that the problems of limited liability within groups cannot be solved by a combination of creditor self-help, general company law strategies such as section 214, or the unfair prejudice remedy[89] and targeted statutory interventions, such as the requirement for group accounts.

CONCLUSIONS

It may be helpful to draw together at this point some threads of the law discussed in this and the previous chapter.

First, we have seen that British law extends the protection of limited liability to all companies incorporated under the Companies Act, and has long permitted even the smallest business to incorporate. This is despite the fact that the traditional rationales for limited liability apply only weakly to small companies. In going in this direction, however, British law follows a common, if not universal, trend in the development of the company laws of other comparable states.[90] Yet, in comparative terms one feature of the British response to the danger of excessively risky behaviour in small companies, created by the broad acceptance of limited liability, does stand out. The traditional response to this danger in the Germano-Latin legal systems has been to insist on a minimum legal capital for all companies. By contrast, common law systems have always been sceptical

---

[87] The CLR proposed a modest version of this idea but, after consultation, did not proceed with it. See *Completing the Structure* (November 2000), paras 10.19–10.57 and *Final Report* (July 2001), Vol 1, paras 8.23–8.28.

[88] Companies Act 1993 (NZ) ss 271 and 272, a solution supported by R Austin, 'Corporate Groups', in R Grantham and C F Rickett (eds), *Corporate Personality in the 20th Century* (Oxford: Hart Publishing, 1998).   [89] See below Ch 8.

[90] M Lutter, 'Business and Private Organisations', in *International Encyclopedia of Comparative Law* (Tübingen: Mohr Siebeck, and Dordrecht: Martinus Nijhoff, 1998), Vol 13, ch 2, 25–9.

of the advantages of the minimum legal capital.[91] However, British company law has not ignored the perverse incentives which limited liability, coupled with control of the company, may create. Rather, it has sought to combat them through the ex post rules relating to wrongful trading and disqualification of directors.

Second, the other area where the traditional arguments in favour of limited liability seem weakly applicable is that of groups of companies and where, equally, a danger of excessively risky behaviour arises through the assignment of high-risk activities to under-capitalized subsidiaries. However, in rejecting the general proposition that a company is liable for the obligations of another company which it controls and in failing to develop a comprehensive set of rules to regulate such liability within groups, British law does not depart from the pattern to be found comparatively. Only very few countries have followed the German lead and legislated for such a code.[92] This is probably because group structures and relationships within groups are highly variable and the appropriate general rules are accordingly difficult to identify.[93] Nevertheless, the result is that group problems are addressed in British law in a rather piecemeal fashion, as the courts struggle to apply general statutory or common law rules in a group context. Without further research it is difficult to assess whether the resulting set of rules addresses the risks of opportunistic behaviour within groups in an efficient way.

Third, like all company laws the British system relies predominantly upon self-help by creditors (usually via contract) to protect themselves against company opportunism generated by limited liability. This is potentially an efficient solution, because, even in the absence of limited liability, large lenders and other creditors will want to secure contractual protections against debtor opportunism, for example, borrowing the money for one purpose but using it for another. Thus, additional contractual protections to deal with the risks generated by limited liability can easily be added to the creditor/debtor contract. A contractual relationship does not have to be created in order to deal with opportunism generated by limited liability; an existing contractual structure has simply to be extended. Worries about excessive creditor self-help relate not so much

---

[91] Ibid 33 and especially the table on p 9, suggesting that all the EC countries except the UK and Ireland have minimum capital rules for all companies and that no common law-influenced country does.

[92] Within the EU only Porugal seems to have followed Germany and some countries which might be expected to do so (eg Austria) have not.

[93] Cf the New Zealand solution mentioned above which involves giving the court a broad discretion at the point of liquidation.

to the taking of promises from borrowers via covenants, but rather to the intra-creditor conflicts created by the taking of security, especially the floating charge.[94]

British law, as elsewhere in Europe, deals with non-adjusting creditors to some considerable extent outside company law, through, for example, compulsory insurance.[95] Assuming that the insurance requirements are appropriately widespread and the premiums sensitive to the risks generated by each company, both of which are empirical questions, then this system can operate to internalize within the company's decision-making processes the costs it imposes on involuntary creditors. However, whilst eschewing minimum capital, British law does use—and always has used—legal capital as a regulatory tool in relation to distributions and, despite arguments to the contrary, that situation seems likely to continue to obtain.

---

[94] Above p 66.   [95] Above p 73.

5

Centralized Management I
Empowering Shareholders in Widely
Held Companies

CENTRALIZED MANAGEMENT AND
DISPERSED SHAREHOLDINGS

In all but the smallest companies one finds that the function of managing the company has become to some degree specialized and separated from that of providing risk capital to companies. The former task is lodged by the law or, as in the case of the UK, by the company's constitution in the hands of the board of directors, whilst the latter is the function of the shareholders. Of course, in the largest companies there will develop an elaborate hierarchy of managers, only the most senior of whom will be members of the board of directors (and can be termed its 'executive directors').[1] It is thus appropriate to describe the board as being 'responsible for the management of the company's business',[2] which leaves open the question of how far the board does the management job itself and how far it delegates it to others. The top executive director in a big company—the managing director in British parlance or the chief executive officer (CEO) in US and, increasingly, international parlance—may become much better known publicly than even the largest shareholders in the company.

Identification of centralized management as a distinct phenomenon was made as long ago as the 1930s by two US scholars, Berle and Means,

---

[1] In contrast to the 'non-executive' directors who do not hold managerial roles in the company.

[2] This is the phrase used in the current model articles for public and private companies (see in each case art 3 of the two models). The previous versions stated, somewhat optimistically in the case of large companies, that the function of the board was to manage the company's business. The current model articles are set out in the Companies (Model Articles) Regulations 2008/3229.

in what must be the most famous English-language company law book ever written, *The Modern Corporation and Private Property*.[3] Their thesis was that, with the fragmentation of shareholdings in large companies, the development of centralized management had caused shareholders to lose control over the company. To what extent this is an accurate picture of the relationship between shareholders and the board in large companies has been a question which has dominated company law scholarship, at least in the US and the UK, ever since.[4] This chapter and the following ones analyse the ways in which the law helps shareholders minimize the costs arising from the emergence of centralized management.

In Chapter 1 I suggested reasons for the development of centralized management.[5] In sum, these reasons were that, in big companies, with a large and fluctuating body of shareholders, decision-making by shareholders was likely to be inefficient. Decision-making would be slow, if it routinely required the convocation of a large number of people to take management decisions. It might be inexpert because there is no reason to suppose that those who are skilled in investing money are the best people to manage the enterprises in which the money is invested. Management and investment are not the same thing, though they are obviously related. Finally, decision-making might be uncommitted. In a large decision-making body, where no one has a large financial stake in the common enterprise, the incentive to free ride, rather than invest substantial time and effort in working out what is the best course of action for the company, is likely to be strong.

What needs to be made clear at this point are some assumptions which lie behind this picture of tardy, incompetent, and detached management of the company by the shareholders. It is premised upon the company in question having a large body of shareholders. Where the shareholding body is small, the first and the third objections to shareholder management are very much lessened, though the second may still prevail.[6] Thus, where the shareholder body is small, the pressures towards centralized

---

[3] New York: Harcourt Brace and World, rev edn, 1968. Berle and Means did not use the term 'centralized management' but rather 'the separation of ownership from control'. The former term is preferred here as leaving open the question how far this development means that shareholders no longer control the company.

[4] For the causes and consequences of the dispersal of shareholdings in the UK see B Cheffins, *Corporate Ownership and Control* (Oxford: Oxford University Press, 2008).

[5] Above p 12.

[6] Thus, even in family-controlled companies the board may provide a locus for installing professional managers who may be better at implementing strategy than the family members and even perhaps better at setting it. No doubt, there will also be family members on the board to keep an eye on what is going on.

management may not operate with the same force.[7] Furthermore, the arguments in favour of centralized management assume that none of the large body of shareholders has a sufficiently big shareholding to give him or her even factual control of the company.[8] If there is a controlling shareholder, the third argument against shareholder decision-making (lack of commitment) is much less likely to hold, and the first argument (slow decision-making) may not apply either. This is because the controlling shareholder can use its votes to appoint its nominees to the board and thus shift decision-making from the large body of shareholders to the small board. Although the board is the locus of decision-making when this happens, this is not a classic example of centralized management, as the term is used in this book, because the board may not be in this case an expression of specialized management separate from the shareholders but rather an expression of the will of the controlling shareholder. The situation of a controller shareholder (or small number of shareholders acting together to control the company) together with a larger number of dispersed shareholders is not uncommon in continental Europe, though less common in the UK.

It is not my purpose to argue that companies with small bodies of shareholders or with large bodies which nevertheless contain a controlling shareholder do not pose important questions for the law arising out of the location of management decision-making. Rather, my argument is that the legal policy issues become clearer if the analysis proceeds in stages. Consequently, we shall analyse in this chapter and the next two the legal issues which arise in companies with large bodies of shareholders where no single shareholder (or associated group of shareholders) has sufficient shares to constitute a controlling block. Here, the arguments for centralized management are the strongest. We shall examine that situation before, in the later chapters, going on to an analysis of the situations where there is a controlling shareholder.

---

[7] Note that a small number of shareholders is not necessarily to be equated with an economically small company. Consider the joint venture between three multinational oil companies (so only three shareholders) which was the subject of litigation in *Multinational Gas and Petroleum Co v Multinational Gas and Petroleum Services Ltd* [1983] 1 Ch 258, CA, which ultimately became insolvent with a deficiency of £113 million (in 1977 prices).

[8] 'Legal control' of the company is a holding of shares which carry 50 per cent or more of the voting rights in the company, ie the proportion sufficient to secure the passage of an ordinary resolution by the shareholders. However, a much smaller shareholding may in fact be enough to secure the passing of an ordinary resolution, because not all shareholders bother to vote on any resolution and some can be persuaded to vote with the block-holder. Takeover regulation often regards one-third of the voting rights as sufficient to provide factual control.

CENTRALIZED MANAGEMENT AND
THE COMPANIES ACTS

Given the advantages of centralized management in companies with large bodies of shareholders and no controlling shareholder, one might have thought that British company law would provide that all important management decisions should be taken by the board (rather than the shareholders) and that the law would pay great attention to the structure, composition, and functioning of the board. In fact, as far as the companies legislation is concerned, this is not the case at all. Certainly, the Act provides ways in which decisions may be taken by the members (shareholders) of the company[9] and requires companies to have directors.[10] To this extent the Act supports the creation of the two decision-making bodies in the company, the shareholders and the board of directors. However, the Act says very little about the division of functions between the shareholders and the board or between the board and the senior management of the company. Certain administrative functions are allocated to the board by the Act, of which the most important is the production of the annual reports and accounts, which we discuss below in this chapter. Also, certain decisions, even if initiated by the board, require shareholder approval (again, as we shall discuss below), but normally these legislative provisions do not require the decision to be initiated by the board, ie the decisions could as well be taken wholly by the shareholders.[11] Moreover, the Act makes no distinction between executive and non-executive directors (ie those with and those without managerial posts in the company), says nothing about the possible functions of the chair of the board, does not mention committees of the board, nor does it stipulate whether the chair of the board should be a different person from the CEO.

How different is all this from, for example, the provisions of German company law about the board structure of public companies (*Aktiengesellschaften*). For a start, the German Act requires the company to have two boards to which different functions are attributed: the managing board (*Vorstand*) and supervisory board (*Aufsichtsrat*). The composition and functions of those boards are specified and, as well, a certain amount of detail on their methods of operation is laid down in the relevant legislation (the *Aktiengesetz*). Finally, the shareholders may decide on matters

---

[9] Essentially shareholders may take decisions at meetings or by circulating a written resolution among themselves outside a meeting, but the latter method is available only to private companies: s 281.   [10] CA 2006, s 154. A private company need have only one director.
[11] *Re Savoy Hotel Ltd* [1981] 3 All ER 646, 657c–g.

concerning the management of the company only at the request of the managing board.[12]

Whilst the Companies Act may be virtually silent on the above matters, it cannot be that the British companies do not have rules governing these fundamental issues. Where should one look? The answer is that the equivalent rules for British companies on the division of powers between shareholders and the board and on the role of the board are located in the company's own constitution or even in rules made by the board itself, for example, concerning the delegation of functions to non-board management. The contents of the articles of association are for each company to decide on, but the importance of the articles in conferring powers on the board is shown by the fact that some 24 (out of 86) regulations in the statutory model articles for public companies are devoted to the board.

Why should so much more be left to private ordering in the UK than in Germany? Partly, it is because the UK uses a single Act to regulate all companies, whereas Germany, in line with most continental European countries, has separate legislation for public and private companies. The German legislation for private companies (the *GmbHGesetz*) gives much more flexibility to private companies as to their internal division of powers and in this respect much more resembles the British Act. This supports the argument we made above to the effect that board decision-making is a universal feature of large companies, whether or not the company is dominated by a large shareholder, but with smaller companies the extent to which decision-making by the board is the efficient regime will vary from case to case. In a rough and ready way the force of this argument is recognized in German law by having separate bodies of statutory law for the two types of company. In the UK, where this approach has been rejected, it follows that a single statute cannot sensibly mandate a unique model of board functioning for all the companies it covers. The UK approach may reflect in part the influence of partnership concepts on early company law, for in the partnership the internal arrangements, too, are a matter for the partners, rather than the law.

Nevertheless, the reluctance in the UK to give statutory guidance on how even large companies organize their management is surprising—and, in fact, today that impression of no guidance is misleading. The Corporate Governance Code—which is the latest version of a succession of Codes for the largest publicly traded companies whose origins can be found with in the 'Cadbury' Code of 1992[13]—now fills the statutory gap, at least to some

---

[12] AktG §119(2).

[13] *The Financial Aspects of Corporate Governance* (London: Gee, 1992).

extent. However, the distinguishing feature of these Codes, which we shall discuss more fully in Chapter 7, is that they are the result of City, professional, and industrial, rather than of governmental, wisdom. In particular, the Code's rules have not been transposed into the legislation and, instead, are enforced mainly through the shareholders' response to the disclosures made under the Code rather than through legal process.

SHAREHOLDER CONTROL OF
THE DIVISION OF POWERS

Since the board's powers depend formally on what the articles say, it follows that the shareholders control the division of powers between themselves and the board (in contrast, for example, to the German situation where the board's powers are derived from the Act). This is what provides the flexibility to adapt the division to the needs of companies of different sizes and configurations, but it is also a fact of theoretical importance because it reinforces the idea that the directors are the agents of the shareholders. However, the legal analysis of that agency underwent a significant change at the beginning of the twentieth century and we ought briefly to make that legal analysis clear before turning to the sense in which economists say there is a principal/agent relationship between the shareholders and the directors.

The dominant nineteenth-century view in the common law was indeed that the directors were the agents of the shareholders, who could, therefore, instruct the board by ordinary majority vote at any time what to do or not to do. In the early twentieth century the courts adopted instead a constitutional view of the board.[14] The articles of association were now regarded as dividing up the powers of the company as between the shareholders and the board, each body being supreme in its own sphere. One important consequence of the new theory was that the shareholders by ordinary resolution could no longer issue instructions to the board. The board cannot interfere, it was now said, with the shareholders nor the shareholders with the board so long as they are exercising their respective powers conferred upon them by the articles. To allow this, as Lord Wilberforce once said, would be to permit either board or shareholders 'to interfere with that element of the company's constitution which is separate from and set against their powers'.[15]

---

[14] The pivotal case was *Automatic Self-Cleansing Filter Syndicate Co v Cuninghame* [1906] 2 Ch 34, CA.

[15] *Howard Smith Ltd v Ampol Petroleum Ltd* [1974] 1 All ER 1126, 1136, PC. See below Ch 6 at p 160 for the implications of this view for the powers of the board.

Thus, directors became the agents of the company, not of the shareholders. However, the significance of the point should not be exaggerated, since the shareholders retain control of the articles of association and so can alter the articles so as to expand or contract the powers of the board. Thus, it is still plausible to view the directors' powers under British company law as deriving from a delegation to them from the shareholders, even if that delegation is now of a formal and constitutional nature.

Of course, this theory does not tell one how powers are in fact divided up between the board and the shareholders. In the light of what has been said about the benefits of centralized management in companies with large shareholder bodies, it is no surprise that the model articles for public companies provide that 'subject to the articles, the directors are responsible for the management of the company's business, *for which purpose they may exercise all the powers of the company*'.[16] Thus, the default model rule is that the directors have all the powers of management, but the articles (and, as we shall see, the Act) may hold certain matters back, either wholly or in part. The model articles also clarify the power of the shareholders to give directions to the board: 'The members may, by special resolution, direct the directors to take, or refrain from taking, specified action.'[17] Thus, the shareholders may amend the directors' powers generally for the future by altering the articles or, by the same majority as is needed for alteration, give the directors instructions in a specific case. It is likely that these model provisions are widely followed in public companies.[18]

It might be thought that all this theory makes very little difference in practice. The board of a company, with a large number of shareholders, whether it is incorporated in the UK, Germany, or Delaware will have extensive powers of management. The differences, it is suggested, arise when the shareholders wish to intervene because they think the board is going down the wrong route. Shareholders in the UK who wish to intervene can do so ad hoc or to reset the division of powers for the future, provided they act by special resolution; Delaware shareholders will normally find they cannot convene a meeting of the shareholders unless the directors want to convene it and cannot change the constitution unless the directors propose it;[19] whilst German shareholders will be told that

---

[16] Above, n 2, art 3. Italics added.   [17] Art 4.

[18] What is more surprising is that the model articles for private companies contain the same default provisions. However, in this case the default is often modified in practice so as to require shareholder sanction for certain business decisions. The reason why this practice is not reflected in the statutory default is probably that the amendments themselves are many and various, so that no alternative default to the public company one could readily be formulated.

[19] Delaware General Corporation Law §§211(d) and 242(b)(1).

management is not their business.[20] We will see throughout this chapter and the next two that British company law is much more pro-shareholder than those of two of its major trading partners. Thus, as we shall see later in this chapter, the power-conferring approach of the common law is strongly reinforced by the statutory provisions enabling the shareholders to remove directors at any time by ordinary resolution.

CENTRALIZED MANAGEMENT AND PRINCIPAL/AGENT COSTS

Historically, centralized management emerged as a form of specialization. It was more efficient for shareholders to hire managers to fulfil that function than for shareholders to do the job themselves, at least outside small companies. As said, hired managers were likely to be more expert, more rapid in their decision-taking, and more committed than a large and fluctuating body of shareholders holding only small stakes in the company. Yet, centralized management is not without its costs for shareholders. The managers might begin to exercise their powers in a way which was, predominantly, in the managers' interests rather than the shareholders' interests. At worst, they might divert corporate assets to themselves or, more likely, set out to achieve goals which were more closely aligned to the promotion of their own interests rather than those of the shareholders. For example, they might seek to maximize the size of the company, because managerial remuneration is, or was, often linked to the size of the company, rather than its profitability.[21] Or the managers might simply shirk. In short, the shareholders could not simply delegate management powers to the board without engaging in some monitoring of how those powers were exercised. On the other hand, if the costs of monitoring exceeded the benefits of centralized management, the whole institution of centralized management would be called into question. A surprisingly large part of company law can be seen as addressing this problem by providing a series of legal strategies whereby the costs to shareholders of monitoring management are reduced. These strategies are the subject-matter of this and the following chapters.

---

[20] Above n 12. Of course, the above sentences are a caricature, but they contain an important truth.
[21] R Marris, *Managerial Capitalism in Retrospect* (Basingstoke: Macmillan, 1998).

A very substantial contribution to the analysis of the benefits of delegation and the costs of monitoring has been made by economists.[22] Less helpful is the phrase used by them to characterize the relationships they are analysing: principal/agent relations. The phrase is unhelpful for lawyers because, first, as we have seen just above, the law regards the directors as agents of the company and not of the shareholder and, second and more fundamentally, as we have seen in Chapter 2, the legal analysis of the principal/agent relationship is one where the agent has authority from the principal to act on the principal's behalf, usually authority to alter the principal's legal position. For the economist, a principal/agent relationship arises out of a purely factual dependency. If the furtherance of A's interests depends upon the actions of B, then A is the principal and B is the agent. In this situation A has an incentive to take steps to secure that B acts in a way which is favourable to A. The economist's conception of a principal/agent relationship is thus very much wider than that of the lawyer.

The legal and economic concepts may coincide exactly, as they did in the nineteenth-century view of the directors as agents of the shareholders. They may coincide substantially, as in the more modern view of the directors as the agents of the company but receiving their powers by virtue of the company's constitution, which is controlled by the shareholders. However, in many cases the two ideas seem at odds with one another, as where, for economists, minority shareholders are the principal and a majority shareholder the agent in respect of decisions taken in shareholders' meetings. The minority shareholders may be factually dependent upon the actions of a majority shareholder, but it is far-fetched to describe the minority shareholders as having conferred any authority on the majority shareholder to act on their behalves. Given these differences in approach between economists and lawyers, why do company lawyers pay so much attention to the economists' theories? A large part of the answer is that situations of factual dependency are much more widespread within companies than legal agency relationships, and the regulation of these situations of factual dependency is a major task for company law and for which the economists' analysis is helpful.

---

[22] The classical analysis is M Jensen and W Meckling, 'Theory of the Firm: Managerial Behaviour, Agency Costs and Ownership Structure' (1976) 3 *Journal of Financial Economics* 305.

A TYPOLOGY OF LEGAL STRATEGIES

It might be objected that there is no need for any legal strategies, beyond freedom of contract, to deal with the principal/agent relationship between shareholders and managers. The shareholders may negotiate with management what constraints they will when they delegate power to the directors via the constitution. However, it is doubtful whether simple contractual solutions are available. It is highly unlikely that shareholders, when deciding the terms of delegation of power to directors, will be able to foresee all the situations which will arise in the management of the company's future business and which will call for an exercise of discretion and thus to identify the full range of situations in which rules will be required. This is the so-called problem of 'bounded rationality'. Even if these situations could be foreseen, the costs of working out an appropriate solution to each one would be high, especially in lawyers' time. This is an example of the problem of transaction costs. So, any contract initially agreed by the shareholders with the managers is likely to be incomplete, and needs to be supplemented at a later date. Thus what is required is one or more legal devices which will steer the parties towards an appropriate solution ex post, even if the ex ante bargaining between shareholders and management has not identified one.

Of course, the fact that long-term relationships require what one might think of as governance structures, broadly conceived, still does not mean the law has to provide them; the parties could design the structures which fit their own situation best. As we shall see, one of the important strategies for controlling agency costs (the reward strategy)[23] does indeed involve the parties designing their own way of aligning the interests of the directors with those of the shareholders, but, as we shall also see, for that contracting process to stand any chance of achieving its goal, it needs to be heavily structured by the law. More generally, we examined above a similar claim for contractual solutions in relation to creditors' rights against the company. We saw there,[24] however, that there were arguments for state-provided default solutions, so that each set of contracting parties did not have to reinvent the wheel. We also saw that in some situations the parties might not be able to contract for their best solution, for example, because on the creditors' side there was such a degree of fragmentation that they were unable to coordinate their positions. Thus, relying wholly on private contracting to produce governance mechanisms is unrealistic,

---

[23] Discussed below in Ch 7.   [24] Above Ch 4 at p 71.

but, equally, the statutory mechanisms need to be adaptable and flexible and to make use of private contracting when this is available.

On examination, it turns out that there is quite a wide range of strategies available to the law to deal with principal/agent problems. A basic division is between legal strategies which focus on enhancing the control of the principal over the agent (then leaving the principal to exercise that enhanced control over the agent in any way desired) and those which seek to influence directly the exercise by the agent of the delegated discretion. Even this banality, however, is enough to demonstrate that the relevant legal strategies go beyond the obvious one of laying down, for example, the requirement that 'agents shall not treat principals unfairly'. That would be an example of a legal strategy constraining the discretion of agents, but it is by no means the only legal strategy which is available. An example of another and very different strategy, focusing on the power of the principal, would be to make it easy for the principal to dismiss an unsatisfactory agent.

In fact, as Figure 1 suggests, there are five pairs of strategies which are available for the regulation of agency relationships, of which two focus on agents and three on principals.[25] This analysis of legal strategies for regulation of principal/agent relations is not confined to shareholder/management relations (therefore, we shall use it in later chapters as well) or even to company law, though of course some types of principal/agent relationship may respond better to some legal strategies than others. We shall say a little about each of the strategies now and then look at each in more detail in this and the next two chapters.

Figure 1 Legal Strategies for the Regulation of Principal/Agent Relationships

Enhancing the principal's control			Structuring the agent's decisions	
Affiliation rights	Appointment rights	Decision rights	Setting agent incentives	Constraining agent decisions
Entry	Selection	Initiation	Trusteeship	Rules
Exit	Removal	Veto	Rewards	Standards

[25] This figure is an earlier version of what now appears in J Armour, H Hansmann, and R Kraakman, 'Agency Problems and Legal Strategies', in R Kraakman and others, *The Anatomy of Corporate Law: A Comparative and Functional Approach* (2nd edn, Oxford: Oxford University Press, 2009), 39.

Proceeding from right to left across the figure, we look first at the agent-focused strategies and the use of rules or standards. To a lawyer, this is perhaps the most obvious legal strategy to use to reduce agency costs, for it involves the stipulation of norms which directly constrain the exercise by the agent of his or her discretion. However, these norms fall into two categories. They may be precise rules or they may be general standards.[26] An example of a rule would be that all shareholders (of the same class) must be paid dividends pro rata to their shareholdings. Such a rule clearly prevents the directors favouring one group of shareholders over another, but only in the matter of dividend payments. An example of a standard is a requirement that the directors must treat all shareholders of the same class fairly. Such a standard catches a wider range of directorial activity, but is much less clear about what behaviour is required of directors and requires an expert judiciary for its effective application. With a standard the legislature is, in effect, sharing the law-making process with the judiciary: the standard is a grant of power by the legislature to the courts to be exercised on a case-by-case basis, because the legislature cannot predict in advance what the proper outcome of those cases should be. We shall see that in relation to shareholders' agency costs standards are more important than rules, precisely for this reason.

The second pair of agent-constraining strategies addresses itself, not to controlling the external manifestations of the conflicts of interest between agents and principals, but to moderating the underlying conflicts of interest and so reducing the incidence of self-interested behaviour. One strategy would be to give the exercise of discretion to an agent who is not exposed (or is less exposed) to the temptation of self-interest (though such an agent may be hard to find). Alternatively, the strategy might seek to align the self-interest of the agent with the self-interest of the principal, most obviously by tying the agent's remuneration to the successful achievement of the principal's goals. The first version of this strategy has been called, albeit at the risk of further terminological confusion, a 'trusteeship' strategy and the second version a 'reward' strategy.

Turning to the three left-hand pairs of strategies, which are based on the idea of empowering the principal, an obvious approach is to give the principal a greater input into the decision-making of the agent. At one extreme the decision-making function could be transferred wholly to the principal, ie the agency relationship could be terminated. However, this is a drastic solution since, in our context, it would deprive the shareholders

---

[26] On this distinction see L Kaplow, 'Rules versus Standards: An Economic Analysis' (1992) 42 *Duke LR* 557.

entirely of the benefits of centralized management. A less extreme form of the strategy would be to leave the initiation of decisions with the agent but require at least certain classes of those decisions to be approved by the principal, thus giving the latter a veto power. These are the two versions of the 'decision rights strategy'.

The other two strategies for empowering principals are closely related. One is to give the principal easily exercised powers in relation to the selection or removal of the agent (the appointments rights strategy), so that the agent will know that divergence from promoting the interests of the principal is likely to lead to swift dismissal and difficulty in obtaining a similar position for the future. A linked strategy is to make it easy for the principal to enter or leave agency relationships of a particular type (not just with a particular agent)—the affiliation rights strategy. In company law terms this means making it easy for shareholders to enter or exit companies. Transferability of shares, for example, promotes this last pair of strategies, allowing dissatisfied shareholders to leave the company, whilst facilitating the entry of, say, a takeover bidder who will shake up or even replace the existing management.

DISCLOSURE OF INFORMATION

The aim of the rest of this chapter and the following two is to analyse these strategies in the context of centralized management in companies with dispersed shareholdings. Before doing this, however, it is important to deal with an immediate objection to the above typology of legal strategies, which is that it is not clear where mandatory disclosure of information fits in, even though a great deal of company and securities markets law is concerned with precisely this topic. We have already seen the importance of corporate financial reporting in facilitating creditor self-help. Disclosure is equally important for shareholders. Indeed,[27] mandatory and regular reporting by directors to shareholders has generally been less controversial with business people than mandatory public filing of those reports, thus making them available to investors and creditors at large (but also to competitors and the public authorities). Thus, it might be asked why disclosure of information is not separately mentioned in the above typology.

The answer, it is suggested, is not that disclosure of information is not important but that it is so important that it is relevant to all the above

---

[27] See n 30 below.

legal strategies. It is difficult to imagine that any of these strategies could operate effectively in the absence of accurate and up-to-date information about the performance of the company. Provisions on disclosure of information thus constitute a method of implementing the above strategies and one that is so important that it plays an overarching role. One consequence of the centrality of information disclosure in company law is that economies of scale are generated: a single set of effective disclosure provisions may facilitate the implementation of a number of (probably all) the above strategies. Perhaps for this reason, information disclosure takes on the appearance of a distinct strategy, but it is suggested that, functionally, it is simply a way of implementing the strategies identified above.

ANNUAL INFORMATION

Over the history of company law, requirements for annual disclosure of financial information to shareholders and to the public have steadily increased. They have also in recent years become increasingly international, as the advantages have become apparent of requiring all companies which operate cross-border or which have substantial numbers of foreign shareholders to produce annual disclosures by reference to internationally agreed standards.[28] Those requirements began with the balance sheet, ie a statement of the company's assets and liabilities at any one time, showing whether its net asset value (assets less liabilities) is positive or negative.[29] They were extended to its profit and loss account (showing income and expenditure over a period of time, normally a year), in order to reveal whether the company is trading profitably or not.[30] The considerable rules governing how the balance sheet and profit-and-loss account are to be constructed are to be found not in the Act but subordinate legislation[31] and in standards produced by independent bodies of standard setters, national or international.[32]

---

[28] For this reason Community law has played an important role in setting both accounting and auditing rules, though its potential inadequacy in this area flows from the fact that it is only a regional body.

[29] First required to be published in 1908. This is referred to as 'a statement of financial position at the end of the period' in International Accounting Standard (IAS) 1.

[30] First required to be published to members in 1929 and to be generally available only in 1948. Referred to as 'a statement of comprehensive income for the period' in IAS 1.

[31] The most important subordinate legislation is the Large and Medium-sized Companies and Groups (Accounts and Reports) Regulations 2008/410. This requires companies choosing national regulation (see following note) to follow the Accounting Standards Board (ASB) standards or explain departures. See eg Sch 1, para 45. This seems to have been the original 'comply or explain' obligation.

[32] National standards are set by the ASB, a subsidiary of the Financial Reporting Council (FRC). International standards are set by the International Accounting Standards Board

Accounting standards even add requirements for further types of financial statement,[33] notably a cash-flow statement for the period in question, since the ability of a company to continue to operate at the day-to-day level often depends, not on its net asset position (that may be positive but its assets illiquid) or even whether it is trading profitably (it may not yet be entitled to payment or its debtors may be tardy in paying up), but on how much cash it can actually lay its hands on at any particular moment.

An innovation in the 2006 Act was to add an obligation on companies other than small ones to report forward-looking, 'soft', non-financial information to supplement the traditional backward-looking, 'hard', financial information. This is the 'business review'.[34] It constitutes part of the directors' report which boards have long been required to produce to accompany the company's financial statements. The business review is designed to provide some context in which the financial statements can better be understood and their implications for the future analysed. For 'quoted companies' (ie UK-incorporated companies whose shares are traded on 'top-tier' markets in the UK, elsewhere in the EEA or on the New York Stock Exchange or NASDAQ) the business review disclosures are heightened.

VERIFICATION

All this disclosure would be of little use, if the information contained in it were unreliable. Although there are general criminal and civil remedies available for misrepresentation,[35] company law has long deployed the additional technique of ex ante verification of the financial statements by a third party (though the reports and accounts remain the primary responsibility of the directors). Except for the smallest companies, an audit of them carried out by a professionally qualified third party is required. The auditors must report whether the accounts present a 'true and fair' view of the company's financial situation and on various other matters of central concern to shareholders.[36] Further, although this obligation is not to

---

(IASB). For certain types of publicly traded company Community law requires the IASB standards to be followed (or at least those standards as endorsed, sometimes after considerable controversy, by the EU). Otherwise, British companies have the option to follow the ASB or IASB standards, which in any case are converging.

[33] See eg IAS 1, para 10. [34] s 417.

[35] However, s 463 removes civil liability (except for fraud) in relation to the directors' report, including the business review. This was done to promote uninhibited disclosure.

[36] s 495.

be found in the Act, accounting standards, national and international,[37] require the auditor to report on whether it is appropriate to value the company on a 'going concern' basis—something which is of crucial importance during an economic down-turn.[38]

But how to ensure that the auditors do a good job? After all, the auditor is paid for by the company and, although the company must normally have an auditor, it does not need to hire any particular auditor: any appropriately qualified person will do. A number of high-profile corporate collapses in recent years have suggested that auditors sometimes get into too cosy a relationship with the corporate managements upon whom they are supposed to report to the shareholders.[39] Traditionally, it was thought that the auditing firms' own business models would lead them to do a good job as 'gatekeepers', on the grounds that their 'reputational capital' was what gave them their competitive advantage as auditors. An auditor with a reputation for laxness would not get hired: even less than respectable management requires for its own reasons an auditor whose opinions carry weight among investors. With the growth of non-audit work for accounting firms, however, the temptation to sacrifice audit rigor for lucrative non-audit work proved too strong in some cases.[40]

The responses to these very unsettling events were various. Essentially, the aim has been to remove the auditors from their dependence on the goodwill of executive management upon whom they are principally to report. Thus, the appointment and removal of the auditors has been made a matter for the shareholders, not the board, ie a decision rights strategy is deployed.[41] Ongoing relations between the auditors and the company are to be monitored by the audit committee of the board, consisting of independent non-executive directors, with whom the auditors

---

[37] Since accounting standards, with which the Act does require compliance, are formulated on the basis that the company is a going concern, they necessarily require this assumption to be tested. See FRC, *Going Concern and Liquidity Risk: Guidance for Directors of UK Companies 2009*.

[38] If the company ceases to trade, its assets are likely to be worth much less than if it is a going concern. This flows from the very fact that the company is a way of bringing together resources which are 'specialized' for the achievement of the company's goals and their value as separate items when this goal is abandoned will typically be less, unless the utility of the assets is easily transferable. So, specialized machinery may have only scrap value outside the company which ordered it whilst cash is fully fungible.

[39] The Enron collapse in the US, where this was thought to have happened, led to a significant overhaul of auditing rules even in the EU, including the adoption of a much stronger Directive on auditing (Directive 2006/43/EC).

[40] See generally in this area J Coffee, *Gatekeepers* (Oxford: Oxford University Press, 2006), esp Part I and ch 5.   [41] CA 2006, Part 16, Chs 2 and 4. This has long been the position.

are required to discuss issues of principle relating to the presentation of the financial statements and which must develop and implement a policy relating to the non-audit work of the auditors.[42] Legislative policy, so far, has stopped short of demanding a complete polarization of audit and non-audit work, ie requiring that both should not be provided by the same firm. Finally, moving outside company law, the regulatory structure for auditors and accountants has been substantially enhanced.[43] Apparently going against these trends, the liability exposure of auditors for negligent work has been reduced. Whereas previously auditors could not contract to limit their liability in such cases, that is now permitted under the 2006 Act, subject to safeguards, notably by way of shareholder approval.[44] This move was probably driven by fear that a very large damages award might drive another of only four remaining multinational accounting firms out of business and the suggestion that the inability to limit liability was discouraging new firms from entering the market for audits of very large companies.

MORE FREQUENT INFORMATION

Annual information about the company, although very important, is not ideal for governance purposes, especially as it emerges only some time after the end of the company's financial year. However, in the case of companies quoted on the main market of the London Stock Exchange the rules of the FSA (in this case its Disclosure and Transparency Rules (DTR)) go beyond the Companies Act reporting requirements. Listed companies must produce (unaudited) half-yearly financial reports to supplement the Act's annual reports and do so within ninety days of the end of the relevant half-year.[45] In addition, as a result of the EU Transparency Directive,[46] listed companies are required to produce quarterly 'interim management statements'.[47] Neither of these sets of reports is required, like the annual reports, to be laid before the shareholders in general meeting, but they

---

[42] This is the 'trusteeship' strategy, which is discussed further in Ch 7 below. An audit committee is required by art 41 of the EC Directive (above n 39) and recommended in a somewhat stronger form by the UK's Corporate Governance Code.

[43] CA 2006, Part 42. The operation of this regulation is the primary responsibility of various subsidiaries of the Financial Reporting Council, such as its Professional Oversight Board, Auditing Practices Board, and Accountancy and Actuarial Discipline Board.

[44] Part 16, Ch 6. This may enable auditors in practice to achieve their long-term goal of being liable only for the damage they cause (proportionate liability), avoiding liability for damage caused by others where both auditor and others contributed to the same loss but the others are now judgment proof (joint and several liability).   [45] DTR 4.2.

[46] Directive 2004/109/EC.   [47] DTR 4.3.

do have the effect of keeping shareholders (and investors generally) up to date with the company's development.

The DTR also require the disclosure of 'inside information', that is, new information about the company likely, when made public, to have a significant effect on the price of the company's shares (or other financial instruments). In particular, this obligation requires the board to issue a 'profits warning' as soon as the directors form the view that the company's profits are likely to be significantly less than the market had expected. Although the additional disclosure requirements contained in the DTR may be motivated primarily by the FSA's desire to ensure accurate pricing by the market of the securities which are traded on it, individual shareholders can also take advantage of the disclosures for the purposes of exercising their internal governance rights.

SHAREHOLDER INVOLVEMENT IN
DECISION-MAKING

We shall devote the remainder of this chapter to an analysis of the legal strategies which address the shareholders' agency problems by aiming to enhance the principal's control. This is the left-hand side of Figure 1. In the following chapters we shall analyse the strategies which aim to structure the agents' decisions, that is, the right-hand side of the figure.

We begin our analysis of the strategies which aim at enhancing the principal's control with what we have termed the 'decision rights' strategy. As already noted, as between directors and shareholders as a class, a strategy of shifting decisions into the hands of the shareholders is very effective at dealing with principal/agent problems but comes with the high price that shareholders are substantially deprived of the benefits of centralized management. Thus, it is not surprising, as we have seen, that company law, in the main, leaves it to shareholders themselves to determine, via the articles, the distribution of decision-making powers as between the board and the shareholders. Nevertheless, there are some instances where the Companies Act requires a shareholder input into the decision by way of approval of the directors' proposal or even permits the shareholders themselves to initiate a decision.

How does this strategy protect shareholders? Where shareholders as a whole may initiate a decision, it may seem obvious that they can shape it so that it furthers their interests. Where they have merely the right to veto the directors' proposal, their position appears less strong, for they will have to engage in bargaining with the directors in order to get the latter to produce a proposal of which the shareholders do approve. The directors may respond to shareholder opposition by withdrawing their proposal, putting nothing in its place, which may not be what the shareholders want. However, even where the shareholders have an initiation right, their reliance upon the directors for management skills to set and implement strategy will in fact often require them to bargain with the directors. The shareholders may formally have the right to decide, but what they want may not be likely to appear in practice unless the directors are committed to it. This is perhaps why the Act often does not make it clear whether it is conferring a veto or an initiation right on the shareholders. In practice, even an initiation right may often turn out to be only a veto right. In any event, we may expect that both initiation and veto rights for shareholders will generate bargaining between shareholders and directors, unless the directors regard the costs of securing shareholder consent as so high that they seek to avoid decisions which require shareholder input.[48]

As indicated, the number of cases where the Act qualifies centralized management by requiring a shareholder input into decision-making is small, though the shareholders remain free, through the articles, to add to that number. Although few, the mandatory cases are instructive. They seem to share one or more of the following characteristics:

- the decision is likely to be an infrequent one (so that the general run of management decisions in the company is not affected);
- the decision is one which the shareholders are likely to be as good at taking as the directors (for example, the decision is as akin to an investment as to a management decision);
- the decision is sufficiently important to the shareholders that they are likely to devote appropriate resources to taking it; and
- the decision is one where there is a high degree of conflict between the interests of the directors and those of the shareholders, so that leaving the decision entirely to the board is particularly risky from the shareholders' point of view.

In other words, the cases where the legislature feels confident enough to insist on shareholder input into decision-making involve decisions which display the converse of the features which argue in favour of centralized management as the normal rule.

Even when based on these general criteria, any attempt to identify the precise range of decisions which should require an explicit shareholder

---

[48] For an analysis along these lines see S Deakin and A Hughes, 'Economic Efficiency and the Proceduralisation of Company Law' (1999) 3 *CFILR* 169, especially at 184–8.

input is likely to be contestable. To require shareholder consent only of decisions which meet all four criteria identified in the previous paragraph would mean very few decisions were subject to this requirement; to require it where only one criterion is met would be to impose shareholder decision-making on a wide scale. Company laws in different countries differ somewhat, though not enormously, in their choice of decisions to be subject to shareholder control.[49] In the UK the main corporate decisions which the Act subjects to shareholder approval are:

- alterations to the company's constitution;[50]
- changes in the type of company (for example, from private to public or vice versa);[51]
- decisions to wind the company up voluntarily;[52]
- decisions by companies to issue or repurchase shares or to alter their legal capital;[53]
- appointment and removal of the company's auditors, whose duty is to verify the financial statements which the company presents annually to the shareholders;[54]
- approval of 'schemes of arrangement', between a company and its shareholders or creditors (a bland name for a useful procedure which can be used for many things, ranging from a merger between two companies to a scaling down of creditors' rights on an insolvency) as well as formal mergers or divisions involving the company;[55]
- approval of certain transactions involving a strong conflict of interest.[56]

As we also saw at the beginning of this chapter, the shareholders, whether or not they alter the articles, are empowered under the model articles to give the directors instructions by special resolution on any particular matter at any time. Nevertheless, giving of ad hoc instructions requires the shareholders to take the initiative to restrict the powers of the board, unlike with the statutory list (above) where the board must seek the approval of the shareholders if it wants to act. Thus, the shareholders' veto under the statutory list comes to them without effort on their part.

---

[49] See E Rock, P Davies, H Kanda, and R Kraakman, 'Fundamental Changes', in R Kraakman et al, above n 25, ch 7. For an intriguing explanation of the pattern see E Rock, 'The Corporate Form as a Solution to a Discursive Dilemma' (2006) 162 *Journal of Institutional and Theoretical Economics* 57.   [50] s 21.

[51] Part 7.   [52] IA 1986, s 84.

[53] ss 549–51, 569–73; Part 17, Chs 8 and 10: Part 18, Chs 2–4.

[54] Part 17, Chs 2 and 4.   [55] Parts 26 and 27.

[56] Discussed further in Ch 6 below.

Somewhat surprisingly, the largest companies, ie in effect those whose shares are traded on the Main Market of the London Stock Exchange, are subject to a longer list of mandatory shareholder approval requirements than are public companies whose shares are not so traded. The Listing Rules, now issued by the Financial Services Authority,[57] extend the principle of shareholder approval to transactions which the company is contemplating simply because of the size of those transactions. Provided the contemplated transaction has a size equivalent to at least 25 per cent of the company's current assets, profits, turnover, market value, or gross capital (the so-called 'Class 1' transactions), prior approval of the shareholders is required.[58] These additional requirements are surprising since the costs of shareholder decision-making are likely to be higher in the largest companies than in smaller ones. The Listing Rules provisions suggest two things. First, as already indicated, the line between decisions where shareholder involvement is appropriate and those where it is not is contestable. The theory behind this rule is presumably that it is likely that a large transaction will significantly alter the nature of the company and is thus as much an investment as a managerial decision. Second, those representing shareholders' interests have had more influence over the setting of the Listing Rules, made by the FSA, than over the legislation made by Parliament.

It is unlikely that the question of whether to include a particular type of decision within the category of those requiring shareholder approval will ever be settled to everyone's satisfaction. For example, despite the requirement in the Act for shareholder approval of share issues and the Listing Rules' requirement for approval of large transactions, in the absence of specific provisions in the articles the directors unilaterally can commit the company to take on large new debt exposures. Notwithstanding its riskiness, the directors do not normally have to seek the shareholders' approval to increase the company's financial leverage.[59]

Of course, a law involving shareholders in decision-making does not guarantee the shareholders are in a position effectively to exercise their decision-making rights. We shall turn to that issue as part of the discussion in the next section of shareholders' appointment rights, since a similar issue arises in relation to that strategy.

---

[57] Before demutualization the Exchange itself issued the listing rules.

[58] LR 10. As we shall see in Chs 6 and 8 below, the Listing Rules are also more insistent than the statute on the principle of shareholder approval in cases of conflict of interest.

[59] LR 10.1.3(4) excludes a transaction to raise finance from the shareholder approval requirement, unless it is part of a transaction to acquire fixed assets for the company.

APPOINTMENT RIGHTS

In the previous section we saw that involving shareholders in corporate decision-making can constitute a way of addressing their agency problems, but only at the potential cost of depriving the shareholders of the benefits of centralized management, which depend upon the exclusion of shareholders from that process. Not surprisingly, therefore, this strategy is sparingly used by company law, at least on a mandatory basis. More promising, it might be thought, is the strategy of giving the shareholders strong legal rights in relation to the selection or removal of the directors. This strategy does not involve the shareholders in decision-making on matters of management, but could allow the shareholders to choose the best people to lead the company and to remove them if their performance fell below what was expected of them. We shall look briefly at the scope of the shareholders' appointment and removal rights and then consider the problems which arise when shareholders seek to use those rights.

Contrary to popular perception, company law does not insist that the directors be elected by the shareholders or that they be periodically re-elected by them, though the Corporate Governance Code applying to the largest listed companies now recommends annual re-election of the directors by the shareholders.[60] Partly, this is because there may be good reasons for giving other groups (for example, creditors) the right to appoint a director in order to protect their interests. Whether appointment rights shall be distributed more widely is a matter for the company, but a mandatory company law rule requiring shareholder appointment only might stand in the way of such broader distribution.[61] However, the absence of a mandatory rule requiring appointment or periodic reappointment by shareholders may simply operate so as to facilitate the entrenchment of incumbent management.

Not only does the company (usually through its articles) decide on how the directors are to be selected and periodically reappointed, but it also regulates the details of the selection and reappointment processes.[62] Although it must be borne in mind that this is a matter of practice rather

---

[60] Corporate Governance Code B.7.1—a provision introduced in 2010.

[61] Equally, though it is rarely done, appointment rights could be given by the company to its employees.

[62] The only significant mandatory rule contributed by the Companies Act is that the appointment or reappointment of directors must be voted on individually (s 160), so that a director who has incurred shareholder disapproval cannot be protected by bundling up his (re-)appointment with that of a director of whom the shareholders think well.

than of mandatory law, it can be said that a typical pattern of directorial selection in large companies is as follows. New directors are approved by the shareholders, either by being elected at an annual general meeting of the shareholders or by being approved at the first AGM after their appointment by the board to fill a vacancy which has occurred in between AGMs. They are then subject to re-election by the shareholders every three years or, in the case of companies which have implemented the Corporate Governance Code, annually, ie the normal term of appointment is such a period. However, it is also usual for the articles to make it difficult for shareholders to appoint their own nominees to the board, as opposed to accepting or rejecting the proposals of the existing board. For example, the articles may require significant prior notice to be given to the board of shareholder proposals for board membership. In practice, what the articles give the shareholders is a veto right, rather than an initiation right, over board appointments and reappointments.

However, the selection and re-selection rules rather fall into insignificance in the light of the rules on removal of directors. Here, British law contains an apparently tough mandatory rule: the shareholders, by ordinary resolution, can at any time remove any director (or, indeed, all of them) without having to assign a reason for so doing.[63] This power overrides anything to the contrary in the company's articles or in any contract with the director, and so removal may occur at any time and not just when the director comes up for reappointment at the end of his or her term of office. The rule applies even to directors not appointed by the shareholders, though if a director appointed by the creditors is removed, that may put the company in breach of its loan covenants and so removal in that case may carry undesirable consequences for the company, such as an obligation to repay the loan. Other company law systems also adopt this tough rule, but it is far from universal. German law, for example, limits the circumstances in which a director can be removed before the expiry of the term of office and US state laws generally permit companies to contract out of the rule of removal at any time by shareholder vote, for example, by a provision in the articles that the directors shall be removable only for cause. However, unlike UK law, they often put a mandatory limit on the length of the director's term.[64]

---

[63] s 168.

[64] For Germany, AktG, art 84; for the United States, see eg the Model Business Corporation Act, ss 8.05–8.08. US laws also provide for the 'staggering' of the terms of the members of the board, so that they do not all expire in the same year; rather, it may take two or three AGMs to remove the whole of an existing board.

The next question we have to ask is whether section 168 is as effective in practice as it appears at first sight to be. Broadly, the question is whether the incentives for shareholders to use their removal power outweigh the disincentives. Two categories of disincentive can be identified: first, steps taken by directors to counteract section 168; second, more general problems which shareholders have in invoking the internal governance machinery of the company.

DEFENSIVE ACTION BY DIRECTORS

Section 168(5) specifically preserves for the dismissed director the right to 'compensation or damages payable to him in respect of the termination of his appointment as director or of any appointment terminating with that as director'. This clearly permits an executive director, who has a service contract with the company,[65] to claim damages if dismissed by the shareholders under their statutory powers but in breach of the service contract. The newspapers are full of reports of dismissed directors receiving sums running into several million pounds as compensation for loss of office, even where the cause of their removal seems to have been the poor performance of the company. Whether such payments do in fact chill the shareholders' use of their powers in the case of companies with multi-billion pound turnovers, is not clear. However, large payments may operate so as to blunt the ex ante impact of the removal power on the director: why bother to avoid a situation in which the shareholders wish to remove you if the financial consequences of removal are attractive? Often, the objection is to the inappropriateness of failed directors receiving large financial rewards. Thus, the issue of large cash payoffs to directors raises issues which relate to the rewards strategy which I discuss in Chapter 7, as well as to the removal strategy. I thus postpone further consideration of the issue until then.[66]

Section 168 deals with only part of the process of the removal of directors. It deals, in essence, with the voting level needed to adopt a removal resolution and the effect of such a resolution. However, the section says nothing about the procedures and processes as a result of which the

---

[65] Whist a director may have a formal contract by which she is appointed director, the more important, financially, will be the management or 'service' contract which an executive director has with the company as a senior manager. It is normal to provide in the articles that the executive position will terminate if the manager is removed from the board. Whether such termination is a breach of the service contract is a matter of construction, but the contract will normally be worded so that it is.

[66] See below at p 209. In Ch 8 (at p 229) I discuss the decision in *Bushell v Faith* [1970] AC 1099, HL, which raises an issue about the effectiveness of s 168 in very small companies.

shareholders come to be assembled at a meeting[67] to consider a removal resolution. For that, one has to look elsewhere. However, unless that prior process works effectively, section 168 will be a dead letter. A shareholder, contemplating summoning a shareholders' meeting to consider a removal resolution, needs three things. The first is reliable information about the company on the basis of which she can decide whether it is in her interests to try and persuade fellow shareholders to remove one or more directors. The second is the legal power to summon a meeting of the shareholders. The third is the support of a sufficient proportion of those fellow shareholders to secure the passage of the resolution. Let us look at what company law says about each of these matters. It should be noted that these issues are not specific to removal resolutions. They arise generally, no matter what the issue is on which the shareholder wishes to initiate a collective decision, and thus they are relevant as well to the decision rights strategy discussed in the previous section.[68]

PROVISION OF INFORMATION TO SHAREHOLDERS

The information rights of individual shareholders as against the company are extremely limited. The Act confers no general entitlement upon individual shareholders to access the information held by the company, and article 83 of the model articles for public companies[69] explicitly provides that the individual shareholder has no right to inspect the company's records, unless the directors or the shareholders by ordinary resolution have conferred such a right. Even at a general meeting of the shareholders, it is only recently, as a result of EU legislation,[70] that an individual member has been given an explicit right to receive an answer to a question which is related to an item on the agenda for the meeting.[71] However, in some cases the common law would imply such a right.[72] Moreover, most listed companies do in practice afford some opportunity for those present at annual general meetings to ask questions, even questions unrelated to any specific item on the agenda, usually in the debate of the annual report

---

[67] The s 168 power can be exercised only by shareholders at a meeting even in the case of a private company. However, the articles may create an additional removal power which can be exercised by written resolution.

[68] Where the shareholders have a veto right, of course, they need not concern themselves with the summoning of the meeting (the board will take care of that) but the information and support problems remain.   [69] Above n 2.

[70] Directive 2007/36/EC on the exercise of certain rights of shareholders in listed companies.

[71] s 319A, but applying only to 'traded' companies, ie those with shares traded on the Main Market of the London Stock Exchange or any equivalent market in the UK or EEA (s 360C).

[72] See following note.

and accounts. However, none of the above helps the shareholder seeking information other than at the AGM.

The important information rights of shareholders under the Act are collective, and fall into two main categories. First, where a resolution is proposed for adoption by the shareholders, the proposers (usually, but not necessarily, the directors) will be obliged in law and practice to provide an accompanying circular to the shareholders which sets out the reasons in favour of the adoption of the resolution. That circular will generally reveal a certain amount of information about the company. If the information given is misleading, the resolution will be invalid.[73] However, this is of little comfort to the shareholder contemplating use of the section 168 powers, since she is the proposer in such a case and, thus, she has to provide, rather than receive, information. However, the shareholder may have gleaned relevant information from previous resolutions on other topics proposed by the board.

The other, and more important, source of collective information under the Act is the periodic and episodic reporting which the board is obliged to make to its shareholders and to the market if it is a listed company. We have discussed these obligations above: they operate both to inform the securities markets and to facilitate the exercise of governance powers by shareholders.

CONVENING MEETINGS

Although the absence of an individual right to have access to the company's information may sometimes prevent a shareholder from knowing whether it is appropriate to attempt to invoke section 168, in one way or another a considerable amount of information about public companies is available, especially if they are also listed companies. But acquiring information is only the first step. Clearly, if the shareholders are to adopt a removal resolution, a meeting of the shareholders must be convened and the removal resolution must be on the agenda of that meeting; equally clearly, the board of the company are unlikely to summon one themselves or put the item on the agenda, if they can avoid it. For this reason, the recent amendment to the Corporate Governance Code (see above) recommending annual re-election of the directors of the largest listed companies may prove very significant, for, if implemented , it gives the shareholders the opportunity to remove a director without themselves having to convene a meeting or secure the placing of this item on the agenda.

---

[73] See *Tiessen v Henderson* [1899] 1 Ch 861, on both the obligation on the proposers to provide information and the legal consequences of failing to provide it fully.

Where the Code does not operate or the company has chosen not to follow its recommendation or the issue is something other than the removal of a director, the Act gives the shareholder two possibilities for laying a resolution before a meeting of the shareholders in the face of an uncooperative board. The first involves piggybacking on the annual general meeting which the directors of public companies are obliged to summon once in each calendar year and with a gap of not more than fifteen months between AGMs.[74] The second consists of the shareholders requisitioning an extraordinary general meeting (an EGM being any meeting of the shareholders which is not an AGM).

The Act empowers shareholders holding 5 per cent or more of the company's voting rights (or 100 or more shareholders each holding shares whose paid-up value is at least £100) to require the company to add to the AGM agenda any resolution which may properly be moved there, together with a circular of not more than 1,000 words in support of the resolution.[75] Unless the company determines otherwise, or unless the company receives the requisition before the end of the financial year to which the meeting relates (ie before the shareholders receive the reports and accounts relevant to that year!) the requisitionists will have to pay the costs of the circulation.[76] However, these should not be large if the resolution goes out with the AGM papers which the company has to mail in any event to those entitled to attend. There is thus some pressure on the requisitionists to get their demand to the company before that time.

In the case of listed companies the date of the AGM is usually known many months in advance and a preliminary announcement of the company's financial results is also likely to have been made to the market long before the AGM. However, the Company Law Review proposed a formal integration of the rules on requisitioning resolutions and the timetable for the company's annual report, at least for quoted companies.[77] Such companies would have to publish their annual report and accounts (including on a website) within 120 days of the end of the financial year. There would then be a compulsory 'holding' period of fifteen days before any notice of the AGM could be sent out, during which period the company would be obliged to accept members' resolutions for circulation at the

---

[74] Failure to hold an AGM is a criminal offence: s 336.

[75] s 338. In the case of a traded company a similar set of members may require the inclusion of an item of business on the AGM agenda which is not a resolution: s 338A. This is again an addition made as a result of the Shareholders' Rights Directive (above n 70). Parallel provisions exist in relation to the circulation of a minority shareholders' statement, for example, one opposing a directors' resolution: ss 314–17.   [76] s 340.

[77] *Final Report*, Vol 1, paras 8.83 and 8.86.

company's expense, provided the thresholds of shareholder support set out above were met. This set of rules would have applied to all appropriate resolutions from members, including removal resolutions. Whilst the requirement for website publication has been implemented,[78] the rest of the reform proposal has not been taken up.

Of course, the triggering event for the shareholders' decision to seek to remove a director may be something other than the contents of the AGM papers, for example, something in a listed company's half-yearly report or in a 'major new developments' statement. In other words, waiting for the AGM may seem an unattractive option for the shareholders who do not want to sit idly by while the company continues its decline. Section 303 offers a solution by permitting shareholders having 5 per cent of the voting rights[79] to requisition an extraordinary meeting of the shareholders to consider a resolution they wish to put before it, which may include a removal resolution. Somewhat surprisingly, the costs of convening the meeting fall on the company. If the directors do not respond quickly, the requisitionists may convene the meeting themselves, their costs must be reimbursed by the company, which must in turn recoup those costs from the fees or remuneration due to the directors at fault.[80]

EXIT OR VOICE?

It thus appears that shareholders holding 5 per cent of the voting rights can move at any time to put a removal resolution before the shareholders. Alternatively, they could make use of the decision rights strategy by giving the directors instructions on how to handle a particular matter, though, as we have seen,[81] instructions require a special resolution (three-quarters majority) whilst a removal resolution requires only an ordinary one (simple majority). Consequently, even if the shareholders wish to give instructions, they may choose to formulate the resolution as a conditional removal one. It seems to be mainly on the basis of these sections that Bob Monks, a leading US authority on corporate governance, characterized the UK as 'easily the world leader' in the accountability of management to investors.[82] However, it may still be the case that shareholders prefer not to use the mechanisms for internal governance, including removal rights, provided by company law and instead to sell their shares if they are dissatisfied with

---

[78] s 430: 'as soon as reasonably practicable'.
[79] The figure was 10 per cent until reduced as part of the transposition of the Shareholder Rights Directive.   [80] s 305.
[81] Above p 109.   [82] *Financial Times*, 17 February 2000, p 18.

the performance of the board, at least where there is an available market in the company's securities. Why should this be? The answer is to be found, once again, in the extent to which the shareholdings in a particular company are concentrated. We have already stipulated that, for the purposes of this chapter, the companies we are considering do not have one or a small number of shareholders acting in concert who have a sufficient block of shares to control the company. So we are assuming there is no block-holder with, say, 50 per cent or even 30 per cent of the shares carrying voting rights in the company. But even where that is not the case, the pattern of shareholding may vary in the extent to which it is dispersed.

Let us assume, first, a pattern of highly dispersed shareholdings, for example, no single shareholder has more than 1 per cent of the voting shares in the company and many have very much smaller shareholdings than that. So, one has a large body of shareholders, perhaps tens of thousands, each with very small holdings. The incentives in such a situation for any one shareholder to seek to put forward a removal resolution against, let us further assume, a determined incumbent board, are weak. That shareholder will have to spend many resources contacting fellow shareholders and persuading them to her view of the company, before there is any question of requisitioning an EGM on the basis of 5 per cent support or passing a removal resolution. Those are costs which are certain to be incurred if the shareholder goes down the removal route. The countervailing benefits may be none, as where the activist shareholder fails to secure enough support to pass the resolution or where the new directors prove to be as ineffective as the previous ones. Or they may be very limited: the incumbent board is replaced, the new board does much better, and the company's share price and dividend levels improve, but our activist shareholder will benefit only to the extent of 1 per cent of those improvements. Even worse, other shareholders have an incentive not to join in with the activist. If they do, they share the costs but for the same limited benefits. If they do not, they obtain their share of the benefits without incurring any costs. So, they have an incentive to 'free ride'.[83]

The above situation may be said to demonstrate what are normally called the 'collective action' or 'coordination' problems of shareholders, ie the difficulties of a large body of people in adopting and maintaining a common position, in the absence of a strong incentive for one of their number (or a third party) to take an organizing role or, alternatively, in the

---

[83] It is true that, by not joining in, any individual shareholder reduces the chances of the activist succeeding, but that shareholder will calculate that the increased chances of benefiting do not outweigh the certain costs of joining the activist.

absence of reliable knowledge as to how one's fellow shareholders will act in the future. At times in the past the shareholding structure of many large British companies seems to have been of this highly dispersed kind and shareholders' use of the internal governance system was at its lowest. The incentives on shareholders in such companies were always to take what the Americans graphically call the 'Wall Street walk', ie to sell the shares, if dissatisfied with the board's performance, and invest elsewhere.

INSTITUTIONAL SHAREHOLDERS AND PARTIALLY RE-CONCENTRATED SHAREHOLDINGS

However, in recent years a limited re-concentration of shareholdings has occurred, not a re-concentration into the hands of personal shareholders but into the hands of what are collectively referred to as the 'institutional shareholders': unit trusts (and similar forms of collective saving scheme), pension funds, and insurance companies. It is clear that the biggest driver behind this growth in institutional shareholding has been the desire of reasonably well-off people to make financial provisions for their retirement (beyond the state provision), and to do so in a way which spread their risks across many types of share (not just one or two companies) and which left the choice of the range of companies to expert fund managers. Indeed, fund management has become an international business, with British investors putting some of their money into shares elsewhere in Europe, in the United States and Asia, whilst equally investors elsewhere in the world put some of their money into the shares of UK companies.

Table 1 Ownership of Listed UK Equities

Beneficial Owner	1963	1969	1975	1981	1989	1993	1997	2001	2004	2008
Individuals	54	47.4	37.5	28.2	20.6	17.7	16.5	14.8	12.8	10.2
Insurance companies	10	12.2	15.9	20.5	18.6	20	23.6	20.0	17.2	13.4
Pension funds	6.4	9.0	16.8	26.7	30.6	31.7	22.1	16.1	15.7	12.8
Other financial institutions*	n/a	n/a	n/a	n/a	1.1	0.6	1.3	7.2	8.2	10.0
Unit and investment trusts	n/a	n/a	n/a	n/a	7.5	9.1	5.4	2.9	3.9	3.7
Banks	1.3	1.7	0.7	0.3	0.7	0.6	0.1	1.3	2.7	3.5
Rest of the world	7.0	6.6	5.6	3.6	12.8	16.3	28.0	35.7	36.3	41.5

*For example, securities dealers, but also includes bank holding companies, which may not be classified as banks.

Source: Office of National Statistics, *Share Ownership Survey 2008*, January 2010.

The table indicates some very interesting facts about the beneficial ownership of listed companies in the United Kingdom over the past forty-five years. First, the proportion of the total market held directly[84] by individuals has declined from over one-half to just about one-tenth.[85] Second, the proportion held by British insurance companies and pension funds taken together rose to over one-half of the market by the middle of the period (1993) but has since declined to just over one-quarter. Third, there has been a steady, even dramatic, rise in the proportion of the market held by non-UK investors over the past two decades.[86] Non-UK investors include overseas pension funds, but also sovereign wealth funds,[87] a novel but important investor in the UK. Fourth, banks are relatively small investors, even if their contribution to 'other financial institutions' is taken into account, but it has grown over the past decade. The table does not exhaust the categories of beneficial owner, but the remainder held smaller proportions in 2008 than the smallest shown in the table (banks).[88]

RE-CONCENTRATION AND ACTIVISM

Concentration at the level of the market does not mean that at the level of individual companies a single institutional shareholder can be found holding a majority of the company's shares. On the contrary, prudential considerations will generally prevent such a situation arising. However, it is often the case that, except in the very largest quoted companies, a coalition of five or six institutional shareholders or of fund managers acting on their behalf, if they could bring themselves to act together, might well control about a quarter of the voting rights.[89] They would

---

[84] Clearly, individuals may invest indirectly, for example through unit or investment trusts or via premiums paid to life insurance companies or contributions to pension schemes. However, such indirect investment rarely gives individuals significant influence over the exercise of voting rights attached to shares.

[85] This does not mean that the value of direct individual investments has similarly declined, since over this period the total value of the market has increased. Again, however, for voting purposes it is the proportion held, not value, which is important.

[86] The second and third points may reflect lower levels of retirement saving the UK (for example, with the close of many defined benefit pension schemes) but a bigger influence has probably been the globalization of investment strategies, with foreign institutions being more willing to invest in the UK and UK institutions more willing to invest outside the UK.

[87] These are investment funds owned by the governments of countries which have chronic trade surpluses and which seek investment outlets for those surpluses. See R Gilson and C Milhaupt, 'Sovereign Wealth Funds and Corporate Governance: A Minimalist Response to the New Mercantilism' (2008) 60 *Stanford Law Review* 1345.

[88] They were (2008 figures): private non-financial companies (3.0), public sector (1.1)— higher at any time since 1993, reflecting government participation in the recapitalization of the Royal Bank of Scotland; and charities (0.8).

[89] Some illuminating, if now slightly dated, factual data on the UK situation is to be found in G P Stapledon, *Institutional Shareholders and Corporate Governance* (Oxford: Clarendon Press, 1996), Parts I and II.

therefore easily be able to summon an EGM under the statutory provisions discussed above, and would stand a good chance of being able to get through a removal resolution (or some other resolution which they thought appropriate). On the other side, a large shareholder may find it difficult to exit the company without driving the share price down to unacceptable levels, so that there is some self-interested pressure towards activism on the part of large institutional shareholders. In fact, it is clear that there is considerably more institutional shareholder activism in relation to the internal governance of companies today than, say, half a century ago.

Three points need to be made about institutional shareholder activism, however. First, to the dismay of the journalistic press, a great deal of the exercise by shareholders of their statutory powers takes place behind closed doors and so is not visible to the outside observer. Shareholders in a position to make a credible threat that they will remove one or more directors are likely to raise the issue first of all with the existing board in a private meeting. If the shareholders can secure a change of policy or a re-constitution of the board through agreement in private with the incumbent board, that has the major advantage that they achieve their objectives without a public row which is likely, in one way or another, to cause damage to the company and involve further out-of-pocket costs for the institutions.

Second, and more important, it is likely, nevertheless, that the level of usage by institutional shareholders of their statutory removal powers in particular and of their governance powers in general is sub-optimal because of competition among institutional shareholders or fund managers and because of conflicts of interest within them.[90] Competition among institutional shareholders and their fund managers means that there is always a temptation for any one shareholder to seek to free ride on the efforts of the others. Conflicts of interest can occur where the fund manager is part of a financial conglomerate which carries on a variety of financial businesses in addition to fund management, for example, providing corporate finance services to companies. The corporate finance arm of a large investment bank may not be best pleased if the fund management arm of the bank is attempting to unseat a board of directors with whom the corporate finance people are doing lucrative business. The Company

---

[90] Analyses of this issue can be found in Stapledon, op. cit., Parts II and IV and in B S Black and J C Coffee, 'Hail Britannia? Institutional Investor Behaviour under Limited Regulation' (1994) 92 *Michigan LR* 1997.

Law Review was impressed with the evidence it acquired about potential conflicts of interest.[91]

Even if the competition and conflicts problems of institutional shareholders could be overcome, it by no means follows that they would choose to exercise their governance powers in all situations where they were in fact able to do so. They might regard it as more attractive, at least in some cases, to sell their shares and invest the money elsewhere. As we shall see in the next section, the law does promote 'affiliation' strategies which facilitate a shareholder's leaving the company. So, one might say that the removal right and the affiliation right give the shareholder, whether institutional or otherwise, a choice between 'voice' and 'exit'. The conflicts of interest which may make the levels of institutional intervention into companies to remove failing management less than optimal by the same token may increase the willingness of institutional shareholders and fund managers to accept takeover bids, where all the shareholders exit on the same terms and without any one of them incurring the costs of organizing the bid (which fall on the bidder).[92]

Third, shareholder activism on the part of pension funds and insurance companies, sometimes referred to as 'long only' investors, has traditionally been of an ex post 'defensive' character, ie after investment things have gone wrong, from the institutions' point of view, which they have sought to put right through their governance rights. More recently, some activist hedge funds have made the activism part of their investment strategy, ie they have decided to invest in order to be active and to reap the rewards of activism.[93] Whilst, as we will see in the next section, government has encouraged activism of the former type, it tends not to mention activism of the latter. Yet, it is unclear that it can facilitate the one without advancing the other.

GOVERNMENTAL ENCOURAGEMENT OF INSTITUTIONAL ACTIVISM

In recent years institutional shareholders have come under governmental pressure to shift the balance of their activity in favour of 'voice'. This probably reflects, on the one hand, government's desire to respond to public

---

[91] *Final Report*, Vol 1, paras 6.22–6.40.
[92] No doubt, the shareholders indirectly carry some or all of these costs in the shape of the price the bidder is prepared to offer to the shareholders, but this cost is borne equally by all the accepting shareholders.
[93] J Armour and B Cheffins, 'The Rise and Fall (?) of Activism by Hedge Funds', ECGI Working Paper 136/2009.

pressure to take action in relation to perceived inadequacies in the performance of company boards (ranging from excessive remuneration for executive directors and failure to give priority to long-term investment to failure of the boards to control the risky activities of banks which contributed to the financial crisis which began in late 2007). On the other hand, government has been unwilling (at least outside the financial area where taxpayer interests are directly at stake) to craft new rules or standards for the direct regulation of corporate boards and has plumped instead for the indirect strategy of pressurizing large shareholders to monitor more effectively the activities of company boards. 'Voice' in this context does not mean solely (or even principally) the exercise by shareholders of their removal rights, but also the exercise of all the decision rights which the Act, the Listing Rules, or the company's constitution give them and, even more generally, the exercise of their oversight powers which are underpinned by these removal and decision rights.

It is, of course, somewhat ironic that governmental pressure on institutions has increased over the very period when it is arguable that their capacity to respond to governmental demands has decreased. As Table 1 showed, the proportion of the overall market held by UK institutional shareholders has fallen by one-half over, roughly, the last two decades, whilst the proportion held by non-UK investors has increased by two and a half times. It is not clear that overseas investors are as exposed to threats of adverse actions by the UK government if they are not more active, as domestic institutions are. Nevertheless, the domestic institutions have still a sufficiently large stake in the domestic market that they find it difficult not to respond to governmental pressure, whilst changes in market ownership make it less certain they have the capacity to achieve the substantive outcomes the government wishes to see.

What have been the manifestations of this pressure? Starting at the modest end, the CLR focused on institutions' incentives to vote and recommended that the Secretary of State should have a reserve power to require institutions and fund managers acting on their behalves publicly to disclose their voting records in the companies in which they were invested ('portfolio' companies).[94] The ostensible aim was to encourage institutional investors seriously to think about their voting policies in portfolio companies, rather than either abstaining from voting or unthinkingly

---

[94] *Final Report I*, para 6.39; now CA 2006, ss 1277–80. The power is a reserve one in the sense that the government is not expected to use it if voluntary moves in the desired direction occur. By 2008 24 institutions publicly disclosed their votes, as opposed to 2 earlier in the decade. See FRC, below n 100, para 2.12.

voting with management. However, public disclosure of voting records is also likely to expose institutional investors to political pressure, not only from governments but also from pressure groups, about the substance of their voting policies.

More fundamentally, the Myners Report of 2001[95] proposed a substantive legal obligation on institutional investors and their fund managers to monitor and attempt to influence the boards of companies where there was a reasonable expectation that such activity would enhance the value of portfolio investments. The institutional investors managed to head off this initiative through the adoption of a voluntary statement of responsibilities under which they undertook to maintain and publish policies on active engagement with portfolio companies, to monitor their performance and to maintain a dialogue with them, and to intervene, where necessary, up to and including the exercise of their removal powers.[96]

However, the government did not rest there. It assessed progress against the goals set by the Myners Report during the following years and the ISC's statement was revised a couple of times. However, a major change came in the wake of the financial crisis which began in late 2007. The Walker Review[97] recommended that responsibility for the statement (now termed a 'Stewardship Code') should move from the ISC to the Financial Reporting Council, a statutory, if practitioner funded, agency, which is already responsible for the Corporate Governance Code.[98] Thus, the institutions lost sole control over their statement of responsibilities. The Walker Review also recommended that authorized fund managers should be made subject to a formal obligation under the rules of the Financial Services Authority to comply with the Code or explain their non-compliance.[99] At the time of writing the FRC was consulting about whether it should simply adopt the ISC Code as its Stewardship Code and about the enforcement of the Code beyond authorized fund managers, ie

---

[95] HM Treasury, *Institutional Investors in the United Kingdom: A Review* (2001). A particular sign of shareholder uninterest in voting is 'stock lending' whereby the shares are temporarily lent to someone else, who may exercise the voting rights without having any beneficial interest in the shares. See on this and on technical problems with voting, P Myners, *Review of the Impediments of Voting UK Shares*, (2007) and H Hu and B Black, 'Hedge Funds, Insiders and the Decoupling of Economic and Voting Ownership: Empty Voting and Hidden (Morphable) Ownership' (2007) 13 *Journal of Corporate Finance* 343.

[96] Institutional Shareholders' Committee, *The Responsibilities of Institutional Shareholders and Agents: Statement of Principles* (2002). The ISC produced its first statement in 1991.

[97] HM Treasury, *A Review of Corporate Governance in UK Banks and Other Financial Industry Entities* (November 2009), ch 5.

[98] The role of the FRC and of the Corporate Governance Code are discussed further in Ch 7 below.

[99] The 'comply or explain' technique is also discussed further in Ch 7 below at p 197.

how the institutions themselves, including foreign investors, should be encouraged to comply with it.[100]

Overall, one can say that the government's solution to the coordination problems of shareholders in UK listed companies is to pressurize the institutional shareholders to take the lead. The coordination problems of institutional shareholders, in its view, are surmountable, though they require sustained governmental pressure if they are in fact to be surmounted. Whether this approach can be made effective in a world of global investing strategies remains to be seen.

AFFILIATION RIGHTS

Affiliation rights constitute a means of empowering shareholders as against the board by enabling them to exit the company by selling their shares and thus substituting new members in their place. Here, the law revolves around that core characteristic of company law which we identified in Chapter 1 as the free transferability of shares.[101] We noted that, from the company's point of view, free transferability is provided by the doctrine of separate corporate personality: the shares in the company can be transferred without any impact on the ownership of the business assets, which remains vested in the company. By contrast, we saw that, from the shareholders' point of view, free transferability is legally much less secure. Company law embodies a presumption that shares may be transferred from one investor to another without the consent of anyone else, but the articles of a company may alter that position, for example, by requiring board consent to transfers or by giving the board or the other shareholders a right to buy the shares at a price which is fixed or can be ascertained (a 'pre-emption' right). Such provisions are common in small companies,[102] but for companies whose securities are traded on a public market, the rules of the market will insist that the shares be freely tradable.[103] In this instance, capital markets law makes up for a deficiency in company law.

However, none of this guarantees that a purchaser will be available to buy the shares of a dissatisfied shareholder at an attractive price. This is hardly surprising: the law cannot act as a market-maker. On the other hand, unless such purchasers are available, the exit right as such is not

---

[100] FRC, *Consultation on a Stewardship Code for Institutional Investors* (January 2010). The Code was adopted in July 2010.
[101] Above p 19.   [102] See above at p 21.
[103] In the case of top-tier markets ('regulated' markets) EU law requires that transferable instruments traded on them be 'freely negotiable': Directive 2004/39/EC on markets in financial instruments, art 40.1.

much protection for the dissatisfied shareholder. This is a deficiency which is supplied by the existence of liquid stock markets. Nevertheless, a mere right of exit even on a liquid stock exchange is of value only to the highly prescient shareholder, one who can predict the unlawful or unwise conduct of the board before it occurs and, even more important, before the rest of the market realizes what is about to happen. In the more likely situation where the shareholder detects the objectionable conduct only after it has happened and has become apparent to the market, the price of the share will now reflect the harm which has been done to the company and the risk that the harmful conduct will continue. In this circumstance, selling the shares may provide the former shareholder with some psychological relief, but not with effective protection against the loss which he or she has suffered. In fact, the sale will simply crystallize the loss.

What, then, can the law do to facilitate the availability of not just a purchaser for the shares (that is the function of a liquid stock market) but of a purchaser who will offer a price above the market price despite the depredations of the incumbent board? The standard answer to this question is that the law should facilitate takeover bids, ie offers by an investor, usually another company, made to the shareholders of company (the target) to acquire all the shares of the target at a price above the prevailing market price. The consideration offered may be cash or may be shares in the offeror company (or a mixture of the two). From the point of view of shareholders, not just in target companies but more generally, the takeover offer (or 'tender offer' in US parlance) has major advantages. Under a legal regime which facilitates takeovers, the threat of the takeover will be a constant pressure on the boards of all companies quoted on public markets to keep the interests of the shareholders centre-stage. Indeed, the threat of the takeover is one of the main drivers behind the, until recently fashionable, concern for 'shareholder value'.[104] Even better, from the shareholders' point of view, the takeover threat requires no input of resources, unlike both the legal strategies discussed earlier in this chapter. If the board does not respond appropriately to this pressure and the shareholders' interests are neglected, the advent of the takeover will enable the shareholders to exit the company at a premium to the (admittedly depressed) market price.[105]

---

[104] P Davies, 'Shareholder Value, Company Law and Securities Markets Law', in K Hopt and E Wymeersch (eds), *Capital Markets and Company Law* (Oxford: Oxford University Press, 2003).
[105] The classic statement of this argument is in H Manne, 'Mergers and the Market for Corporate Control' (1965) 73 *Journal of Political Economy* 110.

However, there is a central puzzle with the takeover offer. Why should the takeover bidder be prepared to pay a higher price for the shares of the target company than other investors in the market? The answer is that, once the bidder has obtained control, it will be able to replace the board of the target (using the powers discussed above) and install its own nominees who will certainly do what the new controlling shareholder wants. In short, concentrated ownership will replace dispersed ownership and the coordination problems of the shareholders will cease to be a relevant issue. The bidder will be willing to share part of the expected benefits of this course of action with the existing shareholders of the target, in exchange for the opportunity to implement its plan.[106] The precise split between the bidder and the existing shareholders of the target will depend on a number of factors, in particular upon whether a competing bidder for the target company emerges.[107]

Since the transaction in a takeover occurs between the offeror (bidder) and the target shareholders, it may seem that the law has to do nothing more than make available the normal rules of contract law in order to facilitate the takeover process. It is in fact quite clear that the takeover cannot succeed if a sufficient proportion of the target shareholders are not prepared to accept the offer, so that they have at a minimum a veto right over the transaction. However, it is also possible for the incumbent board to prevent or discourage an offer being put to the shareholders, or being persisted with, even if the shareholders might well accept it. Indeed, the board has a strong incentive to do so, since they are likely to lose their positions if the offer is successful. The directors' conflict between their personal interests and their duty to promote the interests of the shareholders may reveal itself in a number of ways, for example, by seeking to issue new shares to shareholders who will support the incumbent board or by putting prized assets of the company out of the reach of the bidder, even if it does achieve

---

[106] Takeovers may also be motivated by the prospect of economies of scale or scope, a reason which is not dependent upon any shortcomings on the part of the board of the target. However, this restructuring motivation does provide an additional argument in favour of facilitating takeovers.

[107] It may be wondered why any individual shareholder would accept an offer from a bidder with a value-enhancing plan for the company, since that shareholder will be better off if he or she remains in the company, provided the bid succeeds. This may explain why so much of the potential benefit of takeovers goes to the target shareholders. However, the law may reduce the shareholders' incentives not to sell by permitting a successful bidder to squeeze out non-accepting shareholders. See M Burkart and F Panunzi, 'Mandatory Bids, Squeeze-Out, Sell-Out and the Dynamics of the Tender Offer Process', in G Ferrarini et al (eds), *Company Law and Takeover Law in Europe* (Oxford: Oxford University Press, 2004).

control.[108] In other words, the board may use its powers of centralized management to defeat the bid.

The obvious legal response to this problem is to sideline the board of the company in the decision-making over the takeover bid. The transaction thus becomes one wholly between the bidder and the shareholders of the target. In terms of the decision rights strategy, used earlier in the chapter, the decision on the offer is allocated compulsorily and entirely to the shareholders of the target. This is in fact the strategy adopted in the UK in the Code on Takeovers and Mergers, drawn up and enforced under the auspices of the Panel on Takeovers and Mergers. The Panel was put together by a group of financial institutions, led by the Bank of England, in the late 1960s, in order to ward off the threat of legislation to regulate takeovers. Although the Panel and Code now have a statutory basis in Part 28 of the 2006 Act, its substantive rules still reflect the pro-shareholder orientation of its origins.[109]

From the beginning the Panel, through the Code, has endorsed the principle of sidelining incumbent management in takeover bids. That policy is now enshrined in Rule 21 of the Code, which prohibits the board from taking 'any action which may result in any offer or bona fide possible offer being frustrated or in shareholders being denied an opportunity to decide on its merits'—unless the shareholders give their consent after the emergence of the bid. Thus, management cannot act unilaterally to defeat a bidder. The rule does not prohibit corporate action which has a frustrating effect on the bid but it does require that such action be approved by the shareholders at a general meeting and, crucially, that that approval be given in the face of the bid. Thus, we can see that the Code facilitates an exit right for the shareholders at an attractive price, but does so mainly by removing the constraints which target management might place on the offeror's entry rights. This application of the affiliation strategy is then operationalized through a deployment of the decision rights strategy, ie requiring shareholder approval for that class of board decisions which might have a frustrating impact on the bid.

There are two arguments which might be mounted against the blunt rule embodied in the Code. The first is that, whilst sidelining

---

[108] For an example of the former see *Hogg v Cramphorn* [1967] Ch 254 and for the latter L Gower, 'Corporate Control: The Battle for the Berkeley' (1955) 68 *Harvard LR* 1176.

[109] J Armour and D Skeel, 'Who Writes the Rules for Hostile Takeovers, and Why? The Peculiar Divergence of U.S. and U.K. Takeover Regulation' (2007) 95 *Georgetown Law Journal* 1727.

management deals effectively with the board's conflicts of interest, it also leaves the dispersed shareholders without any help from the board in dealing with the offeror, who may thus be able to exploit the collective action problems which the shareholders have as against the offeror as much as they have against the board of their company. Thus, the offeror may be able to structure the offer in such a way as to pressurize the target shareholders into accepting it, even though they think it is sub-optimal. If the board could play a role in takeovers, it could exclude such opportunistic offers. If the board is sidelined by the takeover rules, however, this cannot occur, and so the rules must go on and address directly the coordination problems of the target shareholders as against the offeror, principally by insisting upon a rule of equal treatment of shareholders in takeovers.[110]

The second argument, or rather group of arguments, raise objections of a more fundamental kind to takeovers. One form of this objection is that takeovers are driven, not by the gains to be made by addressing the shareholders' agency costs (or realizing economies of scale or scope), but by the possibilities takeovers open up for offerors to transfer wealth from stakeholders such as employees or creditors to the bidder as the new owner of the company.[111] Another argument is that they are driven, especially in the case of buyout offers from private equity companies, by financial engineering (notably leverage) rather than the reduction of agency costs.[112] A further objection denies the proposition that financial markets price company's securities accurately. If this is so, transactions which are based on market prices are not necessarily efficient. Finally, it could be argued that takeovers constitute a demonstration, not of the agency problems of the target shareholders, but of the agency problems of the bidders. Bidders embark on takeovers which are not wealth maximizing from the point of view of the *bidders'* shareholders because they fit the interests of the bidders' management, for example, by promoting the aggrandizement of the latter.[113]

---

[110] For further development of this argument see P Davies, 'The Notion of Equality in European Takeover Regulation', in J Payne (ed), *Takeovers in English and German Law* (Oxford: Hart Publishing, 2002) and P Davies and K Hopt, 'Control Transactions', in R Kraakman et al, above n 25.

[111] A Schleifer and L Summers, 'Breach of Trust in Hostile Takeovers', in A Auerbach (ed), *Corporate Takeovers: Causes and Consequences* (Chicago: University of Chicago Press, 1998).

[112] B Cheffins and J Armour, 'The Eclipse of Private Equity' (2008) 31 *Delaware Journal of Corporate Law* 1.

[113] A Kouloridas, *The Law and Economics of Takeovers* (Oxford: Hart Publishing, 2008), 11–13.

We cannot explore the arguments for and against takeovers in this book.[114] What should be pointed out, however, is that the affiliation rights strategy, embodied in the Code, is, in consequence of the debate about the desirability of encouraging takeovers, a highly contested rule.[115]

CONCLUSION

In this chapter we have looked at three legal strategies for empowering shareholders in companies where there is no controlling shareholder: the decision rights strategy, the appointment rights strategy, and the affiliation strategy. Both the first and the third strategy can be used only sparingly. This is true of the decision rights strategy, which turns on involving the shareholders as a body in corporate decision-making, because it is a cure which, if used in relation to a wide range of managerial decisions, may turn out to be worse that the disease. Shifting decision-making into the hands of the shareholders risks making the corporate decision-making process inefficient, even if it protects the shareholders against self-interested behaviour on the part of the board. It is therefore a plausible, widespread strategy only for companies with small shareholder bodies.

The third strategy can be used only sparingly as well, but for a very different reason. As noted, an exit right for the shareholders is not as such much protection. Shareholders need to be able to sell at a price which reflects the value the company would have if it were properly run. As between the board and the shareholders as a class, the law can hardly impose an obligation upon the directors of public companies to buy at a fair price the shares of all the shareholders who have suffered from managerial shirking or self-seeking, or at least it cannot do so without the risk of severely curtailing the supply of businessmen willing to act as directors of such companies.[116] This strategy emerges as a feasible one only in relation to the facilitation of takeover offers, where a third party (the bidder) appears as the willing purchaser at an above-market price. Nevertheless, the takeover bid—or rather the threat of it—is a very powerful corporate

---

[114] For a dispassionate analysis see R Romano, 'A Guide to Takeovers: Theory, Evidence and Regulation', in K Hopt and E Wymeersch (eds), *European Takeovers: Law and Practice* (London: Butterworths, 1992).

[115] The EU was thus able to adopt its Directive on takeovers (2004/25/EC) only by abandoning its original goal of making the no-frustration rule mandatory and by leaving the rules on frustration to a complex system of member state and company choices. See below Ch 10 at p 294, n10.

[116] By contrast, within small companies and as between controlling and non-controlling shareholders, an obligation on the former to buy the shares of the latter at a fair price may be a feasible remedy. See Ch 8 below.

governance tool, though it is much contested whether overall it improves or worsens governance of companies.

By contrast, the second strategy—appointment rights—can be applied generally by company law. Its impact may be lessened, however, by the inability of highly dispersed shareholding bodies to make much use of it, because of their coordination difficulties.[117] The partial re-concentration of shareholdings into the hands of institutional shareholders in the UK in recent decades may have lessened, but it has not removed, this problem. This is an area where the context very much affects the practical impact of the legal rule. Enough has been said to demonstrate, it is hoped, that our enquiry into the legal strategies for controlling principal agent problems as between board and shareholders as a class cannot stop at the strategies for empowering shareholders. We must look, as well, at strategies for constraining directors, and this we do in the next chapter.

---

[117] Appointment rights also facilitate takeovers by permitting the new controlling shareholder quickly to install its preferred management team.

6

Centralized Management II
Directors' Duties

INTRODUCTION

In this chapter we continue our analysis of the legal strategies available for the reduction of agency costs as between shareholders and the board where there is no controlling shareholder and so de facto control lies with the board. In the previous chapter we examined three legal strategies which might be used by the law in this situation to strengthen the hand of the shareholders as a group against the board. These were the decisions rights, the appointments rights, and the affiliation rights strategies. See the left-hand side of Figure 1 on p 113. However, we also saw that only the second of these could be deployed other than in rather special situations, and even the appointments rights strategy is highly dependent upon the ability of shareholders to overcome their collective action problems.

Consequently, it is not surprising that company law has deployed strategies aimed at affecting directly the actions of management, and has not confined itself to strategies which facilitate the imposition of constraints by the shareholders. Thus, it has made use of the strategies listed on the right-hand side of Figure 1. That side of the figure identifies two strategies: (i) a constraints strategy, which comes in the form of either specifying rules for decision-making by the board or (much more common in fact) laying down standards by which board decisions can be reviewed by the courts; and (ii) an incentives strategy, which consists of either trying to avoid directors' high-powered conflicts of interest by excluding them from decision-making (the 'trusteeship' strategy) or realigning those high-powered conflicts with the interests of the shareholders (the 'rewards' strategy).

We will analyse those two strategies in this and the next chapter. However, we do not adopt a simple division between constraints (this chapter) and incentives (the next). Rather, in this chapter we examine the law on 'directors' duties' as a whole, because of its centrality in the structure of British company law. We will see that the law of directors' duties in the UK does indeed make very heavy use of the standards strategy. This is certainly true of the directors' duty of care, their core duty of loyalty, and their duty to act for a proper purpose. However, in relation to conflict of interest situations, the law of directors' duties also makes some use of the 'trusteeship' strategy, especially after the 2006 Act, by excluding interested directors from board decision-making over the issue upon which they are conflicted. Thus, the decision is given to those directors who may be thought not to be subject to high-powered conflicts of interest. Moreover, the law's handling of conflict of interest situations has also traditionally made use of one of the strategies already examined in the previous chapter, ie the decision-rights strategy. The notion here is that, where the board is conflicted, a binding decision on the matter at hand requires the consent of the shareholders.

In sum, one can say that the law of directors' duties in the UK consists of two elements: in the absence of direct conflicts of interest, the law relies on standards; where there is a direct conflict of interest, the law has traditionally relied on shareholder involvement in the decision-making process but today sometimes provides the alternative of board decision-making with the conflicted directors excluded. As can be imagined, the rival merits of these two ways of handling conflicted decisions are highly debated. We will proceed by looking first at those duties where the law relies primarily upon standards and then at the duties imposed in cases of conflicts of interest, where the other two legal strategies are deployed. In the following chapter we will look at ways in which the incentive strategy has influenced company law outside the area of directors' duties, notably its influence on the rules relating to the composition of the board of directors and on the structure of directors' pay.

The law on directors' duties was developed by the courts principally (with only limited input from the legislature). The courts embarked upon this task at an early stage, that is, with the emergence of modern company law in the middle of the nineteenth century, and they often drew on an analogy (not always appropriate) between the director and the trustee. Thus, within case-law, the law of directors' duties was more a matter of equity than of common law in the technical sense of the term. A major change made by the 2006 Act was to embody in Chapter 2 of Part 10 of the Act a 'high-level' statutory restatement of directors' duties (though not of the remedies for breach of those duties), which replaces the common law rules and equitable principles upon which it is based.[1] In taking this step the drafters of the Act followed the recommendations of the Law Commissions and the Company Law Review.[2]

However, it was not intended to stultify the development of the law by the courts. Since the statutory statement is pitched at a fairly high level of abstraction, there is considerable scope for judicial interpretation of the statutory formulae. The courts are instructed to interpret and apply the statutory statement 'in the same way' as the prior common law rules and equitable principles and to 'have regard' to the development of these rules and principles in adjacent areas of law (for example, the law relating to trustees or other fiduciaries) upon which the courts have traditionally drawn.[3] This is all well and good to the extent that the statutory restatement simply embodies the prior case-law in statutory language. However, as we shall see, in a small number of areas the statutory statement reforms the prior law or clarifies matters previously unclear. In these areas, reliance on the earlier case-law needs to be much more circumspect. Overall, the primary purpose of the statutory restatement was to make the law more visible to directors, but in some aspects there was, at least for the Company Law Review, a reform or at least a clarification goal as well.

The duties laid down in Chapter 2 of Part 10 are owed, as at common law, to the company.[4] The significance of this statement is that the duties can be enforced only by those entitled to claim to be 'the company' or to act on its behalf. This means that enforcement action can be taken by the collective decision-making bodies of the company (board, shareholders acting as a body) so long as the company is a going concern, and by the insolvency practitioner who acts on behalf of the creditors when the company enters a formal insolvency procedure. The important question of the extent to which individual shareholders can sue on behalf of the company to enforce its rights (through the derivative action or unfair prejudice remedy) is discussed in Chapter 8 below, dealing with minority protection.

We also discuss in that chapter the separate question of whether directors owe duties to individual shareholders, which the individual should in principle be able freely to enforce in his or her own right and without being subject to the restrictions which may apply when the individual

---

[1] s 170(3).
[2] Law Commission and Scottish Law Commission, *Company Directors: Regulating Conflicts of Interest and Formulating a Statement of Duties*, Cm 4436 (1999); Company Law Review, *Final Report*, Vol 1 paras 3.5–3.27 and Annex C.   [3] s 170(4).
[4] s 170(1).

shareholder seeks to act on behalf of the company to enforce the company's rights. The fact that the duties contained in the statute are owed to the company does not as a matter of logic prevent the development of separate duties owed by directors to shareholders individually. Of course, those duties cannot be grounded in Chapter 2 of Part 10; they are, still, a matter of common law. However, the fact that the statute, like the prior law, sees directors' duties as running only to the company suggests that it did not anticipate a parallel set of duties being owed to individual shareholders. As we shall see in Chapter 8 below, the duties owed by directors to individual shareholders are in fact very much more circumscribed than those owed to the company.

The duties considered in this chapter are owed by 'directors'. This term obviously includes those properly appointed to the board, but the statute suggests that the duties attach also to those who act as directors in fact, whether regularly appointed to that position or not.[5] In modern times, the legislature has explicitly brought within some of the legislation applying to directors a further group of persons. These are 'shadow' directors, ie persons in accordance with whose instructions or directions the directors of the company are accustomed to Act.[6] Although the CLR proposed that the statutory statement of duties should apply to shadow directors,[7] the statute, rather feebly, does not commit itself on that point but rather leaves it to be decided by the courts.[8] If a person falls within the net of being a director, the general duties will apply to all his or her actions on behalf of the company, whether done in the capacity of director or as manager (as in the case of an 'executive' director, who is both a member of the board and the holder of a managerial post within the company). However, a person who is only a manager (ie does not act as a director de facto), albeit a senior one, appears not to be subject to the general duties, though (less rigorous) fiduciary provisions may apply as a result of the common law of the contract of employment.[9]

---

[5] s 250. The section might have been interpreted as covering only properly appointed directors who are given a different name in the company's articles, but it has been interpreted more broadly so as to cover 'de facto' directors.

[6] s 251(1). Note that the majority of the board must be accustomed so to act, not just an individual director. On the distinction between de facto and shadow directors, see *Re Hydrodam (Corby) Ltd* [1994] 2 BCLC 189.

[7] Company Law Review, *Completing the Structure* (November 2000), paras 4.6–4.7.

[8] s 170(5): general statutory duties to apply to shadow directors to the extent that the prior common law applied. However, the answer to this question at common law is very unclear. See *Ultraframe (UK) Ltd v Fielding* [2005] EWHC 1638, which one hopes is not the last word on the question.   [9] *Shepherd Investments Ltd v Walters* [2007] IRLR 110.

Before turning to the substance of directors' duties, it is worth remembering that it is far from clear that those duties constitute the most effective of the legal strategies for dealing with shareholders' agency problems. To deduce this from the fact that the law on directors' duties generates a certain level of litigation would be to adopt too court-centred a view of the impact of law. The relative importance of the different legal strategies discussed in this chapter and the previous one is in fact a question for empirical investigation. We should keep our minds open to the possibility that a quiet word behind closed doors with incumbent management by shareholders who have the power to remove that management may be more effective in changing behaviour than the uncertainties of litigation.[10]

We now turn to the substance of the general duties of directors and look first at those duties which rely on ex post evaluation of directors' actions by the courts. As we have noted before, standards, in contrast with rules, are easy to formulate but difficult to apply. To say that directors must exercise due care, or act for a proper purpose, or promote the success of the company is one thing, but to work out on the facts of a particular case what is required by these precepts is considerably more difficult. In short, with standards the law-making function is shared between the formulator and the applier, whilst with rules it is almost entirely with the formulator. Contrast the rule, drive on the left- (or right-)hand side of the road, with the standards just mentioned. This gives rise to two issues. One is about the expertise of the applier. Does the court have the relevant expertise (or can it acquire it through the process of litigation) to work out the best solution to the issue of what the standard requires? What is the background experience of the judges who will handle the cases? Does the bar contain advocates experienced in such litigation? Does the court receive the relevant cases frequently or only occasionally?[11] The second issue relates to the likely reaction of directors to the prospect of liability for breach of the standards. That they are likely to react in a way which minimizes the prospect of liability is clear, but it is less clear what such behaviour might involve. It might go beyond simple attempts to conform their conduct to the standard. If it is unclear how the standard will be interpreted by the courts ex post, directors acting ex ante may take a cautious view and conform in practice to a standard which is more demanding than that which is apparently contained in the law. This may not be socially desirable.

---

[10] John Armour, 'Enforcement Strategies in UK Corporate Governance: A Roadmap and Empirical Assessment', ECGI Law Working Paper 106/2008.

[11] See further M Klausner, 'Corporations, Contract Law and Networks of Contracts' (1995) 81 *Virginia Law Review* 757, esp Pt III.B.

DUTY OF CARE

OBJECTIVE VERSUS SUBJECTIVE STANDARD OF CARE

Modern company law has never doubted that a director owes a duty of care to the company. The big debate has been over the standard of care required by this duty. There are two views about the appropriate standard, one termed 'subjective' and the other 'objective'. A subjective formulation is one that is specified by reference to what a person with the director's actual abilities is able to achieve. So, a director could be found to have fallen below this standard if on a particular occasion he or she had failed to achieve the level which he or she was reasonably capable of achieving; but no liability would arise if the director could not achieve a higher standard. In other words, the less qualified or more incompetent the director, the less the law would expect of that person. An 'objective' standard is formulated by reference to what a reasonable director in the position of the actual director could be expected to achieve, irrespective of what the actual director was capable of achieving. In this situation, lack of qualification or competence is not a defence to liability for failing to achieve the reasonable standard. On the other hand, a subjective ability to do better than the reasonable standard might lead to an enhancement of the standard required by the law: an exceptionally well-qualified or competent director might be held to a higher standard than other less qualified or competent directors (who would be held only to the reasonable standard).

The story of the development of this branch of British company law is from a largely (perhaps wholly) subjective standard in the nineteenth century to an objective standard (with subjective 'uplift') today. There has been much debate about the precise trajectory of that change, but what is clear is that we have arrived at the 'objective plus' standard today, which is embodied in section 174 of the Act. A director must exercise 'reasonable skill, care and diligence' and that standard is defined by reference to '(a) the general knowledge, skill and experience that may reasonably be expected of a person carrying out the functions carried out by the director in relation to the company and (b) the general knowledge, skill and experience that the director has.' This is clearly an area where reliance on earlier case-law may be dangerous. This change was recommended by both the Law Commissions[12] and the Company Law

---

[12] Above n 2, Part V.

Review.[13] The change in the law probably reflects the professionalization of management in recent decades and a repudiation of the notion of the director as a mere figurehead.[14]

AVOIDING HINDSIGHT BIAS

Although the move to an objective standard of care was well supported by the official bodies which had examined the issue, it is in functional terms a potentially significant change for company law. There is a danger that ex post review by courts of directors' decisions on negligence grounds will, unless carefully handled, slow down the process of decision-making on the part of boards and lead them in the direction of excessive risk avoidance. It is much easier to mount a legal challenge to board decisions to take up business opportunities, which turn out badly, than to decisions to turn down opportunities, except perhaps in those rare cases where the opportunity was virtually riskless. If directors believe that the courts will not be able routinely to distinguish between decisions which turn out badly (for which there should not be liability) from bad decisions (for which they should), they may be less willing to take risky decisions. As the CLR itself said:

> Directors are employed to take risks, often under severe time pressures which prevent the fullest examination of all the relevant factors. Some of these risks will not pay off. The directors' key skill is one of balancing the risk and time factors, recognising that their company's success and failure will depend on their not being unduly cautious as well as avoiding fool-hardiness. What risks are appropriate will depend on a multitude of factors, including the ethos of the company and the character of its business and markets. There may be a danger that the courts will apply hindsight in such cases and reach unduly harsh conclusions based on an alleged absence of care and skill.[15]

Caution would be a desirable result if the directors were truly trustees, for whom the preservation of the capital of the trust was the overriding

---

[13] Above n 2, Annex C at pp 346 (Principle 4) and 353. Section 174 is based on an analogy with s 214 of the Insolvency Act (above p 38) and some first instance decisions had already accepted that this was the position at common law, though that was not firmly established.

[14] In *Re Cardiff Savings Bank* [1892] 2 Ch 100 the Marquis of Bute was held not to have fallen below the required standard of care even though he had attended only one board meeting of the company in his whole life. However, the bank had appointed the Marquis president of the bank when he was a mere six months old. This hardly suggests that the bank expected sage business advice from its new, and indeed leading, board member, but rather wanted him merely as a figurehead. It was the bank, therefore, which, by subsequently suing the Marquis for negligence, sought to depart from the expectations embodied in the appointment.

[15] CLR, *Developing the Framework* (2000), para 3.69.

consideration, but it would be a highly undesirable result for directors of companies in the private sector of the economy whose task is to generate wealth by taking risks, albeit only where the risk/reward ratio is acceptable.

So long as British law adopted a subjective standard of care, the problem of judicial 'hindsight bias' was avoided. For that reason, some have argued in favour of retention of the subjective standard.[16] With that approach now rejected, there is one other device which the law could have utilized to address the issue. It has not been expressly embodied in the legislation but could conceivably be adopted as a matter of judicial interpretation. This, internationally quite widespread, device is the 'business judgment rule'. It is widely adopted in the United States. Formulations of it vary but here is the one from the American Law Institute:[17]

> A director or officer who makes a business judgment in good faith fulfils the duty under this Section [Duty of Care] if the director or officer:
>
> (1) Is not interested in the subject of the business judgment;
> (2) Is informed with respect to the subject of the business judgment to the extent the director or officer reasonably believes to be appropriate under the circumstances, and
> (3) Rationally believes that the business judgment is in the best interests of the corporation.

As can be seen, the essence of this provision is that the director be informed before taking the decision to the extent that he 'reasonably believes to be appropriate'. Provided the director has reasonable grounds for believing him- or herself to be appropriately informed, the decision taken need only pass a 'rationality' test to be accepted by the court, ie provided a director could rationally think the decision promoted the company's business, it will pass court scrutiny, even if not all (or even most) directors, let alone the court, would share that view. The final requirement is that there must be no conflict of interest. This type of provision provides a commodious 'safe harbour' for director decision-making, by focusing the court's attention on the procedure leading to the taking of the decision rather than on its substantive wisdom. Yet the CLR rejected it as a formal requirement of British law,

---

[16] C Riley, 'The Case for an Onerous but Subjective Duty of Care' (1999) 63 *MLR* 697.

[17] *Principles of Corporate Governance*, §4.01(c). Even the procedural approach will not save the directors from some unpleasant surprises. See the notorious decision of the Delaware Supreme Court in *Smith v Van Gorkom* 488 A 2d 858 (1985).

but in the expectation that the courts applying the new section would follow a similar approach. Thus, the passage from the CLR, quoted above, continues:

> This is the argument for creating a specific business judgement defence which is part of US case law and which has been recently introduced in a legislative form in Australia. However, our courts have shown a proper reluctance to enter into the merits of commercial decisions; there are major difficulties in drafting such a provision which would add complexity and is likely to be inflexible and unfair, being too harsh in some cases and allowing too much leeway in others. *The principle as drafted leaves room for the courts to develop this approach....* We therefore oppose a *legislative* business judgement rule. (emphasis added)

DELEGATION AND THE DUTY OF CARE

The business judgment rule protects only directors who take decisions. Those whose alleged negligence consists of a failure to act are not normally protected by it because it applies to directors 'who make a business judgement'—unless of course the decision is a considered decision not to act. Many of the famous cases in the history of this branch of the law in fact concerned failures to act rather than explicit decisions. This issue arises crucially where a director charged with negligence has relied on others (perhaps fellow directors, perhaps subordinate employees) to act properly and they have failed to do so. To what extent is such formal or informal delegation of tasks to others compatible with the objective standard of care?[18]

Whilst the courts have not yet considered this issue under the provisions of the 2006 Act, it has arisen under section 6 of the Company Directors Disqualification Act 1986. This imposes a duty on the court to disqualify for a period a director of a company which has become insolvent if, on the application of the Secretary of State or his appointee, the court finds the director's conduct in the past renders him 'unfit' to be concerned in the management of a company.[19] The courts have interpreted unfitness widely enough to embrace incompetence, at least of the grosser kind. They have

---

[18] At common law the board, as a delegate from the shareholders, could not in principle delegate its responsibilities further, without express provision in the articles, which is invariably given. See eg the Model Articles for Public Companies, art 5. In any event, the model articles no longer describe the board's function as being the management of the company but as being responsible for its management (ibid art 3).

[19] See Ch 4 above at p 90.

held that the board may delegate substantial management powers to one of their number, but even non-executive directors must keep themselves informed of the true financial position of the company so as to be able to check whether the delegated powers have been properly exercised.[20] Boards as a whole may delegate managerial authority to non-board managers, even junior ones, but only on condition that they understand the risks involved in the business so delegated, have in place systems which are designed to reveal whether the risks involved have materialized, and respond appropriately to warnings thrown up by those internal control systems.[21]

REMEDIES

Although the duty of care required of directors was developed by the courts of equity, the modern view is that it is not a duty of a fiduciary character but is to be assimilated to the well-known duty to avoid negligence imposed by the common law. Thus, the directors' duty of care is to be distinguished from all the other duties considered below in this chapter, which are categorized as fiduciary duties or duties of loyalty. Indeed, the division between duties of competence (care) and duties of loyalty (fiduciary duties) is commonplace in Anglo-American company law, though it was suggested above that a better division is between those duties which rely on the standards strategy and those which rely on the trusteeship or decision-rights strategies. In any event, the primary significance of the duty of care not being treated as a fiduciary duty is to be found in the area of the remedies available in case of breach.[22] The principal remedy is tort-like damages for loss caused to the company by the breach of duty rather than an obligation to account for profits made or to restore to the company the value of property misapplied in breach of duty. In the case of failure to act, showing such loss may well be difficult, since the court needs to hypothesize what loss, if any, the company would have suffered, if the director had acted and acted properly.[23]

---

[20] *Re Westmid Packing Services Ltd* [1998] 2 All ER 124, CA.

[21] *Re Barings plc (No 5)* [1999] 1 BCLC 433, approved on appeal: [2000] 1 BCLC 523, CA. In this case none of these conditions was met in a case where a major investment bank was driven into liquidation through unauthorized and undetected derivatives trading of a young employee in a foreign branch of the bank. The courts' approach fits well with the recommendations of the Financial Reporting Council on internal risks: FRC, *Internal Control: Revised Guidance for Directors on the Combined Code* (October 2005).

[22] *Bristol and West Building Society v Mothew* [1998] Ch 1, CA.

[23] See *Lexi Holdings plc v Luqman* [2009] 2 BCLC 1, CA (failure of non-executive director and major shareholder to disclose to the board her knowledge of the convictions for dishonesty

DUTY TO PROMOTE THE SUCCESS OF THE COMPANY

SHAREHOLDERS AND STAKEHOLDERS

The duty to promote the success of the company constitutes the directors' core duty of loyalty. It applies to all the activities of the director, whether or not a conflict of interest exists. It is undoubtedly a fiduciary duty, ie a duty conceived by the law as appropriate to impose upon those who undertake to act for another party in circumstances which give rise to a relationship of trust and confidence between the parties. Here we see the analogy with the law of trusts, for the paradigm case of a fiduciary is the trustee who undertakes to promote the interests of the beneficiaries.

This duty has also provided the main focus in recent years for the British debate between those favouring a shareholder view of the company and those favouring a stakeholder view. The question is, to the furtherance of whose interests should the directors devote their efforts, the shareholders alone or all those whose inputs are crucial for the business success of the company, including but not confined to the shareholders? We consider this debate more broadly in Chapter 9; here, we look only at its impact on the formulation of directors' general duties.

The prior law obscured its answer to this question by requiring the directors to act in the best interests of the 'company'. Since the company is an artificial entity, it can have no interests. The prior law could be made operational only by identifying the interests of the 'company' with one or more sets of human beings involved in it. Probably the majority view was that the company was the shareholders, but perhaps part of the attraction of the prior law (whose formulation can be found in many other jurisdictions) was its very ambiguity on this point. The current provision, contained in section 172, avoids ambiguity. The duty of the directors is to 'promote the success of the company for the benefit of its members'. This is clearly a shareholder-centred statement of the rule.

However, the Company Law Review, which proposed the principle currently to be found in the Act, saw itself promoting 'enlightened

of the managing director, her brother, who misappropriated corporate assets). In this case causation was made out and the defendant held liable to pay nearly £42 million by way of damages to the company.

shareholder value' (ESV).[24] The 'enlightenment' consists in recognizing that the interests of the shareholders can be adversely affected if the interests of other stakeholder groups are not taken into account in appropriate ways by the directors. Thus, section 172 requires directors, whilst acting to promote the success of the company for the benefit of its members, to 'have regard' to a number of stakeholder interests, such as those of the company's employees, suppliers, and customers,[25] as well as the impact of the company's activities on the community and the environment. This formulation constitutes 'enlightened' shareholder value rather than a stakeholder approach because non-shareholder interests are required to be taken into account only insofar as they have an impact on the directors' goal of achieving business success for the benefit of the members (shareholders). The directors are not required to 'balance' the interests of shareholders and other stakeholders so as, for example, to maximize the joint utility of all the stakeholders where this would involve a diminution in shareholder utility.

WHAT DOES THE STANDARD REQUIRE IN PRACTICE?

Despite the ideological debate generated by the core duty of loyalty, there are good reasons for thinking that its practical value in terms of litigation is rather limited. It requires the director, when exercising discretion, to do what he or she thinks *in good faith* will promote the success of the company. It is also clear from the section that the duty does not require the directors to favour the short-term interests of the shareholders as against longer-term ones.[26] This is a subjectively worded obligation, as was the prior law. The directors' duty is, said Lord Greene MR in 1942, to act 'in what they may consider—not what a court may consider—to be the best interests of the company'.[27] Consequently, no matter how eccentric the directors' decision may appear to a court to be from the shareholders' point of view, that is at worst some evidence that the directors did not think their decision was in the best interests of the

---

[24] CLR, *Developing the Framework* (March 2000), ch 3; *Completing the Structure* (November 2000), ch 3.
[25] A notable omission from this list is the creditors of the company. However, s 172(3) says the ESV duty is without prejudice to the operation of any rule requiring directors to consider or act in the interests of the creditors. In fact, creditors' interests are more strongly protected by s 214 of the Insolvency Act 1986, considered in Ch 4 above, which in the vicinity of insolvency substitutes the creditors' interests for those of the shareholders.
[26] s 172(1)(a)—a formulation which, if anything, slightly throws that section's weight on the side of longer-term interests.   [27] *Re Smith & Fawcett* [1942] Ch 302, 304, CA.

company rather than conclusive proof of a breach of duty.[28] Only the careless or naive director[29] is likely to leave direct evidence that they did not consider the interests of the shareholders. Thus, as under the business judgment rule, the directors' decision will be subject to a rationality test (could no reasonable director have acted in the way the particular director did?),[30] but that is far from a reasonableness test where the court has to ask whether it or most directors would have done what the particular director did.

DUTY TO ACT WITHIN POWERS

If British law stopped at the core duty of loyalty considered in the previous section, one could say that the duty of loyalty was a very weak reed. However, the core duty is supplemented by additional equitable rules, which are objectively based and increase the impact of the law. The rest of this chapter will be largely devoted to an analysis of these rules. Yet, the formulation of effective objective rules also faces the fundamental difficulties noted above. Do the courts have the expertise to apply them and how will directors respond to them?

The objective rules considered in this section seek to avoid these problems by basing themselves on rules agreed by the shareholders themselves and embodied in its constitution, normally in its articles of association. This approach has the advantage that the constitution is an example of private ordering, so that building directors' duties on that basis is not open to the objection that inexpert judges are imposing rules from outside; on the contrary, the courts can claim to be reinforcing the rules adopted by the shareholders themselves. Thus developed the general notion that the directors have an obligation to act in accordance with the company's constitution. Even if the directors believe that action contrary to the constitution would promote the success of the company, they are not free to take it. The constitution thus provides the framework within which the directors are required to confine the exercise of their discretion rather

---

[28] See eg *Regentcrest plc v Cohen* [2001] 2 BCLC 80 where a director was a party to a decision, shortly before the company's liquidation, to release his company's claim for £1.5m against another company, in which fellow members of the board had an interest, in return for a speculative consideration. The judge found no evidence of bad faith.

[29] Or their legal advisers, as in *Re W & M Roith* [1967] 1 All ER 427.

[30] The rationality test operates by creating the following Morton's fork argument: if no rational director would have done what the particular director did, then either the particular director was irrational or he did not believe what he did would promote the success of the company.

than being simply an element which they are obliged to take into account. In section 171 of the Act this general idea is expressed in two separate sub-principles: the directors must (a) act in accordance with the company's constitution and (b) only exercise powers for the purpose for which they are conferred. Principle (a) is the more obvious expression of the idea we have just discussed and we turn to that first.

ACTING IN ACCORDANCE WITH THE CONSTITUTION

A duty imposed on directors to remain within the powers which have been conferred upon them by the articles chimes well with the basic proposition of British company law that directors' powers are derived from the articles of association and not, normally, from the Companies Act. The duty reinforces the contractual division of powers within the company. In fact, it almost goes without saying. The directors may also be in breach of duty to the company if they cause it to act in a way which is illegal, either at common law or under the companies legislation. We have already considered an example of this issue in Chapter 4, where directors pay dividends which are unsupported by available distributable income. In both cases, the imposition of liability on the director is uncontroversial, except for one point. This is whether the liability is strict (ie any contravention of the company's constitution or the general law puts the director in breach of duty) or whether it arises only if the director has acted negligently.[31] The decided cases are not clear on the point.

Where the directors act in breach of the articles, the most frequently litigated issue is not, however, their liability to the company but whether their action is binding on the company in favour of third parties. The implication of the directors' exceeding their powers under the constitution is that their decision is ineffective in law, ie it is either void or voidable by the company. However, in an increasing range of cases the directors will be treated as authorized to enter into the transaction in question, despite the breach of the articles, in order to protect the legitimate expectations of third parties dealing with the company through the directors. We discussed this issue in Chapter 2. Indeed, with the transaction now more likely to be enforceable by the third party against the company, despite the provisions in the constitution, the directors' potential liability to the

---

[31] See *Re Paycheck Services 3 Ltd* [2009] 2 BCLC 309, CA. Even if the liability is strict, the director might obtain relief under s 1157, discussed below at p 187.

company acquires an added significance. The directors will be liable for the loss caused to the company from acting without authority, which extends to an obligation to restore to the company the value of assets paid away in breach of the constitution or the general law.[32]

ACTING FOR AN IMPROPER PURPOSE

The above cases involved directors purporting to exercise powers the constitution of the company had not conferred upon them. However, the principle of the directors' duty to act within their powers has been extended to embrace situations where the constitution has conferred the relevant powers on the directors, but the directors have exercised those powers other than 'for the purposes for which they are conferred'.[33] Again, two aspects of this breach of duty are relevant. First, a director who through such a decision causes harm to the company will be liable to reimburse the company for any loss caused to it.[34] Second, a decision taken for an improper purpose is in principle voidable by the company and a shareholder may be entitled to prevent the company from proceeding with action which is in breach of the constitution, but in both cases these propositions are subject to the modern rules protecting third party interests which we discussed in Chapter 2.[35]

The crucial question which the statute poses is, of course, that of how one determines the purposes for which a particular power has been conferred on the directors. It is unusual, though not unknown, for the articles to specify the purposes for which powers are conferred on the directors. This is not surprising, at least in large companies: limiting the powers which the directors are given to pursue the company's business objectives risks depriving the shareholders of the benefits of centralized management. In fact, as we have noted several times already, the articles of companies other than the smallest will normally contain a broad and general delegation of management powers to the board.[36] How can the court tell whether an apparently general power is subject to purpose restrictions?

---

[32] *Re Oxford Benefit Building and Investment Society* (1886) 35 Ch D 502; *Bairstow v Queens Moat Houses plc* [2001] 2 BCLC 531. s 40—protecting third party rights—preserves the liability of the directors to the company for exceeding their powers.   [33] s 171(b).

[34] *Bishopsgate Investment Management Ltd v Maxwell (No 2)* [1994] 1 All ER 261, CA.

[35] *Rolled Steel Products (Holdings) Ltd v British Steel Corporation* [1986] Ch 246. As to the shareholders, subject to third party rights, s 40(4) preserves their right to seek an injunction to prevent the company from proceeding with an action which is beyond the power of the directors. This clearly applies to breaches of the constitution as well as to acting for an improper purpose.

[36] Model Articles for Public Companies, art 3. For the same reason, it is difficult to show in large companies that directors have acted in breach of the constitution, though this was

This issue was considered in a number of 1960s and 1970s cases involving takeover bids, ie offers by a third party to the shareholders of a target company to acquire their shares for an attractive consideration. In one way or another, the board of the target company in these cases sought to defeat the acquirer by issuing new shares to a friendly investor who could be relied upon not to accept the acquirer's offer. The British courts uniformly held that this was an improper exercise of the directors' powers, even though the share issue power in the articles contained no express restrictions on the purposes for which shares could be issued (ie did not say that shares could be issued only to raise capital).[37]

The most elegant rationale for this line of decisions was provided by Lord Wilberforce in the *Howard Smith* case. In large companies, the articles create a division of powers within a company between the board and the shareholders as a body. The integrity of this division of powers is protected, from the point of view of the board, by the requirement that the shareholders can alter it only by going through the special procedure for altering the articles.[38] From the point of view of the shareholders, that division is protected by the proper purposes doctrine, which prevents the board from 'packing' the shareholding body with their supporters through the issue of new shares.

However, one cannot claim the proper purposes doctrine is sharply defined. Even within the area of takeover bids, it is unclear whether the directors have a freer hand to take defensive action if the acquirer is acting 'abusively'. Further, the doctrine, as articulated in *Howard Smith*, applies only to the directors' predominant purpose. If the board's predominant purpose is proper, their decision cannot be impugned on the basis of a secondary improper purpose. This is particularly important in relation to 'pre-bid' defences (ie steps taken by the board of a potential target company before a bid is imminent). A decision which has a good commercial rationale (acquisition of another business, for example) will stand even if, as the board understands and welcomes, that acquisition will render the company less attractive to a potential bidder for its shares. Finally, the implication of the *Howard Smith* approach is that in companies which are not public companies, the directors might have a freer hand to control the

---

established in *Hogg v Cramphorn* (next note): directors attached ten votes to each new share, whereas the articles gave them power to attach only one.

[37] *Hogg v Cramphorn Ltd* [1967] Ch 254; *Bamford v Bamford* [1970] Ch 212; *Howard Smith Ltd v Ampol Petroleum Ltd* [1974] AC 821, PC. Thereafter, litigation in the British courts fell away, mainly because the Takeover Code imposed a 'no frustration' rule on target boards from the late 1960s onwards and the Second Directive restricted the board's powers to issue shares without shareholder approval after 1980.   [38] See Ch 1 at p 15.

composition of the shareholder body because those companies were not set up on the basis of a strict division of powers between shareholders and the board.[39]

Outside the area of upholding the constitution, does the improper purposes doctrine have a role to play? It has been suggested that one way to give the doctrine greater bite would be to treat it as conferring on the courts power to review directorial exercise of discretion by reference to the 'standards expected of a fiduciary office holder'.[40] Even this proposal, however, is a limited one, for it would confine judicial review to the internal aspects of the exercise of directors' discretion (ie the impact of the decision upon distributional issues as between groups of shareholders), where it is suggested that court intervention would be more expert and more acceptable than in the case of the external aspects of the exercise of discretion, which are more intimately connected with the execution of business policy. We shall return to judicial review for the purpose of protecting non-controlling shareholders in Chapter 8.

SELF-DEALING TRANSACTIONS

We now turn to those duties which expressly focus on conflicts between the director's personal interests (usually, but not necessarily, financial) and the interests of the company and, less commonly, on conflicts between competing duties to which the director is subject. It is clear that such conflicts may have been present in the cases already discussed in this chapter. The directors may issue shares in a takeover bid because they fear they will lose their jobs if the acquirer succeeds with its offer or directors may fail to promote the success of the company because they are acting to promote their own interests. However, whether this is so is not central to the applicability of the legal rules discussed above, that is, even if the directors could show there was no conflict, the duty would still apply to them.[41] In

---

[39] *Re Smith & Fawcett* [1942] Ch 302, CA (private company with large overlap between directors and shareholders: directors entitled to use their power not to register share transfers so as to keep out a new shareholder of whom they did not approve); *Gaiman v National Association for Mental Health* [1971] Ch 317 (board of non-profit, campaigning company entitled to use expulsion power to remove members with views contrary to those the company set up to propagate).

[40] R Nolan, 'The Proper Purpose Doctrine and Company Directors', in B Rider (ed), *The Realm of Company Law* (London: Kluwer Law International, 1998) at 19 ff.

[41] Consider the case of a director with a significant shareholding who causes the board to issue shares to defeat the bidder because, although the price offered is a good one and is in cash, he fears the impact of the acquirer on the employees of the target.

the duties which we now consider, however, it is the conflict of interest which is central to the legal regulation and so the conflict (or possibility of it) must be made out for the duty to be triggered.

As we shall see, these duties also mark a change in the legal strategy used to deal with the shareholders' agency problems in relation to the directors. The above duties were articulated through standards (of differing types). As we have seen, open-ended standards create problems for the courts in identifying the basis upon which they should intervene in the affairs of the company. The British courts have tended to identify only limited bases for intervention, although it remains to be seen whether that will continue to be the case in relation to the newly articulated objective standard of care. In relation to conflicts of interest, British law makes little use of standards and employs instead a decision-rights or a trusteeship strategy, ie subjecting the conflicted decision to a special procedure for taking it. This approach continues the policy of reducing the role of the courts in evaluating the conduct of companies' affairs.

The Act identifies four categories of conflict situation, of which two are more important than the other two. The two central conflict situations arise where the director enters into a transaction with the company (section 177) or where he or she diverts a 'corporate opportunity' away from the company (section 175, which also provides the catch-all rules for dealing with any conflict situations not falling within the other three categories). We will look at these two situations first, beginning in this section with transactions with the company or 'self-dealing' cases, before moving on in the next section to look at corporate opportunities and then at the two remaining conflict cases.

A self-dealing transaction can be said to occur where the director deals with his or her company either directly or through a third party in which the director has an interest, for example, where the third party is a company in which the director has a major shareholding or is a partnership of which the director is a member. Consequently, section 177(1) applies 'if a director of a company is in any way *directly or indirectly* interested in a proposed transaction or arrangement with the company' (emphasis added), thus covering both situations.[42] Further, the section takes a wide view of the dealings covered by including arrangements as well as transactions.

---

[42] This formulation—'in any way'—seems wide enough to embrace what in equity are sometimes seen as separate rules, ie the rule against self-dealing and the rule requiring fair dealing. The latter applies where the transaction is with someone connected with the director and crucially allows the director to justify it on the grounds that it was a fair transaction. The

POSSIBLE APPROACHES

There are four approaches which the law might take to the regulation of self-dealing transactions. The first would be simply to prohibit them. Although simple to operate, such a rule might be regarded as an example of overkill. A self-dealing transaction is not in itself objectionable: only if the presence of the director on both sides of the table leads to a deal which is less favourable to the company than an arm's length negotiation would have produced can the shareholders be said to have suffered harm. Moreover, a prohibition might impose more costs on the shareholders than benefits. This is because the director or the third party in which the director is interested might be the best source for the company of the service or good which the company is seeking to acquire. This might be particularly so in the case of private companies where the director might be willing to provide finance to the company on better terms than an outsider, such as a bank, because of the director's better understanding of the company. A prohibition would also mean that a director could never enter into a service contract under which he agreed to work for the company full-time and be remunerated for his work. Thus, either the top managers of a company would have to remain off the board or, on becoming members of the board, they would have to give up their full-time managerial roles. Neither rule is likely to be conducive to the efficient running of the company.

Thus, banning contracting is not likely to be a generally acceptable solution to the self-dealings problem, though it could be used in particular situations where the utility to the company of a particular type of transaction is low and the risk of self-interested behaviour on the part of the director high. It is on this basis that the Companies Act 1948 prohibited loans to a director from the company (and related transactions): experience had shown that directors often abused the facility to receive loans from their company, whilst, if a director was a good risk for a loan, there was no reason why he or she should not get it in the normal way from sources other than the company.[43]

The second approach is to subject contracts with directors to review by the courts by reference to some standard such as fairness or reasonableness.

---

statute appears to require disclosure in both cases, provided the director 'in any way, directly or indirectly' is interested in the transaction.

[43] *Report of the Committee on Company Law Amendment*, Cmd 6659 (1945), para 94. Under the 2006 Act the prohibition has gone, to be replaced by a requirement for shareholder approval (ss 197 ff and below p 172). Ironically, at about the same time a prohibition on loans was introduced by US federal law for public companies as part of the post-Enron legislation. See §13k of the Securities Exchange Act 1934, as introduced by §402 of the Sarbanes–Oxley Act 2002.

On this approach, companies are permitted to contract with directors or third parties in which directors are interested. However, the risk arising from the fact that the director appears, so to speak, on both sides of the bargaining table is controlled by giving the court the power to review the terms of the transaction in case the deal is less favourable to the company than that which arms' length bargaining would have produced. As with all standards, it is an approach which is dependent upon the existence of an expert judiciary to apply them. In the United States, where some use is made of this strategy,[44] there has always been greater confidence in the skills of the judiciary in this regard than in the United Kingdom.

In the UK proof that the transaction was fair to the company is not a defence in a conflict case; the focus is almost wholly on whether the prescribed procedure has been followed.[45] Nor is the court even required to establish the intensity of the conflict of interest to which the director is subject. As indicated above, section 177(1) applies if the director is 'in any way' interested in the transaction or arrangement (though the section does not apply if the interest 'cannot reasonably be regarded as likely to give rise to a conflict of interest').[46] This approach makes it misleading to say (though it is often said, even in the statute) that a director must not put him- or herself in a position of conflict of interest. This sounds like a prohibition. The rule rather is that, if a conflict exists, it must be handled in the appropriate way. There are procedural requirements to be observed which would not exist in the absence of the conflict. If they are not observed the director will be in breach of duty, even if the terms of the transaction are fair; if they are, there will be no breach of duty even if the terms are substantively unfair.

Thus, the British approach is the procedural one of identifying the body within the company which must handle a self-dealing transaction. That task could be given to either the board or the shareholders as a body. These are the third and fourth approaches to the problem. The latter was the traditional technique for dealing with self-dealing transactions, but,

---

[44] R C Clark, *Corporate Law* (Boston: Little, Brown, 1986), 160–1. Even in the US, the rigour of the court review (is it 'entire fairness' or something less?) will turn on the way the decision has been handled within the corporation.

[45] *Re Duckwari plc (No 2)* [1998] 2 BCLC 315, CA: failure of director of the acquiring company to secure the approval of its shareholders for the purchase of a land at a fair market price from a vendor in which that director was interested permitted the company to recover from the director the amount of its loss when the property market subsequently collapsed, even though the acquisition itself could not be reversed.

[46] s 177(6)(a). So, fanciful conflicts of interest are excluded.

on further analysis, it can be seen that the former has made significant progress in the modern law.

DISCLOSURE TO THE BOARD

For conflicted transactions British law can be seen as uncertain of its polarity as between shareholder and board handling of the issue. The common law (or, more precisely, equitable) default rule, as developed in the nineteenth century, was clear: conflicted transactions are permitted provided the conflict of interest is fully disclosed in advance to the shareholders and the shareholders nevertheless approve the transaction.[47] The non-involved members of the board could not give approval because of the further equitable principle that the company is entitled to the unbiased advice of all its directors and, if that is not available because one or more of them is interested in the transaction in question, then the decision reverts to the shareholders in general meeting.[48]

The equitable rule was protective of shareholder interests but potentially imposed an expensive and public decision-making process, at least on large companies, for handling self-dealing transactions. It might operate in practice as a prohibition because of the unwillingness of directors to use the permitted approval process. Consequently, by the end of the nineteenth century, it was becoming common for the articles to modify it.[49] Thus, provisions began to appear in the articles permitting the board to contract on behalf of the company, in the normal way, even though some of its members were interested in the decision in question. In the 1920s the legislature moved to put limits on what the articles could do by requiring at least prior disclosure to the board of the conflict of interest.

We need not go into the details of these developments because section 177 in effect casts the typical upshot of these moves into a simple mandatory rule, which is that the nature and extent of the director's interest in a proposed transaction with the company must be disclosed to the board before the transaction is entered into.[50] The director is not concerned with

---

[47] The requirement for full disclosure can be onerous, including in appropriate cases disclosure of the director's bargaining strategy: *Newgate Stud Co v Penfold* [2008] 1 BCLC 46. This approach will presumably carry over to disclosure to the board under the statute.

[48] *Imperial Mercantile Credit Association v Coleman* (1871) LR 6 Ch App 558, 567–8; *Movitex v Bulfield* [1988] BCLC 104.

[49] Doctrinally this worked because the articles constitute a contract among all the members and the company (s 33) and so all the shareholders agreed to waive the shareholder approval rule in exchange for something different.

[50] s 177(1) and (4). There are some exceptions such as interests and transactions of which the director is not aware or interests of which the other directors are or ought to be aware already: s 177(5)(6).

what the board does with the information, once disclosed. If the transaction in question is one which someone below board level will take on behalf of the company, there is an obvious risk that the information will not reach the decision-taker, but that will not put the director in breach of the self-dealing duty (though conceivably that director and his fellows might be in breach of one of the non-conflict duties if the information were not acted on).

REMEDIES

In equity a director who dealt with the company without full disclosure was not regarded as acting in breach of duty but as being subject to a 'disability', ie of being unable to enter into a legally binding transaction with the company. Consequently, the common law remedies focused on the transaction and in particular on the company's right to rescind (reverse) the transaction where there had been self-dealing. In many cases rescission might work well: with both acquisitions by the company at an overvalue and disposals at an undervalue rescission would both compensate the company (by restoring its consideration and allowing it to contract elsewhere at market prices) and deprive the director of any profit made on the transaction with the company. However, the right to rescind can be quickly lost, for example where the interests of innocent third parties are implicated (as on a subsequent disposal of the property before the self-dealing is discovered), and in any event the right to rescind is problematic where the contracting party is not the director but an entity in which the director is interested.

In the case of disposals the common law found a way to provide the company with a remedy, even if rescission was no longer possible, on the following argument. If a director receives corporate property in breach of trust (in our case as a result of a self-dealing transaction), he or she is under a duty to return it or its value to the company, and that value may well be higher than the fair value of the property at the time of its acquisition from the company. Thus, in *J J Harrison (Properties) Ltd v Harrison*[51] a director acquired property at an undervalue from the company without fully disclosing his interest and later made a further profit when he sold the land on. He was held liable to account to the company for the difference between the acquisition price and the ultimate sale price (less the expenditure necessary to facilitate the onward sale). In the case of acquisitions from a director by the company, however, this argument will

---

[51] [2002] 1 BCLC 162, CA.

not work. Thus, if rescission was no longer available (or if the company wished to keep the property acquired), could the director retain the profit made on the sale to the company? The equitable rule was that the director could, unless the director had been mandated to acquire the property in question for the company. If he or she was selling their own property to the company, the profit made was not illegitimate.[52]

It is unclear whether the above represents the law today. On the one hand, section 178 tells us that 'the consequences of breach... are the same as would apply if the corresponding common law rule or equitable principle applied'. On the other hand, section 177 creates a duty to disclose the nature and extent of the director's interest in a proposed transaction with the company, so that the 'disability' analysis which underlay the equitable assessment of remedies no longer holds. Consequently, it may be that the courts will move to apply to breaches of section 177 the full range of remedies which the legislature has created for those cases where the legislature requires shareholder approval of self-dealing transactions (see below).[53]

The Act imposes the same disclosure rule in relation to existing transactions,[54] but the sanctions here are criminal, not civil. Of course, disclosure at the proposal stage is enough to satisfy this requirement, if there has been such disclosure. Post-event disclosure might be thought to be useless as being too late, but the company may well have a decision to make in relation to a transaction after it has been entered into, for example, whether to terminate a contract for breach by the other party. The director's interest may have changed, or only been acquired, after the transaction was entered into by the company, and so the post-event disclosure requirement is rational, even necessary.

APPROVAL BY THE SHAREHOLDERS

The reader has probably concluded by now that the choice made by British law is to allocate the task of handling self-dealing transactions to the board, on the basis of full disclosure of the conflict in question. One might even

---

[52] *Re Cape Breton* (1885) 29 Ch D 795 (Bowen LJ dissenting); *Burland v Earle* [1902] AC 83, PC. For further helpful analysis see R Nolan, 'Conflicts of Interest, Unjust Enrichment and Wrongdoing', in W Cornish et al (eds), *Restitution: Past, Present and Future* (Oxford: Hart Publishing, 1998), who argues that equitable compensation should be available in this case to put the company economically in the position it would be in, had the transaction been rescinded.

[53] This question, and others, could have been clarified if the Act had produced a statutory statement of remedies as well as of duties: see R Nolan, 'Enacting Civil Remedies in Company Law' (2001) 2 *JCLS* 245, esp at 263–6.   [54] ss 182–7.

go further and assert that the control over such transactions offered by British law is really rather limited. The disclosure rule does not offer either judicial review on grounds of unfairness nor scrutiny by a body of share-holders independent of the board. Instead, the rule relies heavily on fellow directors acting appropriately in response to the conflicts of interest which are brought to their attention. How strong a check this is likely to be one can assess only after looking at the rules on board composition, considered in Chapter 7, but even at this stage it is clear that there are risks with this strategy. The interested director is not even prohibited from voting on the transaction: that is a matter for the company's articles.[55]

Probably more important in practice is not whether the interested director is formally excluded from voting but whether the board develops a cul-ture of approving directors' conflicted transactions without great scrutiny and whether the board feels unable to stand up to a dominant director who seeks approval. Thus, the uninvolved directors may fail to act effectively because of what the Americans graphically, if somewhat disconcertingly, term 'mutual back-scratching', that is, the uninvolved directors may fail to scrutinize closely a particular self-dealing transaction, in the expecta-tion of similar treatment when theirs is the conflict under consideration at some later date. Or, in the face of a dominant chief executive, the unin-volved directors may simply opt for a quiet life. Both courses of action will probably amount to breaches of duty on the part of the uninvolved direc-tors, but the weak ex post threat of suit for breach of duty by the company against the approving directors may do little to induce them to engage in proper scrutiny of proposed conflicted transactions.

However, board handling is not the sole strategy used by the law to regulate self-dealing transactions. In some cases the equitable principle of shareholder approval is reinstated. Self-dealing transactions in four areas require shareholder approval by virtue of Chapter 4 of Part 10 of the Act and a widely defined set of 'related party' transactions requires shareholder approval by virtue of the Listing Rules made by the Financial Services Authority, which apply to companies with a premium listing on the Main Market of the London Stock Exchange, ie in effect the top tier of publicly traded companies. It is in fact quite difficult to say, at least in relation to publicly traded companies, whether the dominant rule is dis-closure to the board, modified in some exceptional cases by a requirement for shareholder approval; or the other way around. Let us look at both sets of provisions requiring shareholder approval.

---

[55] The Model Articles for both public and private companies exclude the director from vot-ing (subject to exceptions). See art 16 of the public model and art 14 of the private model.

Chapter 4 requires shareholder approval for those self-dealing transactions where experience, often in the form of reports from inspectors appointed by the Department of Trade and Industry to investigate the affairs of companies, had shown to be particularly open to abuse. These are, in the order in which they appear in Chapter 4, directors' long-term service contracts, substantial property transactions, loans to directors and analogous transactions, and payments for loss of office. It is worth noting that, in contrast to the general duties of directors, the rules requiring shareholder approval are applied specifically to 'shadow' directors,[56] which may encourage the courts to apply the general duty to them as well. It is very difficult to see on what basis it would be coherent to apply only some of the self-dealing rules to shadow directors.

SUBSTANTIAL PROPERTY TRANSACTIONS

In terms of impact on the conduct of the affairs of companies, at least of private companies, perhaps the most significant area where shareholder approval is required is that of substantial property dealings between a director (or those 'connected with' the director)[57] and the company (or its holding company). Selling assets to the company at an overvalue or acquiring assets from the company at an undervalue is an easy way for a director to expropriate value from the (other) shareholders, since the transaction may appear to be a normal commercial one and the defect in it is revealed only if the values of the respective considerations are investigated. Requiring the director to take the initiative to seek prior shareholder approval of the transaction on the basis of full disclosure thus prevents him or her from taking the benefit of inertia. Crucially, the definition of a 'substantial' transaction is reasonably wide: a non-cash asset falls within the shareholder approval requirement if it has a value of more than 10 per cent of the company's asset value (provided it is worth more than £5,000) or it is worth more than £100,000.[58] The percentage test will catch disposals worth more than £5,000 even in quite small companies,

---

[56] s 223. This may seem an odd thing to do in the case of directors' service contracts and compensation for loss of office, but those provisions include contracts and compensation relating to managerial positions in the company, which a shadow director could hold.

[57] ss 252–6, containing a definition of 'connected persons' etc, are a good example of the complications which the drafter of the Act has to deal with, if the director is not simply to avoid the rule by dealing with the company through another person or business entity, rather than directly.

[58] s 191. 'Asset value' is normally its net asset value, ie assets minus liabilities. Consequently, the more stretched the company's balance sheet, the more likely it is shareholder approval will be required.

whilst the absolute test will catch quite small disposals (relatively) in larger companies.[59]

A particular additional interest of these provisions is that they provide a reasonably elaborate set of remedies for breaches of the statute.[60] The company is provided with the following choices.

1. The transaction entered into in breach of the provisions is voidable and so, in principle, may be either affirmed or rescinded (reversed) by the company.[61] The company may affirm, for example, where it approves of the transaction in principle but objects to its terms (where one of the remedies listed below may be adequate for its purposes). It will want to rescind where it wishes to return to the situation which obtained before the transaction was entered into and, thus, recover the assets disposed of or the price paid for the assets acquired. The company is permitted to reverse the transaction only provided it can restore what it received under the transaction to the other party. Further, the director or connected person may have disposed of the property to a third party before the company learns about the lack of shareholder consent. This does not constitute a complete bar to reversal (which would now occur as against the third party), but a broad category of third parties is protected against reversal. These are those third parties who have acquired rights in good faith, for value and without actual notice of the contravention of the statute (ie innocent third parties who have paid for what they hold). Oddly, the fact that the party to the transaction with the company has acted in good faith, for value and without notice of the breach is not a bar to rescission. It is unlikely that a director party to the transaction with the company could fall into this category, but a person 'connected with' the director might do so.[62]

---

[59] In a company with net assets of only £50k the acquisition or sale of quite a small asset from or to the company will need shareholder approval, whilst in a company with £10m net assets an acquisition or sale at £100k will require shareholder approval even though it represents only 1 per cent of net assets.

[60] s 195. s 213 makes similar provisions in respect of contraventions of the rules relating to loans etc. The CLR proposed taking these provisions as the basis of a codification of the remedies available for breach of duty, but this idea was not taken forward. See CLR, *Final Report* (July 2001), Vol 1, para 15.28 and R Nolan, above n 53.

[61] Affirmation (see s 196) requires a resolution of the company in general meeting 'within a reasonable period' (ie it replaces the prior shareholder authorization which should have been obtained). The decision to reverse the transaction can presumably be taken by either board or general meeting.

[62] To take a far-fetched example, where the contracting party is a company of which a trust holds 20 per cent of the shares (but as a passive investment) and of the thirty beneficiaries of trust one is the estranged son of the director by a previous marriage. See ss 252(2)(c) and 253(2)(c).

2. Whether or not the company avoids the transaction, it may recover from the director any gain made by him 'directly or indirectly' on the transaction.[63] Thus, if the company wishes to keep the property it has purchased from the director, it can affirm the transaction and sue the director for any gain made. However, the company may sue for profit made even if the transaction has been reversed. Suppose the director buys an assets for $£x$, sells it to a connected company for $£3x$, which then sells it to the claimant company for $£5x$. Reversal of the transaction will give the company its $£5x$ back, but it appears the company could recover $£2x$ from the director as a profit made 'directly or indirectly' out of the transaction, at least where the two sales were in contemplation by the director from the beginning and provided the reversal of the sale by the company does not permit the connected company to reverse its transaction with the director. The only defence made available to the director in this situation is that he took all reasonable steps to ensure compliance with the section by the claimant company. The claimant company is thus better off than it would have been had the director committed no breach of the statutory provisions. This shows that the section puts a higher value on extracting an undeserved profit from the director than on exact compensation for the company. This is the so-called 'prophylactic' (or deterrent) aim of the law, though it should be noted that, even when stripped of the profit, the director is financially no worse off than he was before the transaction with the connected company was entered into.[64]

Any profit made directly or indirectly by the connected person may also be recovered by the company. So also may the profit be recovered which was made by any other director of the company who authorized the transaction, whether or not he or she was party to it. By creating liability for the authorizing director, these rules go well beyond the general self-dealing provision (s 177) which, as we have seen, leaves up in the air the question of any liability on the part of the board which, after disclosure, allows the transaction to proceed. Both connected person and authorizing director may benefit from the defence that they did not know of the relevant circumstances constituting the contravention, but this will not help them if they knew the facts but failed to draw the conclusion that shareholder consent was needed.

---

[63] Contrast the more restrictive (or at least unclear) equitable rule discussed above at p 166.

[64] Note the strong contrast with the common law remedies for breach of the self-dealing rule: *Burland v Earle* (above n 52).

3.   Finally, the section permits the company to seek an indemnity from
     the director for loss or damage resulting from the breach of the statu-
     tory provisions. However, if there has been full indemnification of the
     company (from whatever source), the company loses its right to rescis-
     sion. The company's right to seek an indemnity is in addition to its
     right to seek an account of profit from a director or connected person.
     However, it is presumably the case that, often, an account of profits
     will reduce or even extinguish the company's loss; and that a payment
     by way of indemnity will reduce the director's gain. The duty to
     indemnify may also be asserted against those connected with the
     director and any director who authorized the transaction, subject to
     the defences described in the previous paragraph.

OTHER AREAS UNDER THE 2006 ACT

The rules on loans and related transactions are very complex but in
essence track the provisions on substantial property transactions. They
are probably less central to the affairs of the company, in the sense that
transfers of property in and out of the company by directors are a not
uncommon and often legitimate part of the conduct of the affairs of private companies. Loans etc to directors are less evidently part of the conduct of the company's affairs, but the rules regulating them are important
because experience has shown that directors wishing to engage in the
illegitimate extraction of assets from the company often make use of the
'loan' technique.

The other two areas requiring shareholder approval both relate to directors' remuneration, but only to two particular elements of the setting of
that remuneration. Since I discuss the setting of directors' remuneration
more generally in Chapter 7, I postpone discussion of them until then.

RELATED PARTY TRANSACTIONS

Although they apply only to a small number of publicly traded companies
on the London Stock Exchange's Main Market (which are of course economically very important), the Listing Rules' requirements for shareholder
approval do add substantially to the requirements of Chapter 4 of Part 10
of the Act. First, subject to certain relaxations for small transactions,[65]
the requirement applies to all transactions with a related party and not

---

[65]   LR 11.1.10 substitutes for shareholder approval ex ante the provision of information to
the FSA, gatekeeper approval and ex post disclosure to the shareholders in the case of small
transactions, and LR 11 Annex exempts very small transactions entirely.

just to those having a certain subject matter.[66] A related-party transaction includes one in which the company and the director jointly finance an undertaking or asset, so that certain examples of 'corporate opportunities' (discussed below) are also caught by this rule. Second, the concept of a 'related party' is conceived of quite broadly, so as to include directors of all group companies, shadow directors, and former directors (who were directors in the year before the transaction) and also 'substantial' shareholders and persons 'exercising significant influence' over the company, as well as associates of all these.[67] Third, to the requirement for ex ante approval by the shareholders on the basis of full disclosure is added the exclusion of the related party from voting on the approval resolution, whilst the company must also take 'all reasonable steps' to exclude associates from voting.[68] Under the Act interested directors are entitled to vote both on an ex ante approval resolution and on an ex post affirmation vote. These provisions suggest that shareholders, notably the institutional shareholders, have had much greater success in influencing the Listing Rules in their interests than they have had with the general companies legislation.[69]

CORPORATE OPPORTUNITIES AND OTHER CONFLICTS OF INTEREST

We have assumed in the previous two sections that the director's conflict of interest has taken the form of a dealing with the company, either directly or indirectly through another entity in which the director has an interest or another person with whom the director is connected. However, the director's self-interest need not show itself in a manner which involves the company in the transaction. Indeed, the self-interest of the director may lead to the *exclusion* of the company from the transaction. Suppose, for example, that a director learns of a lucrative business opportunity, which the company could exploit. Instead of offering the opportunity to the company, in which the director has only a limited shareholding, the director chooses instead to develop it through a new company wholly owned by her, so that she can capture the whole of the profits arising out

---

[66] Certain specific transactions are exempted, whatever their size, notably 'transactions of a revenue nature in the ordinary course of business' (LR 11.1.5). See also LR 11 Annex.

[67] LR 11.1.4, so that the provisions have a minority shareholder protection function as well. See Ch 8 below at p 234.   [68] LR 11.1.7.

[69] Although the FSA has reviewed the Listing Rules more than once in recent years, the related party rules have survived largely intact.

of the opportunity. Here the self-interest of the director leads to the exclusion of the company from the opportunity. Is it lawful for the director to exclude the company from the opportunity?

This question is dealt with in the Act by section 175, which also provides a general rule for all conflicts of interest not covered by the provisions on self-dealing (considered above) or on independent judgment or on the receipt of benefits from third parties (both considered below). Thus, section 175 begins, rather misleadingly as we have noted, by stating that 'a director of a company must avoid a situation in which he has, or can have, a direct or indirect interest that conflicts, or possibly may conflict, with the interests of the company'[70] and goes on to say that 'this applies in particular to the exploitation of any property, information or opportunity' (section 175(2)). However, although section 175 is the Act's response to the corporate opportunity issue, it deals with only one of the two fundamental questions which corporate opportunities pose for the law. The first (and the one which the section does not address) is, what turns a business opportunity into a 'corporate' opportunity? This is an issue which the prior case-law has considered and, subject to one qualification, the answer to the question is still to be found in the common law. The second question, which the Act does deal with, is the identification of the procedure through which the company considers whether to renounce its interest in the opportunity (so that the director can take it personally) or to exploit it within the company. We will begin with the second question, even though the other question is logically prior.

HANDLING THE CORPORATE OPPORTUNITY

Readers will not be surprised at this point to learn that the common law default rule for the handling of corporate opportunities was that only the shareholders as a body could decide to release the company's interest in the opportunity, typically through an ordinary resolution, unless the opportunity was regarded as the property of the company.[71] However, the

---

[70] This formula could obviously catch self-dealing transactions but those are excluded from s 175 by s 175(3).

[71] *Cook v Deeks* [1916] 1 AC 554, PC (considered further below). The implications of the holding in that case that an ordinary majority could not release the company's interest in a corporate asset in which all the shareholders should share seem to be either that unanimity is required or perhaps even that the shareholders cannot give away corporate assets except through the procedures provided for by law (for example, by way of a distribution). It is very unclear when an opportunity will be treated as the property of the company and when not. The property analysis is on the whole unhelpful.

interested director could vote on the shareholder resolution. In principle, the default rule could be modified in the articles so as to provide something more to the directors' liking, but it was much less common (though not unknown) to do so. In other words, shareholders seemed much more willing to entrust the evaluation of self-dealing transactions to the board than the release of corporate opportunities.[72]

The significance of section 175 of the 2006 Act is that it gives companies a significant nudge in the direction of using the board to handle corporate opportunities, just as the board is central to self-dealing transactions. Whilst the Act elsewhere preserves the shareholders' common law power to authorize directorial action which would be in breach of the section 175 duty,[73] the section itself holds out the prospect of board authorization. Board authorization will relieve the director of any liability to the company,[74] subject to the conditions that (i) the director in question and 'any other interested director' cannot have their votes counted in favour of the board resolution and cannot count towards any quorum requirement of the board;[75] and (ii) where the company is a private company, the company's articles do not prohibit or restrict board authorization or, where the company is a public company, provided the articles permit the board to give authorization in the circumstances and in the manner the board gave approval in the instant case.[76] It appears that the board can approve the taking by the director of any corporate opportunity, even when the opportunity is regarded as an asset or the property of the company, since section 175(2) (quoted above) refers explicitly to the exploitation of the property of the company and the provisions on board authorization cover all potential breaches of the section.[77] Thus, the risks of minority abuse,

---

[72] It was also unclear how far s 310 of the 1985 Act, now s 232, restricted the shareholders' freedom to amend the common law default through the articles.   [73] s 180(4)(a).

[74] s 175(4)(b)—and, where this is relevant, the validity of the transaction is preserved: s 180(1). There may be additional common law requirements, such as full disclosure, which are necessary for board authorization to be effective, insofar as this is not implicit in the section. See the negative wording of s 175(6).

[75] s 175(6)—on quorum requirements below, Ch 8 at p 227.

[76] So, the articles could add to the conditions mentioned in the statute for board authorization.

[77] However, it seems clear that the directors can authorize only specific proposed breaches of duty and not whole categories of proposed future breaches. This is certainly what the CLR intended: *Final Report*, Vol 1, para 3.25. What is much less clear is whether, the board having turned down a specific opportunity for the company, a director can later decide unilaterally to take the opportunity personally or whether the issue must then return to the board. It could be argued that, the board having in good faith rejected the opportunity for the company at the earlier stage, personal exploitation would no longer give rise to a conflict of interest. On the other hand, there are clear risks of opportunistic behaviour by the director. Cf *Peso Silver*

which in the case of shareholder authorization are dealt with by removing some cases from the control of the ordinary majority,[78] are dealt with in the case of board authorization by excluding interested directors from voting (together with the residual control flowing from the general fiduciary duties applicable to the non-excluded directors).

Thus, the Act may be said to have supplemented the common law default rule of shareholder approval with a statutory default rule of board approval, and thus, in our terminology, to make use of the 'trusteeship' strategy whereby the matter is allocated to the directors who are not subject to the high-powered conflicts of interest which beset the director who will take the opportunity if the company rejects it. However, the statutory default displays a vital difference between public and private companies: the public company default is an opt-in rule, whilst the private default is an opt-out rule. In the light of the coordination problems of larger bodies of shareholders, it seems right that the public company default should be an opt-in to board decision-making. In other words, setting the default this way around means that the burden of altering it lies on the board, which is better placed to act than a diffuse body of shareholders. Consequently, if the default is inappropriate for the company, it is more likely that it will be changed if action is down to the board than it would be if the default were the other way around and the onus lay with the shareholders to correct an inefficient default.[79]

However, the central question is whether the move towards board handling of corporate opportunities constitutes appropriate policy. The CLR put its policy arguments in this way: shareholder approval 'is impractical and onerous, is inconsistent with the principle that it is for the board to make business assessments, and stifles entrepreneurial activity'.[80] It is clear, again, that under the proposed rule, the impact of the law will depend heavily upon the integrity of the decision-making of the non-involved members of the board, upon their ability to avoid self-interested decisions and pressure from those seeking approval. No doubt, an approval decision taken by the board other than in good faith can be challenged, but will the courts be able to spot such decisions?

Mines v Cropper (1966) 58 DLR 2d 1, CABC, criticized by S M Beck, 'The Saga of *Peso Silver Mines*: Corporate Opportunity Reconsidered' (1971) 49 Can B Rev 80.

[78] See n 71 above.

[79] For the developed form of this argument see L Bebchuk and A Hamdani, 'Optimal Defaults for Corporate Law Evolution' (2002) 96 *Northwestern University Law Review* 489.

[80] *Final Report*, Vol 1, para 3.23. This is a better argument in relation to public than private companies.

BUSINESS OR CORPORATE OPPORTUNITY?

The second crucial question is, what turns a business opportunity into a corporate opportunity upon which the company has first claim? It would be possible to say that all business opportunities which a director comes across while a director fall into the category of being corporate opportunities. However, it is highly unlikely that this would be an efficient rule. Such a rule would certainly reduce the number of people prepared to take on non-executive directorships, for non-executives are expected to devote only a part of their time to the company. They might not be prepared to run the risk that the company would assert a prior claim over an opportunity which, whilst highly profitable, fell outside any area of activity in which the company operates and which was wholly the result of the directors' efforts in non-corporate time. It is not even clear how far the director and the company could effectively contract ex ante about the issue.[81] What has engendered much debate is how to identify the set of rules which best distinguishes those opportunities which the director may exploit personally from those over which the company has a legitimate prior claim.

CONFLICT OF INTEREST OR NO PROFIT RULE?

The section leaves to the common law the task of settling the criteria for identifying a corporate opportunity, subject to one potentially important qualification. In equity, there are two lines of authority which are capable of being used to define the boundaries of the corporate opportunity. One is to say that the opportunity must first be offered to the company where the exploitation of the opportunity by the director would generate a conflict of interest between the director's personal interests and his or her duty to the company. A second line of authority bases itself upon the rule against secret profits, which is applied by equity to all those in a fiduciary position. Thus, it is said, the director must not make a profit arising out of or in the course of his office as director without that profit having been disclosed in advance to the shareholders and approved by them. The statutory statement of the general duties contains nothing along the lines of a 'no profit' rule. The nearest it comes to that is the rule against accepting benefits from third parties, laid down in section 176 and which we discuss below. The rule dealing with corporate opportunities is contained in a section whose rationale is explicitly one based on conflicts of interest. Thus, the opportunities whose exploitation the section regulates are

---

[81] ss 180(4)(b) and 232(4) appear to preserve freedom of contract via the articles, but these provisions do not cover individual (and non-public) contracting.

those which put the director in a situation of direct or indirect conflict of interest.[82] By implication, it excludes a 'no profits' approach, since a profit which the director makes without putting himself in a conflicted position does not fall within the section.

Does this make any difference? It is clear that the two approaches overlap to a considerable extent. Some of the famous 'no profit' cases would fit happily in the 'no conflict' approach. Thus, in *Regal (Hastings) Ltd v Gulliver*[83] the directors, who were also the majority shareholders, invested in a subsidiary which the company was establishing, and later sold their shares in the subsidiary at a profit. The House of Lords held that the opportunity to invest in the subsidiary and the resulting profit had arisen out of and in the course of the discharge of their duties as directors of the parent, and so they were accountable for the profit made to the parent, which was now controlled, in fact, by the purchaser of the directors' shares, who had acquired that company as well. However, there was also a conflict of interest in this case: the lessor of the assets, which the subsidiary had been set up to acquire by way of long lease, did not care how the subsidiary was financed, provided he had a certain minimum level of security for his rights under the lease. This could be provided by the directors' guaranteeing the subsidiary's obligations, by the company borrowing money from its bank to capitalize the subsidiary at a higher level, or, as happened, by the directors co-investing with the company in the subsidiary. However, the decision among these options was taken by the same directors who stood to benefit if the first two courses of action were rejected on behalf of the company and the third adopted.

However, it does not follow from this example that the two principles of liability are congruent. How far they overlap depends on how rigorously the two rules are interpreted. For example, if the 'no profit' rule catches opportunities arising only *because of* the directorship—and not all those arising *whilst* the person is director—it is less likely to extend beyond the 'no conflict' rule. Equally, the scope of the 'no conflict' rule depends in part on how astute the law is to find potential conflicts of interest. Section 175 takes a fairly strict approach. As we have seen, it applies to directors' 'direct or indirect' interests which conflict 'or possibly may

---

[82] s 175(1)(2).
[83] [1942] 1 All ER 378, HL. The model articles were later modified to permit such co-investment (see Table A of 1985, art 85(b) and (c)), but equally the Listing Rules (see above p 172) treat this transaction as a related party transaction needing shareholder approval. The current model articles do not deal with the issue, probably because board authorization is in principle available.

conflict' with the interests of the company.[84] Even more strongly, in the application of the section we are told that 'it is immaterial whether the company could take advantage of the property, information or opportunity.' It is understandable that the section should provide that it will not necessarily defeat a 'no conflict' claim that the company could not take the opportunity itself, for example, where the director was hired specifically to get that type of opportunity for the company.[85] To provide that it should be 'immaterial' is a very strong statement, for that would seem to imply that there might be a conflict even though it would be unlawful for the company to pursue the opportunity itself. On the other hand, the section provides that the duty created by it is not infringed 'if the situation cannot reasonably be regarded as likely to give rise to a conflict of interest'.[86] These two provisions are somewhat in tension with one another, and it may be that the 'immateriality' provision bites only once it has been established that the situation can reasonably be regarded as giving rise to a conflict of interest. Thus, in the case of an absolute bar on the company taking the opportunity, the situation would be outside the section.[87] Given the strict approach to the 'no conflict' rule by the section, the absence of a 'no profit' basis for a claim may not often matter, but sometimes it will.[88]

Given that the section mandates a 'no conflict' approach, what do the decided cases suggest will fall within its scope? Perhaps the easiest cases are those where the directors make use of corporate information and assets to develop an opportunity and then divert it to themselves once it matures into something with commercial value. In this case, the prior claim that the opportunity be shared with all the members of the company seems strong because the shareholders have in effect funded the development costs involved.[89]

---

[84] This reflects the prior law: *Aberdeen Ry Co v Blaikie Bros* (1854) 1 Macq 461, HL.

[85] See *Industrial Development Consultants v Cooley* [1972] 1 WLR 443.

[86] s 175(4)(a).

[87] The case most discussed in this context is *Phipps v Boardman* [1967] 2 AC 46, HL, a trusts case, where the opportunities taken by the trustees (who were held liable) fell outside the scope of the trust deed—but an application to court to vary the trust deed could have been made by the very trustees who took the opportunities personally.

[88] Cf *O'Donnell v Shanahan* [2009] 2 BCLC 666, CA, a pre-Act case where directors were held liable on the 'no profit' basis because an investment opportunity came to them in the course of their directorships, but the 'no conflict' rule was broken only because their personal interest in this opportunity caused them to deprive the company of commission on the purchase of the investment property. Had the difficulty over the commission not arisen (as it might well not have done), the CA would apparently not have held that the profit to be made on the investment created a conflict of interest, but would still have held the directors liable.

[89] See *Cook v Deeks* (above n 71) and *Canaero Services Ltd v O'Malley* (1973) 40 DLR 3d 371, Sup Ct Canada.

A second group of cases are those where the director has been assigned the task of getting for the company the very type of opportunity he later takes personally. Here, the 'no conflict' analysis seems very powerful, and it should not matter that the chance of the company obtaining the opportunity was very low or that the opportunity did not come to the director because he was director. This was the situation in *Industrial Development Consultants v Cooley*,[90] where the third party offeror of the opportunity (to provide services to the third party) was committed to not contracting with the director's company and offered the director the opportunity personally, not because he was a director of the company, but despite that connection. The director was held liable because he had been hired by the company to obtain precisely this sort of opportunity for the company: anything other than a strict application of the 'no conflict' rule would undermine the director's incentives to try to change the third party's views about the desirability of contracting with the company.

Third, perhaps the most common but also most difficult type of case is where the opportunity does indeed come to the director because he is a director of the company (that is, but for the directorship the opportunity would not have come the way of the director) but neither of the features considered above is present in the case. However, the fact that the opportunity comes to the director because he is a director of the company does not necessarily mean that personal exploitation of the opportunity will create a conflict of interest. Of course, it often will. For example, it is likely that the opportunity comes to the director because it falls within the area of business activity which the company already carries on. If this is so, the company is likely to be in a good position to exploit the opportunity and, if the director takes the opportunity personally, the company will lose that chance. The crucial step in imposing liability on the director is to recognize a duty on the director (for the purpose of the 'no conflict' rule) to offer to the company first opportunities falling within its 'line of business'. This seems an easy step to justify: otherwise the director could in effect run a business competing with that of the company, to which all the best business opportunities were assigned, whilst the company itself invested in the less attractive projects. The same conclusion should follow if the opportunity relates to an area of activity the company has decided to take up, even if it is not already active in the area (the 'expectancy' test). Although the Court of Appeal has recently rejected the 'line of business' test as being irrelevant to directors' liability for corporate opportunities,

---

[90] Above n 85.

this was in the context of the common law 'no profit' rule, which the section does not adopt.[91]

However, it follows from the above analysis that where an opportunity is offered to the director which is not within the company's existing or expected line of business, the director should be free in principle to exploit it personally without the company's permission. To hold otherwise might be thought to be too strong a discouragement for business people to take up non-executive directorships, especially in private companies. The same rule should apply even more strongly if the opportunity does not come to the director in the course of the directorship as well as being outside the company's existing or expected areas of business activity.[92]

REMEDIES

Assuming a corporate opportunity and the absence of approval from the company, what are the company's remedies? The primary one is likely to be an accounting by the director for the profits made out of the personal exploitation, though in some cases the company's interest might be satisfied by a simple injunction preventing further personal exploitation. Going further, the assets resulting from the exploitation of the opportunity may be treated as held on trust for the company, so that the company captures future profits as well. As *Cooley* shows, it is no bar to the recovery of the profit by the company that it could not, or was unlikely to, make the profit itself. The aim is to deprive the director of any incentive to put the company's interests second. On the other hand, the courts will make the director a (sometimes generous) allowance for the skill and time devoted to achieving the profit, at least where the director has acted in good faith.[93] Alternatively, but not additionally (here s 195 on substantial property transactions is more favourable to the company), the company can sue for damages. These may well be less than the profit made, as where the company could not easily have obtained or exploited the opportunity itself. Equally, there might also be cases where the damages were greater than the profit made by the director, as where the director was incompetent and the

---

[91] *O'Donnell v Shanahan*, above n 88.

[92] The decision in *Bhullar v Bhullar* [2003] 2 BCLC 241, CA may seem inconsistent with this proposition, but the main point it establishes is that an opportunity obtained by a director outside his directorship (in this case the director discovered the opportunity whilst on a purely social occasion) is not for that reason inevitably available for personal exploitation. If the opportunity lies in the company's existing line of business, personal exploitation will generate a conflict of interest and duty. Reasonable minds might differ as to whether the opportunity was in the company's line of business in that case, but the appeal was apparently not argued, and was certainly not decided, on that basis. [93] See *Phipps v Boardman* (above n 87).

company well placed to exploit the opportunity (though, even so, the director might have no assets out of which to reimburse the company). There is no case for rescission of contract by the company, since in the cases we are considering here the company has been excluded from the opportunity.

DUTY NOT TO ACCEPT BENEFITS FROM THIRD PARTIES

Section 176 deals with the conflict of interest arising when a director accepts a benefit from a third party given because he is a director of the company or because of his exercise of his powers as director. Such benefits may range from bribes, to payments to directors for appointing the third party's nominees to the board and then resigning themselves, to commissions paid to directors without any corrupt motive. In general, there is no corporate benefit to be obtained from such hidden payments and the CLR did not advance the argument in relation to these payments that the board should be able to approve them. However, the shareholders' power to do so at common law is preserved by section 180(4)(a). Where the benefit is not approved, a full range of remedies is available to the company: the transaction to which the secret payment was linked may be rescinded by the company; and the director and the payer are liable, jointly and severally, in damages to the company or to account for the amount of the payment.[94] Finally, it seems that the liability to account is not just a personal one; the amount of the bribe is held on a constructive trust for the company.[95]

DUTY TO EXERCISE INDEPENDENT JUDGMENT

This duty is imposed by section 173. The situation aimed at here is not one where the director fails to exercise judgment at all (which would fall within the duty of care) but one where the director exercises discretion as directed by a third party (who may, if sufficient directors act in the same way, thus become a 'shadow director'[96] of the company). The section might even cover cases where the director, without being directed what to do, acts in what he or she conceives to be the interests of the third party,

---

[94] *Taylor v Walker* [1958] 1 Lloyd's Rep 490; *Mahesan v Malaysia Government Officers' Cooperative Housing Society Ltd* [1979] AC 374, PC.
[95] *Attorney-General for Hong Kong v Reid* [1994] 1 AC 324, PC.
[96] See p 148, above.

but this will often amount in any event to failure to promote the success of the company, as required by section 172. The scope of the duty is revealed in practice in two situations: that of the nominee director and that of the director whose prior decision limits the exercise of future discretion. As with the duty not to accept benefits from third parties, breaches of this duty may be approved only by the shareholders.

NOMINEE DIRECTORS

The articles of a company or an agreement outside the articles may give a third party the right to appoint or to nominate a representative to the board, usually referred to as a 'nominee' director. As we shall see in Chapter 8, such a right may be a way of protecting the interests of a minority shareholder; it may equally operate to protect the interests of a major creditor to the company.[97] Such 'nominee' directors are obliged to ignore the interests and wishes of their appointer, insofar as these diverge from what is in the interests of the company as a whole.[98] They certainly may not agree to take instructions from the nominator. One may speculate how far this rule is observed in practice by nominee directors.[99]

FETTERING DISCRETION

The implication of the independent judgment rule might be thought to be that the director cannot effectively 'fetter his discretion', ie agree in advance how that discretion shall be exercised. This is certainly the result where the nominee director purports to agree in advance with the appointer to do what the appointer requires. However, it is not obvious that there should be a general rule that a director cannot at time one commit herself as to how she will take a decision at time two. Where directors have committed the company in good faith to a transaction and have undertaken, as part of that contract, to exercise their discretionary powers in a particular way in the future, acting in accordance with the contract should be regarded as a fulfilment of their duties, not a breach of them.

---

[97] Such a director can always be removed by an ordinary majority of the shareholders under s 168, even if such removal would breach the contract with the third party, so the majority of the shareholders retain ultimate control over the composition of the board. The question discussed in the text thus arises so long as the majority are content to have the nominee director on the board.

[98] *Boulting v ACTT* [1963] 2 QB 606, CA; *Kuwait Asia Bank EC v National Mutual Life Nominees Ltd* [1991] 1 AC 187, PC. In return, the nominator is not liable for the negligence or other breach of duty of the nominee. Even so, the risk of being characterized as a 'shadow' director may deter some creditors from appointing representatives to the board.

[99] In particular, there is a good argument for explicitly permitting nominee directors to transmit to their appointers certain types of information which is confidential to the company.

The company should not be able to escape from its contractual commitments nor should the directors be regarded as in breach of duty if they act so as to fulfil those commitments, just because circumstances change after the contract has been entered into and it becomes clear that it would have been better for the company never to have entered into the agreement. If the law did sanction such behaviour, either third parties would be less willing to contract with companies or directors would be less willing to commit themselves to doing the things necessary to carry out the contract on the company's behalf. The 'no fettering' rule would become, in that situation, a fetter on corporate contracting. Not surprisingly, the courts have not interpreted the 'independent judgment' rule so as to permit companies to escape from their contracts or to penalize directors for sticking to them.[100]

However, it is arguable that this robust approach should be applied only where the decision falls within the directors' powers under the principle of centralized management. If under the decisions rights strategy the consent of the shareholders as well is needed to commit the company to a particular transaction, then a more nuanced approach may be called for and, in fact, seems to have been accepted by the courts. In a case involving the sale of substantial assets by a company, where the Listing Rules required shareholder approval for the deal, the directors agreed with the proposed purchaser to recommend the sale to the shareholders. The courts held that there was no breach of contract by the company when the directors changed their minds in the face of the emergence of a better offer before the shareholder meeting called to consider the matter and recommended that better offer.[101] In other words, the contract was interpreted in a way which enabled the director to give the best advice to the shareholders in the circumstances which obtained at the time of the shareholder vote.

These decisions can be explained on the basis that the transaction needed shareholder approval and the ability of the shareholders to play a proper role in the decision-making process depended heavily upon their being given reliable advice by their directors at the time of the decision. Consequently, the directors could not contract out of their duty to give that advice in the way that best promoted the interests of the shareholders, as the directors viewed them at the time the advice was given. It must be admitted that even this rule may chill transactions with the company: some

---

[100] *Fulham Football Club Ltd v Cabra Estates plc* [1994] 1 BCLC 363, CA.
[101] *John Crowther Group plc v Carpets International plc* [1990] BCLC 460. See also *Rackham v Peek Food Ltd* [1990] BCLC 895 where it was the consent of the acquiring company's shareholders which was required.

third parties who cannot reduce the risk of the shareholders' rejecting the deal by signing up the directors to recommend it, come what may, may react by being unwilling to make a proposal to the directors in the first place. However, some risk of this nature is inherent in the strategy of involving the shareholders in the corporate decision in addition to the directors. Accordingly, it is appropriate for the courts to prefer the policy of promoting the integrity of the shareholders' role in decision-making. If this argument is accepted, it can be said to apply *a fortiori* where the third party's transaction is not with the company at all but with the shareholders individually, as in a takeover offer.[102]

COMPETING DIRECTORS

None of the above duties explicitly deals with directors who compete with their company. This is perhaps surprising, since in many continental European systems, where fiduciary duties are relatively underdeveloped, not competing is often a duty explicitly legislated for.[103] However, it may be that the explanation does lie in the developed state of British fiduciary duties. Competing with the company will fall within one of the duties mentioned above, such as the duty to promote the success of the company or the corporate opportunity doctrine (which a director of competing companies will find causes great problems unless the director discloses all corporate opportunities equally to both companies). Nevertheless, it is something of a surprise to find some (admittedly ill-reported) authorities which suggest that being a director of a competing company does not in itself constitute a breach of duty. The better position may be, as indicated by more recent Court of Appeal authority,[104] that acting for a competing company will normally amount to a breach of one of the above duties (including the general no conflict rule of section 175), but in special circumstances competition may be justified.

There is also a countervailing public policy here, ie one against stultifying the talents of the director, where the competition occurs consecutively rather than concurrently. It will generally be of benefit to society if directors can resign and put their expertise and knowledge to work in their own business, provided they do not take with them assets or information of

---

[102] *Dawson International plc v Coats Patons plc* [1990] BCLC 560, CSIH.
[103] For example, AktG (Germany) §88.
[104] *In Plus Group Ltd v Pyke* [2002] 2 BCLC 201, CA. In this case the competing director (found not in breach of duty) had been wrongfully excluded from the claimant company, so that it could be argued no conflict of interest arose.

their former company of which that company has a claim to exclusive use. This is a familiar problem in employment law generally. As far as company law is concerned, it will hold the director liable under section 175 if, as is often the case, the director seeks to give the new business a flying start by diverting the previous company's business opportunities to the new one.[105] However, taking preparatory action whilst still a director to set up a business which can begin trading as soon as the resignation is effective is not as such a breach of duty.[106]

SHAPING THE DUTIES

It is sometimes said that the duties described above are strict, perhaps too strict, being the result of an inappropriate transfer of concepts from the law of trusts into the more commercial area of company law. Moreover, the absence of a 'fairness' role for the courts has made it more difficult for them to adjust the duties to commercial realities. There may be some force in this argument, but it is also the case that the law gives directors and companies freedom to shape the duties into something less strict if they agree that this should be done. Shaping may occur in the face of an actual or proposed breach of duty; or it may occur in advance in relation to a category or categories of duty. In general, the company and the director have greater freedom in the former than in the latter situation, but even in the latter the parties' freedom has been expanded in recent years.

AUTHORIZATION AND RATIFICATION OF
SPECIFIC BREACHES

Shaping in relation to specific breaches of duty may occur before the breach occurs (authorization) or afterwards (ratification). We have already noted the, rather wide, scope for authorization as we have gone through the substantive duties, in particular the increasing role for authorization by the board, supplementing the sometimes unattractive mechanism of shareholder authorization. Little more needs to be said here, except to note that board authorization is available only where the statute specifically provides for it, because the common law accepted only shareholder authorization (on the analogy between the shareholders and the beneficiaries under a trust). Board authorization is a significant adjustment of the law to the 'realities' of commercial life, albeit one that puts a new weight

---

[105] *CMS Dolphin Ltd v Simonet* [2001] 2 BCLC 704 and the express provision on former directors in s 170(2).
[106] *Foster Bryant Surveying Ltd v Bryant* [2007] 2 BCLC 239, CA.

on board decision-making. Also, it may be recalled that it is not entirely clear whether an ordinary majority of the shareholders can authorize all and any proposed breach of duty or whether in some cases a greater level of approval is required.[107]

Ratification is approval given after the breach has occurred. The statute does not provide at all for board ratification, and so ratification is a matter for the shareholders alone. Thus, directors have quite a strong incentive to seek board authorization (where this is available) rather than approval only after the event. At common law the rules on shareholder authorization and ratification proceeded in parallel. However, the statute tightens up the rules on ratification whilst leaving the rules on authorization untouched (though the Company Law Review had recommended that parallelism be maintained). The tightening up consists of the exclusion of the votes of the director whose breach is to be ratified (and of any other 'member connected with him') from the vote on the ratification resolution.[108] This is a measure of minority shareholder protection which I discuss further in Chapter 8.

There is one, perhaps two, further possibilities for post-breach adjustment, this time involving the court. Even if the shareholders do not ratify the director's wrongdoing and in fact initiate litigation, section 1157 gives the court a discretion to relieve a director who has acted 'honestly and reasonably' from liability for breach of the above duties, either wholly or in part. This section, which tracks a similar provision relating to trustees, protects the honest director against swingeing liabilities for what might appear to be largely technical breaches of the above duties, but it has not been used by the courts in an expansive way so as to undermine the substance of the law set out above. Second, if a company goes into liquidation, section 212 of the Insolvency Act 1986 provides a procedural basis upon which a creditor, normally the liquidator acting on behalf of all creditors, can bring an action against present or former directors for breach of duty to the company, and the court may order the director to restore assets to the company or to pay by way of compensation 'such sum . . . as the court thinks just'.[109]

---

[107] See above n 71.

[108] s 239. The 'connected person' definition, already noted in relation to substantial property transactions, is used, with modification, here as well: s 239(5)(d).

[109] On the interrelationship between this section and s 1157 of the CA 2006 see *Re Paycheck Services 3 Ltd* [2009] 2 BCLC 309, CA, where the judges disagreed whether s 212 added substantially to the discretion available under s 1157.

AUTHORIZATION OF CATEGORIES OF BREACHES

Shaping of the duties occurs much more radically where the company authorizes what would otherwise be breaches of categories of duties, rather than specific proposed breaches. As we noted in relation to self-dealing transactions, company law provides a ready vehicle for conferring such category approval, namely, provisions in the articles of association. Even though the introduction of such provisions into the articles requires shareholder consent under the normal rules for amending the articles, shareholders' collective action problems mean that they might acquiesce in such changes even when it is not in their best interests to do so. This at least was the view the legislature took in the 1920s when it amended the legislation so as to introduce the provision which now appears in section 232. This renders void any provision in the articles (or in any contract with the company) which exempts a director from liability for breach of duty to the company (subject to exceptions we consider below). This is a very significant provision, because it renders the provisions on directors' duties mandatory, not default, rules, at least as far as general exemptions from the duties are concerned. Thus, it is not possible for British companies to do the thing which Delaware companies (and companies incorporated in many other US states) are specifically permitted to do, ie to exempt directors from liability in damages in the case of breaches of the duty of care.[110] It was precisely the presence of such provisions in the articles in a notorious case[111] of the 1920s which caused the British legislature to introduce what is now section 232.

The 1920s rule was later made subject to two major exceptions. In 1989 it was amended so as to permit insurance against the director's liability to the company to be purchased at the company's expense and for the benefit of the director.[112] Taking out such insurance will normally be a decision for the board. Although such insurance has the unattractive feature of shareholders paying to protect their representatives against the consequences of wrongs done by those representatives to the shareholders, it is unlikely that insurance is available in respect of wrongdoing intentionally aimed at the company because of the moral hazard problems arising in such insurance. Outside the area of intentional wrongdoing, the board might well take the view that, without such insurance, senior persons might be unwilling to come forward for directorships or would require

---

[110] Delaware General Corporation Act §102(b)(7), though the Delaware courts have shown some reluctance to apply the provision at face value.
[111] *Re City Equitable Fire Insurance Co Ltd* [1925] Ch 407.   [112] Now s 233.

even higher remuneration so that they could purchase their own insurance. The latter is perhaps the crucial point: since insurance against civil liability is permitted by the general law, the only question is whether the company pays for it directly or indirectly via an increase in the director's remuneration. The former is likely to be more cost effective. The downside of such insurance, both for the director and the company, is that the presence of insurance may actually encourage litigation.

Since 1994 the ban has also been subject to the qualification that the company may promise to indemnify a director in respect of liabilities arising in favour of third parties (ie other than the company).[113] Thus, in respect of liabilities to the company insurance remains the only exception, perhaps because purchasing insurance brings home to the company the cost of its decision through its obligation to pay premiums to the insurance company. A promise to indemnify a director against liabilities which may or may not arise in the future may appear costless at the time it is given (since the contingency may never arise which will cause the company to pay out). The indemnity in respect of liabilities to third parties is not of great importance to this chapter (since directors' duties are owed to the company) and the policy of making it available seems to have been driven by the perceived threat of US, class-action based shareholder litigation arising out of duties owed by directors to shareholders or investors more generally.

Finally, section 232 is qualified by the new provision in the 2006 Act that it does not 'prevent the company's articles for making such provision as has previously been lawful for dealing with conflicts of interest'.[114] Like other formulae of this type in the Act its meaning is highly obscure. Most likely it is intended to give cover to provisions in the articles permitting directors to deal with conflicts of interest by withdrawing from decision-making on issues where they are subject to such a conflict.

ENFORCEMENT

Since the statutory general duties of director are owed to the company, they are enforceable only by those who can claim to be the company or to act on its behalf. This clearly includes the board, but if the board contains the alleged wrongdoers, it may be unsafe to rely on it alone.[115]

---

[113] Now s 234.   [114] s 232(4). See also s 180(4)(b).

[115] It may be a new board, of course, as in *Regal v Gulliver* (above n 83) or the wrongdoer may have left (as in *IDC v Cooley*, above n 85) or the company may have gone into winding up so as to permit action by or on behalf of creditors (see p 147 above).

Alternatively, it appears the shareholders as a body can initiate litigation against the wrongdoers.[116] However, they may be loath to do this, if the alleged wrongdoers are major shareholders, especially as no ban of voting by interested directors applies when the question is not whether the wrongdoing should be ratified but whether the company should sue to enforce its rights. This gives rise to an issue of majority protection and in particular to the question of the appropriate role of the derivative claim, which I discuss in Chapter 8. However, even if there is no controlling shareholder but rather a large body of dispersed shareholders, it is likely that their collective action problems will prevent effective exercise by the shareholders of their power to initiate litigation. The directors may simply sit quiet, not seeking ratification nor in any other way to put the issue before the shareholders in general meeting. In this situation, the burden of convening a meeting falls on the shareholders and they may not be well placed to discharge, or even to secure the addition of an item to agenda of the annual general meeting. In short, the risk is that, in a substantial number of cases, the company will never give proper consideration to the question whether the wrongdoing directors should be sued, because they control the board and the shareholders' meeting, in practice, does not consider the issue.

An obvious solution to this problem might be thought to be to empower individual shareholders to enforce the company's rights. I discuss this technique in Chapter 8 in the context of minority shareholder protection. Suffice it to say here that, since the full panoply of directors' duties is owed only to the 'company', individual shareholders have no *right* to enforce the company's claims against errant directors and British law has traditionally been cautious in permitting such action (by way of 'derivative' claims). However, the 2006 Act may be producing change in that area.

CONCLUSION

The substantive law of directors' duties maps well onto the principal/agent analysis of the relationship between the board and shareholders, and the shareholders' consequent incentives to reduce their management agency costs. The shareholder-centric formulation of the duties, even with the adoption of 'enlightened shareholder value', means that

---

[116] The common law rule excluding shareholders from bringing derivative claims where the wrongdoers were not in control of the general meeting of the company does not make sense unless the general meeting, in the absence of wrongdoer control, could be safely relied upon to take the litigation decision.

the shareholders are the primary beneficiaries of the duties. However, although the shareholders collectively are the prime beneficiaries of directors' duties, this is not to say that those duties are optimally formulated for the reduction of the shareholders' agency costs. Two opposite criticisms can be made. The first is that, in relation to conflicts of interest, the transposition of duties of loyalty from trustees to directors is over-constraining of directors and will discourage talented persons from taking up directorships, especially non-executive directorships. Whilst there is some force in this argument in relation to the taking of business opportunities, the 2006 Act may operate as a corrective through its apparent abandonment of the 'no profit' rule. More generally, in relation to all the different forms of the conflict-based duties, there is considerable scope for the company and the director to shape the duties so as to mitigate any undue severity—and some protection for directors who inadvertently fall foul of the duties whilst acting honestly and reasonably in section 1157 of the Act. Moreover, enforcement of the duties has traditionally been weak so that the impact in practice of the duties is much less than the severity of their substantive formulation might suggest.

The opposite criticism is sometimes advanced of the non-conflict-based duties (care, promotion of the success of the company, duty to remain within powers) ie that they impose rather limited constraints on the exercise by directors of their discretionary powers. This is probably traditionally true, but understandable in the light of the courts' worries as to whether they can make better decisions than boards. An important question for the future will be whether the courts will maintain their deference to boards' decision-making in relation to the objective standard of care promoted by the 2006 Act.

7

Centralized Management III
Setting the Board's Incentives

In this chapter we conclude our analysis of the legal strategies available to reduce the agency costs as between shareholders and the board in large companies with no controlling shareholder. In the previous chapter we considered the strategy of constraining agent decisions through the use of liability rules of one sort or another (brought together under the heading of 'directors' duties'), a development to which, as we saw, company law has devoted considerable attention over the years. In this chapter we analyse further uses of one of the strategies we considered in the previous chapter, namely that of 'Setting Agent Incentives' in particular through use of the trusteeship strategy.[1] Of course, in a broad sense the duties considered in the previous chapter set incentives for directors. For example, the prospect of liability, so far as it exists, will give directors an incentive to abide by the law relating to directors' duties. However, what we cover in this chapter are those incentives, provided by the law, which encourage directors to act in the best interests of the shareholders, whether or not any legal sanctions are attached to their not so doing. With this strategy, the interests of the shareholders are internalized, so to speak, by the directors, not imposed on directors from outside, by way of the threat of legal sanctions.

The incentive setting strategy takes two, very different, forms. It may operate negatively, by reducing or removing the self-interest of the directors, so that the competition between that self-interest and the interests of the shareholders is mitigated or even eliminated. This we have called 'trusteeship'. We saw one example of this in the previous chapter where the non-involved members of the board can sometimes authorize breaches of duty by a director. We now consider uses of that strategy outside the area of directors' duties. Alternatively, the self-interest of the directors may be given free reign, but the shareholders benefit from this

---

[1] See Figure 1 above p 113.

because that self-interest is aligned with the interests of the shareholders. By benefiting themselves the directors benefit the shareholders. This is the rewards strategy. As applied to any one director, these strategies are mutually exclusive, though both could be, and normally are, applied to the board, non-executive directors being subject to the former and executive directors to the latter strategy. We shall look at each strategy in turn.

TRUSTEESHIP AND NON-EXECUTIVE DIRECTORS

THE NATURE OF 'TRUSTEESHIP' ON THE BOARD

The 'trusteeship' strategy has been a central element of the reforms which have resulted from the modern 'corporate governance' debate.[2] These reforms are based on the insight that the most powerful incentives to self-interested behaviour on the part of directors stem, not so much from holding a directorship, but from holding a directorship in conjunction with a full-time executive position in the company as a senior manager, especially as CEO. Such a person not only has an obvious interest in raising his or her reward package to the highest levels possible, but also may be able to exercise his managerial powers in a wide variety of other ways so as to confer private benefits which do not advance the interests of the shareholders. A trivial example might be the private or doubtfully business-related use of a private jet; a more serious one the diversion of corporate opportunities from the company. However, the distorting private interests of full-time executive directors may not be primarily financial. A leadership position in a large company gives frequent opportunities for the exercise of power or for public display, which do not clearly advance the interests of the shareholders. A dominant chief executive may wish, for example, to launch a takeover offer which will expand her business empire, but, because she overpays for the target company, the profitability of the combined enterprise suffers. Or she may give lavish support from the company's coffers for a sport which she personally enjoys, even where market research suggests that equally effective promotion of the company's image could be obtained much more cheaply by other means.

So long as the company is a going concern, it may be difficult to demonstrate from outside that the company could have been run differently and better from the point of view of the shareholders. Indeed, some

---

[2] Above Ch 5.

non-shareholder stakeholders in the company may benefit from a partial setting aside of the shareholders' interests, as where the enlarged company increases employment. However, in the late 1980s a number of sudden corporate failures occurred which seemed to be in part attributable to the CEO of the company being insufficiently accountable to his or her board of directors, those collapses hitting hard at the interests of all the stakeholders in the company and not just the shareholders. The remedy, it was proposed, was to increase the number of, and the importance of the roles performed by, non-executive directors (NEDs) and, in particular, by *independent* NEDs, ie those not otherwise currently or recently connected with the company. Such directors have only their directorships and thus no managerial positions in the company; are part-time and so their lives are not wholly bound up in the company; and are modestly remunerated, at least by corporate standards.

Whilst one may accept that such directors are not subject to the high-powered incentives of executive directors to put self-interest above shareholder interest, one might wonder what incentives they have to act as a check on those directors who are subject to the high-powered incentives of self-interest. The answer which is given is that they are motivated by low-powered reputational incentives to do a good job of controlling headstrong executive directors. Those seen to have acted as effective non-executives will enjoy the public esteem of being so regarded and, of course, will be more in demand in this role for other companies. It has to be said that, at present, the jury is still out on the empirical question of whether low-powered reputational incentives can act as an effective counterweight to self-interested executives or whether even well-motivated non-executive directors have sufficient knowledge of and power within the company to challenge dominant executives except in rather clear cases.[3]

The problem was pointed up some time ago by Professors Gilson and Kraakman,[4] writing from a US perspective, where the drive for

---

[3] Thus, in the wake of the recent financial crisis a government-commissioned review of corporate governance in banks and other financial institutions ('BOFIs') put down the losses suffered by BOFIs in significant part to failures by the non-executive directors to spot the risks BOFIs were running, and it proposed in consequence enhanced corporate governance rules for the boards of BOFIs. However, it is far from clear that the independent directors could realistically have spotted risks not seen by the executive directors or could easily have changed the executives' assessment of the risks which were identified, still less that they would have been thanked by the shareholders for so doing when the activities appeared at the time to be so profitable. See HM Treasury, *A Review of Corporate Governance in Banks and Other Financial Entities* (the Walker Review) (November 2009), chs 2–4.

[4] R Gilson and R Kraakman, 'Reinventing the Outside Director: An Agenda for Institutional Investors' (1991) 43 *Stanford Law Review* 863.

non-executive directors has been taken much further, to the point where they usually constitute the overwhelming majority of members of the board.[5] They suggest that the crucial step is not to make the non-executives independent of the management but dependent upon the shareholders, ie that the appointments rights strategy is likely to be more effective than the trusteeship strategy. On the supply side, this would involve creating a cadre of persons whose activities as directors would consist only of being non-executive directors of companies (though they would probably have other non-directorial but business-related activities as well). On the demand side, institutional investors would involve themselves in appointing and liaising with such non-executive directors. In the UK, however, the Cadbury Committee (see below) rejected a proposal for closer shareholder involvement in the selection of non-executives, probably because it did not want to alienate management from its proposals, but it is less clear why institutional investors have not pressed for it. The answer may be found in the conflicts of interest which face institutional investors or, more likely, in their unwillingness to accept the legal and, more important, the political risks associated with appearing to become the monitors of British industry.[6]

THE ORIGINS OF THE CORPORATE GOVERNANCE CODE

Although the appropriate role for NEDs on the board has been much discussed publicly in recent years, this debate has had very little impact on the companies legislation. As far as the Act is concerned, it is perfectly proper for all the directors to be executives or non-independent. Unlike many, perhaps most, other comparable systems of corporate law, British company law says virtually nothing about the structure or composition of the board. When the modern corporate governance debate was launched in the UK in the early 1990s, that occurred through a business initiative, albeit with governmental support, rather than within the civil service. It seems that the government thought the whole issue too much of a 'hot potato' for legislation, but wanted to have some influence on how this important public policy matter was handled. The result was

---

[5] See D DeMott, 'The Figures in the Landscape: A Comparative Sketch of Directors' Self-Interested Transactions' (1999) 3 *Company, Financial and Insolvency Law Review* 190, 194: the average US board had 'two "inside" (or executive) directors and nine "outside" directors'.

[6] However, as the recent economic crisis shows, it may not be possible for institutional shareholders to avoid this responsibility, whether or not they seek to make non-executive directors dependent on them. See above Ch 5 at p 136.

business-sponsored committees, but serviced by civil servants. The public policy arguments in favour of NEDs will always be associated with the Report of the Cadbury Committee.[7] That Committee set out the basic arguments in favour of increasing the number and importance of NEDs. Its ideas were refined, though not fundamentally altered, during the 1990s by the subsequent Greenbury[8] and Hampel[9] Committee reports. There were then two further significant crisis-driven reviews. The first came in the wake of the Enron and associated scandals in the United States early in the new millennium. This generated the Higgs Committee,[10] which had a significant impact in terms of increasing the stringency of the initial Cadbury recommendations. The recommended proportion of independent directors on the board was increased from one-third to one-half; their role on crucial board committees (nomination, remuneration, and audit) was enhanced; and more emphasis was placed on the role of the chair of the board (as a countervailing force to the CEO) and of the senior independent director. It was the first review committee formally to be established by government.[11] The second significant review of this century came in the wake of the recent economic crisis and it emphasized further the role of the chair of the board but it also emphasized the importance of board behaviour (as well as composition), that is, the need for non-executives to have an independent character as well as independence in the largely negative sense of not being beholden to others.[12]

Because these Committees, at least initially, were private-sector initiatives, their output was not legislation but codes of practice, which have been brought together in a single Code, now referred to as 'the UK Corporate Governance Code'.[13] However, with the new Stewardship Code,[14] the Code is not entirely lacking in binding force as far as publicly traded companies are concerned. Companies, whether incorporated in

---

[7] *The Financial Aspects of Corporate Governance* (London: Gee, 1992).

[8] *Report of the Study Group on Directors' Remuneration* (London: Gee, 1995).

[9] *Final Report of the Committee on Corporate Governance* (London: Gee, 1998).

[10] DTI, *Review of the Role and Effectiveness of Non-executive Directors* (January 2003).

[11] See P Davies, 'Enron and Corporate Governance Reforms in the UK and the European Community', in J Armour and J McCahery (eds), *After Enron* (Oxford: Hart Publishing, 2006).

[12] Financial Reporting Council, *2009 Review of the Combined Code: Final Report* (December 2009). The FRC, a statutorily recognized but largely privately funded body, now has charge of keeping the Code under review. It regularly reviews it. More fundamental changes have been proposed by the Walker Review for the corporate governance of banks etc. See n 3 above.

[13] References are to the 2010 version of the Code. Previously, it was referred to as the 'Combined Code' because it was the joint product of the Cadbury, Greenbury, and Hampel Committees, and before that—and often still today—simply as the 'Cadbury Code'.

[14] Above p 137.

the UK or elsewhere, with a 'premium' listing[15] of equity shares in the UK are required to state in their annual report to shareholders how they have complied with the Main Principles of the Code and whether they have complied with the Provisions of the Code, explaining any examples of non-compliance ('comply or explain').[16] The 'Main Principles' are stated at such a high level of abstraction that non-compliance with them is hardly an issue. The 'Provisions' are more detailed and it is there that the flexibility of the 'comply or explain' approach is relevant. In an attempt to encourage greater use of the flexibility inherent in 'comply or explain' the Financial Reporting Council puts the relationship between Principles and Provisions in the following way: 'The provisions describe one route by which the principles might be met, but not the only route.'[17]

The argument for applying the Code only to companies with a 'listing' is largely pragmatic, namely that such listing happens to identify the subset of public companies for which the Code rules are appropriate. The CLR largely accepted this argument, though it proposed to extend the Code to all companies whose securities are publicly traded.[18] This has not happened so that the Code applies only to a subset of publicly traded ones (albeit the most economically important).

THE CONTENT OF THE CORPORATE GOVERNANCE CODE

What, concretely, does the UK Corporate Governance Code[19] require in the way of board structure? Its requirements can be summarized as follows:

- The board has a dual function, both to 'lead' and to 'control' the company.

  The board's role is to provide entrepreneurial leadership of the company within a framework of prudent and effective controls which enables risk to be assessed and managed. The board should set the company's strategic aims, ensure that

---

[15] This is the top level of listing. Since it is open to companies to choose 'Standard' listing instead, there is a double sense in which the Corporate Governance Code is not binding. In effect, companies choose 'premium' listing in order to obtain the reputational enhancement of compliance with higher standards.

[16] Listing Rules 9.8.6(5). There are also 'Supporting Principles', in relation to which the LR are unclear about the company's obligations.   [17] FRC, above n 12, 2.8.

[18] CLR, *Completing the Structure* (November 2000), para 4.44. The essence of the present restriction is that the Code applies to companies with the relevant level of listing on the Main Market of the London Stock Exchange but does not apply to companies listed on junior markets, such as the Alternative Investment Market (AIM), which is also run by the LSE but for which the admission requirements are less demanding than those for the Main Market.

[19] It is most conveniently available on the website of the FRC: <http://www.frc.org.uk/>.

the necessary financial and human resources are in place for the company to meet its objectives and review management performance.[20]

- Except in small listed companies, at least one-half of the board, excluding the chair, should be independent NEDs, but there should be an 'appropriate combination' of both NEDs and executives on the board.[21] This was the major change made by the Higgs Report, but the latest version of the Code somewhat softens the approach by emphasizing that the Principle in question is that the board should 'consist of directors with the appropriate balance of skills, experience, independence and knowledge of the company to enable it to discharge its duties and responsibilities'.[22] The 'one-half' recommendation is seen as promoting, but as not being the only way of achieving, this goal.

- Independence is to be assessed by the board itself and the names of those so characterized disclosed. The board is required to explain its characterization of a director as independent if that director has (or had) certain types of relationship with the company (such as an employment relationship within the previous five years, a material business relationship within the previous three, a relationship from which the director derives remuneration other than the directors' fee, if the director acts as the representative of a significant shareholder), but even if no such relationship exists the board must ensure that independent directors are 'independent in character and judgement'.[23]

- As with the board as a whole the NEDs have a role both in setting the company's strategy ('leading') and 'controlling' it. The strategy-setting role, however, is emphasized in Principle A.4 (NEDs should 'constructively challenge and help develop proposals on strategy'), whilst the monitoring role is mentioned in the Supporting Principle. In the case of the non-executive directors, the Supporting Principle makes it clear that 'controlling' includes monitoring the performance of the company's executive directors and—especially important in the light of recent events—ensuring that 'financial controls and systems of risk management are robust and defensible'.

---

[20] Code A.1 Supporting Principle.
[21] Code B.1 Supporting Principle and Provision B.1.2. A typical FTSE 350 board consists of five non-executives and three executives.   [22] Code Principle B.1.
[23] Provision B.1.1.

- There should be committees of the board to deal with certain matters likely to generate high-powered conflicts of interest for the executive directors, on which independent NEDs should be the only or the majority of the members. These are the audit,[24] remuneration,[25] and nomination[26] committees (but there is no requirement for a separate 'risk' committee, unlike in the banking area under the FSA's rules).

- There should be a formal statement of the matters on which the board's decision is necessary.[27]

- NEDs should have access to appropriate outside professional advice and to internal information from the company[28] and should themselves be in a position to make adequate commitments of time to the company.[29]

- A theme of both the post-2000 reviews has been an increasing emphasis on the role of the chair of the board as a counterweight to the CEO. 'There should be a clear division of responsibilities at the head of the company between the running of the board and the executive responsibility for the running of the company's business. No one individual should have unfettered powers of decision.'[30] It follows that these two roles should not be performed by the same person, and the independence criteria (above) indicate that a retiring CEO should not go on to be chair of the board.[31] This is a prohibition to which retiring CEOs are sometimes reluctant to conform. In a nod towards this fact, the Code states that where, exceptionally, the CEO does go on to be chair of the board, 'the board should consult major shareholders in advance and should set out its reasons to shareholders at the time of the appointment and in the next annual report.'[32] The division of responsibilities between

---

[24] Code C.3. Entirely independent. Monitors relationship with the external auditors and the company's internal audit function, and also the company's internal risk controls, unless that is done by another committee of independent NEDs or the board as a whole.

[25] Provision D.2.1. Entirely independent, but the chair, if independent on appointment, may also be a member. The remuneration committee's role is considered further below in this chapter.

[26] Ibid B.2.1. Majority independent. Responsible for making recommendations to the board on new appointments.   [27] Ibid A.1.1.

[28] Main Principle B.5.   [29] Ibid B.3.   [30] Ibid A.2.

[31] Provisions A.2.1 and A.3.1. The chair is expected to be independent on appointment, though it is recognized that, such is the depth of their involvement in the company thereafter, they are not expected to continue to meet the independence criteria.

[32] Ibid A.3.1. The strong emphasis of the separation of the role of the chair and the CEO is one of the major differences between British and US corporate governance recommendations. However, in the US, where separation is not required, it is also the case that the executive

the chair and the CEO is to be set out in writing and agreed by the board.[33] The chair is responsible for the leadership of the board and ensuring its effective operation.[34]

• Another innovation of the Higgs report was special mention of a 'senior non-executive director'. Partly, he or she is to be a crisis-manager, that is, to provide a conduit between the other NEDs and the chair or between the shareholders and the chair/CEO when the direct and normal methods of communication have broken down for some reason. The senior NED should also lead one meeting a year at which neither executives nor chair are present, in order to appraise the chair's performance in that role.[35]

This account of the requirements of the Code in the area of board structure makes clear the importance of the 'trusteeship' strategy in its approach to this issue. Independent NEDs are to be a significant part of the board as a whole and dominant on the committees where the conflicts of interest of the executive directors might be expected to be most prominent: the remuneration, audit, and appointment committees. Further, the chair of the board, who must be independent on appointment and probably remains in fact less subject to high-powered conflicts of interest thereafter, acts as a counterweight to the CEO.

THE IMPACT OF THE CODE IN PRACTICE

It is more than usually difficult to assess levels of compliance with the Code. This is because, as we have stated, the Code is a set of 'best practice' recommendations. The only 'hard' obligation which applies to the company is that set out in the Listing Rules, that is, to explain how the company has complied with the Code's Main Principles and to disclose how far it has complied with the Provisions of the Code, explaining areas of non-compliance. Thus, non-compliance with one, or even several, Code Provisions is not a ground for criticism of the company, provided it explains the non-compliance and provided it still can show compliance with the Main Principles. Indeed, perhaps the main purpose of the flexibility in relation to the Provisions is to enable the company *better* to achieve the goals of the Main Principles by departing from certain of the

directors form a much smaller proportion of the board than in a typical British company. See n 5 above. The chair of the board is not even mentioned in the New York Stock Exchange's provisions on corporate governance.

[33] Ibid A.2.1.   [34] Main Principle A.3.   [35] Code Provision A.4.1–3.

Provisions. Whether departure from the Provisions is a sound step for any particular company to take is to be judged by its shareholders, who, if they think differently, may respond by selling their shares or seeking to exercise their governance rights. However, even an ill-judged departure from the Provisions involves no breach of a rule by the company, provided the departure is fully explained.

In short, compliance with the Listing Rules is mandatory; compliance with the Code Provisions is not. Consequently, non-compliance with the Provisions cannot by itself be a criticism of companies covered by the Code. For this reason, it has been suggested that the principle underlying the Code should be 'apply or explain' rather than 'comply or explain', but the latter phrase seems too established now to be discarded.[36] However, one can reasonably ask about companies' compliance with the obligation in the Listing Rules. This is not a straightforward exercise either, because it is necessary to identify not merely departures from the Provisions which are not explained but also departures which are inadequately explained. A study covering the period 1998 to 2004 showed that over this period as a whole companies chose on average not to follow 1.57 of the eight Code recommendations studied but provided, in the authors' assessment, adequate explanations for their conduct only in relation to 1.38 of the recommendations not followed, thus leaving a group of unexplained departures and, arguably, breaches of the Listing Rules.[37] The FRC's 2009 review of the Code accepted that 'investors remain concerned in particular about the quality of explanations provided by companies that do not comply with one or more of the Code provisions' but did not propose a more active enforcement role for either itself or the FSA.[38] This seems difficult to justify, since effective engagement by shareholders with management over corporate governance is likely to be less productive if adequate explanations are not given. More positively for the Code, research by the same authors found that 'companies that depart from governance best practice because of genuine circumstances outperform all others and cannot be considered badly-governed at all', thus providing powerful support for the 'comply or explain' approach.[39]

[36]   FRC, above n 12, paras 3.90–3.92.
[37]   S Arcot and V Bruno, 'In Letter but not in Spirit: An Analysis of Corporate Governance in the UK' (May 2006), Table 7. Available at SSRN: <http://ssrn.com/abstract=819784>.
[38]   Above n 12 at paras 3.65–3.68.
[39]   S Arcot and V Bruno, 'One Size Does Not Fit All, After All: Evidence from Corporate Governance' (15 January 2007). Available at SSRN: <http://ssrn.com/abstract=887947>.

Turning to companies' choices whether to depart from the Code's provisions, these display a fairly high level of acceptance of the Code's recommendations, though, as noted, the separation of the positions of CEO and chair of the board has often been controversial[40] and choices in favour of the Code are less strong among the smallest listed companies. Slightly fewer than half the companies covered claim compliance with all the recommendations of the Code and non-compliance does not usually reach beyond two Code recommendations.[41] This level of compliance seems to have been in large part due to the support given to the Code by the institutional investors.

THE CODE AND TWO-TIER BOARDS

The effect of implementing a trusteeship strategy on the board is to distinguish firmly between executive and non-executive board members. Besides the participation of the NEDs in the board tasks of setting and monitoring the execution of the company's business strategy, the NEDs have a role of monitoring the performance of the executive directors and the senior non-board managers of the company. In execution of strategy the executive directors will take the lead, and even in its formulation the executive directors, especially the CEO, will be prominent. The non-executives are thus potentially in an uncomfortable position: they are both responsible for the company's business strategy (with the executive directors) and responsible (against the executive directors) for assessing the performance of the executives in setting and implementing that strategy. This might be thought to be an argument in favour of institutionalizing the two functions, by creating a supervisory board (consisting wholly of non-executives) and a management board (consisting of executives). However, those leading the corporate governance reviews in the UK have uniformly shown antipathy to the idea of adopting a two-tier board system. Moreover, it can be argued that the discomfort of the non-executives on a unitary board is a price worth paying for the better access to information which membership of the single board gives to the non-executives.

---

[40] At the end of 2000 it was said that 20 or more companies among the 350 largest listed companies had the same person as CEO and chair of the board, including Marks & Spencer and Powergen: *Financial Times*, 10 October 2000.

[41] Grant Thornton, *Moving Beyond Compliance: Embracing the Spirit of the Code* (February 2010). The two most commonly missed recommendations were the one-half requirement for independent NEDs throughout the year (because of unexpected departures during the year) and the failure to have a person with appropriate financial experience on the audit committee.

Nevertheless, British company law does not prohibit the creation, de facto, of a two-tier board and the CLR found evidence that some large companies were creating informal management boards beneath the formal board on which the non-executives were represented.[42]

NEDs AND DISINTERESTED DIRECTORS

There is one final, but important, issue to be considered here, which is the interrelationship between independent NEDs and the exclusion of 'interested' directors from voting on the board resolution to approve the taking of corporate opportunities etc by directors , as discussed in Chapter 6.[43] The two things are clearly not the same. For the purposes of authorization of a breach of duty, a director is excluded from voting if he or she is the director whose proposed breach of duty is to be approved or is another director interested in that opportunity.[44] The excluded director might be an executive or a non-executive director of the company, and be independent or not independent—and, more important, so might the authorizing directors fall into any of those categories. Thus, an independent NED might be an 'interested' director, as where it is he or she who has come across and wishes to exploit personally the opportunity in which the company has a legitimate interest. Equally, an executive director who is not involved in the proposed exploitation of the opportunity is not 'interested' as far as the law on directors' duties is concerned.

Nevertheless, the theory underlying the Code's recommendations on NEDs and the Act's use of disinterested directors seems similar: in both cases decision-making is said to be transferred to a sub-group of directors who, it is hoped, are not tempted to prioritize self-interest over the interests of the shareholders. In the narrow sense of interest in the particular decision in mind, the argument is undoubtedly right. However, as with independent NEDs, so also with disinterested directors, it is less clear that they are free of self-interest when the broader decision-making context is examined. Just as independent NEDs may have an interest in high levels of executive remuneration because they are executive directors of other companies (see below), disinterested directors may support a

---

[42] CLR, *Developing the Framework* (March 2000), para 3.152: 'the practice of delegating day to day management and major operational questions to a "management board" is becoming increasingly common in this country.' And it adds: 'It is, of course, perfectly legal and gives many of the advantages of the two-tier board.'   [43] Above pp 174–6.
[44] s 175(6).

relaxed attitude to board approval of the taking of corporate opportunities because they may benefit from that policy in the future when they are the interested directors.

THE REWARD STRATEGY AND EXECUTIVE REMUNERATION

The reward strategy has an entirely different point of departure from the trusteeship strategy. The self-interest of the executive director is here accepted as a powerful motivator of his or her behaviour, but the attempt is made to align that self-interest with the interests of the shareholders. Normally, this is done by tying a significant part of the executive director's earnings from the company to the advancement of the shareholders' interest. In principle, this strategy has potential, not least because it does not need an elaborate legal framework for its implementation. The incentives for the directors are normally embodied in a contract between him or her and the company. The strategy suffers, however, from two drawbacks.

The first is the difficulty of identifying an appropriate indicator of the shareholders' welfare to which the directors' remuneration can be attached. A traditional mechanism is the share option scheme, whereby the director is given an option to subscribe for a certain number of shares in the company at some point in the future (normally three years or more) at the market price prevailing at the time the option is granted. If over the three-year period the shares do well, the director will exercise his or her option at the relevant time, probably sell the shares immediately and pocket the difference between the option price and the market price prevailing when the option is exercised. It is said that the shareholders should be pleased about this because their shares will have increased in value over the period as well.

However, a thoughtful shareholder might wonder about this argument. If the market for shares as a whole increases in value over the period in question, because it is a period of economic boom, the value added to the company's shares might not be attributable at all to the efforts of the directors, so that it is unclear why they should be especially rewarded for it. Equally troubling to the thoughtful shareholder may be the insight that, if over the period the market as a whole declines, the directors will receive no reward, even though they have worked especially hard and have taken some astute business decisions. Of course, there are ways around this problem. The rewards of the directors may be attached to the relative performance of their company as against appropriate comparator companies, so that the directors are rewarded if they do better than the comparators, whether the market as a whole is going up or down. Such schemes may involve a move away from share options towards other forms of long-term incentive plans ('ltips'). Considerable ingenuity has been devoted by the business schools and by remuneration consultants to the invention of appropriate schemes. However the ltip is structured, there is a risk that it will generate an incentive for senior management to maximize (even manipulate) the figures on which the incentive plan turns at the particular point in time at which it matures, and it may be only coincidental if this leads to a maximization of the welfare of the shareholders over any longer period.

The second disadvantage takes us back to territory we have already covered in Chapter 6, that of conflicts of interest. In the past, executive directors have had a considerable input into the design of their own remuneration packages. Whilst the traditional arrangement (as seen, for example, in the model articles in their 1985 version) was that directors' fees required shareholder approval, the remuneration paid to directors for the discharge of managerial functions was in the hands of the board as a whole, which therefore set the primary sources of the remuneration (executive salaries, annual bonuses, long-term incentives) of executive directors.[45] Although the current model articles are less explicit on the point, it seems that, in principle, the board still fixes the executives' remuneration as a result of the general grant of authority to the board and their power to delegate their functions to others 'on such terms and conditions as they think fit'.[46] This arrangement thus created a very high-powered conflict of interest on the board, even if, as usually was the case, any particular executive director was excluded from voting on his or her own remuneration package. Very few groups in society are in a position to set their own pay.[47]

This conflict of interest over directors' remuneration, which has long been present, was exacerbated by the move towards greater reliance on performance-related pay to align directors' interests with those of the

---

[45] Table A 1985, art 84.

[46] Model Articles for public companies, arts 3 and 5. The reticence of the current model is probably due to the need for certain listed companies to comply with the Corporate Governance Code's provisions on remuneration committees, discussed below. Art 19 of the current model facilitates adjustment to what the Code requires by permitting the directors, subject to the articles, to 'make any rule which they think fit about how they take decisions'.

[47] For a trenchant critique see L Bebchuk and J Fried, *Pay without Performance* (Cambridge, Mass.: Harvard University Press, 2004).

shareholders. The performance-related elements were capable of sub-stantially enhancing the value of directors' remuneration packages, but was the extra pay in fact a reward for better performance? The crucial factor, for distinguishing whether performance-related pay achieves its ostensible goal effectively or is simply a mechanism whereby the executive director extracts an even higher level of remuneration from the company than is represented by his salary and other benefits, is to be found in the rigour of the performance criteria which trigger the reward. The Code commits itself to the value of performance-related pay ('A significant proportion of executive directors' remuneration should be structured so as to link rewards to corporate and individual performance')[48] but also to the need for demanding criteria for deter-mining pay-outs ('The performance-related elements of executive directors' remuneration should be stretching and designed to promote the long-term success of the company').[49] It is easier to state this prin-ciple than to ensure that it is applied in practice. The financial press has long contained complaints from institutional shareholders that a number of companies have adopted performance-related pay with undemanding performance criteria, whilst the general press has com-plained that much directorial pay is too high, even if it is performance related. More recently, the Walker Review has blamed remuneration systems in banks for encouraging reckless risk-taking by executives and senior employees which, it is said, led to the collapse or near-insolvency of those institutions.[50]

The cumulative effect of these pressures was to cause government and others to devote more attention to the regulatory structure for setting directors' remuneration in general (and not just its performance-related elements, though those have remained the most controversial). Over the years, a range of techniques has been deployed to address these concerns, some of these techniques being found in the Act, others in the Code, and yet others in the Listing Rules. The main idea underlying them, how-ever, is the notion that the setting of remuneration packages should be

---

[48] Main Principle D.1.   [49] Supporting Principle D.1.

[50] Above n 3 ch 7. Of course, even if pay is closely linked to performance, this does not fully answer the question of how much executives should be paid. Salary may be linked to demanding performance targets but should the amount achievable by good performance be £100,000, £1 million, or £10m or even more? The distributional question cannot thus be made to disappear through the 'pay-for-performance' mantra. The point is current since it seems the CEOs of Britain's largest 100 companies were paid 81 times the average pay of full-time workers in 2009, up from 47 times in 2000 (*Financial Times*, 3 April 2010, p 9). And see J Gordon, 'Executive Compensation: If There's a Problem, What's the Remedy' (2004–5) 30 *Journal of Corporation Law* 675.

taken out of the hands of the board as a whole and in particular out of the hands of the executive directors, whose conflict of interest in the matter is obvious, and be lodged in the hands of the non-executive directors, the shareholders, or, more recently, at least in relation to financial companies, a regulator.

REMUNERATION COMMITTEES

It is not surprising to find that the Corporate Governance Code puts its faith very much in non-executive directors as the solution to the remuneration problem, for this technique fits well with its general view that non-executive directors have an important role to play in corporate governance. As we have noted already, the Code requires the companies it covers to establish a remuneration committee consisting of independent NEDs and, usually, the chair of the board. That committee should set the remuneration of the executive directors and the chair (*not* simply make recommendations to the full board) and it should recommend to the board the remuneration levels for senior management immediately below board level.[51] The Code provides some guidance on the setting of the performance-related elements of the remuneration package, including a recommendation that variable compensation should be reclaimable 'in exceptional circumstances of misstatement or misconduct'.[52] It also deals with the desirability of avoiding the payment of excessive compensation when a director is removed during his or her term of office, the so-called 'rewards for failure' issue.[53] This latter could be regarded as a perversion of the reward strategy (ie rewarding failure rather than success) but it should be remembered that from an ex ante perspective a 'golden parachute' may induce a person to take on a major but risky role in a company which is in difficulties and which needs to be turned around. Without the parachute, the person to be appointed may simply require an even higher basic salary, which might turn out to be more expensive for the shareholders in the event.

The impact of the remuneration committees, by themselves, has been muted, though they may be more significant when combined with greater shareholder 'say on pay', as discussed below. If the test in this area is the exertion of a downward pressure on executive salaries, achievements since remuneration committees were introduced in the 1990s[54] have been modest. If anything, the Code seems to have been associated with the upward rise of remuneration packages. The explanation for this state of

---

[51] Provision D.2.2.   [52] Schedule A.   [53] Provisions D.1.4–5.
[54] Notably after the Report of the Greenbury Committee in 1995 (above n 8).

affairs may be that the main source of non-executive directors is executive directors of other companies. Although independent of the company of which they are non-executives, they are likely to share a 'high compensation' culture with the executives of that company because of their executive positions elsewhere. This analysis, if it is correct, indicates the problems with implementing a trusteeship strategy, ie the difficulty of finding non-executive directors who are both effective (which will necessarily involve business experience) and free across the whole range of issues from the self-interest to which the executive directors are prone.

SHAREHOLDER 'SAY ON PAY'

Where a policy-maker has concluded that the board, or some subset of its members, has proved inadequate as a decision-maker on a certain topic, the conventional next move within company law is to give that decision to the shareholders, notwithstanding the potential costs involved in shareholder decision-making. This is the development we have seen in relation to directors' remuneration, which culminated in a statutory reform of 2002 putting the remuneration package of executive directors of 'quoted' companies[55] to an advisory vote of the shareholders at the annual general meeting.[56] However, even before that, certain elements of the remuneration package had been (and still are) subject to an approval vote of the shareholders, not originally because of concerns relating to the overall level of remuneration of directors but for more targeted reasons. We look first at those areas where shareholder approval is required.

As we saw in Chapter 6, the general rule for self-dealing transactions is disclosure to the board,[57] but in certain cases the statute restores the common law principle of approval by the shareholders because of the abusive potential of the particular form of self-dealing. Two of those instances relate to directors' remuneration.[58] A directors' service contract, whose effective term is longer than two years, requires shareholder approval.[59] Without it the contract is deemed to be terminable at any time

---

[55] This means mainly companies listed on the Main Market of the London Stock Exchange, though it also covers UK-incorporated companies listed on equivalent exchanges anywhere in the European Economic Area or on the New York Stock Exchange or NASDAQ: s 385.

[56] Now ss 439–40 of the 2006 Act.

[57] s 177. In fact, in most cases the board will be treated as knowing about the terms of the directors' actual or proposed service contract without those that have to be disclosed by the director in question. See s 177(6)(b)(c).

[58] The rules on loans etc to directors dealt with in Chapter 6 at p 172 could also be relevant here as constituting a form of disguised remuneration.

[59] ss 188–9. Before 2006 the period was five years. The provision was introduced by the Companies Act 1980, s 47, because it was thought that very long service contracts were

on reasonable notice, despite the term to the contrary. This provision directly relates to the 'rewards for failure' debate. However, in the case of companies covered by the Corporate Governance Code, the recommendation is that notice periods should be no more than one year, except in the case of 'new hires' who may initially be given longer contracts.[60]

Second, the Act requires shareholder approval for payments to dismissed directors by way of compensation for loss of office, including loss of executive positions in the company.[61] These provisions extend to payments by third parties where the dismissal occurs in connection with a sale of corporate assets (ie payments by the purchaser) or the acquisition of shares in the company (payments by the acquirer), perhaps via a takeover bid. Non-approved payments are void and are held in trust by the receiving director, normally for his or her company, but in the case of share acquisition for the selling shareholders.[62] These provisions, too, are relevant to the 'rewards for failure' debate, but it should be noted that they catch payments made by an acquirer to the former directors of the acquirer's new subsidiary, even where the directors of the target have done a good job of negotiating a high price for the former shareholders on the sale of their shares to the acquirer. The risk of the directors short-changing the shareholders in order to obtain a reward from the acquirer could be said to justify the approval rule for 'golden parachutes'.

However, whether applied to payments by the company on a simple dismissal of an unsatisfactory executive director or to payments by an acquirer of the company's share capital, the sections are, with one exception, limited to gratuitous payments. Contractual payments (or payments by way of compensation for breach of contract) are not caught, thus giving directors an incentive to agree substantial severance payments in advance with their companies. The exception arises where the contractual entitlement was negotiated in the face of the events giving rise to the removal.[63]

These two sets of Companies Act provisions, which apply to all companies incorporated under the companies legislation and which pre-date the current debate on directors' remuneration,[64] are supplemented by Listing Rules provisions, applying only to UK companies with a premium listing

---

becoming a way of chilling the use by shareholders of the power to remove directors (now s 168).

[60] Provision D.1.5. [61] ss 215–26.

[62] s 222. The assumption in the share sale case is that the acquirer would have paid more to the selling shareholders if the payment had not been made to the director.

[63] s 220(2). On the other hand, pension payments are exempted from the approval requirement, even if gratuitous, provided made in good faith: s 220(1)(d).

[64] The loss of office provisions go back at least to s 150 of the Companies Act 1929.

on the London Stock Exchange. These require shareholder approval of any share option scheme (if the option is exercisable at less than the then prevailing market price) or long-term incentive scheme, unless, in either case, the arrangement is open on similar terms to all the employees of the company.[65] It is the scheme which needs approval, rather than particular grants made under it to individual directors. The requirement arose originally in relation to share option schemes and was driven by concerns about dilution of non-director shareholders, rather than by worries about overall levels of remuneration. It was extended to ltips in the wake of the Greenbury Committee's report, thus moving its rationale in the direction of the control of performance-related remuneration.[66]

Of these three specific controls, the Listing Rule requirement for shareholder approval of ltips is the most important for large companies. Removal of directors before the end of their term is necessarily an episodic event and in most cases the contract will provide more than adequate compensation for the departing director. Whilst term provisions of some sort are necessary in any service contract for a director, the fact that the Corporate Governance Code recommends a maximum term (one year), which is only half the period at which the statutory shareholder approval requirement bites, suggests the statutory requirement is marginal. However, in the light of the Code's commitment to performance-related pay, most listed companies will have in place long-term incentive plans and will want to modify them from time to time, thus generating repeated requirements for shareholder approval.

Even the Listing Rule requirement, however, demands shareholder approval only when the ltip is proposed or later amended, not for specific grants under the plan. The general statutory shareholder approval mechanism, introduced in 2002, by contrast, generates an annual vote on the whole of the directors' remuneration package. That vote is both mandatory and advisory. On the mandatory side, it is a vote which must be held,[67] so that shareholders in quoted companies are given, without organizational effort on their part, an opportunity to vote on the issue. Moreover, it is a vote which is informed by a Directors' Remuneration Report (DRR) which the directors of quoted companies must produce and circulate to shareholders with the annual financial statements.[68]

---

[65] LR 9.4. Companies can choose to have a premium or a standard listing, the latter involving compliance with minimum standards, increasingly set by EU law, and the former the higher standards which the Listing Rules have traditionally required.

[66] Greenbury Committee, above n 8, paras 6.26 and 6.33.   [67] s 439(1).

[68] ss 420–2. The detail of what is required to be in the DRR is laid out in the Large and Medium-sized Companies and Groups (Accounts and Reports) Regulations 2008/410, Sch 8.

The required resolution is for the approval of the DRR. The DRR must contain information (which is audited) about the payments by way of remuneration (of all types) made to directors in the year in question together with information (which is not audited) about the directors' (or, more accurately, the remuneration committee's) policy approach to the setting of the various elements in the executive directors' pay packages (basic pay, bonuses, long-term incentive schemes, provision for compensation on termination) and some information of a comparative kind designed to show how well (or badly) the company is doing on a comparative basis.

The vote is advisory in the sense that even a defeat for the board on the approval resolution does not render unenforceable any director's contractual rights against the company.[69] However, it would be a brave board which continued with its policy unchanged in the future in the face of an adverse vote. Experience, with both the statutory advisory vote and the Listing Rules' approval requirement, has shown that companies suffer occasional defeats; somewhat more often face public shareholder revolts which are unsuccessful but bring home to the company the force of shareholder opposition; and most often companies anticipating controversial changes in remuneration seek in advance to consult with major shareholders and modify what is proposed, if it does not meet with approval, before a formal motion is put to the shareholders' meeting. What is less clear is whether, overall, the 'say on pay' rules have produced a lower rate of growth in executive pay than would otherwise have been the case or higher levels of alignment between shareholders' and directors' interests.[70]

However, the current state of the law is probably not the final one. In his review of corporate governance in banks Sir David Walker proposed to extend the significance of a substantial, but not majority, vote against the DRR in banks by proposing that a vote against the DRR of more than 25 per cent should have the consequence that the chair of the remuneration committee would have to stand for re-election at the following year's

---

[69] s 439(5)—though clearly director and company could agree that the package be conditional on a favourable vote of the shareholders.

[70] See M Conyon and G Sadler, 'Shareholder Voting and Directors' Remuneration Report Legislation: Say on Pay in the UK' (2009), available at SSRN: <http://ssrn.com/abstract=1457921> and W Alissa, 'Boards' Response to Shareholders' Dissatisfaction: The Case of Shareholders' Say on Pay in the UK' (2009), available at SSRN: <http://ssrn.com/abstract=1412880>. Both papers concentrate on the relationship between voting on DRR resolutions and other outcomes, which may not capture all of the pre-proposal negotiations between company and shareholders.

annual general meeting.[71] As noted in Chapter 5, however, the recommendation in the 2010 Corporate Governance Code that all directors be re-elected annually has somewhat overtaken this suggestion.

REGULATORY APPROVAL

Remuneration has traditionally been regarded as a private matter for companies, or more precisely for shareholders as principals and directors as agents. However, the near or actual collapses of banks and other financial institutions in 2007 and 2008 showed that the interests of other principals were implicated in remuneration systems, namely, the interest of creditors and, in particular, of taxpayers as the ultimate guarantors of the stability of the financial system. A strong theme of the Walker Review[72] was that the remuneration systems, not only for directors but for many senior employees as well, had encouraged excessively risky trading activities whose benefits were taken by those senior employees in the good times but whose losses fell on the taxpayers in bad ones (with the senior employees largely holding onto their gains). The criticism here was not of long-term incentive plans but of short-term bonus schemes, which paid out for immediate past performance even if the deals achieved turned out in the longer term to be loss-making. Following Walker the FSA responded with a Remuneration Code for BOFIs, designed to bring remuneration structures into line with the institution's avowed risk profile. Since it is not clear that shareholders have a strong incentive, at least in the short term, to police compliance with the Remuneration Code, the FSA has taken oversight of its implementation within financial institutions.[73] For the time being, and probably for the long term, this supervisory oversight remains a technique deployed only in relation to banks and other financial companies.

CONCLUSIONS ON BOARD/SHAREHOLDER STRATEGIES

In this chapter and the previous two we have examined the application of the strategies, set out in Figure 1 in Chapter 5, for the regulation of principal/agent problems in general to relations between shareholders

---

[71] Above n 3, paras 7.39–7.42. A proposal to make the vote no longer simply advisory was thought to be 'impractical'. It would certainly put British companies at a disadvantage when seeking to recruit talented directors in a global labour market, because no deal struck would be binding on the company unless later (perhaps quite a lot later) ratified by the shareholders. [72] Ibid, ch 7. [73] FSA, *Senior Management Arrangements, Systems and Controls*, 19.2.

and the board. That figure identified three strategies for empowering shareholders as against directors (the decision rights, appointment rights, and affiliation rights strategies) and two strategies for directly structuring agents' decisions (the constraining and the incentive strategies). What these chapters have shown is that British company law makes use of all five strategies to reduce shareholders' agency costs. This is perhaps not surprising. None of the five strategies is so obviously effective on its own (and all have costs as well as benefits) that it would be wise for the law to put reliance on only one or a small number of them. Is it possible to go beyond the statement that British company law makes some use of all these strategies?

One thing that seems clear is that British company law does not make equal use of all the strategies. At least in terms of the formal statement of the rules, the British system seems more wholeheartedly committed to the appointment rights and affiliation rights strategies (both considered in Chapter 5) than any of the others. The shareholders' removal rights as against directors are strongly formulated: only an ordinary resolution is required and there is no need to wait until the end of the director's term of office.[74] As for affiliation rights, we have seen that the City Code is firmly committed to the sidelining of incumbent management during takeover bids and placing the decision on the offer in the hands of shareholders of the target company, thus promoting both the exit rights of existing shareholders and the entry rights of the bidder.[75]

However, analysing the formal rules is only part of the task. In relation to the appointments right strategy, we have noted that there is reason to think that shareholders still face collective action problems in companies without a controlling shareholder over the use of their removal rights. Even if shareholders' traditional collective action problems have been mitigated in recent decades with the rise of institutional shareholders, there remain the conflicts of interest among institutional shareholders which are likely to reduce the level of their intervention below what is optimal.[76]

As for the disciplinary effects of takeovers, the latest evidence for the UK suggests that takeovers do operate so as to change the management of badly performing companies, but that, across the board, takeover targets are not noticeably badly performing companies.[77] This suggests that takeovers are more often motivated by synergistic than disciplinary

---

[74] Above p 125.   [75] Above p 141.   [76] Above p 134.

[77] J Franks and C Meyer, 'Governance as a Source of Managerial Discipline', in P Butzen and C Fuss, *Firms' Investment and Finance Decisions* (Cheltenham: Edward Elgar, 2003).

reasons, but this fact is not necessarily conclusive in an assessment of the disciplinary impact of takeovers, which relies as much on the threat of the bid as on the actual bid. However, this evidence is consistent with the view that the threat of a takeover provides an incentive to the boards of companies only to avoid the worst levels of performance and not to maximize shareholder utility. In other words, the takeover threat may put a floor under board performance but may not do much to influence the level of performance above that floor.

Despite the weight of legal analysis which it is necessary to undertake in order to understand the law on directors' duties (considered in Chapter 6), it is doubtful how effective the law is in practice. Insofar as the law of directors' duties relies on standards (as it does in relation to the duty of care, the duty to promote the success of the company, and the restriction on acting for an improper purpose), it depends heavily on litigation to bring cases before the courts so that the potential for liability is realized. Enforcement, however, as we saw at the end of Chapter 6, is probably the Achilles heal of directors' duties. Cases are brought, of course, but overall the area is probably under-litigated. Where the law of directors' duties relies on the trusteeship strategy, ie excluding interested directors from voting, there are reasons to be sceptical about the effectiveness of the law. The distinction between interested and not-interested directors is essentially ad hoc and issue-specific, so that a director on one occasion is on the interested side of the divide and the non-interested on another. This gives rise to incentives for all directors to act in favour of those who are interested on any particular occasion. In companies traded on the Main Market of the London Stock Exchange, where the (different) independent/non-independent distinction is formalized in the composition of the board, reliance on the independent directors may work better, but in relation to all but this small elite set of top companies the Corporate Governance Code does not operate.

As for the two, very different, aspects of the incentives strategy (considered in this chapter), they are relative newcomers to the regulation of boards and apply only to the top set of listed companies. The relationship, if any, between director independence and good corporate performance still has to be demonstrated.[78] However, there is some evidence that splitting the roles of the CEO and the chair of the board is associated with more rapid replacement of the former in underperforming companies.[79] As for

---

[78] S Bhagat and B Black, 'The Non-Correlation between Board Independence and Long-Term Financial Performance' (2002) 27 *Journal of Corporation Law* 231.

[79] J Franks and C Meyer, above n 77.

the reward strategy, as can be seen from the above discussion, the question of whether performance-related pay is a solution to or a manifestation of the shareholders' managerial agency problems is still heavily debated.

Finally, the decision rights strategy (the first strategy we considered, in Chapter 5) has turned out to play a curious role. As a general strategy, it is clearly hopeless, because it involves solving the agency problem by ending the agency relationship. However, as a solution to particular problems it has an enduring role to play and, as we saw, it kept on emerging as a possible solution for dealing with the difficulties which the other strategies encounter in coping with conflicts of interest. The attraction of involving the shareholders, compulsorily, in the decision-making process is that the law thereby insists upon a procedure in which the shareholders have a good chance of protecting themselves, without the law having to determine, substantively, the point at issue. That was the approach of the common law to self-dealing transactions and its enduring value is shown by its partial reinstatement by Chapter 4 of Part 10 of the Companies Act;[80] the adherence to it by such modern codes as the Listing Rules (for related-party transactions and long-term incentive schemes);[81] and its adoption by the government through an advisory vote as a solution to one of the most intractable of company law issues (companies' remuneration policies).[82]

The five strategies discussed above all focus on the shareholder/director relationship and aim either to enhance the shareholders' control or to structure the board's behaviour in favour of the shareholders. However, it is possible that the shareholders may also benefit, indirectly, from strategies whose ostensible aim (and, indeed, effect) is to advance the interests, as against the board, of principals other than the shareholders. We noted in Chapter 4 that large lenders have an incentive to establish contractual mechanisms which permit them to monitor the performance of the boards of companies to which they lend money and to intervene to replace the management of the company in extreme cases. Particularly in companies with highly geared capital structures (that is, a high proportion of debt to equity), the shareholders may well benefit from the monitoring activities of the lenders. Although, logically, the lenders are interested solely in the company generating enough cash to pay the interest due on the loans and to repay the capital and do not care whether there is anything left over after that for the shareholders, it may in fact be difficult for the creditors to monitor the board with that degree of precision and

---

[80] Above p 169.   [81] Above pp 172 and 210.   [82] Above p 210.

so the shareholders benefit indirectly from the creditors' activities.[83] This reverses the traditional argument that, so long as the company is a going concern, the creditors do not need to be involved directly in the monitoring of boards, because monitoring in the interests of the shareholders will indirectly protect the creditors. It is the high degree of risk for lenders in highly leveraged capital structures which leads to this reversal, and there is, indeed, some empirical evidence that replacement of boards is associated in the UK with high levels of leverage.[84]

Finally, the shareholders may be protected by markets, rather than by legal strategies, and again this protection may be provided directly or indirectly. Indirect protection for shareholders may arise out of, for example, strongly competitive product markets. If the markets into which the company sells its products are competitive, at least some forms of board disregard of shareholder interests (for example shirking) will carry major penalties for the board itself, which may see the company driven into insolvency or become a takeover target (with the consequent loss of the directors' jobs) if the company does not operate effectively so as to meet the interests of its customers. More direct protection for shareholders may arise in the case of a company which needs regular access to the capital markets for fresh injections of equity finance. Investors may be reluctant to provide additional funding for the company if the board's record is one of disregard of the existing shareholders' interests and the board, anticipating this, will give the shareholders' interests a high priority.

The impact of the capital market as a check on board performance is strengthened in the UK by the rule that new equity capital, issued for cash, must normally be raised on a 'rights' basis, ie the new shares must first be offered pro rata to the existing shareholders.[85] This reduces the risk that the board will do an implicit deal with the new investors, whereby the board issues new shares at a substantial discount to the current market price in exchange for the support of the new shareholders against the existing shareholders, who are the ones who sustain the loss inherent in the dilution of the company's capital through the new issue at less than the current market price. The importance attached by institutional shareholders to their pre-emption rights is demonstrated by the supplementary rules, which they have sponsored, applying to such issues. Although the Act permits the pre-emption rights of the shareholders to

---

[83] J Drukarczyk and H Schmidt, 'Lenders as a Force in Corporate Governance: Enabling Covenants and the Impact of Bankruptcy Law', in K Hopt et al (eds), *Comparative Corporate Governance* (Oxford: Clarendon Press, 1998), ch 10.
[84] Franks and Meyer, above n 77.   [85] Companies Act 2006, Part 17, Ch 3.

be disapplied by the articles or a shareholder vote for periods of up to five years, the Pre-Emption Group's *Statement of Principles*[86] indicate the limited circumstances in which the institutional shareholders will support such resolutions as a matter of course. The Principles, which are essentially the result of bargaining between the institutional shareholders and companies and their advisers, with some government input, indicate that institutional shareholders will normally accept waiver of their statutory rights if the company (a) restricts the new shares to be issued for cash to 5 per cent of the issued ordinary shares in any one year and 7.5 per cent over any rolling period of three years, and (b) restricts the discount on any issue to 5 per cent—but will otherwise need a special case to be made out. Although the Guidelines came in for some criticism for slowing down the process of recapitalization by banks in the recent crisis, they survived that crisis largely unscathed.[87]

Thus, we can see that overall the agency problems of the shareholders (as a class) as against the board are addressed through a portfolio of legal strategies as well as through the operation of markets, whose effectiveness is sometimes supported by company law rules, such as those on pre-emptive rights. Given the variety of circumstances in which those problems can arise and the lack of conclusive empirical data about which strategies are most effective, implementing a range of strategies seems a wise approach for the law. The balance among the strategies, however, will always be a matter for public policy debate and something which is likely to be subject to change.

---

[86] These can be found at: <http://www.pre-emptiongroup.org.uk/principles/index.htm>.

[87] See HM Treasury, *A Report to the Chancellor of the Exchequer by the Rights Issue Review Group* (November 2008). The CLR also recommended the retention for corporate governance reasons of the pre-emption rule: CLR, *Developing the Framework* (March 2000), para 3.160.

8

Majority and Minority Shareholders

In the previous three chapters we analysed the legal strategies available for dealing with the agency problems of the shareholders as a class as against the board of directors. That analysis assumed a shareholding structure in which no shareholder had a controlling stake in the company, ie the shareholdings were dispersed. Suppose, however, that is not the case, ie that there is a controlling shareholder but equally, unless the company has only one shareholder, there will be non-controlling shareholders as well. Here, the crucial relationship upon which the law focuses is that between the controlling and non-controlling shareholders, or in principal/agent terminology, the non-controlling shareholder is the principal and the controlling shareholder the agent.[1]

Control of a company by a single shareholder or small group of shareholders acting in concert is not common in the largest listed British companies, though it is not unknown even at this level. This is one of the contrasts between the shareholding structures of British and US companies, on the one hand, and the structures of large companies in most other parts of the world, especially continental Europe,[2] where a controlling block-holder or controlling group is common even in the largest listed companies. However, such control certainly becomes more common in the UK when one examines the smaller, publicly traded companies, public companies whose securities are not publicly traded and, especially, private companies. Thus, the problems generated by majority/minority shareholder relationships throw up a widespread set of issues, even in British companies.

What, however, do we mean by a non-controlling shareholder or—the equivalent term normally used in British writing—a 'minority'

---

[1] This is counter-intuitive for the lawyer, but remember that in law and economics analysis the agent is the person whose actions affect the welfare of the principal, and so in the controlling/non-controlling shareholder relationship, that potential lies with the controlling shareholder, who is thus the agent.

[2] M Becht and A Röell, 'Blockholdings in Europe: An International Comparison' (1999) 43 *European Economic Review* 1049; F Barca and M Becht (eds), *The Control of Corporate Europe* (Oxford: Oxford University Press, 2001).

shareholder? A minority shareholder can be said to be a person who finds him- or herself in the position where (a) he or she cannot command sufficient votes to be sure of being able to secure the passage of a resolution by the shareholders which the minority favours and (b) there is another shareholder (the 'majority' shareholder) or group of shareholders acting together who can achieve the passage of the resolutions they favour.[3] The Companies Act tells us that the default rule is that a shareholder resolution requires the consent of 50 per cent plus 1 of the votes cast (ie a 'simple' majority or an 'ordinary' resolution),[4] so that is the test normally used to determine whether one has a controlling or non-controlling position. The Act itself raises the majority required for certain fundamental decisions by stipulating for a 'special' resolution (75 per cent of the votes cast) and the articles of association may do so in other cases. A special resolution may seem even worse than an ordinary one from a small shareholder's point of view because that shareholder has even less chance of securing the passage of a resolution it favours. However, the requirement for a special resolution does in fact protect the non-controlling shareholder, because it makes it easier for small shareholders to block a proposal from the large shareholders and thus potentially gives the small shareholders some bargaining leverage with the large shareholders. We look in more detail at the circumstances in which special resolutions are required below.

Nevertheless, the fact remains that a shareholder who cannot command enough votes to secure the passing of an ordinary resolution faces being constantly outvoted on most business issues which come before the shareholders, if there is another shareholder who does command those votes. Even worse from the non-controlling shareholder's point of view, in one crucial area the Act insists that an ordinary resolution is all that is required for shareholder decision. The shareholders by ordinary resolution may at any time remove any of the directors for any reason,[5] and, inevitably, the provisions in companies' articles concerning the appointment of directors will normally track this majority requirement. Thus, a minority shareholder may be unable to get its way at shareholder meetings and face a board which is responsive to the interests of the majority shareholder (its members are in effect the majority shareholder's nominees)[6] and neglectful of those of the minority. It also follows that, if the law is to protect

---

[3] If only condition (a) obtains, then we have a situation of dispersed shareholding.
[4] s 281(3).   [5] s 168—discussed above at p 125.
[6] The duty to exercise independent judgment (above p 182) and other fiduciary duties will constrain directors from the unthinking obedience to the wishes of the majority shareholder but will not fully correct the pro-majority bias in board decision-making, especially in areas of business policy.

minorities, it will need mechanisms which operate on both shareholder and board decisions.

Should the law do anything to rescue the minority shareholder from this position? There is an obvious argument for doing nothing. Since the rules for shareholder decision-making are well known, a person who makes a minority investment in a company run by a controlling shareholder knows the risk he or she is running when making such an investment. The investor will assess the risks involved and reduce (discount) the price he or she is prepared to pay for the shares to reflect the risk. Of course, investors' risk assessments may not always be correct, but across the board there is no reason to suppose they will be systematically inaccurate. So, it can be argued, reduction of the price the investor is prepared to pay ex ante (before investment) provides a functional substitute for legal protection ex post (after investment).

Although a powerful argument—and an antidote to the view that every ex post adverse treatment of a minority shareholder is unfair; it may be what the majority has already paid for—there are equally powerful counter-arguments. First, it is not clear that it is against the interests of majority shareholders to be constrained from treating minorities unfairly. Ex post, the majority shareholder may see only gain from treating the minority unfairly. Ex ante, however, a majority shareholder is able to obtain risk finance on better terms if it is committed to not treating the minority unfairly, ie the minority will no longer discount (or will discount less) the price payable for the shares.[7] And legal rules may facilitate more credible commitments by the majority than purely contractual mechanisms. Society, too, may prefer the situation in which the majority is constrained from unfair treatment. Companies' contribution to the wealth of society is likely to be promoted by the availability of risk capital at a lower price. Permitting unfair treatment raises the cost of capital for companies (if minority investors accurately discount the risks involved or overestimate them) or facilitates wealth transfers from minority to majority (if the risk is underestimated), from which no societal benefit appears to flow.

---

[7] Of course, this is not to say that majority shareholders will necessarily be better off by giving up exploitation of minorities: the question (for them) would be whether the benefit of a lower cost of capital outweighed the benefits obtainable from exploiting minorities. See A Dyck and L Zingales, 'Private Benefits of Control: An International Comparison' (2004) 59 *Journal of Finance* 537 who show that the premium paid (above market price) on the sale of a controlling block of shares varied enormously from country to country, a result partly explicable by variations in levels of minority protection. See also R Gilson, 'Controlling Shareholders and Corporate Governance: Complicating the Comparative Taxonomy' (2006) 119 *Harvard Law Review* 1642.

Thus, doing nothing to protect minorities is probably not sensible policy. However, working out the level of protection which should be provided is no simple task. Nevertheless, it is easy to justify one protective step: if the majority and the minority wish to contract to provide a higher level of minority protection than the general law provides, then the law should surely provide mechanisms through which their agreement can be rendered effective. We begin the legal analysis in this chapter by looking at the contracting mechanisms which British company law provides to this end. Beyond that, British law places its faith largely in standards, ie in ex post judicial assessment of the acceptability of what the majority has done according to some broad test. This approach is best exemplified by the 'unfair prejudice' provisions of Part 30 of the Act, whereby a member of the company can complain that the affairs of the company have been conducted in a way which is 'unfairly prejudicial' to his interests. Even here, as we shall see, the courts have been most comfortable in finding against company controllers where it can be shown that their action was in breach of some informal agreement or understanding among the incorporators as to how the company should be run.

Beyond protecting contracting and broad standards for the review of the majority's conduct, the pattern is more fragmented. Use is made, but in specific areas, of many of the strategies identified in Figure 1.[8] Some use is made of decision rights strategies (putting the decision in the hands of the minority), of exit strategies (enabling the minority to leave the company on acceptable terms), of sharing strategies (requiring benefits to be distributed to majority and minority pro rata), and of trusteeship strategies (putting the decision in the hands of persons not subject to high-powered conflicts of interest). As we shall see, some of these strategies are implemented through rules which we have already examined in connection with board/shareholders-as-a-class relations. Thus, directors' duties may perform a role in constraining both boards which are not responsive to shareholder interests at all and those which are responsive to the interests of only majority shareholders.

FACILITATING CONTRACTING FOR MINORITY PROTECTION

British law provides a number of mechanisms whereby the majority can commit (bond) itself to treat minorities fairly. We will look at class rights, shareholder agreements, and entrenching provisions in the articles of association.

---

[8]   Above p 113.

CLASS RIGHTS

Chapter 9 of Part 17 of the Act provides a mechanism whereby a company can create a further class of share, to which different rights are attached from those attached to the shares already in issue, and bind itself not to alter the rights of that further class without the consent of that class. To take a simple situation,[9] suppose a company has one class of (ordinary) shares which follow the standard model whereby the shareholders will receive dividends only if the directors declare them. Holders of such shares run the risk that directors will not distribute dividends but rather retain corporate earnings for investment in future projects. The shareholders may be happy with this arrangement, especially if they have confidence in the ability of management to develop the business successfully. However, other groups of investors may prefer a guarantee of a distribution if profits are earned, perhaps because they need regular income to meet their own obligations. One way of providing that is through an issuance of preference shares under which, for example, they are entitled to an 8 per cent dividend each year, if sufficient profits are earned.[10] The issuance of the preference shares creates a contract between the company and the preference investors, the terms of which are usually set out in the company's articles.

The class rights provisions of the Act provide a mechanism whereby when the company (ie the existing ordinary shareholders) decide to contract to issue the preference shares, they can bond themselves not subsequently to alter the new shareholders' rights (for example, to reduce their dividend entitlement) without their consent. Specifically, the Act[11] lays down a default rule that a variation of the rights of the preference shareholders will require a special resolution (ie supermajority consent) of the preference shareholders meeting separately as a class. The risk which the preference shareholders would run, in the absence of this protection, is that their rights, which are typically to be found in the articles, could be altered to their disadvantage by the standard mechanism for altering the

---

[9] A company may issue further classes of share even though it has a number of classes of share already in issue; preference rights may come in many different packages. Such facts may complicate the picture but do not alter the essential analysis.

[10] The requirement for profits, which is imposed by s 830 of the Act, differentiates the dividend entitlement of a preference shareholder from the interest entitlement of a bond-holder: interest normally has to be paid whether profits are earned are not and so interest payments are constrained only by the company's cash flow.

[11] s 630(2). Even if the class passes a special resolution approving the variation, a dissenting minority of at least 15 per cent of the class may appeal to the court to have the variation cancelled (s 633)—a use of the trustee strategy discussed below.

articles, ie by way of a special resolution of the shareholders.[12] The class vote rule gives the preference shareholders protection beyond that contained in the standard procedure, in two ways. First, the separate consent of the preference shareholders is required, so that the preference shareholders' views cannot be swamped by a greater number of ordinary shareholders. Second, in many cases preference shares are issued without voting rights,[13] so that, if this is so, the class rights protection gives the preference shareholders the right to vote on variations of their rights when, without it, they would be disenfranchised.

So attractive is the class rights protection that the company may create a second class of shares, not for corporate finance reasons, but purely to take advantage of the class protection provisions. For example, there may be a class of A ordinary shares, held by the majority shareholder, and a B class, held by the minority, with identical financial entitlements, but with the B class having the right to appoint a person to the board. B cannot then be deprived of its board appointment right without its consent.

As befits a rule designed to facilitate contracting, however, the class rights protection provision just described is only a default rule. If there is an express variation provision in the articles, that will govern.[14] Thus, the parties may agree something different and embody their agreement in the articles.[15] That agreement may confer a higher level of protection (for example, the consent of all the preference shareholders) or a lower one (for example, consent of only a simple majority of the preference shareholders) or even, it seems, alteration of class rights through the normal procedure for altering the articles. However, if nothing different is agreed,

---

[12] s 21.

[13] This is justified on the basis that voting rights are compensation for the absence of contractual rights, so that the ordinary shareholders, with no right to a dividend, should have the vote, whilst preference shareholders, with a contractual right to a dividend, should not have it. Whether and in what circumstances preference shareholders have voting rights is a matter for negotiation between the company and the investors upon issue of the shares.

[14] s 630(2)(a). Machiavellian readers may see the possibility of the company changing its articles *after* the issuance of the shares so as to substitute a lesser protection than that contained in the default rule, thus defeating the default rule. But the drafter of the section was not naive. The introduction of a variation provision into the articles (and the amendment of an existing one) are themselves treated as variation events and so as attracting the default protection: s 630(5). So, it would be necessary for the company, *before* issue, to insert a provision into its articles permitting it to introduce, in some easy way, a variation procedure *after* issue for the default protection to break down.

[15] If there is a large class of potential investors in the preference shares, direct negotiations between company and investors may be difficult. In that case, the company will state its proposed terms of issue and try to establish through financial intermediaries whether an issue on such terms is likely to attract investment at the price sought. If not, the company may adjust its proposed terms. So, there is bargaining here, but it is not face to face.

the default rule described above applies.[16] Thus, the burden is properly put on the company to contract out of the default protection rather than on the investors to contract into it.

The third—probably unintended—way in which the class rights provisions encourage bargaining arises out of the ambiguity of the statute and its interpretation by the courts. As to statutory ambiguity, the Act does not make clear what a class right is. Is it all the rights attached to the class, only the ones which are unique to that class, or all the important rights, whether shared with other classes or not?[17] Since this is not clear, the parties have an incentive to agree a definition. As to the courts, they have interpreted a 'variation' of rights narrowly, so as to include only formal changes to the rights and to exclude corporate actions which reduce the practical significance of the right but leave the formal right unchanged. So, where both preference shareholders and ordinary shareholders have voting rights, a decision to increase the number of ordinary shares in issue would not be a variation of the rights of the preference shares. The preference shareholders would have the same formal voting rights as previously, even though their weight in the company is now reduced.[18] This again generates an incentive to the investors and the company to spell out what is meant by a variation. The courts have facilitated bargaining of this type by accepting that the company can use the articles, not only to alter the procedure for varying class rights, but also to determine what constitutes a class right or a variation of it. However, the articles must clearly show an intention to move beyond the statutory default. But if the articles are clear, the courts will give effect to them.[19]

SHAREHOLDER AGREEMENTS

Judging by the amount of litigation over the years, the ability of the company (ie its existing controllers) to bond themselves not to alter the rights of investors in a new class of shares without the latter's (majority) consent

---

[16] s 630(2)(b).

[17] In *Cumbrian Newspaper Group Ltd v Cumberland and Westmorland Herald Newspaper* [1997] Ch 1 Scott J favoured the second and narrowest interpretation, thus accentuating the parties' incentive to bargain to expand the scope of the protection.

[18] This is a simplified version of what happened in *White v Bristol Aeroplane Co* [1953] Ch 65, CA.

[19] Contrast *House of Fraser plc v ACGE Investments Ltd* [1987] AC 387, HL (where the articles were ineffective) with *Re Northern Engineering Industries plc* [1994] 2 BCLC 704 (where they achieved their objective). In both cases the question was whether a repayment of preference shares at par was a variation of their rights and so needed class consent. In the absence of an extended provision in the articles such repayment would not be viewed as a variation of rights but as treating the preference shareholders in accordance with their rights (assuming the shareholders had no entitlement to surplus assets in a winding up): *Scottish Insurance Corp Ltd v Wilsons and Clyde Coal Co Ltd* [1949] AC 462, HL.

has been an important tool in facilitating investment in companies. However, it is a reasonably complex mechanism and, where a separate class of shares does not need to be issued, one might expect some simpler bonding mechanism to be available. And, indeed, it is.

The very simplest mechanism is that of the ordinary law of contract. The shareholders reach an agreement (outside the articles) as to the conduct of the company in the future and the courts will give effect to it, by injunction if necessary. Thus, in *Russell v Northern Bank Ltd*[20] a bank and four executive directors of the company were its only shareholders but with the bank holding 120 shares to the executives' 20 each. An agreement among the shareholders provided among other things that they would not vote in favour of a shareholder resolution to increase the company's capital or to issue new shares unless all of them had declared in writing that they were in favour of the resolution. The aim was to preserve the existing balance of influence among the shareholders unless they all agreed to alter it. The House of Lords would have been prepared to issue an injunction to restrain a majority of the shareholders from voting in favour of such a resolution without the consent of all the shareholders having been given.[21] The shareholders were thus permitted to contract out of the standard procedure laid down in the Act for voting on capital increases (an ordinary resolution), even though the Act did not expressly contemplate this.

Shareholder agreements may also be used to regulate proceedings at board level. Thus, in *Breckland Group Holdings Ltd v London & Suffolk Properties Ltd*[22] a company had only two shareholders, a majority and a minority. The majority shareholder was entitled to appoint two members to the board and the minority one, but certain matters, including the institution of legal proceedings, required the consent of one director appointed by each 'side'. The majority shareholder sought to circumvent the provision by causing legal proceedings to be instituted by shareholder decision. The judge restrained the company from proceeding with the shareholder-authorized proceedings for 'the shareholder agreement points to its being accepted by the both parties that consent of both parties to the institution of legal proceedings at a board meeting was a requirement for such valid institution.'[23]

---

[20] [1992] 1 WLR 588, HL.

[21] The court issued only a declaration as to the validity of the agreement, because the claimant did not in fact object to the share increase but wished to establish only the principle that consent of all was required.   [22] [1989] BCLC 100.

[23] At p 104b. It is much debated whether, even in the absence of a shareholder agreement, the shareholders could have validly authorized the litigation, in the light of a provision in the articles conferring general management powers on the company. The judge considered this issue but it is doubtful whether his views, given 'at 4.20 on a Friday afternoon', can be considered the last word.

PROVISIONS IN THE ARTICLES

Despite the courts' willingness to give shareholders wide powers to regulate company affairs by agreement outside the articles, shareholders' agreements do suffer from the defect that they are not suitable for large bodies of shareholders (because initial agreement will be difficult to obtain) or for shareholder bodies where frequent transfer of the shares and the admission of new shareholders is anticipated. This is because ordinary contract law provides no mechanism whereby new shareholders automatically become parties to the shareholder agreement. It is easy to think of mechanisms which might be deployed to achieve this result, such as an obligation on the parties to the agreement to require a transferee of a share to agree to become a party to the agreement. However, these mechanisms are likely to break down in practice at some point. What remedy would the other shareholders have if the transferor failed to obtain the transferee's agreement or if the transferee broke its promise to adhere to the agreement?

These problems are exacerbated by the decision in *Russell v Northern Bank* (above) for the House of Lords, whilst giving full effect to the agreement as between the shareholders, held that the company could not contract out its statutory power to increase its capital by ordinary resolution, and so it had to be severed from the shareholders' agreement. So long as all the shareholders are parties to the agreement, the statement that the company cannot contract out of its statutory powers has no practical bite, for all those who might act as the company to approve an increase are bound by agreement not to do so. However, if some shareholders were not so bound, a shareholder vote in favour of an increase could conceivably be obtained. Indeed, the court was concerned to open up precisely this possibility by severing the company from the agreement. Otherwise, the company might be bound by the agreement not to put a resolution forward to the shareholder meeting, even if there were now in existence shareholders who had never become parties to it and even if there was only a single shareholder who was any longer party to the agreement with the company.

To avoid the practical difficulties of binding new members, it may be more attractive to the shareholders to embody their agreement in the company's articles, for the articles do automatically apply to new members,[24] even if the articles have the potential disadvantage of being a public

---

[24] s 33. By operation of law the articles constitute a contract between the company and its members for the time being.

document,[25] whilst the contents of a shareholders' agreement can be kept private. British company law gives shareholders very broad powers to regulate the internal affairs of the company through the articles of association. There are endless ways in which the articles can be constructed so as to protect minority interests. One example will suffice, involving the use of 'quorum' requirements in the articles (ie stipulations as to the minimum number of people who must be present at a meeting for that meeting validly to transact business). In *Ross v Telford*[26] a husband and wife were the only shareholders and only directors of two companies (but they were not equal shareholders in one case). The articles of association of both companies provided that the quorum for both shareholder and board meetings was two, so that the companies were potentially deadlocked if one person stayed away from meetings or, to put it another way, the companies could proceed only with the consent of both husband and wife. On the basis that the investors had deliberately chosen to adopt this deadlock arrangement, the court refused to use its statutory powers to break a deadlock which in fact arose in the course of divorce proceedings between husband and wife.

In addition to the potential disadvantage of publicity, however, putting agreement in the articles suffers from another possible shortcoming. A contract such as a shareholders' agreement, in principle, can be amended only if all the parties to it agree; the articles of association can be amended by special resolution, ie by something short of unanimity.[27] An agreement embodied in the articles is thus less secure than a shareholders' agreement, unless, perhaps, it is supported by a shareholders' agreement relating to amendments of the articles. But, if the purpose of putting the agreement in the articles was to avoid resort to a shareholders' agreement, the solution of a supplementary shareholder agreement is not an attractive one. What is needed is some way of entrenching provisions in the articles, so as to produce the effect of an external contract.

Section 22 is the modern version of such entrenching mechanisms, which have long existed. This permits the articles themselves to intensify the normal alteration rule in relation to particular provisions therein, up to and including requiring the agreement of all the members of the company (so that, therefore, a 'dead hand' provision, rendering a provision completely unalterable, is not permitted).[28] Consequently, minority protection

---

[25] ss 9(5) and 26.

[26] [1998] 1 BCLC 82, CA. The power which the court refused to exercise is now s 306: power of court to order meeting of the shareholders if it is 'impracticable' for one to be called under the provisions of the articles.   [27] s 21.

[28] Presumably the entrenching provision will itself have to be specified as one of the provisions which cannot be changed except in accordance with the enhanced rule.

provisions in the articles, which are entrenched, can replicate the effect of a shareholders' agreement. (One might note that not all minority protections need entrenchment: in *Ross v Telford* either shareholder could defeat a proposal to alter the articles to amend the quorum requirements through the simple expedient of not attending the shareholder meeting.) Because of the potential impact of entrenchment on the company's ability to adapt to changes in its business environment, it is intended that entrenchment provisions can be introduced only if all the shareholders agree (either on incorporation or later).[29] Otherwise, a majority shareholder might secure a special resolution to introduce entrenchment of a provision which benefits him, just before he sold down his majority holding. Entrenchment might then give him a veto power over changes which his shareholding no longer justified, so that entrenchment became an instrument of oppression.

CONCLUSION

If the parties see the problems of minority protection in advance, the law provides effective mechanisms for them to implement any agreement they may come to as to how these problems are to be dealt with. The class rights protection is particularly strong, since the law there provides a default protection, out of which the majority must negotiate its way, if they do not like it, rather than a protection into which the minority must contract, as is the case with shareholders' agreements and provisions in the articles.[30] But, under all three mechanisms, the scope given to the contracting parties is striking. In some cases, rules in the Act, which might be thought to be mandatory rules, turn out to be default rules, at least where the default is changed in an upwards direction. *Russell* demonstrates that rules in the Act which allow the company to proceed by ordinary resolution can be changed into unanimity rules (or something else more demanding than an ordinary resolution) by shareholders' agreement, and *Ross v Telford* shows the same impact of a provision in the articles.[31]

So committed are the British courts to freedom of contract that in one famous—and perhaps not typical—case the House of Lords permitted the

---

[29] s 22(2)—a provision not in force at the time of writing because of fears that, as drafted, it goes beyond what was intended.

[30] For an analysis of the significance of setting default rules on an opt-in or opt-out basis see L Bebchuk and A Hamdani, 'Optimal Defaults for Corporate Law Evolution' (2002) 96 *Northwestern University Law Review* 489.

[31] Formally, the provision in the Act remains the same, but the shareholders can agree not to put the company in a position where it can take the relevant decision through the statutory procedure, unless some further condition is satisfied, and the courts will enforce that agreement.

articles to override an expressly mandatory rule of the Act. Section 168 of the Act allows a simple majority of the shareholders to dismiss a director, and that provision is said to operate 'notwithstanding anything in any agreement between it [the company] and him [the director]'. Nevertheless, in *Bushell v Faith*[32] the court allowed this provision to be sidestepped. The case concerned a company with three equal shareholders (two of whom were its directors) whose shares normally carried one vote each. A provision in the articles gave a director proposed to be dismissed three votes per share on a resolution to dismiss, thus producing a situation in which a director could not be removed against his or her will.

STANDARDS

Although contracting powers are widely used, especially in small companies, to avoid minority problems in advance, this technique is of value only to those who do anticipate future difficulties at the time of contracting and who think it is worthwhile to invest the resources necessary to produce a solution to possible future problems at that time. In many cases it is too difficult or, more likely, too costly, in relation to the value of the business, to incur the expense of identifying the issues and generating solutions, by negotiating customized articles or a shareholders' agreement.[33] Thus, the courts will be presented with the problem after it has arisen and without the parties having negotiated a customized solution. The most general (though not the only) ex post legal strategy which British law has developed to address minority problems is judicial review of the majority's actions by reference to some broad standard of fairness. In fact, the law has generated three such mechanisms, of which only the unfair prejudice provisions have had a significant impact. We will look at each of the mechanisms in turn—as well as at one which has not been developed.

Broad standards of review by reference to fairness are easy to formulate, but difficult to apply. They shift a substantial part of the process of lawmaking from the formulator of the standard to its applier.[34] (In the case of court-generated standards, these may be the same institutions, though

---

[32] [1970] AC 1099, HL.

[33] A Schwartz, 'Relational Contracts in the Courts: An Analysis of Incomplete Agreements and Legal Strategies' (1992) 21 *Journal of Legal Studies* 271. The model articles are inevitably of little use here: minority issues are company specific so that even a default general solution is difficult to draft, though the attempt has been made. See CLR, *Developing the Framework* (March 2000), paras 4.102–4.104, disagreeing with Law Commission, *Shareholder Remedies*, Law Com No 246 (1997), Part 3.

[34] L Kaplow, 'Rules Versus Standards: An Economic Analysis' (1992) 42 *Duke LJ* 557.

possibly situated at different levels within the court hierarchy.) As we shall see below, the British courts have struggled to solve this problem, for they have doubted their own expertise to intervene wisely in business affairs, whilst fearing to leave the minority wholly to the mercies of the majority.

REVIEW OF DECISIONS TO ALTER THE ARTICLES

In the light of the importance of the articles in protecting minority interests, it is perhaps not surprising that this was the area upon which the courts focused when developing a standard at common law for review of majority decisions. This standard of review is still to be found in the common law, ie it has not been transposed into the 2006 Act in the way that the high-level law on directors' duties has been. The Court of Appeal, more than a century ago in *Allen v Gold Reefs of West Africa Ltd*,[35] laid down a standard by which the actions of the majority in deciding to alter the company's articles could be reviewed. Such alterations, it was said, perhaps in a conscious echoing of the rule applicable to directors, should be made 'bona fide for the benefit of the company as a whole'. Thus, as far as alterations of the articles are concerned, the law imposes, not only a supermajority requirement, but also gives individual dissenting shareholders the power to have the majority's decision reviewed against a standard. If the review is successful, the decision taken no longer binds the company and, indeed, it would be improper for the company to act on it.

However, the judges have had tremendous difficulty articulating what this standard requires of majorities. They have vacillated between two approaches. One is to interpret the standard as requiring simply good faith of the majority, ie the majority should have acted for the purpose of promoting the company's business and not, for example, in order to confer an advantage on themselves from which the minority was excluded. On the good faith test, the *effect* of what the majority did might be to confer an advantage on themselves, but that would not necessarily be fatal to the legality of their action. On the other hand, an objective approach would permit the court to assess whether the majority's actions struck a fair balance between the interests of majority and minority. The latter test would potentially confer more protection on minorities than the former but allocates to the courts the uncomfortable task of developing substantive criteria for distinguishing between legitimate and illegitimate action.

---

[35] [1900] 1 Ch 656, CA. In *Clemens v Clemens Bros Ltd* [1976] 2 All ER 268 the *Gold Reefs* test was applied, without comment, to a shareholder decision to increase capital and issue shares (not involving an amendment of the articles) but the CLR (*Final Report*, July 2001, 7.59–7.60) recommended the doctrine should not be so extended.

At an early stage the judges did seem prepared, by interpreting the test as having an objective element, to use it to impose an external standard on the majority of what fairness to the minority required.[36] Quite soon, however, the Court of Appeal interpreted the test as a subjective one,[37] although in one case the subjective test was given, confusingly, objective elements in terms of a requirement on the majority to have regard to the interests of the 'individual hypothetical shareholder'.[38] Today, subject to one possible qualification, the subjective approach based on good faith seems to dominate. In *Citco Banking Corp v Pusser's Ltd*[39] the company had two large shareholders, the chairman with 28 per cent of the shares and the appellant bank with 13 per cent, the remainder being dispersed among many small shareholders. The company was in financial diffi-culties and the chairman arranged rescue finance, which, however, was conditional upon the chairman taking control of the company. The share-holders adopted a resolution to issue a new class of shares with multiple voting rights, all of which were to be allocated to the chairman. The Privy Council turned down the challenge to the resolution altering the articles on the grounds that there was no evidence that the shareholders voting for the resolution had acted in bad faith.

How can bad faith be shown? In the absence of extrinsic evidence, the test, the court said, was whether no reasonable shareholder could consider the alteration to be for the benefit of the company or, to put the same point in a different way, whether there was any reasonable ground for thinking that the proposal was for the benefit of the company. If this test (put either way) was satisfied, the decision was a matter for the shareholders, not the courts. As we have seen in relation to directors,[40] this rationality test is how the subjective test is made operational in practice. The court obvi-ously cannot simply accept statements from the witness box by the major-ity, some time after the decision, that they acted in good faith when taking it, but the 'no reasonable person' test sets the hurdle which the majority's action has to overcome at a low level.

In particular, the mere fact that the amendment leaves some of the shareholders worse off than before does not in itself constitute a breach

---

[36] *Brown v British Abrasive Wheel Co Ltd* [1919] 1 Ch 290; *Dafen Tinplate Co Ltd v Llanelly Steel Co Ltd* [1920] 2 Ch 124.

[37] *Sidebottom v Kershaw, Leese & Co* [1920] 1 Ch 154, CA; *Shuttleworth v Cox Bros & Co (Maidenhead) Ltd* [1927] 2 KB 9, CA.

[38] *Greenhalgh v Arderne Cinemas Ltd* [1951] 1 Ch 286, CA.

[39] [2007] 2 BCLC 483, PC (the judgment was delivered by Lord Hoffmann). The tests approved in this case were taken directly from the judgments in *Shuttleworth v Cox Brothers*.

[40] Above p 152.

of the principle. Otherwise, the amendment procedure could not be used to resolve a straightforward conflict between majority and minority.[41] The one possible exception, where a higher standard might be applied, is where the effect of the resolution is to require the minority to surrender its shares (to the company or to another shareholder) at a fair price. (If the price is not fair, even the subjective test would be very hard to satisfy.) A more rigorous approach has been applied in this situation in Australia. The Australian High Court in *Gambotto v WPC Ltd*[42] invalidated a change in the articles so as to effect a compulsory acquisition of shares made in good faith which would have left the minority economically no worse off and the majority considerably better off. However, the British courts have shown no enthusiasm for this approach and the Company Law Review thought that it should not be adopted in the United Kingdom.[43]

What protection does the subjective test give to minorities? It will at least pick up those cases where the majority vote as they do to obtain some collateral benefit not available to the minority. Thus, in *Re Holders Investment Trust Ltd*[44] a trust having 90 per cent of the preference shares voted at a class meeting in favour of a reduction of capital which would lead to the cancellation (at par) of the preference shares. (At a class meeting the *Gold Reefs* principle is amended so as to refer only to the members of the class.) The trust also held 52 per cent of the company's ordinary shares, which would benefit from the cancellation of the preference shares. Fortunately for the challengers, there was written evidence available that the trust had been advised that the value of its holdings overall in the company would be advanced by voting in favour of the cancellation resolution. The court refused to approve the reduction of capital.

UNFAIR PREJUDICE

History

Even if the courts had adopted an objective view of the *Gold Reefs* principle and applied it to all shareholder decisions (not just changes to the articles), it would still have suffered from a major limitation as a minority protection standard. It does not reach board decisions, which, as we have

---

[41] *Peter's American Delicacy Co Ltd v Heath* (1939) 61 CLR 457, H Ct Aus; *Redwood Master Fund Ltd v TD Bank Europe Ltd* [2006] 1 BCLC 149. This approach seems finally to discard the objective elements of the largely subjective *Greenhalgh* decision (above).

[42] (1995) 127 ALR 417.   [43] CLR, *Final Report* (July 2001), 7.54 and 7.59.

[44] [1971] 1 WLR 583. See also *British America Nickel Corporation Ltd v O'Brien* [1927] AC 369, PC, for an even more blatant example of a collateral benefit. The case also shows that the *Gold Reefs* principle applies to *bond-holders* voting on a resolution which will bind them all to accept a variation of their rights against the company, the rights being contained in this case in a trust deed.

noted, are likely to be highly responsive to majority interests because the holder of a simple majority of the votes can select all the members of the board. A review standard which holds out the prospect of being effective must thus embrace board as well as shareholder decisions.

In fact, from the earliest days of modern company law the legislation has contained one tool of intervention, namely, the power compulsorily to wind the company up if the court thinks it is 'just and equitable' to do so. This power is now to be found in section 122(1)(g) of the Insolvency Act 1986, and we examine it further below. This review power, however, had little impact, in part because of its remedial inflexibility. The only remedy the court could give the minority was through the dissolution of the company and the disposal of its business, a costly procedure which might well not realize the full value of the business. However, the threat of value destruction through liquidation might mean that the prospect of winding up would induce the majority to offer the minority something more appropriate.[45]

In 1948 Parliament decided to meet this argument about remedial inflexibility by introducing a remedy alternative to winding up. By virtue of s 210 of the 1948 Companies Act, where the company's affairs were being conducted in a manner which was oppressive to some part of the members and the circumstances were such that a just and equitable winding up would be available but it was inappropriate to grant this remedy, the court could instead grant such other remedy as it thought fit. The impact of this new section was to bring the full force of litigants' and judges' attention to bear on what was meant by 'oppression', the scope of which concept would determine the rigour of the standard by which the majority's conduct was reviewed. In the end, the courts took a cautious line and so that section had less impact than the legislature had probably hoped.

In section 75 of the Companies Act 1980 the legislature had another go: the test for intervention was now stated to be that the affairs of the company were being conducted in a way which was 'unfairly prejudicial' to the interests of any of its members; the express link to the winding-up remedy disappeared; but the wide remedial flexibility of the section was retained. Section 75 became s 459 of the Companies Act 1985 and is now section 994 of the 2006 Act—but it remained unamended in its essentials, except on one point. Thus, in 1980 the legislature had laid down a standard by which the courts might review, on a broad basis, the conduct of those controlling companies, but the question remained as to the use which the courts would make of their powers.

---

[45] In practice, counsel for the minority, having obtained a winding-up order, would immediately ask the court for its implementation to be suspended for a period to see if something mutually more attractive could be worked out.

Judicial development: enforcing informal agreements and arrangements

In fact, the judges this time reacted more positively, perhaps because the recent generations of judges are less conservative than their predecessors and perhaps because the legislature's reiteration of the principle of minority protection in 1980 made it clear that it took the matter seriously. In any event, the judges quickly accepted that the section was wide enough to cover acts done by the majority, whether as shareholders or directors, and done to the minority, whether as shareholders or directors.[46] The courts also concluded that the section permitted the court to review actions of the majority which they were, apart from s 994, entitled to take, such as decisions by the majority to exercise their statutory power to remove a minority shareholder from the board. Doubt on both these points had severely reduced the impact of s 210.[47]

With this ground-clearing task performed, the courts then squarely faced the need to articulate the bases upon which their review of controllers' decisions under the heading of 'unfair prejudice' was to proceed. This was no easy task. However, the courts have been able to identify one clear basis for intervention. Here, the courts act to support the private agreements or arrangements made by the shareholders and where, thus, the courts are at their least interventionist. In the light of the available express contracting mechanisms outlined above, it may be wondered why this role for the unfair prejudice provisions has proved to be so important. The answer is that in small businesses it is not uncommon for the entrepreneurs, setting up a company, to have a clear understanding of how the company is to be run, for example, on the basis that all the shareholders are to be involved in the management of the company by being directors of the company, but to fail to embody that expectation in the company's articles of association. As we notice above, this may be for cost reasons (it's cheaper to operate

---

[46] Or indeed, in appropriate circumstances, action taken in a managerial capacity: *Oak Investment Partners XII LP v Broughtwood* [2009] 1 BCLC 453. Whilst the action complained of must prejudice the interests of the petitioning member, that prejudice to a member's interests may arise out of acts done to him or her as director, for example, where a person has secured a seat on the board in order to protect the investment made as shareholder in the company but is later removed from the board. See *Re A Company* [1986] BCLC 376. This development was helped by a 1989 amendment which made it clear that the prejudice did not have to affect all the members of the company, provided it affected the petitioner's interests as a member. Under s 210 of the 1948 Act oppression of someone as director was sharply distinguished from oppression of a member and did not trigger statutory relief.

[47] Ironically, the inspiration for this change of heart in relation to unfair prejudice was a watershed decision of the House of Lords taking the broader view of its 'just and equitable' winding-up powers: *Ebrahimi v Westbourne Galleries Ltd* [1973] AC 360, HL.

through a company bought 'off the shelf' with a standard set of articles rather than customized ones) and partly because the shareholders are not psychologically in a position to contemplate their later falling out.[48]

Thus, the crucial step which the courts have taken in their interpretation of the unfair prejudice provisions has been to recognize and enforce informal agreements and arrangements existing outside the articles. The courts have given legal backing to such arrangements by granting the minority a remedy if the expectations generated by the informal agreement are later ignored by the majority without good reason. In this respect, the courts can be said to have extended the reach of the parties' freedom to contract about the running of the company. Even informal arrangements between majority and minority will be given legal protection via section 994. The typical case—though many different fact situations are found in practice—is where a small number of entrepreneurs come together on the basis that all are to be involved in the running of the company (ie will be directors as well as shareholders). Later, there is dissension and the majority use their statutory powers to remove the minority from the board by ordinary resolution. The minority will be able to claim a remedy under the unfair prejudice provisions, provided it can be shown that there was indeed an informal arrangement that all would be involved in the running of the company and the minority had subsequently done nothing to deserve exclusion. Although this development could be criticized for reducing the incentives for the parties to contract formally and explicitly about the future running of the company, experience had shown that this incentive was rather weak and insistence on formal contracting would simply leave many reasonable expectations unprotected.

This use by the courts of the unfair prejudice power is relatively uncontroversial. The section is being used in support of private ordering, not to contradict it. Will the courts be willing to go beyond this basis of intervention? In its first decision on the section, *O'Neill v Phillips*,[49] the House of Lords was particularly concerned not to allow the concept of 'legitimate expectations' to be dissociated from what the parties had (informally) agreed amongst themselves and to be used as a general tool to assess the fairness of the majority's conduct. For that reason the court preferred the phrase 'equitable considerations' to denominate the exercise the courts were engaged in when scrutinizing the majority's actions. The crucial question,

---

[48] D Prentice, 'The Theory of the Firm: Minority Shareholder Oppression' (1988) 8 *OJLS* 55. The informal understanding need not be reached when the company was set up but may emerge only at a later stage, for example, when a new investor joins the company.

[49] [1999] 1 WLR 1092, HL.

the courts have said, is to identify the basis upon which those involved in the small company came together. If the basis of association is 'adequately and exhaustively laid down in the articles',[50] then fair treatment is likely to mean only compliance with the articles. If, as is likely in small companies, there is 'a fundamental understanding between the shareholders which formed the basis of their association but was not put into contractual form',[51] then an allegation of unfair treatment can be based on that fundamental, if informal, understanding. Beyond that, however, one reaches the limits of legitimate expectations or equitable considerations.

Reducing the costs of litigation

The main difficulty which arises out of the use of the unfair prejudice provisions to support informal agreements among the shareholders is the cost of litigation, because establishing what the parties originally agreed and whether the majority have subsequently unjustifiably departed from that agreement may involve an extensive trawl in court through the company's life history. For example, the minority's subsequent conduct may have justified a departure from the original arrangements. The courts have sought to encourage minorities to accept pre-litigation offers to buy them out at a fair price, under threat that, if the offer is refused, the majority's conduct will no longer be seen as unfairly prejudicial.[52]

This approach is aligned well with the fact that, if the petition is successful, the remedy the court overwhelmingly orders is that the petitioner be bought out at a fair price by either the company or the majority.[53] Although section 996 gives the courts very wide remedial powers, these are used rather sparingly. The divorce analogy is often used to explain this: the relationship among the entrepreneurs having broken down, it is beyond the powers of the court to put it back together again and to police it into the future; instead all the court can do is settle the financial terms of separation. Yet, this remedy can be harsh. An entrepreneur who has teamed up with a financier to develop a product, for example, and who is, in effect, squeezed out before the product is successfully brought to market, may think that the potential of the business was undervalued when the fair price was fixed and also feel that he has been excluded from the future development of something which is not just a financial asset but an expression of his creativity and even humanity.

---

[50] *Ebrahimi v Westbourne Galleries Ltd* [1972] 2 All ER 492, 500.

[51] *Re Saul D Harrison & Sons plc* [1995] 1 BCLC at p 19 (*per* Hoffmann LJ).

[52] The conditions that such an offer has to meet to have this effect are set out in some detail in *O'Neill v Phillips* (above).

[53] Ordering the unfairly prejudiced petitioner to be bought out may not be appropriate in a joint venture; rather it may be appropriate to give total control of the venture to the petitioner: *Boughtwood v Oak Investment Partners XII LP* [2010] EWCA Civ 23.

Other cases?

One implication of the approach to the unfair prejudice rules outlined above is that they provide remedies for companies with small and relatively stable bodies of shareholders and therefore, typically, for companies which are small in economic terms. Outside such companies, even informal agreement will be rare because, the larger the shareholder body, the more difficult it will be to demonstrate that such informal agreement exists, and has been maintained, amongst *all* the shareholders.[54] In the absence of such informal agreements, can any other basis of intervention under section 994 be identified? It is suggested that there are two. First, one may predict that the courts would grant a remedy under the unfair prejudice provisions in respect of the sort of self-seeking conduct on the part of the majority which would constitute a breach of the *Gold Reefs* rule, discussed above, whether or not the conduct infringed an informal agreement among the shareholders. In fact, cases falling under the *Gold Reefs* principle are more likely to be brought as unfair prejudice petitions today than as common law claims. Further, the reach of section 994 in such cases would be longer because the section is not confined to majority action consisting of changes to the articles of association.

Second, the unfair prejudice provisions may be used to seek redress if the directors of the company act in breach of their duties to the company but are protected by the principle of majority rule from any action against them by the company. We discuss this use of the unfair prejudice provisions below.[55]

It would be rash to predict that the courts will never be willing to go beyond these three categories of unfairness, but it is highly likely that they will be cautious in so doing.[56] The provisions are very widely drafted and it is clear that the limits placed on them are the result of judicial policy, not of any inherent restriction in their wording. The fear of ending up managing 'every alehouse and brew-house in the kingdom'[57] is clearly one which continues to motivate the courts, and probably rightly so. The CLR was happy with the *O'Neill* decision, on the grounds that 'it is not desirable that, when members of companies fall out, all manner of allegations may be made which might possibly sustain a contention that a particular situation is unfair. This can lead to enormously lengthy and expensive proceedings, which are unsustainable for small companies, producing

---

[54] See *Re Posgate & Denby (Agencies) Ltd* [1987] BCLC 8 and *Re Blue Arrow plc* [1987] BCLC 585.   [55] See p 251.

[56] For a creative use of the courts' powers in a case which does not fit easily into any of the categories see *McGuinness v Bremner plc* [1988] BCLC 673.

[57] *Carlen v Drury* (1812) 1 Ves & B 154, 158, *per* Lord Eldon.

potentially unfair results at wholly disproportionate expense.'[58] In other words, in relation to private companies, where the CLR saw minority remedies as having the greatest significance, 'clarity, accessibility and cost-effectiveness' were more important than formally perfect justice.[59]

WINDING UP ON THE JUST AND EQUITABLE GROUND

As we noted above, this statutory ground for petition, contained in the Insolvency Act 1986, still exists. Petitioners are discouraged from using it where an unfair prejudice claim is available, unless winding up is the remedy they really seek (winding up remaining a remedy the court cannot grant under section 996, despite recommendations to the contrary). A petition to wind up the company can operate unfairly on the majority for it tends to make the day-to-day conduct of the company's business impossible or very difficult, because the company's assets come close to being frozen. Hence the discouragement. However, petitioners would have an incentive to use the winding-up remedy (and the courts could hardly refuse it) if the grounds upon which the courts could make a winding-up order were wider than those leading to an unfair prejudice remedy. This is at present uncertain. On the one hand, it would be extremely odd if the effect of the *O'Neill* decision, restricting the grounds of unfair prejudice, were to drive litigants to seek the less appropriate remedy of a winding up. On the other hand, the just and equitable provision has traditionally been used to provide a remedy for company deadlocks (where trust and confidence among the shareholders has broken down) which have arisen without any fault on the part of those involved. It is at present unclear how the courts will balance these two considerations, but it seems highly unlikely that they will develop the winding-up remedy so that it captures a wide range of situations which are not within the unfair prejudice powers.

FIDUCIARY DUTIES

This is an underused strategy in British law. In the US company laws have long regarded majority shareholders as directly subject to fiduciary duties by virtue of their controlling position, which duties they owe both to the company and, more important here, to minority shareholders. British law has never taken this step. Even if a majority shareholder puts itself in the position of being a shadow director, we have seen that it is uncertain how far directors' general duties apply to shadow directors.[60] British law has thus focused on the fiduciary duties of directors, not shareholders.

---

[58] *Completing the Structure* (November 2000), para 5.78.   [59] Ibid 5.60.
[60] Above Ch 6, p 148.

Nevertheless, since the board members are likely to be appointed by the majority shareholder, it would be a constraint on that shareholder if the board members owed fiduciary duties to the minority shareholders, whether or not the majority shareholder itself was subject to those duties. But this step the British courts have also not taken. The general duties of directors, as section 170(1) tells us, are owed to the company. The debate in British law has thus focused mainly on the circumstances in which an individual shareholder can enforce the duties owed to the company by directors. If the individual shareholder can do this, it will undoubtedly constitute a form of minority protection. This is the 'derivative claim' problem, which we discuss below.[61]

Nevertheless we should look here in a little more detail at the exceptions to the rule that directors owe duties only to the company. Section 170 reflects the prior common law and the basic proposition, that directors do not owe duties to individual shareholders, famously associated with the decision in *Percival v Wright*.[62] This rule can be defended on the grounds that it preserves the collective nature of corporate decision-making. It is therefore appropriate to apply it to directors' decisions relating to the conduct of the company's business, but less obvious that it should apply where the directors, whether as part of the conduct of the company's affairs or not, are dealing with the shareholders in relation to their shares (ie, in relation to the property of the shareholders rather than the property of the company). Imposing duties on directors when dealing with share-holders individually does not necessarily undermine the collective nature of the company.

However, one can still ask why should directors and shareholders deal-ing with each other in relation to the latter's shares not be treated as oper-ating at arm's length, so that no fiduciary duty is owed by one party to the other. Within the Commonwealth, the principled answer to this ques-tion was first provided by the New Zealand Court of Appeal in *Coleman v Myers*,[63] where it was found in the monopoly of the majority shareholder/directors over up-to-date information about the affairs of a private com-pany, coupled with a consequent situation of long-term reliance by the minority on the majority, as both sides recognized. In this situation, the controllers were regarded as under a fiduciary duty, in particular a duty to disclose to the minority non-public information which was central to the

---

[61] Below p 247.   [62] [1902] Ch 421.

[63] [1977] 2 NZLR 225. Of course, *Percival v Wright* (previous note) was itself a case where the directors dealt with the shareholders in relation to their shares, but in that case the interaction was initiated by the shareholders and was held not to put the directors in a fiduciary position.

valuation of the shares of the minority which the controllers were negotiating to buy from them. This 'special facts' exception to the *Percival v
Wright* rule that directors do not owe fiduciary duties to individual shareholders seems now to be fully part of English law as a result of the decision
of the Court of Appeal in *Peskin v Anderson*.[64]

Thus, the cases in which directors owe duties to individual shareholders are likely to remain exceptional. *Coleman* was, like so many of the cases
discussed in this chapter, a small company case. In the case of a publicly
traded company, where statutory disclosure requirements are extensive,
there would be little scope for the application of the exception on the basis
of information asymmetry. On the other hand, where the directors of a
public company give advice to the shareholders as to whether they should
sell their shares (as in a takeover offer) or how they should vote (as in a
merger), the courts have recognized a duty on the directors, owed to the
shareholders individually, to give advice in the interests of the shareholders (and not, for example, in their own interests or to promote their view
of the company's interests).[65]

Finally, minority shareholders might benefit indirectly from duties owed
by directors to the company, even if the duties are not owed to them. As we
have seen, the directors' core duty of loyalty requires them to have regard to
the need to 'act fairly as between members of the company'.[66] Given the subjective structure of that section, however, this seems to amount to no more
than a good faith requirement and, even then, fairness as between members
is only one of the factors to which the directors must have regard.[67]

DECISION RIGHTS

Although British law has placed most reliance on ex ante contracting and
ex post standards to address minority issues, examples can be found of
other strategies being deployed. Decisions rights for minority shareholders are quite widely found, but are not as extensively deployed as standards strategies, mainly because, in one way or another, they undermine the
collective view of the company, ie the presumption that all the members of
the company (or at least all the members of the same class) are entitled to
participate equally in shareholder decisions, unless they have contracted

---

[64] [2001] 1 BCLC 372, CA. However, the directors were not dealing with the shareholders
over their shares in this case. It was simply that their (undisclosed) dealings on behalf of the
company would have had an effect on the share price, had they been disclosed. Since there
were good reasons for the non–disclosure, no breach of duty was found.

[65] *Re A Company* [1986] BCLC 382.   [66] s 172(1)(f).

[67] For a pre-Act case in which the minority sought unsuccessfully to invoke this principle
see *Mutual Life Insurance Co of New York v Rank Organisation Ltd* [1985] BCLC 11.

for something different. A mandatory rule which displaces this presumption thus needs justification.

In fact, three different types of decision right can be identified of which British law makes use. These are (in ascending order of severity): requiring supermajority approval for certain decisions; excluding the majority from voting; and giving decisions to individual shareholders. As the severity of the technique increases, so does the infrequency of its incidence.

SUPERMAJORITY REQUIREMENTS

A supermajority is any majority required for a shareholder resolution greater than a simple majority. In the Act supermajority requirements are associated with 'special' resolutions, where 75 per cent of those voting must support the resolution for it to pass.[68] As we explained above,[69] the special resolution does protect a minority which can command at least 25 per cent of the votes likely to be cast by, in effect, requiring the majority to obtain the consent of the minority to the resolution. In other words, a 25 per cent minority obtains a veto right where a special resolution is required which an ordinary resolution would not give it. A special resolution is thus more difficult for the minority to propose than an ordinary resolution but more easy to oppose.

This technique is in fact widely adopted by the Companies Act. We have seen above that the Act requires certain decisions to be approved by the shareholders (ie they cannot be wholly delegated to the board) and in many of those cases shareholder approval is to be given by special resolution. Thus, looking again at the list, given on p 122, of decisions the Act requires to be taken by the shareholders, one sees that the Act requires supermajority consent in the cases of changes to the company's constitution, alterations in the form of the company, decisions to wind the company up, and schemes of arrangement, as well as other cases. It is probably impossible to give a wholly coherent account of why the Act requires shareholder approval in some cases and not others, and why in some cases approval by ordinary resolution and others by special resolution. Underlying the requirements seems to be a notion that fundamental decisions should receive shareholder approval and the potentially more important the decision, the higher should be the majority required.[70]

---

[68] s 283.   [69] Above p 219.

[70] Despite the imprecision of the reasoning in the text, jurisdictions do display a surprising degree of uniformity over the matters they subject to shareholder approval and even in the level of approval required, though in US state laws a simple majority of all the outstanding shares is often used instead of three-quarters of those voting. The two may well produce similar results in practice. Continental European jurisdictions often use two-thirds rather

VOTING CAPS

Special resolutions protect only rather large minorities. An alternative technique for preventing the overreaching of minorities on shareholder votes is to cap the percentage of the votes which any one shareholder and its associates may cast. For example, the rule might be that no one shareholder may cast more than 5 per cent of the votes, no matter how large its shareholding. The articles of companies may impose such a cap and it was not uncommon to do so in the nineteenth century.[71] However, voting caps are not required by law and are in fact uncommon in practice today, perhaps because their impact is unpredictable and perhaps because they may well exacerbate the agency problems as between the board and the shareholders as a class.[72]

MAJORITY OF MINORITY REQUIREMENTS

A more far-reaching form of protection would be to exclude the majority from voting and to seek the approval only of (a majority of) the minority shareholders. In fact, no current rule excludes the majority from voting just because it is a majority. However, shareholders are in a few cases excluded from voting because they have some other quality, which may in particular situations turn out to equate with being a majority shareholder.

However, it should be made clear that the starting point of British company law is that the right to vote is a property right because it is one of the rights which may be conferred upon a shareholder by the share and a share is the holder's property. Consequently, the right to vote can be exercised in principle for purely selfish ends and the shareholder may vote on a resolution even though he stands in a position of conflict of interest in relation to it. In the nineteenth-century case of *North-West Transportation Co Ltd v Beatty*[73] the Privy Council said: 'every shareholder has a perfect right to vote upon any such question, although he may have a personal interest in the subject-matter opposed to, or different from, the general or particular interests of the company.' It is this characterization of the right to vote (and other rights attached to shares) which has made British law resistant

---

than three-quarters as the benchmark. See R Kraakman et al, *The Anatomy of Corporate Law* (2nd edn, Oxford: Oxford University Press, 2009), ch 7.

[71] The model articles of association of 1856 (Table B, reg 38) applied a form of 'progressive taxation' to votes in order to give small shareholders more influence. Each share had one vote for the first ten held by a shareholder, then one vote for every five shares for the next ninety, thereafter one vote for every ten shares. So, a shareholder with 200 shares could be outvoted by three shareholders with 50 shares each.

[72] Precisely for this reason they are popular in some continental European systems, as a defence against the takeover bid.   [73] (1887) 12 App Cas 589, PC.

to the notion of applying fiduciary duties to controlling shareholders (see above). As we have seen, even the non-fiduciary review standards have been developed cautiously by the courts, probably for the same reason.

Nevertheless, in some modern developments under the Act and in relevant bodies of law outside the Act the notion of excluding interested shareholders from voting has made some headway. The CLR proposed that on decisions by shareholders to authorize or ratify breaches of duty by directors, the wrongdoing directors (and their associates—always a difficult term to define) should be excluded from voting. The Act implements this proposal in relation to ratification (ie post breach approval) decisions, discounting the votes of the director 'and any member connected with him'.[74] Thus, a majority shareholder cannot vote as shareholder to ratify his or her own wrongdoings as a director.

The Listing Rules, as applied to companies with a premium listing on the Main Market of the London Stock Exchange, also make significant use of the principle that interested persons should not vote on shareholder resolutions. In respect of transactions between the company and 'related parties' the prior approval of the shareholders is required and the related party's votes are to be excluded by the company, which must also take all reasonable steps to ensure that the related party's associates do not vote either. Here, then, the exclusion of the interested party applies to prior authorizations. Moreover, the definition of a 'related party' includes not only directors (and shadow directors) of any group company but also substantial shareholders, defined as someone able to control 10 per cent or more of the votes.[75] Thus, large shareholders are excluded from voting when they are interested in the transaction with the company, even if they play no formal role in the management of the company. This approach no doubt reflects the perception that large shareholders are well placed to influence corporate policy by informal means outside the board. The Listing Rules display much more openness to the principle excluding interested shareholders from voting than does the Act.

INDIVIDUAL SHAREHOLDER DECISION-MAKING

This is the decision rights strategy which is most corrosive of collective decision-making. It is a denial of collective voice, because any individual

---

[74] ss 239(3) and 252–4. This section does not apply to authorization (ie shareholder approval given before the breach) though it is clear that the CLR intended its proposal to apply to both: *Completing the Structure* (November 2000), 5.85–6 and 5.101. Nor does the exclusion rule apply to shareholder 'affirmation' of substantial property transactions or loans under Ch 4 of Part 10. See ss 196 and 214.   [75] FSA, Listing Rules 11.1.

shareholder can decide to take the decision in question. It is a strategy which, accordingly, is sparingly used. The strategy can take two forms. A shareholder may be able to veto a decision of the company with which he or she does not agree. In other words, the corporate decision is subject to a unanimity requirement. Or the individual shareholder may be able to initiate corporate action, whether the other shareholders agree or not. This is a much stronger form of the idea of individual shareholder decision-making.

Since even veto rights for individual shareholders are likely to hobble corporate adjustments to the changing business environment by creating 'hold-ups', they are rarely found in the Act. The shareholder with the veto will be tempted not to cooperate with the other shareholders to reach a decision which best advances the business of the company but to seek instead some special benefit for giving up the veto. Since, with individual vetoes, all the shareholders have the veto, agreement on any proposal may be very difficult to reach.

The writer is aware of only two individual veto provisions in the Act. A member of the company cannot be required by an amendment to the articles made after he or she joined the company to contribute further capital to it, without individual agreement.[76] The level of one's financial investment in the company is thus a matter of individual decision. However, the company may put pressure on a shareholder to take up new shares by offering them at a favourable price to others (either existing shareholders or outside investors).[77] Second, a private limited company cannot re-register as unlimited without the consent of all its members. Because of the potential impact of this decision on the shareholder's personal liabilities and creditworthiness, limited liability cannot be foregone except on the basis of individual consent.[78]

Enforcing the articles

Turning to initiation rights, it might be thought that giving the individual shareholder the right to initiate action would be regarded as so corrosive of corporate decision-making that it should never occur. Is not a decision about, for example, the commitment of corporate assets an issue for shareholders as a whole (or the board), not individual members? Of course,

---

[76] s 25.

[77] Institutional shareholders seek to combat this development in listed companies by insisting on pre-emption rights and also that those rights be tradable. See E Ferran, *Principles of Corporate Finance Law* (Oxford: Oxford University Press, 2008), 134 ff.

[78] s 102. It may be wondered why this requirement is not applied to public companies: they, however, come by stipulation with limited liability (s 4).

the answer is that it is. However, it may be rational to give shareholders (or members generally) individual enforcement rights in relation to the procedures by which the company is required to operate. The individual shareholder, it might be argued, should be able to insist that the company follows the correct procedure, even if he or she cannot determine the outcome which will be reached if the proper procedure is followed. In this situation the individual shareholder is not taking a decision on the company's behalf to commit its resources, but rather is taking action against the company to secure adherence (by the majority) to proper procedure. Proper procedure constitutes a form of minority protection: in many cases an overbearing majority could not have got what it wanted had it stuck by the correct procedure.

The validity of this argument British company law has long accepted, and has given effect to it by recognizing the articles of association (the company's 'rule-book') as constituting a contract between company and members which, subject to certain restrictions, any member can enforce.[79] This is currently provided by section 33 of the Act. The unfair prejudice provisions (above) now provide a ready mechanism for individual shareholders to secure compliance with the articles. If departure from informal understandings can constitute unfair prejudice, failure to comply with the articles can certainly do so (unless, of course, there was an informal agreement that the articles should not be complied with).[80]

However, direct enforcement of the articles as a contract has long been accepted though it is somewhat more problematic than an unfair prejudice petition. The courts have generated two hurdles for the shareholder who wishes to enforce the section 33 contract, of which the first is probably justifiable and the second is not and, indeed, is incoherent. The first is that only 'membership' rights and not 'outsider' rights can be enforced under section 33.[81] A membership right is one which is held in common by all the shareholders of the company or, at least, all the shareholders of a

---

[79] Of course, the member can enforce the contract only as it is for the time being. If it is validly altered, the amended articles become the rule-book. The courts have not applied the law of contract fully to the articles, because it constitutes a public statement by the company (above n 25) as well as contract among the members and the company: *Bratton Seymour Service Co Ltd v Oxborough* [1992] BCLC 693, CA; cf *A-G for Belize v Belize Telecom Ltd* [2009] 2 BCLC 148, PC.

[80] That observance of the articles could be enforced through this procedure was established even under the 'oppression' regime of the 1948 Act: *Re H R Harmer Ltd* [1959] 1 WLR 62, CA. For a case where the unfair prejudice petition failed, even though there had been extensive breaches of the company's constitution and, indeed, company law, because all those involved had consented to them, see *Jesner v Jarrad Properties Ltd* [1993] BCLC 1032, CSIH.

[81] *Hickman v Kent or Romney Marsh Sheepbreeders' Association* [1915] 1 Ch 881.

particular class. Thus, a right to vote, attached to a class of voting shares, is a membership right, whilst a right to be a director of the company, conferred by the articles on a particular individual, is an outsider right and not enforceable by suit under section 33. The strongest argument in favour of this rule is probably that, if the individual is not a member of the company, there is no question of being able to use section 33 to enforce the entitlement,[82] and that it is not rational to change this position if the outsider happens to become or to be a member of the company.[83] The CLR was content to keep this restriction.[84]

The second hurdle is more problematic. Even if the claimant is seeking to enforce a membership right, the claim may fail on the ground that what he or she is seeking to complain of is a 'mere internal irregularity' (which can be put right by a decision of the majority of the shareholders) rather than breach of a personal right. It is wholly unclear why a breach of the articles should be subject to majority control. It is one thing for the majority to forgive a wrong done to the company, quite another for them to purport to forgive a wrong done by the company to the individual shareholder.[85] Perhaps for this reason, the cases have failed to produce a reliable test for predicting which breaches will be regarded as giving rise to complaints of mere irregularities and which of rights.[86] In principle, the individual shareholder should always be able to insist on correct procedure being followed, unless it is clear that, even if the proper procedure had been followed, the meeting would have arrived at the same conclusion. This last point can be catered for by the court not granting a remedy in any case where this is the situation, rather than by depriving the individual shareholder of the right to sue by some ex ante and arbitrary categorization of the articles into those generating rights and those not. The CLR proposed reform along these lines,[87] but the Act remains, like its predecessors, silent on the point.

---

[82] It should be noted that s 6(2) of the Contracts (Rights of Third Parties) Act provides that that Act does not apply to the s 14 contract

[83] Professor Wedderburn once famously proposed a way wholly to subvert the distinction, by suggesting a membership right to have the affairs of the company conducted in accordance with its articles. See [1957] CLJ 194 at 212.

[84] Above n 74, 5.66–5.67. In any event the well-advised outsider can protect his position by entering into a separate contract (ie outside the articles) with the company.

[85] R Smith, 'Minority Shareholders and Corporate Irregularities' (1978) 41 *MLR* 147.

[86] The conundrum is exemplified in two similar cases of the 1870s, where the courts went in different directions: *MacDougall v Gardiner* (1875) 1 Ch D 13, CA and *Pender v Lushington* (1877) 6 Ch D 70 (Master of the Rolls). The modern tendency is perhaps to prefer the rights analysis: *Wise v USDAW* [1996] ICR 691.

[87] Above n 58 at paras 5.70–5.74 and *Final Report*, Vol 1, paras 7.34–7.40. It may be that the point is not of practical significance because of the availability of the unfair prejudice remedy.

THE DERIVATIVE ACTION:
STANDARDS AGAIN

THE NATURE OF THE PROBLEM

An individual shareholder right to enforce, whether through the unfair prejudice provisions or otherwise, informal arrangements as to how the company is to be run or formal arrangements set out in the company's articles seems correct in principle. However, it is much less easy to square an individual shareholder decision to commit the company to a course of action which requires the deployment of corporate resources with the collective nature of the company. Yet, this is the consequence which the derivative action is capable of having. A derivative action arises where a member of a company seeks to enforce the *company's* rights against direc-tors for breach of their duties to the company and thus to obtain relief on behalf of the company.[88] Since the rights are the company's rights and the company is the potential beneficiary of the litigation, the company may—perhaps typically will—have to pay for the litigation.[89] Thus, if the individual shareholder could initiate litigation against allegedly wrong-doing directors, he or she would be committing the company to expend its resources in a particular direction and, given that resources are finite, in that direction rather than another.

This would be all well and good if it were possible to say that it is always in the company's interests to enforce its rights against the directors for breach of duty. However, it may well not be. It may be debatable whether the com-pany will be able to prove in court the things it says the directors have done; the matters about which the company feels aggrieved may not turn out to be illegal; the directors may not be worth suing; the company may suffer reputational harm through the publicity associated with the suit; the man-agement may have better value projects to spend their time on than litiga-tion. So, whether it is in the company's interests to sue the directors requires a situation-specific assessment in each case. Why should that assessment (and the concomitant decision to commit corporate resources) be given to the individual shareholder rather than to the body which normally takes business decisions (the board) or to the shareholders collectively?

---

[88] ss 260(1) and 265(1). Ch 1 of Part 11 applies to derivative claims in England and Wales and Northern Ireland, ch 2 to derivative proceedings in Scotland. The differences relate largely to matters of civil procedure rather than principle.

[89] *Wallersteiner v Moir (No 2)* [1975] QB 373, CA; Civil Procedure Rule 19.9E; *Wishart v Castlecroft Securities Ltd* [2009] CSIH 65 at [49]–[71] and [2010] CSIH 2.

The answer, of course, is that we do not necessarily trust the board and the shareholders to act in a disinterested way. The board may contain the wrongdoers, who may be able to influence the board decision inappropriately (despite the fiduciary duties of directors).[90] This is especially likely if the directors have been appointed by a majority shareholder and that shareholder is involved in the wrongdoing, but this situation may arise simply from the dominance of the wrongdoers on the board, even in a dispersed shareholding company. The wrongdoers may also be able to influence the shareholders if the wrongdoers include a majority shareholder or his agents, so that shareholder decision-making may be no more reliable than board decision-making. The directors are no longer permitted to use their votes as shareholders to ratify their own directorial wrongdoing, but could use them to pass a resolution that no litigation should be embarked on by the company.[91] Where shareholdings are dispersed, the shareholders may never overcome their coordination problems so as to manage to summon a shareholder meeting, put a resolution to initiate litigation on the agenda, and secure its adoption. In this case the shareholders will simply never address the issue of whether litigation should be brought.

In short, the fear is that confining the right to sue to the collective corporate bodies will lead to sub-optimal levels of litigation, as the interests of the company may be undervalued in the decision-making processes of both board and shareholders. So, giving to the individual shareholder the right to sue on the company's behalf is a way of redressing the balance. Yet, this is a course of action which carries its own risks of inappropriate decision-making. Since recovery in a derivative action is by the company, rather than the individual shareholder, a shareholder suing on behalf of the company will benefit from the success of the litigation only to the extent that the increase in the value of the company's assets is reflected in the share price. In a non-publicly traded company, where there is no liquid market for the company's shares, it may be very difficult for the minority shareholder to realize that gain. Even in a publicly traded company, where any gain can easily be realized, it may be of a very small magnitude, unless the minority shareholder has a significant holding in the company. Thus, the prospect of corporate recovery may

---

[90] Of course, the board may no longer contain the alleged wrongdoers (see *Regal (Hastings) Ltd v Gulliver* [1942] 1 All ER 378, HL) or may have been replaced by an administrator or liquidator, in which case this problem does not arise.

[91] A decision not to sue seems not to fall within s 239 restricting the interested director from voting on a ratification resolution (above n 74). A decision not to sue leaves the wrong intact but resolves that nothing should be done about it, at least by the company.

not provide a strong incentive to the shareholder to incur the effort of organizing litigation.[92] Thus, individual decision-making may still not generate litigation where the company's interests suggest suit should be brought. Even worse, there may be a suspicion that, where the individual does sue, the litigation is driven by some personal interest of the shareholder (perhaps some independent disagreement with the majority shareholder) rather than the financial or other interests of the company.

THE COMMON LAW AND PART 11 OF THE 2006 ACT

In the trade-off between facilitating individual suit (in order to maximize the enforcement of directors' duties) and discouraging litigation not in the interests of the company, the common law chose to stand decisively on the side of discouraging litigation. Under a set of rules, known compendiously as the 'rule in *Foss v Harbottle*', the individual shareholder could proceed with litigation on behalf of the company only in very restricted circumstances. Only if the breach of duty complained of was not ratifiable by the shareholders as a body (ie was a 'fraud on the minority'), only if the wrongdoers had control of the company, and only if the majority of the non-involved shareholders were not against the litigation could the individual proceed with the litigation. Very little derivative litigation resulted. By the 1990s the view was gaining ground that the common law balance discouraged derivative actions disproportionately. In this situation the Law Commission,[93] whose recommendations were accepted substantially by the Company Law Review,[94] proposed a conceptually bold move, albeit one already taken in a number of other jurisdictions,[95] which has found its way into the 2006 Act.

Under Part 11 of the Act the individual shareholder is free to commence derivative litigation in respect of any breach of directors' duties, whether ratifiable or not.[96] In particular, this permits derivative action to be commenced over allegations of the breaches of directors' duty of

---

[92] This problem could be overcome by giving the lawyers a strong incentive to organize the litigation against the company, as under the 'contingent fee' arrangement in the US. However, the British 'conditional fee' arrangements incentivize the lawyers less strongly and it is at present unclear whether British civil procedure rules will move in the US direction.

[93] *Shareholders' Remedies*, Cm 3769, 1997, Part VI.

[94] *Developing the Framework* (March 2000), paras 4.112–4.139.

[95] P van Nessen, S Goo, and C Low, 'The Statutory Derivative Action: Now Showing Near You' [2008] *JBL* 627.

[96] Of course, if the breach of duty has been properly ratified or authorized, there can be no litigation in respect of it by or on behalf of the company, however brought. See ss 263(2)(b)(c) and 268(1)(b)(c).

care. However, the individual cannot proceed beyond the initial step of issuing a claim form unless he or she obtains the consent of the court to continue further with the litigation. So, the court acts as a 'gatekeeper' for the litigation.

The crucial question is what tests the court should apply when determining whether to open the gate or keep it closed. Although Part 11 is procedurally somewhat complex,[97] the essence of the test which the court has to apply—and it seems the appropriate one—is whether it is in the interests of the company that the litigation be brought. This test is deployed in a negative and a positive way. Negatively, the court must refuse permission to proceed with the litigation if a director acting in accordance with the section 172 duty to promote the success of the company would not continue with it.[98] If the claimant passes this test, the court considers a wide range of factors to determine whether it is in the company's interests for the litigation to proceed.[99] They include the importance a director acting in accordance with section 172 would attach to continuing the litigation (so that a merely trivial benefit to the company would count against permission being given), whether the claimant is acting in good faith (rather than, for example, pursuing a collateral grievance), and the factors which the common law put up as bars to litigation but which now appear as factors which the court should consider. Thus, the court must consider the likelihood of the breach being authorized or ratified, whether the company has decided not to pursue the claim, and 'in particular' the views of the shareholders with no personal interest in the decision. It must also have regard to whether there is an alternative remedy which the claimant could pursue in his or her own right which would achieve the desired result.

Whether this reform will move derivative litigation in the UK from its previously sub-optimal level towards the optimum remains to be seen. Some have taken a very gloomy view of whether the courts will apply the legislation in a purposive way.[100] The present writer is less pessimistic, but only time will tell. However, even if the courts do their job well, one may wonder whether the new structure generates

---

[97] Partly in order to save the company the costs of being involved in the litigation until the claimant has shown a prima facie case for being given permission and partly because the Act deals with not only the initiation of derivative litigation but also the taking over by an individual shareholder of litigation begun by the company or by another shareholder.

[98] s 172 is considered in more detail in Ch 6 above at p 155.

[99] ss 263(3)(4) and 268(2)(3).

[100] A Reisberg, 'Shadows of the Past and Back to the Future: Part 11 of the Companies Act 2006 (In)Action' (2009) 6 ECFR 219.

sufficient incentives for shareholders to bring the matter before the court in the first place.

COMPLAINING OF BREACHES OF DUTY THROUGH THE UNFAIR PREJUDICE MECHANISM

The derivative action is not the only mechanism available for the individual shareholder to complain about directors' breaches of duty. The unfair prejudice provisions (discussed above) can be used to this end as well. In *Re Saul D Harrison & Sons plc*[101] Hoffmann LJ (as he then was) explained how this development was linked to the contractual view of the unfair prejudice jurisdiction which he and other judges were then developing.

> Since keeping promises and honouring agreements is probably the most important element of commercial fairness, the starting point in any case under s [994] will be to ask whether the conduct of which the shareholder complains was in accordance with the articles of association. The answer to this question often turns on the fact that the powers which the shareholders have entrusted to the board are fiduciary powers, which must be exercised for the benefit of the company as a whole. If the board act for some ulterior purpose, they step outside the terms of the bargain between the shareholders and the company.

This was a very important conceptual step for the courts to have taken. This use of section 994 complements (indeed echoes) the *Gold Reefs* principle[102] by permitting individual shareholders to challenge on general fiduciary grounds (the requirement to act 'for the benefit of the company as a whole') decisions taken by company controllers at board level as well as the shareholder decisions. Consequently, it is very common to find that the unfairness alleged in section 994 petitions points to acts the majority have done in their capacity as directors in breach of the duties imposed on them, as well as (perhaps even instead of) breaches of informal understandings and arrangements.

The unresolved question is what relief the shareholder can obtain by means of a section 994 petition and, specifically, whether relief for the company (which is what the derivative action produces) can be obtained through an unfair prejudice petition. Or is the petitioner confined to personal relief such as an order that his shares be bought at a fair price? It is clear that there is one way in which an unfair prejudice petition can lead to corporate relief, since one of the orders a court may make if an unfair prejudice petition is successful is to 'authorise civil proceedings to be brought in the name of and on behalf of the company by such person

---

[101] [1995] 1 BCLC 14, CA at 18.   [102] Above n 35.

or persons and on such terms as the court may direct'.[103] However, to bring and succeed in one set of proceedings (the unfair prejudice petition) in order to obtain permission to bring another set of provisions (the derivative claim) is not likely to prove an attractive course of action, as contrasted with going directly to the court to obtain permission to bring a derivative claim under the provisions discussed above. The petitioner might well prefer to see the corporate relief granted immediately the unfair prejudice petition is successful.

However, there are strong reasons for thinking that such a step would not normally be consistent with the scheme of the Act. The Act provides that 'a derivative claim may only be brought (a) under this Chapter [Chapter 1 of Part 11] or (b) in pursuance of an order of the court in proceedings under section 994.'[104] The second part of this provision seems to refer to the order mentioned above.[105] There are good policy reasons for thinking that an unfair prejudice petition should not lead directly to corporate relief. The Act requires a person bringing a derivative action under Part 11 to demonstrate to a court that the litigation is in the company's interests and chokes it off at a preliminary stage, if this is not the case. It would be odd if, by the expedient of recasting the claim as an unfair prejudice claim, the court could be required to hear and determine the substantive allegations, without a decision whether the litigation is in the company's interests. There are a number of pre-Act unfair prejudice claims in which corporate relief has been granted directly,[106] but, naturally, they did not address the point made in this paragraph. That point has been considered, however, in Hong Kong under similar but, on this point, less explicit legislation by that jurisdiction's Court of Final Appeal. After an exhaustive review of the British cases Bokhary PJ concluded that allowing corporate relief to be pursued through an unfair prejudice petition would be appropriate only in 'rare and exceptional' situations.[107] If this analysis is correct, individual decision-making with regard to the enforcement of directors' duties will be channelled through

---

[103] s 996(2)(c).   [104] s 260(2).

[105] This is absolutely clear in the Scottish provisions, which are differently constructed but surely intended to have the same effect. Having stated that derivative proceedings can be begun only under Chapter 2 of Part 11 (s 265(2)), the section makes an exception for 'the court's power to make an order under section 996(2)(c) or anything done under such an order' (s 265(6)(b)).

[106] Notably *Clark v Cutland* [2004] 1 WLR 783, CA; *Bhullar v Bhullar* [2004] 2 BCLC 241, CA.

[107] *Kung v Koo*, FACV No 6 of 2004. For strong argument in the same direction see A Reisberg, *Derivative Actions and Corporate Governance* (Oxford: Oxford University Press, 2007), ch 8.

the derivative action, if corporate relief is sought, but may express itself in the unfair prejudice remedy if relief for the shareholder personally is the goal.

AFFILIATION STRATEGIES

We have noted above that the two main strategies which British law uses to protect minorities (ex ante contracting and ex post court review by reference to a standard) work most effectively only in relation to small bodies of shareholders and therefore, normally, economically small companies. Perhaps for this reason, the Listing Rules of the FSA make greater use than does the Companies Act of the 'majority of the minority' decision rights strategy in order to address the issue in large companies.[108] However, the leading technique for the protection of minorities in publicly traded companies is the exit right. To some extent use is also made of laws which facilitate entry into the company—the other branch of the affiliation rights strategy. We will look in this section at two exit rights and two 'entry' rights.

The exit rights are to be found in their strongest form in the Takeover Code,[109] which is administered by the Panel on Takeovers and Mergers.[110] An exit right is, of course, the remedy provided most often by the court after a finding of unfair prejudice has been made under the provisions analysed above. Here, however, we examine exit rights made available without any finding of unfair prejudice and therefore without any attribution of misconduct or blame to the majority. Moreover, the exit rights now examined arise without court adjudication: if certain circumstances exist there is an exit right and any dispute about whether those circumstances have arisen will be determined by the Panel and its appeal mechanisms, with only very limited rights of appeal to the court. The Panel also normally makes its adjudications in 'real time', not after the event.

THE MANDATORY BID RULE

As their names suggest, the Code and the Panel are concerned with takeover bids, which are offers by a third party (the acquirer or bidder) addressed

---

[108] See above p 243.

[109] 9th edn, March 2009, as amended, available at: <http://www.thetakeoverpanel.org.uk/the-code>. The Code, although formally of somewhat wider ambit, applies in practice to publicly traded companies.

[110] The Panel was initially a self-regulatory body. It now has statutory status under Ch 1 of Part 28 of the Act, but the takeover rules are still mainly adopted by the Panel rather than laid down by Parliament in the Act.

to all[111] shareholders of a company (the target) proposing to acquire their shares for a consideration (in cash or securities of the acquirer) which is normally superior to the current market price of the target's shares. In the normal course of events, a bid is voluntary, that is, the rules of the Code are triggered only if the acquirer decides to make (or is at least contemplating making) an offer for the target's shares. Whether the acquirer takes this decision is normally a matter for it alone.

However, Rule 9 of the Code requires a person who acquires, either alone or together with others acting 'in concert' with it,[112] shares carrying 30 per cent or more of the voting rights in the company to make an offer in cash for all the outstanding equity shares of the company (whether voting or non-voting), the price in the offer to be fixed at the highest level paid by the acquirer or those acting in concert with it for the various classes of the target's shares over the previous twelve months. This is the mandatory bid rule: if the acquirer crosses the 30 per cent threshold, it must make an offer for all the outstanding shares, whether it wishes to or not. In consequence, acquirers rarely breach the 30 per cent threshold; instead, they sit just below it and wait until they are in a position to make a general offer and then proceed with a voluntary bid.[113]

Although subject to exceptions,[114] the mandatory bid rule constitutes a very strong form of minority protection. For example, it permits a shareholder in a dispersed shareholding company to exit the company at an attractive price when its shareholding structure changes to one of having a controlling shareholder (as measured by the 30 per cent rule). This suggests that the Code's rule-makers held two views: one is that the move from dispersed to concentrated shareholding is potentially highly disadvantageous to non-controlling shareholders and, second, that the ordinary provisions of company law would not effectively protect the (new) minority against such adverse developments. Of course, the rule comes with a cost for the shareholders. In effect, the rule makes it impossible for someone to acquire control of the company without making an offer for

---

[111] Other, of course, than itself, if the acquirer already holds, as it normally will, shares in the target.

[112] The 'acting in concert' rules are highly complex and, as the note to Rule 9.1 says, 'the majority of questions which arise in the context of Rule 9 relate to persons acting in concert.'

[113] The main advantages to the acquirer of this way of proceeding are that it retains control over when the bid is launched and over the setting of the acceptance condition (see below). The price offered in the voluntary bid is likely to be calculated in the same way as in the mandatory offer, if there have been substantial pre-bid purchases (Rule 11), as is the range of share classes which must be offered for (Rule 14).

[114] See the note to Rule 9: these are essentially situations where other policy objectives (such as rescuing the company from insolvency) outweigh the policy of protecting minorities.

all the shares, so that there are likely to be fewer offers for the shares than would be the case if the mandatory bid rule did not exist so that partial bids were permitted. Swiss law, for example, responds to this point by permitting the shareholders, subject to safeguards, to modify or exclude the mandatory bid rule through provisions in the company's articles of association.[115]

However, it will be noted that the mandatory bid rule applies, not only when the third party acquires 30 per cent of the votes from dispersed shareholders, but also when the acquisition is from an existing block-holder. Here the minority protection argument is less strong, because the dispersed shareholders are already subject to a controlling shareholder and the transfer of the block has not brought about a change in that position. An argument might be mounted that the nature of the risks to which the non-controlling shareholders are subject might change significantly on a transfer of control to a different controller. However, the costs for the non-controlling shareholders and for society in imposing a mandatory bid rule, at the highest price paid, on a transfer of control are much larger than in an acquisition of control. This is because the highest price rule will discourage block-holders from selling out at all if they cannot secure a premium for their controlling shares.[116] This issue has probably not concerned the drafters of the Takeover Code extensively, because controlling blocks are quite rare in British listed companies.

THE SELL-OUT RIGHT IN TAKEOVERS

For all types of bid (voluntary and mandatory) the Code in certain situations gives the minority a right to require the bidder to acquire his or her shares. Since the takeover bid is an offer by the bidder to the shareholders to acquire their shares, one might well wonder why such a right is needed. The answer to the question can be seen by considering the position of the shareholder who does not think the acquirer's offer an attractive one and so would be expected not to accept it. However, sufficient of the other shareholders may take a different view, so as to give the acquirer the number of shares it wants and, in the Code's terminology, enable the acquirer to declare the bid 'unconditional as to acceptances'.[117] However,

---

[115] See Kraakman et al, above n 70, at p 255.

[116] L Enriques, 'The Mandatory Bid Rule in the Proposed EC Takeover Directive: Harmonization or Rent-Seeking', in G Ferrarini et al (eds), *Reforming Company and Takeover Law in Europe* (Oxford: Oxford University Press, 2004), pointing out that the mandatory bid rule operates to discourage inefficient transfers of control but also efficient ones.

[117] The offer from the bidder will be subject to a condition relating to the proportion of acceptances from the offerees, so that, if that condition is not met, the bid lapses. The Code

the non-accepting shareholder may discover this only once the offer has closed and so cannot any longer be accepted. This means that the shareholder who does not think the offer attractive may nevertheless choose to accept it for fear of being left as a minority shareholder in the company if the bid succeeds.[118] Rule 31.4 requires the acquirer to keep the offer open for fourteen days after it has been declared unconditional as to acceptances, so as to enable the dissenting shareholders to maintain their opposition right to the end, but then to change their minds. This right is thus a form of minority protection which is designed to maintain the integrity of the 'shareholder choice' model for determining the fate of takeover offers which is embodied in the Code.

Even before the Takeover Code was adopted in the late 1960s, the Companies Act 1948, too, provided a sell-out right.[119] The statutory sell-out right is less attractive than the Code right in one major respect: it operates only at the 90 per cent level. This is a rather high threshold. A bidder might well be content with control based on fewer voting rights and thus defeat the shareholders' statutory sell-out right. On the other hand, the statutory right is available for longer (at least three months from the close of the offer)[120] and the statutory right embraces the full range of choices that were available to the shareholders who accepted the offer.[121]

BUYOUT RIGHTS

The shareholder's sell-out right at the 90 per cent level, which has existed since 1948, was in fact pre-dated as a legislative reform by the acquirer's right, introduced in the 1920s, to compel a non-accepting minority to sell their shares to it, once it had acquired 90 per cent of the shares (the so-called 'squeeze-out' right).[122] The squeeze-out right is interesting because it constitutes a recognition on the part of the legislature of the potential 'hold-up' power of the minority,[123] where the acquirer needs to obtain 100 per cent control. Here the legislature addresses the agency problems of the *majority* by permitting them to appropriate the minority

---

requires the acceptance condition to be one which gives the bidder at least 50 per cent of the voting rights in the company (when taken with the shares the bidder holds pre-bid: Rule 10) but beyond that, at least in a voluntary bid, the acquirer has a fairly free hand as to when to declare the bid 'unconditional as to acceptances'.

[118] L Bebchuk 'The Pressure to Tender: An Analysis and a Proposed Remedy' (1987) 12 *Delaware Journal of Corporate Law* 911.   [119] Now in ss 983 ff of the 2006 Act.

[120] s 984(2). Normally, the period is somewhat longer.

[121] s 985(3). The Code allows certain alternatives to the bidder's main offer to be 'shut off' under certain conditions and thus not be available to a shareholder who exercises the Code's sell-out right: Rule 33.2.   [122] Now in ss 979 ff.

[123] See above p 244.

at a fair price. In some other European jurisdictions, there is a buyout right for an overwhelming majority shareholder (for example, one holding 95 per cent of the shares), whether or not that position has resulted from a takeover offer.[124] There is no equivalent provision in the British Act, but it may be possible in some cases for the majority to use the unfair prejudice provisions to review the conduct of the minority, whether it is a 10 per cent minority or, for example, a larger one which has blocked the passing of a special resolution.[125]

APPRAISAL RIGHTS

Whilst the Takeover Code contains a strong version of the shareholder's right to exit upon a change of control, the Companies Acts in recent times have shown little interest in this technique, ie giving the minority an exit right if the majority take a particular type of decision. Perhaps this is not surprising. Unlike with the mandatory bid rule (where the bidder picks up the cost of the exit right), appraisal rights triggered by, for example, fundamental corporate changes would throw that cost onto the company or directly onto its non-exiting shareholders and thus make such changes less likely.[126] Nevertheless, appraisal rights (ie the right to leave the company by cashing in one's shares rather than accepting the fundamental change and remaining in the company or selling out in the market) are quite widely used in some jurisdictions, notably in the United States and Japan. However, they are often hedged around in such a way as to make the rights less attractive in practice than they might seem at first sight.[127]

The principal British example is to be found in a set of rules, dating from 1862 and now contained in Chapter V of the Insolvency Act 1986. Sections 110–12 of that Act permit the liquidator of a company being wound up voluntarily[128] to transfer the company's business to another company in exchange for shares in the transferee company, which shares are then distributed among the shareholders of the transferor company.

---

[124] See Forum Europaeum Corporate Group Law, 'Corporate Group Law for Europe' (2000) 1 *European Business Organization Law Review* at 225 ff.

[125] The majority shareholder is not in terms excluded from using s 994 but what he or she complains of must amount to the 'conduct of the affairs of the company' by the minority and the majority must be unable to obtain redress in another way. Cf *Parkinson v Eurofinance Group Ltd* [2001] 1 BCLC 720: majority shareholder successfully petitioned in respect of the board's conduct in removing him and selling the company's business before the petitioner could exercise his s 168 rights to remove them.

[126] Of course, investors can contract for an exit right and in small companies sometimes do.   [127] Kraakman et al, above n 70, pp 200–2.

[128] Any company can thus make use of this mechanism by the shareholders agreeing to wind the company up.

In effect, the businesses of the transferor and transferee companies are merged and the shareholders of the transferor company become shareholders in the combined enterprise. Any shareholder who did not vote in favour of the special resolution needed to implement the scheme may notify his objection to the liquidator within seven days, and the liquidator must then either abandon the scheme or buy out the dissenting shareholder's shares at a price to be fixed by arbitration. The procedure seems to be popular for reconstructing private companies or groups of companies, where there is agreement among the shareholders about what is to be done. However, if shareholder dissent is a potential threat to the scheme, it can normally be implemented through other mechanisms which do not provide an 'appraisal right' for dissenting shareholders, such as a scheme of arrangement[129] or a takeover offer.

ENTRY RIGHTS

In contrast to exit rights, entry rights facilitate investor decision-making over whether to become or remain shareholders in a company. For minority shareholders the rules relating to publicly traded companies require the provision of two types of information which may be helpful to investors seeking to determine where control in the company lies.

The first concerns disclosure of the beneficial ownership of large shareholdings. Although the share register is a public document[130] (and few companies in the UK issue bearer shares), the register is not all that helpful in determining who controls or influences the company because it lists those with the legal title to the shares but not necessarily those with the beneficial interest. In other words, by vesting my shares in a nominee (who may be a bare trustee for me) I cause the nominee's name to appear in the register and keep my beneficial ownership hidden. Since there are good cost reduction and prudential reasons for using nominees, even in the absence of any particular desire to hide ultimate ownership, a large proportion of the share register may simply reveal nominee holdings.

However, British law has long required the disclosure of 'large' shareholdings. Now those provisions are partly in the Financial Services and Markets Act 2000[131] but mainly in rules (Disclosure and Transparency Rules) made by the FSA which apply to publicly traded companies. Although these rules are rather complex, the essence is that they require,

---

[129] This will require the scheme to be restructured. If it remains a simple exchange of the transferor's assets for shares in the transferee, the court is likely to insist that the IA procedure, with its appraisal right, be used: *Re Anglo-Continental Supply Co Ltd* [1922] 2 Ch 723.

[130] s 116.   [131] s 89B.

in relation to voting shares, disclosure at the 3 per cent level (and every 1 per cent thereafter, upwards or downwards), the disclosure to be made within two days of the event giving rise to the obligation to disclose. This is a low threshold with quick disclosure. Further, the triggers for disclosure go beyond mere acquisition or disposal of shares (so that acquisitions through others are caught) and now include the acquisition or disposal of purely economic interests in shares (through 'contracts for differences' or 'equity swaps') as well as ownership interests in them.[132] Thus, for publicly traded companies it is very difficult for changes in control or even shifts in influence among shareholders to go undetected by the market for very long—something, of course, which helps the management of potential takeover targets as well as investors.

Second, as a result of Article 10 of the Takeover Directive[133] a company whose securities are traded on a 'regulated market'[134] must disclose annually (in the directors' report) information about the structure of the company's capital, about its large holders, about restrictions on voting and transfer rights, and about special control rights which may exist. The information is required mainly to facilitate takeovers, but it may also be of use to those thinking of taking or maintaining a minority shareholding in such a public company. The control structures of British companies traded on regulated markets are not typically complicated and so not much may have to be disclosed under these provisions.

INCENTIVE STRATEGIES

There remain two sets of legal strategies which we have so far not considered: incentive strategies (coming in trusteeship and reward forms) and appointment strategies (coming in selection and removal forms). They can both be dealt with fairly briefly, since neither is heavily used by British law.

SHARING RULES

Non-use of the reward strategy (in the form of a sharing rule) is perhaps surprising. Since a major fear of minority shareholders is that the controlling shareholder will take a disproportionate share of the company's

---

[132] DTR 5.3.1 and 5.3.3(2).

[133] 2004/25/EC, transposed in the UK in the Large and Medium-sized Companies and Groups (Accounts and Reports) Regulations 2008/410. Sch 7, Part 6.

[134] This is the 'top tier' of public markets, so this disclosure obligation does not apply to all publicly traded companies.

earnings, a sharing rule might seem well crafted to meet this concern. There are a number of sharing rules to be found in company law but they are all default rules. The Act[135] lays down a default rule of 'one share, one vote', but allows that provision to be displaced by contrary provisions in the articles; it also lays down a somewhat stronger sharing rule when shares are issued for cash, requiring them to be offered first to the existing shareholders, but that rule, as well can be disapplied;[136] whilst, most relevantly, the model articles lay down a sharing rule for dividends (but no company has to follow the model).[137] The reason for this reluctance to adopt strong sharing rules is that it is easy to think of situations in which it would be sensible to depart from them, and so the law prefers to give companies the freedom to do so.

By contrast, the Takeover Code is committed to strong expressions of the sharing principle. We have just noted that the mandatory bid rule requires controlling shareholders to share their bid premium with the non-controlling shareholders, and other rules in the Code require equal treatment for those who accept the offer with those who sell to the bidder in the market, whether before or after the bid is launched. However, as we have already indicated, these rules are probably more driven by the need to allow shareholders to decide dispassionately on the offer from the acquirer than by a policy of minority protection from the majority shareholders.[138]

Besides default sharing rules, general company law deploys the two principal strategies (already identified) to protect minorities. Shareholders can contract for the sharing rules they wish to have, and their informal understandings in that regard will be protected through the unfair prejudice mechanism.[139] Otherwise, legal principles already discussed elsewhere in the book may come to the minority's aid. For directors (whether acting on behalf of controlling shareholders or not) to take assets out of the company through related party transactions or to divert to themselves corporate opportunities will be a breach of their duties as directors and the minority may seek redress through the derivative action or the unfair prejudice remedy. Equally, the rules on disguised distributions may catch attempts by company controllers to acquire corporate assets at

---

[135] s 284.   [136] s 95.

[137] Companies (Model Articles) Regulations 2008/3229, Sch 1, para 30(4) and Sch 3, para 70(4).

[138] P Davies, 'The Notion of Equality in European Takeover Regulation', in J Payne (ed), *Takeovers in English and German Law* (Oxford: Hart Publishing, 2002).

[139] *Irvine v Irvine (No 1)* [2007] 1 BCLC 349.

an undervalue, at least where the company has no distributable profits,[140] whilst simply giving the corporate assets away is something the company does not have power to do.[141]

TRUSTEESHIP

The other version of the reward strategy is trusteeship, ie giving the decision to someone who does not suffer from high-powered conflicts of interest. In the case of minority shareholders this would mean placing the decision, wholly or partly, in the hands of persons not beholden to the majority shareholder. That 'trustee' may be someone internal to the company or external to it.

As far as internal trusteeship is concerned, the board as a whole could be thought of as performing that role. At the beginning of the last century the courts moved from seeing the board as agents (in law) of the shareholders, who could at any time by an ordinary majority give instructions to the board, and instead began to treat the board as a constitutional body whose powers could be altered only by a sufficient majority to change the articles (ie a supermajority). Part of the argument in favour of this change was that it was a way of protecting the minority because the board was removed from continuous and direct accountability to the majority shareholder.[142] However, since in 1948 Parliament reintroduced that direct accountability by making the directors removable at any time by ordinary resolution,[143] that argument seems to have fallen away.

A better argument might be constructed on the basis of the requirement that half the board be independent non-executive directors, and a director is not classified as independent if he or she 'represents a significant shareholder'.[144] However, this requirement applies only to companies listed on a regulated market, where majority shareholder dominance is not widespread, and not to private companies, where it is. In any event, since the removal power is still vested in the majority shareholder, it is very unclear how independently minded the independent director is likely to be in the face of a controlling shareholder.

The trustee might be external, typically the court. There are a number of transactions regulated by the Act where the court's approval is necessary (for example, reductions of capital in public companies, schemes of arrangement) so that the court has a veto power over the transaction. In

---

[140] See above p 79, n 22.   [141] *Re Halt Garage (1964) Ltd* [1982] 3 All ER 1016.
[142] *Automatic Self-Cleaning Filter Syndicate Co Ltd v Cuninghame* [1906] 2 Ch 34, *per* Collins MR.   [143] Now s 168.
[144] Corporate Governance Code B.1.1.

other cases, dissentient shareholders can place the matter before the court (for example, even if a supermajority of the class approve a variation of class rights under the provisions discussed above, a 15 per cent dissenting minority can prevent the change occurring unless the court confirms it[145]). It may be wondered what the difference is between a court reviewing a decision of the company by reference to a standard and a court deciding whether to confirm a company decision. The answer lies in the fact that, with a standard, the grounds for court review are laid down in the standard, whereas, as trustee, the court has an open-ended discretion. However, it has to be conceded at once that the line between these two can be very narrow, as where the standard is imprecise, on the one hand, and the courts acting as trustee have adopted a narrow view of how they will exercise their discretion, on the other.

Thus, the court as trustee is a feature of British company legislation, but these provisions have made relatively little impact. In 1948, in a case concerning a reduction of capital, a senior Scottish judge, Lord President Cooper, said: 'Nothing could be clearer than and more reassuring than those formulations of the duties of the court. Nothing could be more disappointing than the reported instances of their subsequent exercise.'[146] He was referring to the dearth of cases in which the courts had refused to confirm a reduction on the grounds that it was substantively unfair (though they are more willing to turn a proposal down on procedural grounds, such as the failure to make full disclosure of relevant facts at the prior meeting of the shareholders). However, perhaps this should not surprise us. The confirmation provisions present to the court in specific contexts precisely the difficulties which the courts have faced more generally under the open-ended standard embodied in the unfair prejudice remedy, which has also produced limited results.

APPOINTMENT RIGHTS

In Chapter 5 we saw that British company law attaches great weight to appointment rights, especially to removal rights, as a strategy for dealing with the agency problems of the shareholders as a class as against the board. It would be possible to extend this strategy so as to use it to deal with minority/majority agency problems, by ensuring that minority shareholders were able to have one or more representatives on the board. In this way, the board would be prevented from becoming simply the expression of the views of the controlling shareholder; the minority shareholders

---

[145] s 634.
[146] *Scottish Insurance Corp v Wilsons & Clyde Coal Company*, 1948 SC at 376.

would have access to more, and more current, information about the way the company's business was being conducted; and the minority might be able to influence the substantive decisions taken by the board. In short, minority shareholders would have access to centralized management.

It is always open to minority shareholders to contract for such representation, and, as we have seen, frequently small companies proceed on the basis that all involved will be directors, no matter what their shareholdings. However, British company law has never insisted upon such rules, in contrast to US state laws, which, at one stage, imposed the principle of 'cumulative voting' on a reasonably wide scale. The essence of cumulative voting is that, on the election of the directors, each voting share is allocated a number of votes equivalent to the number of directors to be elected. Those votes may be cast by the shareholder in any way he or she wishes across the directors to be elected, but a sufficiently large minority shareholder, by concentrating her votes on one or a small number of directors, will be able to ensure that her candidates are elected.[147]

Cumulative voting could be said to represent the application to the company of the principle of proportional representation which is often urged in the political sphere. However, this may be the very reason why it has fallen out of favour even in the United States, where today only a very small number of economically unimportant states insist on it. It can be argued that the board is not the place for the expression of competing interests among the shareholders or, at least, if it does become so, its effectiveness in setting and monitoring the company's business strategy is likely to be impaired. It is therefore unlikely that British company law will adopt mandatory cumulative voting, even though the partial re-concentration of shareholdings amongst institutional shareholders in recent years has provided a situation in which cumulative voting could work effectively.[148]

CONCLUSIONS

First, the law gives shareholders who anticipate conflicts between majority and minority considerable latitude to rearrange the internal decision-making procedures of the company through formal contracting.

---

[147] The mathematics of this process are rather complicated and need not detain us here, except to note that in the US formulae were worked out which indicated to minority shareholders of different sizes how they should cast their votes for maximum effect.

[148] See J Gordon, 'Institutions as Relational Investors: A New Look at Cumulative Voting' (1994) 94 *Columbia Law Review* 124. This article contains much interesting material on the rise and fall of cumulative voting in the US. On the likely reluctance of British institutions to make use of cumulative voting, were it introduced, see above p 195.

Second, the unfair prejudice provisions have extended contractual protection to informal agreement and arrangements to which all shareholders are party.

Third, the impact of the unfair prejudice provisions has been extended to embrace redress for the minority where the controllers act in breach of their duties as directors.

Fourth, for publicly traded companies the Listing Rules and the Takeover Code are much more important protective mechanisms than contracting, whether formal or informal. In particular, requiring shareholder authorization of related-party transactions and excluding interested persons from voting on the required authorization (Listing Rules) and the mandatory bid rule (Takeover Code) are powerful minority protection strategies.

Fifth, there is conceivably a gap in the protection of minorities where the company's securities are not publicly traded (so that neither Listing Rules nor Takeover Code apply), but where the number of shareholders is too large for contracting effectively to occur.

Sixth, whether the new statutory derivative action will become an important tool for the enforcement of directors' duties remains to be seen.

9

Shareholder Control

BRITISH COMPANY LAW AND
SHAREHOLDER PRIMACY

In Chapter 1 we identified shareholder (or member) control as one of
the core features of company law. It has now become clearer what are
the main features of shareholder control. First, the shareholders have
control of the company's constitution, since those who establish the
company and who become its first members also adopt its articles and
the members may change the constitution subsequently.[1] Through the
articles, the shareholders determine the division of powers between
themselves and the board, so that the directors are beholden to the
shareholders for the formal grant of their functions. Unlike in many
other systems, the directors' powers derive, in the main, from the company's constitution, not from the companies legislation. Second, the
shareholders' formal power over the directors is affirmed by their right
to remove the directors at any time without cause by ordinary majority vote.[2] Third, shareholder influence over management is powerfully
reinforced by the market for corporate control and the prohibition on
the directors taking defensive measures which might frustrate a takeover bid.[3] Finally, and consistently with the previous two points, the
directors' core duty of loyalty is to promote the success of the company
for the benefit of its members.[4]

Thus, as far as the allocation of powers within the company is concerned and the accountability of those who exercise management
powers, the law places the shareholders in the driving seat. The British
rules are probably uniquely powerful in this respect. Of course, the fact
that shareholders have formal control of the company does not mean
that they are always in a position to exercise it, for example, because
of their collective action problems where the shareholder body is large

---

[1] Above p 15. [2] Above p 125. [3] Above p 141. [4] s 172, above p 155.

and dispersed, though that problem has been mitigated somewhat in recent years through the ability and willingness on the part of institutional shareholders to concert activities.[5] More important, the market for corporate control is a powerful accountability mechanism which does not rely on shareholder organization for its effectiveness. All the shareholders need to do is decide whether to accept the bidder's offer.[6] Therefore, the substantive question needs to be addressed of whether and how shareholder control can be justified.

The justification question stands out since it is quite clear that the business which a company carries on requires inputs from a number of groups of people other than its shareholders in order to function successfully. Even within company law itself, the role of creditors and senior managers is recognized, in connection with the doctrines of limited liability and centralized management. Beyond that, one does not need to be an expert in business organization to see that the contribution of further groups—employees, suppliers, customers—are also crucial. So, why does UK company law place shareholders centre stage, give creditors and senior management only a supporting role, and say virtually nothing about employees, suppliers, and customers? The old argument that the shareholders have these rights because they are the owners of the company now carries little sway, because its premiss is false: shareholders own their shares, not the company. The question is why ownership of shares usually carries control rights over the company: the answer to that question cannot be deduced from the proposition that shareholders own shares in the company.

It is the aim of this chapter to argue that there are good reasons for shareholder control of companies (ie that this model of allocation of control rights is not arbitrary); that, however, different allocations of control rights are perfectly conceivable and are to be found in practice, both in the UK and more so in some other European jurisdictions; and that the choice among the various possible allocations of control depends on one's view of how large organizations are best structured for the production of goods and services in the modern economy. In answering this last question, one should bear in mind the not unlikely possibility that there is no one best solution and therefore no one best set of company laws.

---

[5] Above p 133.
[6] They are likely to get a better offer if they can negotiate collectively with the bidder, but the target management has an incentive to do that on their behalf.

SHAREHOLDERS AS RESIDUAL CLAIMANTS

The standard argument, and one of the most powerful, in favour of shareholder control of companies is that the shareholders come last in line in their claims on the company's revenues. This is true when the company is wound up. Section 107 of the Insolvency Act 1986 provides that in a winding up the company's property shall be 'applied in satisfaction of the companies liabilities pari passu and, subject to that application, shall (unless the articles provide otherwise) be distributed among the members according to their rights and interests in the company'. This rule means that, if a company is wound up with more property than is needed to meet the claims of the non-shareholders, then the whole of the surplus goes to the shareholders. On the other hand, since the company's liabilities have to be met before the shareholders become entitled to anything, it is the residual payment to the shareholders which first is diminished if the company has performed poorly. So, on a winding up, the shareholders go first as far as losses are concerned and go last as far as surplus is concerned.

In the more common context where the company is a going concern the position is a little more complicated. As we have seen in Chapter 4, the company is permitted to make distributions to its shareholders even though not all the claims of the creditors have been discharged, but the rules setting maximum levels of distribution are designed (and may have the effect) that distributions to shareholders do not prejudice the chances of the creditors being paid in the future. In this context too one can say therefore that the shareholders come last in the sense that an increase in the company's liabilities (or a fall in the value of its assets) will reduce, perhaps eliminate, its freedom to pay a return to its shareholders whilst the company is a going concern. As the levels of distribution made by the company fall, so also will the price of its shares, so that the financial impact of the company's lack of business success will be felt immediately by the shareholders, whether it is being wound up or not.

COST OF CAPITAL

The argumentative move from shareholders being residual claimants to their having control rights can be made in two ways. First, it can be said that the shareholders' position at the end of the queue makes them more dependent on the economic success of the company than any other group. If the shareholders did not have control over the management to which has been delegated the task of adopting and implementing the strategies upon which that success depends, equity investment would be a less attractive proposition. The price equity investors would be prepared to pay for shares would decrease and thus the company's costs of raising share capital would increase. So, the argument is that shareholder control reduces the company's costs of production by reducing its cost of capital.

That there is a link between the investor's exposure to the success of the company's business strategies and control rights over the management which sets that strategy is suggested by considering the position of preference shareholders and bond-holders. Preference shareholders with an entitlement to a fixed dividend are often not granted voting rights, except when their dividends are in arrears. Of course, even preference shareholders are not fully insulated from the company's economic success. Preference dividends, like any other distribution, are payable only out of the company's profits, so that if the company earns no profits the dividend entitlement will fall away, either temporarily or permanently.[7] Bond-holders by contrast, who have lent money to the company normally in exchange for an entitlement to a periodic interest payment, are almost never given votes, but their entitlement to interest is not dependent on the company having earned profits. So, bond-holders are at one further remove from the economic success of the company, and this may explain their lack of votes. Nevertheless, as we saw in Chapter 3, lenders (including bond-holders) may and often do contract for negative governance rights over companies (ie covenants requiring lender consent for certain managerial decisions) or for positive obligations on management to observe certain financial ratios. And, if the company's obligations to the lenders are not met, because the company runs out of cash as well as profits, the lenders will likely get control over the company through insolvency law. In insolvency the board appointed by the shareholders is replaced by an insolvency practitioner whose duty is to promote the interests of the creditors. Further, as we saw in Chapter 4, as insolvency approaches the duties of directors begin to reflect in the interests of the creditors.[8] Thus, bond-holders have an attenuated form of control over the company because they have an attenuated, but real, exposure to the company's economic success—and when that exposure begins to manifest itself control rights for creditors are on the law's agenda.

Thus, it is possible to discern a variety of typical 'packages' for investors' relations with the company, the common feature of which is that, the

---

[7] It is a matter of contract whether a dividend which is not paid in a particular year because of lack of profits has to be paid in a future year if profits return as well as the preference dividend due in that year. If so, the preference shares are said to have a 'cumulative' dividend. Equally, because of this dependence on management, preference shareholders may want to negotiate for voting rights in all cases.   [8] Above p 88.

more exposed the investor is to the success of the management's strategies, the stronger will be the control rights which the investor has over the
company.[9] Typically, ordinary shareholders with the strongest exposure
have the strongest form of control, followed by preference shareholders
with some form of contractual entitlement to a return out of distributable
profits, to bond-holders dependent on the company's cash-flow.[10] Non-
voting ordinary shares may appear to be an exception to this pattern, but
it is suggested that they are not. They are typically issued by a company
which has a controlling shareholder which wishes to keep control whilst
raising further equity capital. A prospective investor in non-voting shares
has then to decide whether the block-holder can be trusted to monitor
the management effectively on behalf of all the ordinary shareholders,
voting and non-voting alike. If the answer is positive, then in effect the
non-voting ordinary shareholders have delegated their control rights to
another group of ordinary shareholders. Alternatively, an investor may
be prepared to buy non-voting shares where she concludes that the company will have to come back to the market periodically in the future for
more capital and so will have to treat the shareholders well if it is to raise
risk capital in the future at a reasonable cost. This is shareholder control
through the market rather than through legal rights, but it is still shareholder control.[11]

What are the implications of the cost of capital argument for the policy
of the law towards shareholders' voting rights? They are probably no more
than that the law should permit those establishing or later controlling a
company to assign all the voting rights in the company to the ordinary
and perhaps other shareholders, but not require it. There may be a cost
of (equity) capital penalty to be paid if equity shareholders are not given
voting rights, but the company's management may think this a price worth
paying in particular situations for other benefits. Generally that sort of
trade-off is left by the law to the management of the company. There is
no mandatory rule of company law that management must minimize its
cost of equity capital. Thus, if a company wishes to raise large amounts

---

[9] Shareholders and lenders can contract for more or less whatever range of rights the company is prepared to grant them. The 'packages' discussed in the text are thus factually typical,
not legally required.

[10] This is assessing control rights from an ex ante perspective. Ex post, for example
if the company nears insolvency, the bond-holders' control rights will trump those of the
shareholders.

[11] Even so, non-voting ordinary shares will normally trade at a discount in the market
to voting ordinary shares, because of their holders' exposure to controlling shareholder
opportunism. See Ch 8 above at p 220.

of finance by way of debt (ie 'leverage' the company), this will typically raise its cost of equity capital because the residual available for distribution to the shareholders is likely to become more volatile. However, that is regarded as a decision for the company, not the law.

Facilitating but not mandating shareholder control, it could be said, is the stance which British company law adopts. Shareholder control is permitted, even assumed by the Act as the typical situation, but it is not mandatory. We noted in Chapter 1 that the Act provides for one form of company (the company limited by guarantee) which has no shareholders.[12] Even in shareholding companies, there is no obligation to issue all or any of the voting shares to the suppliers of risk capital. We noted that in small quasi-partnership companies there may be no significant equity capital and the allocation of control rights is essentially to those who are going to manage the company, as is the case in limited liability partnerships used to run professional firms (the LLP being mainly governed by company law).[13] The same arrangement is possible in larger businesses but much less commonly found. A large company with an appropriate business model might raise its long-term finance through debt and allocate the voting rights elsewhere—probably to members rather than shareholders.[14] Possibly, it could even issue non-voting ordinary shares to the providers of risk capital and the voting shares could be allocated elsewhere (say, to employees) for a nominal consideration. However, that course of action would run up against the reluctance of institutional investors to buy non-voting shares, ie there would be a cost of capital penalty to be paid. In some cases, successful entrepreneurs, reaching retirement without any obvious successors in the family, have handed over the shares to a trust for the benefit of the employees, an arrangement which often comes near to entrenching the management of the company. An example is the retailer, John Lewis. The law's main mandatory contribution, it might be said, is to *deprive* shareholders of the control rights they have contracted for from the company at the point where their investment has disappeared, ie upon insolvency or even when insolvency is unavoidable.

---

[12] Above p 26.   [13] Limited Liability Partnership Act 2000, ss 1 and 15.
[14] See eg Glas Cymru which describes itself as 'a single purpose company formed to own, finance and manage Welsh Water' so that 'under Glas Cymru's ownership, Welsh Water's assets and capital investment are financed by bonds and retained financial surpluses'. This is possible because in the regulated business of supplying water to customers the costs and revenues of the business are highly predictable. Otherwise, this would be regarded as a company with an unduly high level of leverage. Even so, the covenants in the loan contracts are likely to be particularly demanding.

EFFICIENT MONITORING

A second way of moving from the ordinary shareholders as residual claimants to shareholders as holders of control rights is to focus on the comparative efficiency of shareholders as monitors, in comparison with the other groups to whom control rights could be allocated. The argument here is that, because of their position as residual claimants, shareholders have a greater incentive to use their monitoring powers to see that management minimizes the company's costs of production than any other group to whom monitoring rights might be assigned. Minimizing the value of the company's inputs and maximizing the value of its outputs maximizes the company's contribution to the wealth of society, so that shareholder monitoring serves social goals. Shareholders' incentives to maximize their own wealth are to be promoted, not because shareholders benefit from their monitoring, but because everyone else does too.[15] Whatever view one takes of 'sustainability' or the benefits or otherwise of economic growth, there would seem to be no reason to be in favour of using more resources to achieve a given level or type of output than is otherwise possible.

By contrast, groups with fixed claims against the company—whether preference shareholders, bond-holders, employees, customers, or suppliers—have a lesser incentive to drive down the company's costs of production because, beyond the level of corporate performance needed to ensure the satisfaction of their claims, these other groups do not benefit from extra monitoring effort. Only ordinary shareholders benefit from extra monitoring across the whole range of potential monitoring effort, up to the point where the marginal extra costs of monitoring exceed the extra benefits therefrom. This argument is probably not undermined by the accurate observation that some groups with fixed claims may also have non-fixed interests in the company's performance which would be advanced by efficient monitoring. For example, employees with fixed claims in respect of their current jobs may have a greater chance of promotion if the company prospers. However, this incentive is normally less direct and less powerful than the immediate pay-offs to ordinary shareholders from

---

[15] 'The appropriate goal of corporate law is to advance the aggregate welfare of all those affected by the firm's activities . . . That is what the economists would characterize as the pursuit of overall social efficiency . . . Focusing on the maximization of shareholder returns is, in general, the best means by which corporate law can serve the broader goal of advancing overall social welfare . . . Whether in fact the pursuit of shareholder value is generally an effective means of advancing overall social welfare is an empirical question on which reasonable minds can differ.' (J Armour, H Hansmann, and R Kraakman, 'What is Corporate Law', in R Kraakman et al, *The Anatomy of Corporate Law* (2nd edn, Oxford: Oxford University Press, 2009), 28–9. This argument, of course, goes back to Adam Smith.

effective monitoring. Consequently, any reform which makes the board accountable, wholly or in part, to some monitoring group other than the shareholders is likely to reduce the pressures on management to minimize the company's costs of production, even if the issue of conflicts between the monitoring groups could be satisfactorily solved.

A commonly advanced counter-argument is that monitoring by shareholders leads to concentration on short-term goals. Some shareholders undoubtedly have short-term goals. For example, hedge funds which buy shares in a takeover target after a bid has been launched have a very short-term interest in that company, namely that the bid for it should succeed. They will not mind if the bidder overpays for the target; indeed, they may sell the shares of the bidder short in order to benefit from that aspect of the deal as well.[16] However, it is not at all clear why the interests of all shareholders should be regarded as short term. Insurance companies and pension funds, which now hold a substantial proportion of the shares of publicly traded companies, have very long-term horizons.[17] Such an investor will not benefit if shares currently have a higher value, if the cost of that is a lower value in five years' time. It might also be possible to structure the control rights of shareholders so as to give greater weight to long-term holders, though it is not easy to devise techniques which do not have adverse side effects.[18]

An alternative or additional set of arguments in favour of shareholder monitoring is that the ordinary shareholders have a greater homogeneity of interest than any other monitoring group or, of course, a monitoring group made up of a number of different monitoring classes. The shareholders' interest can be reduced to an interest in the value of the share and votes are usually allocated according to the shareholder's financial interest in the company. Both points make for a clear monitoring focus. Monitoring by other groups, such as employees, is likely to involve a greater range of interests as between different classes of worker, which may result in

---

[16] M Kahan and E Rock, 'Hedge Funds in Corporate Governance and Corporate Control' (2007) 155 *Pennsylvania Law Review* 1021; H Hu and B Black, 'Hedge Funds, Insiders, and the Decoupling of Economic and Voting Ownership: Empty Voting and Hidden (Morphable) Ownership' (2007) 13 *Journal of Corporate Finance* 343.

[17] Moreover, the hedge fund strategy in a takeover cannot work if the existing, non-hedge fund shareholders are not willing to sell out at something less than the bid price, so they must perceive the price offered by the bidder as a fair valuation of their shares.

[18] French law permits companies by shareholder decision to confer double voting rights on those shareholders who have held their shares for two years, thus giving them greater weight in shareholder decisions, but also in takeovers giving greater weight to the decisions of long-term shareholders who do not sell out as against those who do, who can pass on only the standard voting right to the acquirer (Commercial Code, Art L225-123).

a dispersal of or even ineffective monitoring effort.[19] Of course, within these other groups, particular sub-groups of persons could be chosen as the monitors, such as skilled workers.

The implications of the efficient monitoring argument for legal policy are somewhat more robust than those flowing from the cost of capital argument. The implication is that there would be an efficiency (cost of production) loss in any departure from shareholder monitoring and that this is a cost which would fall on society as a whole as well as on the shareholders. In this situation, it might be said, the law should not adopt a neutral attitude to replacing shareholders with other monitors or even with a system in which shareholders shared control with others; it should as a minimum lean against anything other than shareholder monitoring. This might be said to be a better description of current UK company law than the neutral approach to non-shareholder involvement in monitoring, suggested above. Although it is by no means impossible to assign control rights elsewhere under current company law, current law does not facilitate it. Its strong default rule is (exclusively) shareholder control.[20]

EMPLOYEES AND CORPORATE CONTROL

THE NATURE OF THE EMPLOYMENT CONTRACT

The argument based on shareholder monitoring might be thought to have the implication that the law should not merely lean against any other system but should positively impose shareholder monitoring. The arguments made above suggest that a move away from shareholder monitoring in favour of employees or any other group, at least in companies requiring significant equity funding, would have adverse efficiency implications for society through less productive use of resources. Society's only concern, it might be said, should be to ensure that shareholder governance is not overly concentrated on short-term considerations. This might be said to be an accurate characterization of the state of things currently in the UK. The Companies Act and the Takeover Code strongly support shareholder

---

[19] This case is powerfully argued by H Hansmann, *The Ownership of Enterprise* (Cambridge, Mass., and London: Harvard University Press, 1996).

[20] Of course, British law does make a number of non-company legal vehicles available where control rights are given to groups other than shareholders, such as cooperatives, building societies, community benefit societies (formerly friendly societies), but these are essentially vehicles for businesses which do not use significant, if any, amounts of equity capital. They are indeed often inefficiently run, in cost of production terms, because no one has a strong incentive to monitor their management.

primacy, and the government leans on institutional shareholders to engage with investee companies on a long-term basis.[21]

However, even within this costs-of-production paradigm, an argument could be made for employee participation in corporate governance if the efficiency gains to the company arising out the inclusion of employee interests in a reformed employee governance system were greater than the losses arising out of downgraded shareholder monitoring. The section will explore how such an argument could be constructed. It is unlikely that the argument can be made to stand up in the market economy if control rights were shifted entirely from shareholders to employees, and so we will concentrate on mechanisms which involve the sharing of control between shareholders and employees. It is also unlikely that the argument could be made to stand up, generally, in relation to any other group of stakeholders than the employees, since stakeholders other than employees (including in fact shareholders) can reduce their exposure to the company by diversifying their commitments across a number of companies.[22] The only other reasonably prominent alternative to exclusive shareholder control found in European economies is state control. This model will not be considered in this chapter, partly because it is in retreat in the UK as a permanent feature of the economic organization[23] and partly because, in its heyday, the legal vehicle for carrying on state-controlled enterprises tended not to be a company formed under the Companies Act but a corporate body created specifically by statute for the activity in question. So, the focus for the rest of this chapter will be on a comparison between exclusive shareholder control and a system in which governance rights are shared between shareholders and employees.

The standard argument for excluding employees from control rights in the company is that, even if they are in a uniquely poor position among stakeholders to diversify their risks by having a number of concurrent

---

[21] See above p 135.

[22] Of course, there can be cases of sole suppliers or sole customers, but the problems arising can normally be addressed through contractual provisions or by adjusting the boundaries of the firm, ie by the company acquiring its supplier or customer or vice versa. The argument in this chapter also proceeds on the basis that a stakeholder is someone whose contribution is necessary for the productive success of the company and does not extend to groups who are simply affected by the company's activities.

[23] Clearly, in the 2007 paralysis of the banking system temporary state control of certain banks and building societies has been part of the government's policy to prevent the collapse of financial institutions whose failure presented systemic risks to the economy. However, the government's stated aim is to sell off the stakes when market conditions make this appropriate, if only to help redeem some of the government debt issued to acquire the stakes in the first place.

employers, they can protect themselves through the contract of employment. The contract of employment does indeed give employees fixed claims against the company by way of remuneration and other benefits which take the employees out of the category of being pure residual claimants. However, on the task side the contract of employment is typically rather open-ended, in terms of specifying what the employee has to do or how to do it. This is because it has to regulate a potentially long-term relationship. Labour lawyers have long recognized the indeterminacy of the task side of the employment contract[24] and the fact that this indeterminacy benefits employers as much as, probably more than, employees. Within broad parameters the employer wishes to remain free to specify amended tasks as circumstances change. What the employer will wish the employee to do in even the short-term future is normally unknowable with any precision at the time the contract is entered into. Even if circumstances do not much change, the employer will want to leave many employees significant discretion in the discharge of the work tasks, for the employee will be in a much better position to identify the most efficient way of discharging those tasks at the level of fine detail than the employer. It is conceivable that these considerations could be addressed—and in the past have been addressed—by means of the employer reserving in the contract a wide formal power to tell the employee what to do[25] and employing supervisors to monitor how well the employee does the task. However, close monitoring is an expensive exercise for the employer and, as jobs become more sophisticated, the level of employee performance may not be immediately observable by even dedicated supervisors (and who is to monitor them?).

Thus, there is an argument from the employer's point of view for developing a commitment on the part of the employee to employer's goals for the employment: internalization could conceivably replace close monitoring. However, the employee's willingness to engage in this process is likely to be affected by the availability of reciprocal commitments on the side of the employer—most probably to address employee concerns relating to the maintenance of the employment relationship. Commitment by the employee to the goals of the employment relationship as the employer sees them is, in short, likely to be more forthcoming where that approach is

---

[24] 'Compared with that of many other types of contract, the content of personal work or employment contracts is to a very large extent dependent upon implied terms... In this respect, the law creates or confirms a regime in which the content of personal work or employment contracts is usually not specified fully or directly as part of the initial act of contract making, that is to say at the point of engagement for work or appointment to employment.' (M Freedland, *The Personal Employment Contract* (Oxford: Oxford University Press, 2003), 119.

[25] In the shape of an implied (or express) duty on the employee to obey all lawful orders.

reciprocated by the employer. The aim, it is sometimes said, is to produce a 'high trust' relationship between employer and employees: the employer trusts the employee to work without close supervision to achieve the goals of the enterprise as the employer sees them; the employee trusts the employer to take the employees' interests into account when taking strategic decisions about the direction of the firm and implementing that strategy.[26]

This dynamic is more likely to develop where the company needs to induce employees to make firm-specific human capital investments (FSHC) in order to extract the best use from the tangible and intangible assets the firm holds. FSHC involves the acquisition by employees of skills which are of no or lesser value outside the firm but which are valuable within the firm. The need for FSHC investments strengthens the employees' incentives to gain some control over some strategic decisions by the firm. Since the skills are specific to the firm, they cannot be sold to good effect on the market (by finding an alternative job). Further, since the skill has to be acquired first, the employee is at risk of subsequent opportunistic behaviour by the employer which deprives the employee of the value of the investment, for example, by plant closures or changes in technology. On the other hand, the employer has an incentive to induce the employees to acquire the relevant FSHC in order to maximize the productiveness of the firm.

GOVERNANCE STRUCTURES FOR THE EMPLOYMENT RELATIONSHIP

The above argument suggests the basis for a deal between employees and employer: acquisition of FSHC in exchange for higher wages and job protection or, even where no FSHC is acquired, freedom from close supervision (and presumably therefore greater job satisfaction) in exchange for internalization of the employers' goals for the employment relationship. Since the deal, if it is possible at all, occurs in the context of a potentially indefinite employment relationship, it is very unlikely that its terms can be spelled out in detail in advance—for the same reasons that the task side of the employment contract cannot be spelled out in detail. What is needed is a governance structure for the employment relationship through which each side can protect its legitimate interests whilst maintaining the trust basis of the relationship, as changes occur in markets and technologies.

[26] This argument was first developed at length in the British literature in A Fox, *Beyond Contract: Work, Power and Trust Relations* (London: Faber, 1974).

Governance structures for the employment relationship are, of course, of long standing. Three main types exist. First, there is collective bargaining, conducted by a trade union on behalf of its members, though de facto for the benefit of all the employees in respect of whom the union is 'recognized' by the employer for the purposes of collective bargaining. Collective bargaining may be conducted with single employers or with multiple employers (employers' associations), and the latter may occur on a regional or national basis within an industry. Second, there are works councils, based at the level of the firm and representing all the employees in the firm and having a variety of possible relationships, cooperative or competitive, with the trade unions, if any, operating in the same area. Works councils normally draw their strength from legislation giving them rights as against the employer rather than from the decisions of workers to join a trade union and support its policies, as is the case with collective bargaining. Third, governance may be provided through employee representation on the board of the company, sometimes on a single tier board, sometimes on the upper tier of a two-tier board,[27] with the proportion of seats allocated to the employees varying but not being above one-half (parity).

Collective bargaining

What is the potential for the generation of high-trust relations of the three employee governance mechanisms identified above? Collective bargaining probably has the least potential for generating high-trust relationships. Its staples are essentially distributional issues as between employees and managers/shareholders, for example, the division of the economic surplus of the company as between wages, pay-outs to the shareholders, and retentions by the managers for reinvestment. Distributional issues inevitably generate adversarial attitudes and these are likely to hinder the development of high-trust relations even in relation to matters where the benefits of cooperation are significant. This is not to say that collective bargaining is wholly an adversarial process. Rather, it contains elements of both cooperation and conflict, but it is perhaps true to say that only in rather particular situations do the cooperative elements predominate and predominate in a sustainable way.[28]

---

[27] See Ch 7 above at p 202.
[28] J Bélinger and P Edwards, 'The Conditions Promoting Compromise in the Workplace' (2007) 45 *British Journal of Industrial Relations* 713, identifying technology, exposure to the market, and institutions as the operative factors.

Works councils

Works councils, whose members are normally elected by the workforce as a whole, are not necessarily likely to do any better than collective bargaining in generating high-trust relations, if they have to deal with high-powered distributional issues as well. However, in a number of continental European countries one can see a division of function between the works council, on the one hand, and collective bargaining through a union, on the other, in which the most adversarial issues are allocated to collective bargaining, leaving works councils to concentrate on areas of potential cooperation for the mutual benefit of both parties to the employment relationship. However, the works council probably needs quite close links with the union in order to obtain the expertise to be an effective counterparty in discussions with the employer.[29] Thus, relations between works council and union need to be particularly sophisticated in order to give the works council space to develop areas of cooperation with the employer without infection from the adversarialism of collective bargaining, but also without cutting the works council off from the union entirely, for in that case it will probably not operate effectively as either a representative of the employees or as a negotiating party for the employer.

Currently, the arrangements most closely approximating this desideratum seem to exist, probably more by accident than design, in Germany.[30] What is the evidence about the impact of works councils in Germany on the production costs of German firms? Economic modelling suggests the potential gains from mandatory works councils to the firm are substantial, arising out of better information flows from management to employee representatives which moderate worker demands in poor times and reduce the incentives to inappropriate behaviour (by either management or workers) based on misunderstandings about the other party's position; the production of better solutions to new problems faced by the firm; and greater job security which encourages FSHC investment by employees.[31] Empirical

---

[29] R Gumbrall-McCormick and R Hyman, 'Embedded Collectivism? Workplace Representation in France and Germany' (2006) 37 *Industrial Relations Journal* 473.

[30] See W Müller-Jentsch, 'Germany: From Collective Voice to Co-management', in J Rogers and W Streeck (eds), *Works Councils* (Chicago and London: University of Chicago Press, 1995), ch 3. However, it is necessary to avoid taking too static a view of the German system. It is constantly evolving and could evolve away from the dispositions best suited to generate high-trust relations. See G Jackson, M Höpner, and A Kurdelbusch, 'Corporate Governance and Employees in Germany: Changing Linkages, Complementarities and Tensions', in H Gospel and A Pendleton (eds), *Corporate Governance and Labour Management* (Oxford: Oxford University Press, 2005).

[31] R Freeman and E Lazear, 'An Economic Analysis of Works Councils', in Rogers and Streeck (eds), above n 30, ch 2.

evidence bears out the model. Even the most unfavourable assessment of works councils finds works councils to be associated with higher labour productivity, higher wages, and lower profitability. However, because the research could not identify the relative importance of these effects, it could not say whether the profit effect dominated the productivity effect to yield a reduction in the joint surplus of employees and shareholders or not.[32] More recent research has suggested that works councils 'foster the generation as well as the distribution of rents that would otherwise not occur'.[33]

Under the influence of European Community legislation,[34] the United Kingdom has recently introduced a form of works council legislation in the shape of the Information and Consultation of Employees Regulations,[35] which require the employer, on an application from a sufficient number of workers, to set up a mechanism within the firm to inform the employees about the economic situation of the firm and the state of its activities and their likely development; to consult them on matters relating to employment levels in the firm, threats thereto and any measures the firm envisages taking; and to consult them 'with a view to reaching an agreement' on decisions likely to lead to substantial changes in work organization or contractual terms. Evidence to date is that the take-up of this new representational mechanism has been low.[36] This is consistent with the view, discussed further below, that step-changes in workplace governance arrangements do not occur easily.

In the UK, where collective bargaining through a union, underpinned by the threat of industrial action, has been the dominant form of governance of the employment relationship since the industrial revolution, a move to a mechanism based on legal entitlements to information and consultation attached to the employees rather than the union requires considerable adjustments on the part of employees, union officials, and managers if the mechanism is to be used effectively. Even with the decline

---

[32] J Addison, C Schnabel, and J Wagner, 'Works Councils in Germany: Their Effects on Establishment Performance' (2001) 53 *Oxford Economic Papers* 659.

[33] B Frick and E Lehmann, 'Corporate Governance in Germany: Ownership, Codetermination and Firm Performance in a Stakeholder Economy', in H Gospel and A Pendleton (eds), above n 30 at 135.

[34] Directive 2002/14/EC ([2002] OJ L80/29) establishing a general framework for informing and consulting employees in the European Community.

[35] Information and Consultation of Employees Regulations 2004/3426, especially reg 20.

[36] M Hall et al, *Implementing Information and Consultation: Evidence from Longitudinal Case Studies in Organisations with 150 or more Employees*, Department for Business, Innovation and Skills, Employment Relations Research Series 105 (December 2009). Consultation mechanisms have existed on a voluntary basis in the UK for many years. What the research establishes is that the Regulations had not (yet) altered their limited role in the conduct of British industrial relations.

in the coverage of collective bargaining, which has been in train for over a quarter of a century, substantial growth in effective consultation mechanisms has not occurred. Even if it did, it is far from clear that it would operate so as to expand the areas of cooperation between management and workers. In a system, like that in the UK, where collective bargaining is also firm based, rather than multi-employer, as in Germany, it may be difficult to insulate the consultation mechanism from the adversarialism of collective bargaining, where collective bargaining exists in the firm,[37] or for the consultation mechanism to work effectively where there is no union presence. The development in the UK of cooperative relations through consultation mechanisms might be trapped in this dilemma, even if the statutory mechanism were to become more widespread.

Worker representation on the board

With mandatory worker representation on the board we come to the final of the three mechanisms with a capacity for generating high-trust relations between employer and employees but the first that makes use of the structures of corporate law to this end. The employees' agency costs as against the company (management or shareholders, as the case may be) are addressed by giving them appointment rights in respect of the board.[38] By the same token, this mechanism is confined to firms which carry on business through the company vehicle, but since mandatory appointment provisions are confined in practice to firms with large numbers of employees, and therefore to firms which are large economically, and since the corporate form is the vehicle of choice for large businesses,[39] this potential limitation on the scope of the mechanism is not significant.

The potential advantage of the board representation mechanism as against the other two is that the board provides the forum in which the company's strategy is set, whereas collective bargaining and works councils handle the consequences of strategic decisions and can thus be said to secure employee input into decision-making too late in the process. Just under half the member states of the European Union require large

---

[37] 'Councils fit better in labour relations systems where pay and other basic components of compensation are determined outside the enterprise...[this] may help to explain why councils are found largely in economies with relatively centralized collective bargaining.' (Freeman and Lazear, above n 31, p 32.) See also O Hübler and U Jirjahn, 'Works Councils and Collective Bargaining in Germany: The Impact of Productivity on Wages' (2003) 50 *Scottish Journal of Political Economy* 471.

[38] Lesser rights could be envisaged and are found in some jurisdictions, for example, a right for employees to veto shareholder appointment decisions in respect of a certain proportion of the members of the board. For simplicity, we will focus on the employee appointment right.

[39] See Ch 1 above at p 21.

companies operating in the private sector of the economy to grant appointment rights to the employees in respect of a proportion of the members of the board.[40] In the overwhelming majority of cases these rights exist only in relation to a minority of the seats on the board, typically one-third or fewer. Even where the employees can be outvoted on the board, their board presence may play an important role in facilitating the flow of information about the company's strategic choices to lower-level representation mechanisms, such as the works council or, less often, the union for collective bargaining.[41] Thus, board level appointment rights for employees do not constitute a fully coherent strategy on their own but only in conjunction with either collective bargaining or works councils (or both).

However, discussion centres around the unique system of parity codetermination required of large companies in Germany (ie those employing more than 2,000 workers).[42] It is clear that parity codetermination has a significant impact upon the behaviour of the board, even if the shareholder representatives are likely to get their way in a deadlock because the chair of the supervisory board has a casting vote and that person will be a shareholder nominee. The most notable governance change flowing from parity board representation is that the supervisory board becomes a less effective body for setting and monitoring overall corporate strategy. Rather, it focuses much more heavily than would otherwise be the case on strategic issues of concern to the employees.[43] In a system of concentrated ownership, which is what Germany generally has, controlling shareholders may not worry about the functions of the board being so confined, because a large shareholder will always have direct access to the top management of the company and does not need to rely on the supervisory board to monitor

---

[40] 'Arrangements for employee representation at board level in the EU countries plus Norway can be divided into three groups. There is a group of ten countries where there is no board level representation and a further group of six, where board level representation is limited to state-owned or recently privatised companies. However, the biggest group of 12 states provides for employees to be represented on the boards of private companies, once they have reached a certain size. These thresholds vary greatly as do other elements of the national arrangements.' (European Trade Union Institute, available on <http://www.worker-participation.eu/National-Industrial-Relations/Across-Europe/Board-level-Representation2>).

[41] R Kraakman et al, above n 15 at 110. Consequently, a crucial element about the functioning of such arrangements can be whether the appointment rights are conferred upon the employees as a whole, the works council, or the trade union—or some combination of these.

[42] For companies employing between 500 and 2,000 workers a one-third system is required. Below the 500 threshold employee representation on the board is not mandatory.

[43] K Pistor, 'Co-Determination in Germany: A Socio-Political Model with Governance Externalities', in M Blair and M Roe (eds), *Employees and Corporate Governance* (Washington, DC: Brookings, 1999), 163.

the management of the company. In fact, a block-holder may welcome the de facto narrowing of the supervisory board's functions, since it implies a diminution of the areas upon which the employees will have an influence. The losers in this process may appear to be the minority shareholders, but, in the absence of a system of cumulative voting or something similar,[44] it is not likely that the supervisory board is an effective mechanism for the protection of their interests, even in the absence of employee representation.

As to the impact of parity codetermination on the productive efficiency of the firm, the evidence is rather inconclusive. One piece of research found that the shares of companies with parity codetermination traded at a 31 per cent discount compared with those with one-third representation. This indicates that parity codetermination carries a significant cost of capital penalty, but does not demonstrate that gains in terms of labour productivity fail to outweigh this penalty.[45] In other words, the discount might be simply a reflection of the distributional effect of parity codetermination (lower dividends for shareholders; higher wages for employees) rather than evidence of an overall higher cost of production. On the other hand, overall higher costs of production might be the driver of the share price discount. By contrast, other research has shown an increase in both profitability and productivity in the move from one-third to parity codetermination.[46]

PATH DEPENDENCY

It is clear from the above discussion that a number of patterns of employee governance can be found across the EU, involving different roles for collective bargaining, works councils, and appointment rights for the employees at board level. Can member states simply pick the combination of these mechanisms which will most effectively reduce the firm's costs of production? There are two reasons why this is a more difficult exercise than it might seem. First, the empirical evidence about the impact of appointment rights at board level is rather mixed. A government of a state without such rights might well take the view that it would need much stronger evidence of the benefits of introducing appointment rights for employees before it

---

[44] See Ch 8 above at p 263.

[45] G Gorton and F Schmidt, 'Capital, Labor and the Firm: A Study of German Codetermination' (2004) 2 *Journal of the European Economic Association* 863.

[46] S Renaud, 'Dynamic Efficiency of Supervisory Board Codetermination in Germany' (2007) 21 *LABOUR* 689, which usefully summarizes earlier research showing varying results.

was convinced of the utility of such a move or of the chances of overcoming the political opposition that such a move would likely generate.

Second, even clear empirical evidence of the benefits of mandatory appointment rights for employees in Germany would not answer the question about the likely impact of the introduction of such rights in, for example, the UK. The impact of a governance system will depend on characteristics of the society in which the mechanism is embedded, ie this is pre-eminently a question of path dependency.[47] Let us assume that a high-trust relationship between employer and employees entails lower costs of production than a low-trust relationship. Whether the benefits of moving from low to high trust can be captured at all in a specific context will depend on the costs of moving to a high-trust relationship. The costs of moving may be so high as to wipe out the benefits to be expected from high-trust relationships. If the tradition in a particular country is that employee relations are highly adversarial, then the costs of changing the adversarial system (assuming it can be done at all) may be very high. For example, the bases of worker power may have to be destroyed or the workers heavily bribed to abandon adversarialism. The former may produce social conflict which makes it impossible for firms to operate effectively and the latter may involve costs for the firm which exceed the gains from high-trust relations.[48]

It is possible that, over time, institutions originally designed to be expressive of one view of relations within the firm adapt themselves to express another, as the institution responds to changes in the wider society.[49] Nevertheless, history suggests that radical changes in governance arrangements for the employment relationship occur mainly as a result of the exigencies of fighting a major war,[50] the need to adjust to the

---

[47] See L Bebchuk and M Roe, 'A Theory of Path Dependence and Complementarity in Corporate Governance', in J Gordon and M Roe (eds), *Convergence and Persistence in Corporate Governance* (Cambridge: Cambridge University Press, 2004), ch 2 and R Schmidt and G Spindler, 'Path Dependence and Complementarity in Corporate Governance', ibid, ch 3.

[48] Similar examples could be envisaged in relation to managements which did not accept the legitimacy of the collective representation of employees.

[49] For a classic analysis of the changing social function of works councils in the period after the Second World War see W Streeck, 'Works Councils in Western Europe: From Consultation to Participation', in J Rogers and W Streeck (eds), above n 30, ch 11. For the theory underlying institutional adaption see K Renner, *The Institutions of Private Law and their Social Function*, trans. by A Schwarzschild, with an introduction by Otto Kahn-Freund (London: Routledge & Kegan Paul, 1949, repr 1976; repr in *International Library of Sociology* 1996).

[50] For example, the commitment of the British government to promote collective bargaining across the economy during and immediately after the First World War. See P Davies and M Freedland, *Labour Legislation and Public Policy* (Oxford: Oxford University Press, 1993), 38–43.

circumstances created by losing such a war,[51] or the need to buy off significant social unrest.[52] Thus, despite the elements of mutual benefit in principle obtainable from a move from a low-trust to a high-trust relationship, it
is unlikely that the introduction of new employee governance mechanisms
for this purpose will occur often on a voluntary basis. The uncertainty of
the benefits and certainty of the costs involved in the process are likely to
deter all but the far-sighted and fortunately placed employee leaders and
managements from attempting the change. Moreover, there may well be
steps which would facilitate the change which lie outside the competences
of either of the parties to the employment relationship, such as changes in
the law.

However, uncertainty about the existence or the magnitude of the net
benefits from making the change are also likely to discourage governments
from imposing changes in governance arrangements outside crisis periods. In fact, across-the-board reforms are more risky than experiments
within single firms. Further, governments will know that they cannot
generate high-trust relationships between employees and employers by
legislative fiat. All they can make mandatory is the use of certain governance arrangements for the employment relationship which offer the best
chance of facilitating a move from low trust to high trust, if the parties to
the relationship wish to make it. Government may view the risk of failure
as high, ie that all they will achieve is an enhancement of the bargaining
position of the employees in a system which remains adversarial or low
trust. This view is likely to be reinforced if those companies that wished to
avoid the reforms could do so by reincorporating outside the UK, whilst
continuing within the UK whatever operations they wished to carry on in
the jurisdiction.[53]

Thus, paradigm shifts in employee governance structures are risky
moves and are unlikely to occur except under strong political pressure
for change. This view can be based more formally on the notion of 'complementarities' existing between the corporate governance and employee
governance systems. This means, for example, that a set of rules in which
management accountability to the shareholders is constrained fits with a

---

[51] For example, the introduction of parity employee representation requirements for the
boards of companies in the iron, coal, and steel industries in Germany in 1951. At this time
employers' political power was weak because of their previous association with the Nazi
regime.

[52] The social unrest of the late 1960s led to a revival and extension of the functions of works
councils at that time (Streeck above n 49 at 321–7) and even to proposals (not adopted) for
mandatory worker representation on the boards of large companies in the UK (Davies and
Freedland, above n 50, at 396–404).   [53] See Ch 10 below at p 295.

set of institutions which facilitates FSHC investments by employees (and, of course, vice versa). Let us suppose—to take the opposite hypothesis to the one considered above—that there might be gains to be made in terms of a lower cost of capital and closer monitoring of management, if managerial accountability to shareholders were strengthened. Those gains might be outweighed by the losses caused by reduced incentives for employees to make FSHC investments, if stronger management accountability to shareholders made it more difficult for management to enter into credible commitments to the employees. If this were so, increasing accountability to shareholders would appear to be a policy error.

However, if we move onto a second period in which, greater accountability to shareholders having been introduced in the first period, the labour governance system adapts to the new shareholder accountability regime, so as to recoup some of the losses in terms of lower labour productivity incurred in the first period, then the overall assessment of losses and gains might be different and more favourable to reform at the end of the second than the first period. However, this makes the reform process a longer and more risky one. Governments would embark on the period one reforms only if reasonably certain that the period two reforms could be introduced and be made to work as well. Thus, the longer or more complex the set of reforms required, the less likely the reforms are to occur, even if at the end of the periods, society would be better off if all the reforms had been implemented. In this way, states may get stuck in a higher cost of production equilibrium.[54]

The argument above that reforms which require changes in complementary institutions are less likely to occur than reforms confined to a single set of institutions (which means that incremental change is more likely than radical change) took as its example a move to increase management accountability to shareholders, but it applies equally to a reform aimed at reducing managerial accountability to shareholders. That might not bring the expected gains in FSHC investment without period two reforms in labour governance, for example, the abandonment by a union movement of an ideology which did not regard private ownership of productive capital as legitimate.

[54] Of course, it might be the case that gains would outweigh losses even in period one but that change might not occur because of the political power of the incumbents who benefit from the current system. We do not consider political issues systematically in this chapter, but we need to bear in mind that a change will not necessarily occur because it is of benefit to society as a whole to make that change, if groups who would be disadvantaged by it are in a strong enough political position to veto the change. See M Roe, *Political Determinants of Corporate Governance* (Oxford: Oxford University Press, 2002).

In recent important work Hall and Soskice[55] have offered some hope for those states apparently stuck in unattractive equilibria by arguing that there is not a single combination of governance arrangements (meaning both shareholder and employee governance) which is required for success in a globalized world. Firms require different overall governance arrangements according to their needs for large quantities of capital, FSHC investments, and flexibility to meet rapid changes in the market. In other words, productive activities and governance systems become adapted to each other, and states display different combinations of these. Hall and Soskice distinguish between 'coordinated' and 'liberal market' economies. In liberal market economies, of which the USA and the UK are the primary examples, the provision of the inputs necessary for the business to function is made predominantly through a process of market contracting rather than close coordination. Only those without any contractual protection, such as ordinary shareholders, obtain institutional positions of influence instead. In coordinated market economies, such as Germany and Japan, a bigger role is played by institutions, sometimes state institutions, oftentimes not, which align the actions of those providing the necessary inputs. In the latter type of economy, representation of non-shareholder interests on the board has a natural affinity with other organizational structures for coordinating activities, existing outside company law, whereas in liberal market economies institutional representation seems an unnecessary addition to contractual arrangements.

Further, neither type of economic organization can be said to be better in all circumstances in discharging the tasks facing a modern economy. Each has its strengths and weaknesses and each is associated with specific types of productive activity. Of course, this argument makes proposals to move a particular state from a liberal market to a coordinated economy (or vice versa) even more problematic. A change in shareholder governance may require a change in employee governance and both may require a change in the balance of productive activities in that state's economy if, at the end of the day, the gains from reform are to exceed the losses.[56]

---

[55] P Hall and D Soskice, 'Introduction', and S Vitols, 'Varieties of Corporate Governance: Comparing Germany and the UK', in P Hall and D Soskice (eds), *Varieties of Capitalism* (Oxford: Oxford University Press, 2001).

[56] The extent to which this analysis leans against radical reform has been the subject of controversy. See C Crouch, *Capitalist Diversity and Change* (Oxford: Oxford University Press, 2005).

FREEING MANAGEMENT FROM ACCOUNTABILITY

It has been argued in the previous paragraphs that complex reform proposals, involving changes in more than one complementary institutions, are likely to occur only where there are extensive potential benefits to outweigh the costs of the reforms. However, there is a set of changes which could be made to company law which would not involve any reforms to the employee governance system and in particular would not involve the presence of employee representatives on the board. The aim of these reforms would be to reduce significantly the accountability of management to the shareholders, in the expectation that this would permit the board to balance the interests of the various stakeholders in the company in such a way as to maximize their joint welfare. It would probably be enough, as far as British law is concerned, to reverse (a) the rule that the board cannot take defensive measures against hostile takeovers;[57] (b) the rule that the shareholders can by ordinary resolution dismiss the members of the board at any time,[58] and (c) the focus of the core duty of loyalty on the interests of the shareholders, coupled perhaps with restrictions (d) on the freedom of shareholders to insert themselves into decision-making other than where the Act requires this[59] and (e) on executive compensation provisions which hold out the prospect of large financial pay-outs to executives upon a change of control.[60] It can be argued that this was, in practice, the set of rules under which large British companies operated in the 1950s, ie before the emergence of the hostile bid and the market for corporate control and when shareholdings were dispersed so that shareholders' coordination problems made the exercise of their formal governance rights a rare event.[61] Further, it has been argued that this is an accurate characterization of current US company law, which is much more management friendly than British law.[62]

However, whilst the above steps would clearly reduce the level of board accountability to the shareholders they would not obviously produce board behaviour which maximized the joint welfare of the stakeholders.

---

[57] Above p 141.   [58] Above p 125.   [59] Above p 108.

[60] Above p 209.

[61] See P Davies, 'Shareholder Value, Company Law and Securities Markets Law', in K Hopt and E Wymeersch (eds), *Capital Markets and Company Law* (Oxford: Oxford University Press, 2003), ch 11.

[62] M Blair and L Stout, 'A Team Production Theory of Theory of Corporate Law' (1999) 85 *Virginia Law Review* 247.

In fact, the mechanism which would induce the board to exercise its new-found discretion in the desired way (rather than, for example, in their own interests) is not easy to identify. The obvious candidate is a reformulation of the core duty of loyalty of the directors so as to require them to balance the interests of all stakeholders (or, at least, of those whom the reformer wished to protect). However, this would be very unlikely to be ineffective. So long as the core duty was formulated in largely subjective terms, as it currently is,[63] it would be virtually impossible to show that any particular balance which the directors chose to adopt was outside the range of rational decisions which the directors could take whilst still complying with their duty. Alternatively, if the duty were reformulated in objective terms, the effect would be to shift into the hands of the court the decision as to how the company should balance the interests of shareholders, employees, and other stakeholders—a task which the court is ill-equipped to undertake. In short, accountability to a range of stakeholders with diverse interests is in practice accountability to no one.

One may speculate that, in the absence of effective legal accountability mechanisms, the strongest influences on the behaviour of corporate management would stem from markets. In highly competitive product markets the incentives on management to reduce the costs of production in order to survive commercially might be such that the lack of strong accountability to shareholders was not much noticed. Society's interest in least-cost production would thus be promoted by the product market rather than the law. If it were also the case that companies needed regular access to equity capital, it might also be that shareholders' interests were well protected by a market mechanism. This analysis suggests that freeing management from legal mechanisms of accountability to shareholders and, in effect, to any stakeholder group would benefit or disadvantage stakeholders according to their market position as against the company. For example, if globalization has worsened the market position of some types of worker by exposing them to competition from workers overseas, management would not take greater note of their interests if accountability to shareholders were reduced. What one would predict with some confidence under the above proposal is that management's ability at the margin to increase its own rents from the business would be improved.

---

[63] See p 156 above.

CONCLUSIONS

The strongly shareholder-centred nature of British company law makes the position of the shareholders in the company a recurring issue in public policy debates. Strong and exclusive accountability to shareholders finds its rationale in the goals of reducing the company's cost of capital and maximizing pressure on management to produce the company's output at least cost. These goals are of benefit to the shareholders but also to society as a whole. It is by no means impossible, however, to construct a system in which accountability of management to the shareholders is downgraded (and the costs of this step incurred) and control rights for employees are made mandatory, with the result that the company's overall costs of production are reduced, because the company now acquires its labour inputs on a less costly basis. The cost reduction on the labour side is greater than the increase in the cost of capital and the costs of less effective monitoring. Germany may be an example of a jurisdiction where sharing of control arrangements works in this way. However, empirical evidence on the cost implications of employee governance arrangements is not conclusive, especially that element of the arrangements which involve mandatory appointment rights to the board for employees. The cost calculation in respect of such rights is heavily influenced by the effectiveness of the linkages between the board level representatives and lower-level forms of employee representation (collective bargaining and works councils) and on company's requirements for high-trust relations with its employees in order to achieve its productive goals. Moving to appointment rights for employees (other than of the cosmetic type, of which plenty of examples exist in the EU) from a system of exclusive shareholder control is thus a bold reform step which, it is suggested, societies take only at times of considerable stress, when it is clear that the benefits will outweigh the costs of the move.

International Company Law

Some UK-incorporated companies have always operated across borders (ie in other countries) and sometimes their business operations have been located almost wholly outside the UK. The same is true for companies incorporated in foreign countries. With the dismantling of trade barriers since the Second World War, first on a regional basis and then across the developed and developing world, the incidence of such activity has increased. A number of company law issues arise in this context which we explore in this chapter. In particular, the appropriate role for company law made by the European Union, rather than by the member states, becomes an important issue here.

OVERSEAS COMPANIES

The UK has never applied a general rule that, in order for a company to conduct business in the UK, the company has to be incorporated in one of the UK jurisdictions. Companies incorporated elsewhere are normally free to operate in the UK subject only to disclosure provisions where the company has an 'establishment' in the UK. Such companies, rather quaintly and perhaps reflecting the UK's imperial past, are referred to as 'overseas' companies, though it may be that only a very narrow strip of water, such as the English Channel or St George's Channel, separates the foreign country of incorporation from the UK. These disclosure provisions are designed to ensure that similar information is available about the foreign company (especially in relation to its annual reports and accounts) as would be available in relation to a UK-incorporated company.[1] With the UK's accession to the European Community in 1972

---

[1] See now Part 34 of the Act and the Overseas Companies Regulations 2009/1801. If the company does not even have an establishment in the UK (for example, it advertises its goods on the internet and ships its products directly to customers in the UK from a location outside the UK), not even these disclosure provisions apply.

companies established elsewhere in the EU acquired a Treaty right to establish themselves in the UK,[2] and the disclosure provisions, mentioned above, are now harmonized in an EU Directive.[3] However, given its prior stance, these Community rules had rather little impact on British law. In 2009 there were just over 2,000 companies which had registered in Great Britain as overseas companies from elsewhere in the EU (one-quarter from the Netherlands), just under 2,000 Commonwealth companies (one-third from the Cayman Islands), and nearly 4,000 from the rest of the world (two-thirds from the USA), as well as just over 1,000 Channel Islands and Isle of Man companies.[4]

One crucial question, to which we shall return below, is how far this process can be taken. For example, is it possible to incorporate in a foreign jurisdiction a company the whole of whose activities are intended to be and are conducted in the UK? UK company law has no difficulty with such a step. The UK conflicts of law rule for corporate law is that the company is governed by the law of its place of incorporation, so that a foreign-incorporated company will be subject to that foreign company law, even if it operates wholly in the UK. The effect of this rule is to apply competitive pressure on the UK legislature and courts to produce company law which is attractive to companies. Otherwise, the situation could arise in which British company law was of declining relevance to companies in fact operating in the UK because they incorporated elsewhere. Some countries apply a conflicts of law rule whereby the company is governed by the law of the country in which its 'seat' is located, a not entirely clear term but one which clearly refers to something like its headquarters or main place of operation. Under this approach, the company in our example would be in danger of being treated by the courts of the country in which it had purported to incorporate itself as having failed to do so because its seat was not there—and, by extension, being treated by the UK courts also as a nullity because it had not achieved incorporation.

The 'seat' rule protects jurisdictions which adopt it from competition from other countries' laws at the point of company incorporation.

---

[2] See now arts 49 and 54 of the Treaty on the Functioning of the European Union (TFEU).

[3] See the Eleventh Company Law Directive 89/666/EEC, [1989] OJ L395/36. This is a 'maximum harmonisation' directive, ie member states may not apply national provisions which either fall below or go above the Directive's requirements. It applies to companies, wherever incorporated, which set up establishments (or 'branches'—the term used in the Directive) in the EU.

[4] BERR, *Statistical Tables on Companies Registration Activities 2008–09*, Table E1. The Channel Islands and the Isle of Man are Crown Dependencies and are not part of the UK.

However, even the UK approach does not expose the law-maker to the full force of competitive pressure. For that to happen, a company would have to be free to choose, not only its applicable law upon incorporation by choosing the country in which to incorporate, but also to alter that law by later reincorporating in another country. Later reincorporation, sometimes referred to as jurisdictional migration, is not provided in any simple form by British company law, though the Company Law Review thought it should be.[5] We will return to this issue after we have examined the EU's programme for harmonizing company law.

HARMONIZATION OF COMPANY LAW BY THE EUROPEAN UNION

Somewhat surprisingly, company law received an explicit mention in the original Treaty of Rome of 1957. The current Treaty provides that 'in order to attain freedom of establishment' the Community should have the power to issue Directives with the objective of 'coordinating to the necessary extent the safeguards which, for the protection of the interests of members and others, are required by Member States of companies or firms... with a view to making such safeguards equivalent throughout the Union'.[6] Seizing this power, the European Commission set off in the late 1960s down the road of implementing an elaborate plan to harmonize the company laws of the member states through a series of 'company law' directives. By the late 1980s the programme had more or less run into the sands. Nine directives—a not inconsiderable number—had been adopted but the Commission's proposals had failed to secure sufficient support from the member states in a number of the crucial areas of corporate law.[7] There is nothing significant in the series which addresses the central company law questions of the relations between directors and shareholders, between majority or minority shareholders or the question of shareholder enforcement of directors' duties, for example, through derivative actions.[8] Whether one regrets the failure of the company law

---

[5] CLR, *Final Report* (2001), ch 14. British law does not provide a simple way to migrate even within the three British jurisdictions.   [6] Art 50(2)(g) TFEU.

[7] The legislative base for the directives does not require unanimity among the member states but does require a 'qualified' majority of the member states to be in favour of the Commission's proposals. See art 238(2) TFEU.

[8] The best the Community has been able to produce in these areas are non-binding Commission Recommendations on directors' remuneration and the role of non-executive directors.

harmonization programme to achieve its full objectives or regrets the fact that it was undertaken at all depends upon one's view of the assertion that 'freedom of establishment' required company law harmonization.

Article 49 TFEU says that 'freedom of establishment shall include the right . . . to set up and manage undertakings, in particular companies or firms within the meaning of the second paragraph of Article 54, under the conditions laid down for its own nationals by the law of the country where such establishment is effected'. Since member states already allowed companies incorporated in other jurisdictions to operate in their territories before the Treaty of Rome, why was freedom of establishment seen to require a greater harmonization of member states' company laws than previously existed? There were two main rationales put forward for the harmonization programme in the context of the new freedom of establishment. First, it might be said that a uniform system of company law would reduce transaction costs in the single market, because those dealing with companies would have to make themselves familiar with just one system of company law and not several. There are reasons to be sceptical about this argument. The most important is that it is fully persuasive only in a situation where there is one and only one efficient rule for all the member states or it does not matter what the rule is, provided there is a rule. Then uniformity has distinct benefits over multiple rules in a single market. But if, as suggested below, there is no single most efficient company law rule for the member states, then imposing a single rule comes with considerable costs, ie costs for companies in those jurisdictions where the common rule is inefficient. The costs of an inappropriate rule, at least for a number of member states, may well outweigh the benefits of harmonization.

The most obvious divergences across the member states relate to whether shareholdings are concentrated or dispersed and whether a particular state seeks to achieve a close coordination of its governance systems for dealing with shareholders' and employees' agency costs or not. So, it is difficult to design an efficient common rule for a UK listed company with dispersed shareholdings and no employee representatives on the board and a German one with concentrated shareholdings and mandatory parity board representation, whilst proposals to eliminate these differences by legislative fiat face the uncertainties we examined in Chapter 9. This is perhaps why the company law directives which were adopted dealt with topics which did not raise these problems (for example, company formation or annual reports and accounts and their audit) and could even be said to offer benefits to cross-border investors (through the comparability of financial statements).[9] For the same reason, there was a failure over many years to adopt the proposed Fifth Directive on the internal structure of large companies, where the Commission's initial proposals for mandatory board representation of employees on a two-tier board were not acceptable to enough member states to get the proposal over the qualified majority requirement. That proposal appears now to have been abandoned by the Commission. Because of the programme's failure to tackle the core problems of company law, and for a number of other reasons, the harmonization resulting from it has been characterized as 'trivial'.[10]

The second rationale for the harmonization programme was that, without it, there would be regulatory arbitrage. Company incorporations would gravitate to the state with the least demanding rules and companies would conduct their business in other member states from there. This is the argument against creating a 'European Delaware'.[11] The irony of this rationale is that, during the time that the harmonization programme was on foot, the possibilities for regulatory arbitrage in the EU were extremely limited because many member states maintained the real seat rule and all states made jurisdictional migration difficult. A further piece of irony is that since the series of company law harmonization directives was abandoned, decisions of the Court of Justice of the European Union (CJEU) have made regulatory arbitrage a more plausible development in the EU than it previously was. The effect of regulatory arbitrage (choice by companies of the applicable company law) is to increase the competitive pressures on member states in relation to their company laws (jurisdictional competition). Thus, it is necessary to address head on

---

[9] The audit directive was substantially expanded post the Enron scandal and is now the important Directive 2006/43/EC, [2006] OJ L157/87 on statutory audits of statutory accounts and consolidated accounts. The accounting directives have been rather overtaken by the move towards global accounting standards, though not without a certain amount of kicking and screaming by the Commission. None of the other directives was significant except, in a negative way, the Second Directive on legal capital which has stood in the way of experiments with different rules for protecting creditors. See above Ch 4.

[10] L Enriques, 'EC Company Law Directives and Regulations: How Trivial Are They?' (2006) 27 *University of Pennsylvania Journal of International Economic Law* 1. Another example of failure to reach agreement on a core issue is the Takeovers Directive, originally proposed as the Thirteenth Directive in the company law series. This was ultimately adopted but only on the basis that the core contentious issue (the freedom of target management to take defensive measures against a hostile bid) was left to be settled at member state or company level, thus favouring the status quo over harmonization. See P Davies, E Schuster, and E Van de Walle de Ghelcke, 'The Takeover Directive as a Protectionist Tool?' ECGI—Law Working Paper No. 141/2010 (2010). Available at SSRN: <http://ssrn.com/abstract=1554616>.

[11] Delaware, despite its small size, is the state of incorporation of about one-half of the largest US companies.

the merits and demerits of competition among the company laws of the European Union.

THE CONDITIONS NECESSARY FOR REGULATORY ARBITRAGE

In order for a 'European Delaware' to emerge it is suggested that three conditions need to be satisfied.[12] First, companies must be legally free to choose their corporate laws without that choice of law imposing on them other efficiency-reducing requirements. An obvious example of such a requirement is being able to choose corporate law only by locating or moving the corporate headquarters to the country whose law is preferred—a potentially costly and disruptive move. Choice of applicable company law will be much facilitated if a company can move its registered office alone (thus altering the applicable law) but leave its productive activities where they are. Second, one or more member states must have an incentive to attract incorporations from companies exercising their legal freedom under point one. If member states do not care whether companies incorporate in their jurisdiction or not, they will have no incentive to design corporate laws so as to attract incorporations or reincorporations. Finally, companies must perceive that the choice of another corporate law to regulate their affairs confers benefits on them which exceed the disadvantages.

FREEDOM OF ESTABLISHMENT

In a pair of judgments at the turn of the century the Court of Justice interpreted the freedom of establishment provisions of the Treaty so as to confer upon incorporators the power to choose the applicable law at the point of company formation. In its famous *Centros* decision[13] the CJEU held that the Danish authorities were wrong to refuse to recognize in Denmark a British private company formed by Danes solely for the purpose of conducting business in Denmark. In *Inspire Art*[14] the Court held the Dutch

---

[12] For the classic analysis see J Armour, 'Who Should Make Corporate Law? EC Legislation versus Regulatory Competition', in J Armour and J McCahery (eds), *After Enron* (Oxford: Hart Publishing, 2006) (also in (2005) 48 *Current Legal Problems* 369).

[13] Case C-212/97, *Centros Ltd v Erhverus-og Selkabsstyrelsen* [1999] ECR I-1459.

[14] Case C-167/01, *Kamer van Koophandel en Fabrieken voor Amsterdam v Inspire Art Ltd* [2003] ECR I-10155. The additional requirements, relating mainly to minimum capital, failed to pass the Community justification test of being necessary in the public interest (the so-called *Gebhart* test). It does not follow that all pseudo-foreign requirements would fail that test, for example, a requirement that a UK company operating wholly in Germany comply with the German codetermination requirements.

authorities had acted unlawfully in applying to a similar British private company provisions of Dutch law dealing with 'pseudo foreign' companies. The aim of the pseudo foreign rules was to require foreign-incorporated companies, which carried on their business wholly in the Netherlands, to comply with certain provisions of Dutch company law, even if those provisions were not present in the law of the state of incorporation. However, it should be noted that the UK is an 'incorporation' theory state.[15] It does not necessarily follow that this arrangement would have been possible had the UK been a 'real seat' state. In that case, the headquarters of the company would have had to be in the UK as well as its registered office, and the choice between incorporation and real seat theories seems to be a matter for the member states.

Empirical studies[16] have shown that these decisions of the Court had a significant impact on the number of EU entrepreneurs from outside the UK seeking to incorporate in the UK, mainly because the UK imposes no minimum capital rules for private companies but also because its incorporation processes are speedy and cheap. It seems that relatively small cost savings at the point of incorporation will drive quite large shifts in entrepreneurs' decisions about the place of incorporation, especially as incorporation agents appeared in other EU countries to facilitate the use of the UK law by foreigners. Subsequently, the law-makers in the countries in which the entrepreneurs were based felt the pressure to respond to this loss of domestic incorporation activity and in recent years France, Germany, the Netherlands, and Spain have all removed or lowered minimum capital requirements. It is not absolutely clear why countries should worry if small companies operating in their jurisdiction are incorporated elsewhere, especially as the cost of bringing them back to domestic incorporation was to mimic or move towards the provisions of UK law. Perhaps it can be said that the take-up of UK incorporation had demonstrated to the foreign law-makers that their rules were in this respect inefficient. If so, it would be rational for a member state to make the better company law available to all its domestic entrepreneurs, whether they were prepared to incorporate in another country or not.

However, Delaware is not particularly noted for the number of small companies which incorporate there. As far as one can tell, incorporations

---

[15] Above p 291.
[16] Notably M Becht, C Mayer, and H Wagner, *Where Do Firms Incorporate? Deregulation and the Cost of Entry*, ECGI Law Working Paper No. 70/2006, available on <http://ssrn.com/abstract=906066>.

in the US tend to occur in the state in which the company intends to carry on business. The remarkable fact about Delaware is the high proportion of large and usually publicly traded companies which are incorporated there. This occurs, normally, not through initial incorporation in Delaware but through subsequent reincorporation in Delaware from another state. Technically, this is usually achieved by forming a new company in Delaware and then merging the existing operating company into it, ie this is reincorporation through cross-state merger. The extent to which such a manoeuvre is protected by the freedom of establishment provisions of the Treaty is unclear. In its *Cartesio* decision,[17] the court considered a case which in some ways is the opposite of the situation we are interested in, ie the company moved its head office from Hungary to Italy but wished to retain Hungarian company law as the applicable law. The Hungarian authorities refused to regard the company as any longer subject to Hungarian law because its headquarters were no longer in Hungary. The court held that this stance was permitted by Community law since it was up to each member state to define the criteria which connected a company to its company law.

However, the court indicated that it would have been a breach of Community law for a member state to insist that a company, which wished to move its headquarters as part of a scheme to change its corporate law by changing its registered office as well, should wind itself up in the transferor state and have its assets acquired by a new company formed in the transferee state. This method of changing the state of incorporation, which of course is always available, is highly unattractive to companies because of the tax liabilities likely to be triggered on a winding up (in addition to the fact that the winding-up process is a rather cumbersome mechanism). However, it is unclear whether the exiting state could impose requirements short of winding up (for example, tax liabilities).[18] Even more important, it is unclear what the implication of these dicta are for a company which wishes to move only its registered office and not its head office. Thus, the issue of midstream reincorporation by moving the company's registered office alone is surrounded with many unsolved questions, so that further Court of Justice decisions will be needed before it can be said that reincorporation is substantially free from legal doubt.

---

[17] Case C-210/06, *Cartesio Oktató és Szolgáltató bt* [2008] ECR I-9641.
[18] See Case 81/87, *Queen v HM Treasury and Commissioners of Inland Revenue ex parte Daily Mail and General Trust plc* [1988] ECR 5483.

MEMBER STATE INCENTIVES

Second, to produce a 'Delaware effect' in the EU, not only must established companies be legally free to move to another state purely to obtain that state's company law, but member states must have an incentive to offer good company law in order to attract them. It is far from clear that the UK—or any other member state—has a strong incentive to compete for incorporations, unlike Delaware. A substantial fraction of the revenue of the state of Delaware comes from annual franchise taxes which companies incorporated in that state pay.[19] No such taxes are imposed on companies incorporated in the UK—indeed, they are forbidden by Community law except by the state where the company has its centre of management.[20] Of course, there is a benefit to national economies from having large companies headquartered in the jurisdiction, but much less so from having companies simply incorporated there but with their headquarters elsewhere. There are two potential replacements in the case of the UK for the financial incentive which the franchise tax generates in Delaware. First, the large London law firms have an incentive to increase the number of companies incorporated in London, because that will increase the number of their clients, to whom they may be able to sell legal services beyond the narrow area of corporate law, especially as they are likely to have offices in the company's headquarters state as well. So, they will lobby the British government to keep British company law attractive to foreign incorporators.[21]

Second, the UK government might see itself as having a strong incentive to provide efficient corporate law to companies incorporated and operating in the UK. Companies not operating in the UK, if legally able to do so, might take advantage of that law by incorporating here. This might be seen as a 'spill-over' effect of the push to provide efficient company law for domestically operating companies.[22] In order for this argument to produce a 'European Delaware', however, there would need to be further analysis to show that the UK—or some other member state—was under unique incentives to provide efficient company law to domestically operating companies, which did not apply to other member states. In fact,

---

[19] M Roe puts the figure at 20 per cent ('Delaware's Competition' (2003) 117 *Harvard Law Review* 588, 608–10. A franchise tax is an annual tax based on the value of the shares issued or the amount of the company's assets.

[20] Council Directive 69/335/EEC [1969] OJ L249/25.

[21] Armour, above n 12 at 519–20.

[22] 'Company law provides the infrastructure which enables people to collaborate in productive business relationships, generating the wealth on which the whole community depends…Its effectiveness impacts on us all.' (Company Law Review, *Final Report*, 2001, para 3.)

it is probably right to conclude that these two 'substitute' incentives generate less strong pressure on the UK government to produce attractive law for out-of-state companies than the prospect of substantial state revenue from franchise taxes.

CORPORATE BENEFITS FROM REINCORPORATION

The ability of member states to offer an attractive company law regime for out-of-state companies (assuming they want to) and the benefits to the out-of-state companies contemplating a change of corporate law may be constrained by structural differences in companies across Europe. Thus, one can see that UK public company law is designed to deal with the agency problems of shareholders in large companies without block-holders but with a high level of institutional shareholding across the market as a whole. These rules may not be attractive to block-holder-controlled companies or be efficient for such companies, even if they are attractive. For example, on the one hand, block-holders whose position is not entirely secure may not want to commit to a rule which prevents the target board (ie the block-holders) from taking defensive measures against a hostile bid,[23] whilst, on the other, the British minority protection mechanisms may be inadequate because they do not address minorities in public companies.[24]

Equally, companies incorporated in those continental European jurisdictions which require a close coordination between the shareholder governance and employee governance systems, for example, through employee representation on the board, may incur overall costs by choosing a legal system without such mandatory rules, even if, ex ante, the absence of such requirements appears attractive and reincorporation occurs in order to escape the mandatory appointment rules for employees.[25] In the US neither of these major structural variations across the continent exists. In short, the imperative for member states to produce company law which suits their fully domestic companies may constrain that state's ability to produce law attractive to out-of-state companies.

Finally, there is a question of jurisdiction. A company whose only connection with a state is the use of its company law may find it inconvenient to sue in that jurisdiction. The courts of the headquarters state will normally have jurisdiction over company law issues as well, but the courts in that state, if the choice of law has been effective, will apply the law of the state of incorporation, and companies may wonder how well that task will be discharged.

---

[23] Above p 141.   [24] Ch 8 above at p 237.   [25] See above Ch 9.

A RACE TO THE BOTTOM?

What all this suggests is that the emergence of a European Delaware is unlikely. What is more likely is that, either there will be no regulatory competition at all,[26] because changing the state of incorporation is seen as too difficult, or there will emerge a small number of leading states offering efficient company laws for different types of company structures, for example, those with concentrated and those with dispersed ownership; those which display close complementarities between the shareholder and employee governance systems and those which do not.[27] Indeed, even the leading states may not attract large numbers of out-of-state incorporations if the 'abandoned' states move quickly to align their law with that of the leading states, in order to provide better laws for their entrepreneurs. We have already seen a minor example of this process with minimum capital rules. Nor is this a new process. Even without the ability of companies to choose their corporate laws, jurisdictions still compete with each other to offer their entrepreneurs the most suitable company laws, which are perceived as a competitive advantage. Thus, when in 1892 Germany produced a form of company law well adapted to the needs of small and medium-sized companies (the GmbH law), France and the UK reacted by amending, in different ways, their company laws, which had previously been aimed at large companies, so that they became better suited to the needs of smaller companies. In this way, the distinction between public and private companies was born in the UK in 1907.[28] Freedom of companies to choose their corporate laws sharpens this competitive pressure on the states, but does not introduce an entirely new factor. Unless, as seems unlikely but is not impossible, a state was prepared in effect to contract out its company law to another state and to encourage its businesses to incorporate in that other state, then states will be under a continuing pressure to modernize their company laws in order to obtain competitive advantages for their domestic businesses—or at least in order not to put them at a competitive disadvantage.

This vision of the future of company law within the European community is much more attractive than the harmonization model because (a) as suggested above, a single efficient company law across all European jurisdictions is a goal incapable of realization and (b) even if it were, the

---

[26] L Enriques, 'EC Company Law and the Fears of a European Delaware' (2004) 15 *European Business Law Review* 1283.   [27] Armour, above n 12 at 524.

[28] R Drury, 'Private Companies in Europe and the European Private Company', in J McCahery, T Raaijmakers, and E Vermeulen (eds), *The Governance of Close Corporations and Partnerships* (Oxford: Oxford University Press, 2004), 375–81.

Community may make mistakes in identifying that law and such mistakes are difficult to rectify, given the 'stickiness' of Community law.[29] By contrast, regulatory competition allows a number of approaches to be tried out and tested against alternatives and the choices made are more easily reversible, because only the national law-maker has to be convinced that the original decision was misplaced.

The major argument against regulatory competition is that it would mean 'a race to the bottom'. Of course, there is a great deal of debate in the US about whether the Delaware effect has involved a race to the bottom or a race to the top. Insofar as there are fears of a race to the bottom in the US, they arise out of an analysis which says that Delaware law is too pro-management because it is the managers/directors of the company who decide whether to transfer the company's incorporation to Delaware, rather than its shareholders. Delaware thus has an incentive to offer companies pro-management corporate law.[30] The way to address the question is through the design of the decision-making process which is laid down for taking the transfer decision. It ought to be easy enough to build into the decision process a say for the shareholders and whatever other groups are thought to need protection to ensure that the decision is wealth enhancing from their point of view.[31]

THE PROPER ROLE FOR COMMUNITY LEGISLATION

The argument above has been in broad terms that the Community's plan to produce an overall harmonization of member states' company law 'from the top down' by means of directives was misconceived and, further, that regulatory competition among the company law jurisdictions could be successfully managed so as to produce harmonization 'from the bottom up' without prior commitment to the adoption of a single company law system across the Community and with greater scope for experimentation with different solutions to important problems. Regulatory competition, insofar as it exists, has been the product of the Treaty provisions and the

---

[29] See the great difficulties in obtaining even minor amendments to the Second Directive on legal capital despite strong arguments that legal capital is not the best way of protecting creditors.

[30] L Bebchuk, 'Federalism and the Corporation: The Desirable Limits on State Competition in Corporate Law' (1992) 105 *Harvard Law Review* 1435.

[31] See the CLR proposals, above n 5, which involved a director proposal, a special majority approval of the shareholders, a solvency statement, and the right of creditors to apply to the court if their interests were likely to be harmed by the transfer.

Court of Justice's interpretation of them. However, this does not mean that rules produced by the Community legislature should have no role in shaping company law in the EU. In fact, after the general harmonization programme had reached exhaustion at the end of the last century, a crucial role was played by the High Level Group of Company Law Experts[32] in refocusing the efforts of the Community on those matters where it genuinely has an advantage over legislation produced by the member states.

These matters are sometimes referred to as 'cross-border' issues, by which is meant that there is a need to coordinate the laws of the member states in order that a transaction involving parties in different member states can occur easily. The clearest example is a cross-border merger, where company A in jurisdiction X wishes to merge with company B in jurisdiction Y, so that the resulting company is either company B (company A disappearing without being wound up, its assets and liabilities having been transferred to B) or a new company, C (both A and B disappearing). In the latter case C may be formed, if the parties wish, in neither X nor Y but jurisdiction Z. All member states provide for mergers to happen where the companies involved are all incorporated in the jurisdiction.[33] Where, however, companies in different jurisdictions are involved, their merger laws need to be coordinated for the cross-border merger to happen at low cost. This issue the Community legislator tackled in its directive on cross-border mergers,[34] though not without having been given a hefty nudge in this direction by the Court.[35]

Of course, cross-border amalgamations have always been possible by way of takeovers. Since a takeover involves simply an offer by company A to the shareholders of company B to acquire their shares and no corporate decision by either A or B is required for the transfer to occur,[36] coordination of company laws is not required for the share transfer, even if A and B are in different jurisdictions. However, jurisdictions vary on the extent to which the board of B can take defensive measures, ie exercise their powers of centralized management so as to frustrate the offer.[37] The Community legislator tackled this issue in its Takeover Directive,[38] but, as we have

---

[32] *Report of the High Level Group of Company Law Experts on a Modern Regulatory Framework for Company Law in Europe*, Brussels (November 2002).

[33] UK law does this primarily through the more general scheme of arrangement (Part 26 of the Act) which can be made to produce a merger.

[34] Directive 2005/56/EC, [2005] OJ L310/1, on cross-border mergers.

[35] Case C-411/03, *SEVIC Systems AG* [2005] ECR I-10805.

[36] Company A must take a corporate decision to make the offer, of course, but that is a decision by it alone and generates no cross-border issues.   [37] Above n 10.

[38] Directive 2004/25/EC, [2004] OJ L142/12 on takeover bids.

noted above,[39] agreement on the Directive was secured only on the basis that this crucial issue was left, in effect, for the member states to decide. Mergers, unlike takeovers, require either in law or in practice that the management of the 'target' company consent to the transaction as well as its shareholders. Thus, management, and by extension, national government opposition to amalgamations initiated by foreign companies is less pronounced when they are effected by mergers rather than takeovers.

Apart from the cross-border mergers directive, the other achievement of the Community legislator to date in the core company law area post the High Level Group's Report was the adoption of a directive on shareholder rights.[40] Like the Takeover Directive, this directive was not formally confined to cross-border voting by shareholders (ie where shareholder and company were in different jurisdictions), though this was the driving force behind the directive. Nevertheless, a proxy for the cross-border element was provided by the directive being confined to companies whose securities were traded on 'regulated' markets (ie top-tier public markets), where the incidence of cross-border voting was likely to be significant.

However, focusing on cross-border issues does not necessarily mean that the adoption of a particular proposed directive will be easy. Thus, the proposed fourteenth directive on the transfer of a company's registered office to another jurisdiction, although strongly recommended by the High Level Group and clearly necessary in the light of the uncertainties in the Court of Justice's case-law, has not been adopted and the Commission has currently abandoned any attempt to push it forward. This is probably on the basis that agreement among the member states would be difficult to secure, because the competitive pressures which would be unleashed through freedom of establishment beyond the point of incorporation are strongly resisted in some quarters.

COMMUNITY LEVEL LEGAL VEHICLES

The European Public Company (SE)

Until recently, a submerged theme in Community company law activity has been the creation of Community-level corporate vehicles which incorporators could choose to adopt instead of national forms of incorporation. In 2001, after decades of trying, the Community adopted a Regulation on the Statute for a European Company,[41] in effect a Community form of incorporation for those wishing to set up a public company. Why should a

---

[39] Above n 10.
[40] Directive 2007/36/EC, [2007] OJ L184/17, on shareholders' rights.
[41] Regulation 2157/2001, [2001] OJ L294/1.

Community level form of incorporation be thought to be something that would help foster the single market, given that some other cross-state markets, such as the US, manage perfectly well without one, ie incorporation takes place there at state rather than federal level? The main argument in favour of the SE[42] was that it would facilitate cross-border mergers by large companies. For this reason the Regulation provides that the founders of an SE must be existing companies (ie individuals cannot form an SE) and the founding companies must be able to show some evidence of existing cross-border activity.[43] This argument was somewhat undercut by the subsequent enactment of the cross-border merger Directive, discussed above, which facilitates cross-border mergers without the need for the resulting company to be an SE. It should be noted that the SE was not designed to promote free corporate choice of law, because of the rule that the SE's head office must be located in the jurisdiction of incorporation.[44] A further argument was that within corporate groups the Regulation would permit the bundling together of a number of national subsidiaries into a single SE, which would reduce the costs of running group enterprises.

What do we know about the take-up of the SE? There have been two important pieces of research on this, one by Dr Kirshner[45] and one by Professor Eidenmuller and colleagues.[46] Dr Kirshner's research, based on case studies, suggests that the intra-group impact of the SE has been fairly limited. Combining subsidiaries in order to reduce the administrative costs of running separate subsidiaries has not proved a major incentive towards the SE. However, she did find that in industries subject to regulation there was a move towards the single SE model, because that reduced compliance costs. The rules of only one regulator had to be understood and complied with. So, reducing regulatory costs seems to have been a

---

[42] The acronym from the Latin for European company: *Societas Europaea*.

[43] Regulation, art 2 and Title 2. The height of cross-border hurdle to be surmounted varies according to the method of formation. Formation by 'transformation' (ie an existing national company transforms itself into an SE) is subject to the highest requirement, ie the transforming company must have had for at least two years a subsidiary governed by the law of another member state.

[44] Regulation art 7, though the Commission is under a duty to review this rule.

[45] J Kirshner, 'Regulatory Competition in Europe?—The Societas Europaea', forthcoming in *European Company and Financial Law Review*.

[46] H Eidenmüller, A Engert, and L Hornuf, 'Incorporating under European Law: The Societas Europaea as a Vehicle for Legal Arbitrage' (2009) 10 *European Business Organization Law Review* 1. See also B Keller and F Werner, 'The Establishment of the European Company (SE): The First Cases from an Industrial Relations Perspective' (2008) 14 *European Journal of Industrial Relations* 153.

bigger incentive than reducing administrative costs. Of course, these findings also suggest a rather limited role for the SE.

The survey by Eidenmüller and colleagues confirms that in many member states there are rather few SEs and even fewer if one counts only active SEs.[47] However, the findings also show considerable variation across the Community. In particular, the researchers found a surprising number of SEs in Germany. It seems that modification of the domestic codetermination rules was very often a reason for the formation of an SE. This is a very interesting finding because German fears that SEs would allow domestic companies to escape from national rules on mandatory board appointments rights for employees by becoming SEs delayed adoption of the Regulation for many years. First, it was proposed that board level appointment rights for employees should be mandatory for all SEs, but this was not accepted by states without any such domestic requirements. Eventually, the principle of 'no escape, no extension' was adopted whereby the applicable rules on board composition in the SE depend on the rules applying under the national laws of the companies forming the SE. This solution was embodied in a Directive which accompanies the Regulation.[48]

The delay caused by the codetermination issue to the adoption of the Regulation is a vivid example of the problem mentioned above of the impossibility of producing a single rule for divergent company law systems. The research suggests, further, that the 'no escape' strategy of deriving the applicable rules from the national laws applying to the founding companies was not fully successful. Although an SE formed by a German company subject to German board appointment rules would be subject to the German rules in principle, certain modifications of those rules could be obtained by moving to SE status. Three modifications were available in particular. The SE could choose to have a smaller board than German law required (so that the number, if not the proportion, of employee appointees was reduced). The representatives would

---

[47] As of March 2009, there were 14 SEs registered in Great Britain, of which 9 had been registered in 2008/9 (BERR, *Statistical Tables on Companies Registration Activities 2008-09*, Table E3). There are some 400 across the EU.

[48] Directive 2001/89/EC, OJ L294/29, on involvement of employees in the Statute for a European Company. This principle, although simple to state, was immensely complex to implement, in part because the founding companies might be subject to different board appointment rules for employees and in part because management and union can by agreement in most cases opt out of them. See P Davies, 'Workers on the Board of the European Company?' (2003) 32 *Industrial Law Journal* 75.

be appointed by the whole of the workforce of the SE and not just by its German employees. This was a deliberate policy of the SE Statute but it might have the effect of diluting the influence of the German representatives who might be the ones best placed to make use of the appointment rights. Finally, the SE rule would be the one applicable to the German company at the time of the formation of the SE and it would not alter if, later on, circumstances changed in such a way as would have triggered a change in appointment rights under national law. Most obviously, the employees of a German company with 1,000 employees would hold appointment rights to one-third of the board seats. That entitlement would increase to one-half if the number of employees doubled, if German law still applied.[49] If in the meantime the German company had become an SE, the proportion would remain fixed at one-third.[50] So, the SE has been an interesting development, but it is difficult to say that it has been a success from the point of view of the Commission's goal of encouraging cross-border activities by companies; and at least one main driver of the use of the SE has been a factor (modification of board appointment rights for employees) which the Community legislator positively wanted to exclude.

The European Private Company (SPE)

Despite the limited impact of the SE, the Commission, after much hesitation and under prodding from the European Parliament, has recently produced proposals for a European Private Company (SPE). The goals of this proposal and its structure are, however, significantly different from those which drove the SE. The aim here is not to promote cross-border mergers between small and medium-sized enterprises but to permit small companies to form subsidiaries in other countries which would be subject to the same law as the parent company because they would all be SPEs. The proposal is thus aimed at reducing the transaction costs of setting up subsidiaries in other jurisdictions. It is in fact pretty unclear that this is a significant transaction cost, but leaving that aside, the achievement of this goal requires that the law pertaining to the SPE should be uniform across the member states. This result was not achieved in the case of the SE. Although the SE Regulation contains some rules, which are directly

---

[49] See above p 281 and n 42.

[50] These problems occur also in relation to cross-border mergers where the resulting company is formed in a jurisdiction without mandatory appointment rights for employees but one of the disappearing companies was subject to such rules. The solution adopted in the cross-border merger directive is similar, but not identical to the one in the SE Directive (see art 16 of the Cross-border Merger Directive).

applicable in the member states, and the SE Directives other rules which the member states must transpose into their national legal orders, many of the crucial rules applicable to it are determined by the public company rules of the law of the state in which it is registered.[51] So, one can say that there is not a single SE law but as many SE laws as there are member states of the European Union.

The SPE rationale demands a high level of uniformity in the applicable rules across the member states for otherwise the cost-reduction goals in relation to the formation of subsidiaries will not be met. On the other hand, the SPE has to be an attractive form of incorporation for entrepreneurs, otherwise they will simply stick with national forms of incorporation. Thus, the SPE will be most successful if its rules are determined at Community level and it contains few mandatory rules. The Commission's initial proposals approximated to this ideal.[52] However, the SPE proposal presents a major challenge to the domestic private company laws of the member states, because the cross-border requirements for forming an SPE are either non-existent (as in the Commission's initial proposals) or exiguous, as in later variations. Consequently, the SPE bids fair to be a full competitor to domestic private company laws and thus to constitute regulatory competition, this time not from other member states but from the Community. This raises the obvious question of whether the member states are willing to accept such competition, given their unwillingness, noted above, to promote regulatory competition through the adoption of the proposed fourteenth directive.[53] The member states are in a good position to reduce the competitive potential of the SPE because its adoption requires unanimity of the member states.[54] It is no surprise to learn that the SPE negotiations are bogged down in the familiar perennial problems: must the SPE be incorporated in the jurisdiction where its seat is located, is it to be subject to an SE-like solution to the issue of mandatory board representation for employees, and what minimum capital rules should be applied to it? None of these problems is insoluble, but it is doubtful if they are soluble whilst maintaining the uniform and non-mandatory nature of the initial SPE proposals.[55]

---

[51] See art 9 of the Regulation.
[52] Available on: <http://ec.europa.eu/internal_market/company/docs/epc/proposal_en.pdf>. [53] See p 303.
[54] The Regulation has been proposed under what is now art 352 TFEU.
[55] See P Davies, 'The European Private Company (SPE): Uniformity, Flexibility, Competition and the Persistence of National Law', ECGI Law Working Paper 154 (May 2010), available on <http://ssrn.com/abstract=1622293> for a critique of the SPE proposal.

CONCLUSIONS

The full potential of the European Community in the areas of company law has not been realized, as yet. The original top-down general harmonization programme was a mistake and was eventually perceived by most people to be so. Bottom-up regulatory competition is by no means fully in place and may not be for many years. Nevertheless, the Community will always play a role in steering some aspects of member states' company laws but may lack a coherent rationale for its activities until the regulatory competition issue is faced head on.

Index